ENCYCLOPAEDIA OF
COMPUTER SCIENCE AND TECHNOLOGY

ENCYCLOPAEDIA OF COMPUTER SCIENCE AND TECHNOLOGY

Kamal Sharma

ANMOL PUBLICATIONS PVT. LTD.
NEW DELHI - 110 002 (INDIA)

ANMOL PUBLICATIONS PVT. LTD.
H.O.: 4374/4B, Ansari Road, Daryaganj
New Delhi - 110 002
Ph.: 23278000, 23261597
B.O.: No. 1015, Ist Main Road, BSK III Stage
III Phase, III Block
Bangalore - 560 085 (India)
Visit us at: www.anmolpublications.com

Encyclopaedia of Computer Science and Technology

First Published, 2007

PRINTED IN INDIA

Printed at Mehra Offset Press, Delhi.

Preface

The aim of this encyclopaedia is to give, in the light of present knowledge and opinion, definitions of terms that are of importance in computer science and technology. It is a encyclopaedia of computer technology terms, written by specialists, partly for other specialists but more particularly for the man-in-the-street, and for students and interested workers of all kinds and ages: indeed, for all who wish to understand what computer is all about.

A very well written dictionary of computer terms, language definitions, Internet definitions, standards, and computer interface devices, connectivity, etc. Terms are easy to find and the definitions are exact and to the point and where needed are explained in detail. The description of connectors is particularly helpful.

Whether a complete beginner, a college student, or a seasoned professional, this book will fill the gaps in background knowledge and make computers easy to understand for everyone.

The goal is to explain, not just define. That is, it's not a book about words, it's a book about computers. We have taken half a page or more to explain every important concept, and we have included useful information, from emoticons to mathematical symbols, ASCII codes, cable connections, web languages and much more. Thus we have covered not only business software, personal computers, and the Internet, but also such fundamentals as computer architecture and binary arithmetic.

Further to serve the needs of the teacher, student and worker in the field of computer science, as well as in related fields, a considerable number of terms have been included from the subject-areas bordering on computer science and technology, such as applied electronics, applied electricity, etc. Obviously, all the terms in computer technology cannot be defined adequately in a book, or for that matter in a library. The objective of editors and contributors has been the more modest one of providing a book useful as a general reference in computer science and technology, helpful even to the specialist in regions outside of his domain of specialized knowledge

Clarification of the meaning of terms, precision in their use, and uniformity in usage among workers in computer science and technology and related fields are essential in the growth of a science.

The aim of this volume is to provide a concise repository of number of major concepts in this field. In preparation of this book, the author has freely consulted large number of books and journals so no authenticity is claimed. Author is specially thankful to M/S Anmol Publications for shaping this book in its final form.

Suggestions for further improvement of this book are not only welcome but also greatly appreciated.

Author

A

A/d converter A device used to convert analog data to digital data. Analog data is continuously variable, while digital data contains discrete steps.

A/V (audio/video) Marriage of big screen television with movie-theater-like audio in homes and classrooms.

AAL Connection Association established by the AAL between two or more next higher layer entities.

AAL-1 (atm adaptation layer type 1) AAL functions in support of constant bit rate, time-dependent traffic such as voice and video.

AAL-2 (atm adaptation layer type 2) This AAL is still undefined by the International Standards bodies. It is a placeholder for variable bit rate video transmission.

AAL-3/4 (atm adaptation layer type ¾) AAL functions in support of variable bit rate, delay-tolerant data traffic requiring some sequencing and/or error detection support. Originally two AAL types, i.e. connection-oriented and connectionless, which have been combined.

AAL-5 (atm adaptation layer type 5) AAL functions in support of variable bit rate, delay-tolerant connection-oriented data traffic requiring minimal sequencing or error detection support.

AAP DTD A DTD for a standard SGML document type for scientific documents, defined by the AAP.

AAP The Association of American Publishers Engaged in standardisation efforts in document preparation.

Aautoexec.bat A root directory batch file that is responsible for executing commands at system startup.

AB roll editing The transfer of portions of two video sources into one master videotape. For example, one source may be a VCR and the other source a video camera.

AB style switches Analog switchers that are designed to be used in applications whenever multiple computer sources must be connected to a single display device such as a monitor, projector, or LCD panel. For example, multiple VGA or SVGA PCs may be connected to a single data projector or PCs and Macs may be connected to a single data projector.

Abacus An ancient counting device that probably originated in Babylon around 2,400 B.C.E.

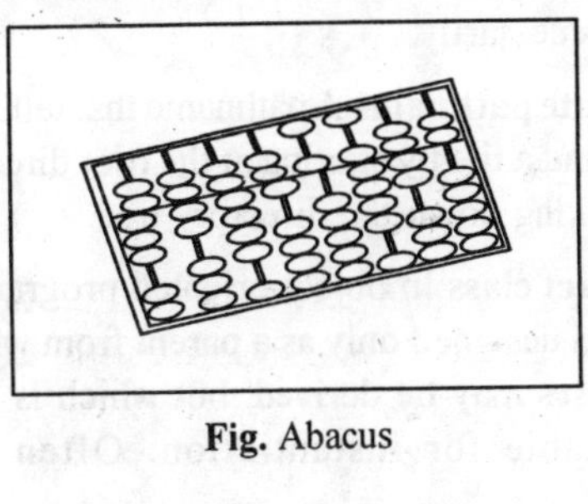

Fig. Abacus

Abend When Novell's NetWare network operating system crashes, it will usually toss up a message that starts with the term abend, which stands for abnormal End. Much like the Windows NT BSOD (Blue screen of death), the abend screen signifies a problem condition that the operating system cannot handle. Most often, this term is used in phrases like "The server abended!" or "The server stopped abending after I updated the NIC drivers."

ABI (application binary interface) The interface by which an application program gains access to operating system and other services, designed to permit porting of compiled binary applications between systems with the same ABI.

ABIOS (advanced basic input/output system) A set of firmware service routines built into the IBM PS/2 series of computers that use the Micro Channel Architecture (MCA) to support multitasking operating systems such as OS/2.

ABR (available bit rate) ABR is an ATM layer service category for which the limiting ATM layer transfer characteristics provided by the network may change subsequent to connection establishment. A flow control mechanism is specified which supports several types of feedback to control the source rate in response to changing ATM layer transfer characteristics. It is expected that an end-system that adapts its traffic in accordance with the feedback will experience a low cell loss ratio and obtain a fair share of the available bandwidth according to a network specific allocation policy. Cell delay variation is not controlled in this service, although admitted cells are not delayed unnecessarily.

Absolute pathname A pathname that tells you how to find a file by starting at the root directory and working down the directory tree.

Abstract class In object-oriented programming, a class designed only as a parent from which sub-classes may be derived, but which is not itself suitable for instantiation. Often used to "abstract out" incomplete sets of features, which may then be shared by a group of sibling sub-classes, which add different variations of the missing pieces.

Abstract syntax notation one (ASN.1) The OSI language for describing abstract syntax, which is a description of data structures independent of machine orientation.

AC (alternating current) A type of electrical current that reverses its direction at a regular interval, and can be represented by a sine wave. Alternating current is the type of current typically found in a wall outlet. You plug your TV, computer, refrigerator, etc. into alternating current. These devices then change the alternating current into direct current (DC) so that they can use the current properly. Alternating current is the reason that we need such complex power supplies, or power bricks, to regulate the flow of current in electronic devices.

AC-3 (dolby digital) This digital surround-sound format for home audio is called Dolby Digital in theaters. It is a 5.1 format, with six separate audio tracks. AC-3 has been chosen as the official sound format for digital TV, and is already encoded on many DVDs and Laserdiscs.

Accelerated graphics port (AGP) A dedicated expansion port that began to show up on motherboards in the second half of 1997. It bypasses the PCI bus and allows higher throughput from the graphics card to the processor and memory for speedier 3D graphics. Original AGP cards were "1x" versions that ran at 66MHz, offering 266MB/second throughput; but now AGP supports up to 8X data transfer speeds, which means the card still runs at 66MHz, but transfers 8x as much data per clock tick, upping the throughput to 2.1GB/second. Although the throughput is much greater, most graphics cards have a large amount of local memory and thus do not get much of a bonus from faster AGP speeds.

Accelerator board An add-in printed circuit board that replaces the main processor with a higher-performance processor, so you can upgrade your system without replacing monitor, case, keyboard, and so on.

Using an accelerator board can reduce upgrade costs substantially. However, there are other factors to consider, such as disk access time, in determining the overall performance of your system.

Most modern computers are designed to accept simpler upgrades. Built into the motherboard is a socket in which the CPU sits. It is usually possible simply to remove the CPU and replace it with a faster model. This is particularly easy if the socket is a zero insertion force (ZIF) socket.

Acces mechanism In a floppy or hard disk drive, the component that positions the read/write head over the surface of the disk, so that data can be read from or written to the disk.

Access bandwidth The ability of a communications network to provide bandwidth dynamically so users will receive service regardless of the bandwidth their service request requires.

Access concentrator A device that efficiently forwards data, handling incoming calls for a network point of presence (POP) In general, an access concentrator supports dial-in modem calls, ISDN connections, nailed-up links, frame relay traffic, and multiprotocol routing.

Access control list (ACL) Defines the roles that are required to execute a method. Defines the user or group IDs of people who do (or do not) have explicit access to a file or directory.

Access control The management of permissions and restrictions for logging onto a computer or network. Systems typically employ individual profiles that specify which network-attached resources are available to which users. The profiles are maintained in a database, such as RADIUS.

Access Microsoft's advanced database creation and maintenance software. It is very popular among developers who maintain online databases with Windows NT.

Access point A hardware device or a computer's software that acts as a communication hub for users of a wireless device to connect to a wired LAN.

Access provider The company that provides you with Internet access and, in some cases, an online account on their computer system.

Access rate The data rate of the user access channel.

Access router An access device with built-in basic routing protocol support, specifically designed to allow remote LAN access to corporate backbone networks. Not designed to replace backbone routers or to build backbone networks.

Access server Same as RAS(remote access server) Any device that enables multiple remote users to access a network.

Access speed The average amount of time it takes for a floppy drive, hard drive, CD drive, or other drive to find any particular piece of data on a disk and send it to your PC. Access speed is typically listed in milliseconds (ms).

Access time The period of time that elapses between a request for information from disk or memory, and the information arriving at the requesting device. Memory access time refers to the time it takes to transfer a character from memory to or from the processor, while disk access time refers to the time it takes to place the read/write heads over the requested data. RAM may have an access time of 80 nanoseconds or less, while hard disk access time could be 18 milliseconds or less.

Account An e-mail account is the arrangement you've made with an ISP or network administrator in which space is allocated on a server for your mail, and in which you're assigned the right to send and received e-mail. ACE Advanced Computing Environment: a consortium to agree on an open architecture based on the MIPS R4000 chip.

Account boot disk A disk used to load DOS into the computer when it is turned on.

Accuracy /accuracy vs. precision If the actual value is 4.321 and you say that it is 4.30, then you are precise to the first decimal place but inaccurate by .021. If a value is represented as a bulls-eye on a target, a group of guesses or measurements represented by closely grouped points have a high degree of precision. If that group is near the center, it is highly accurate as well. On a bullseye, think of accuracy as how close to the center your arrow hits, and your measurement of precision as how closely you can group your shots. Accuracy is how close to the actual value you are. For example, if the number you are representing is 4 and you say it's 3, you are inaccurate by 1.

ACK (acknowledge) An acknowledgement (approval) from an authorized contact for a domain name record that a requested modification to a domain name's registration information should be completed. When a modification request is received from a source that is not an authorized contact/agent, the request will be rejected by the InterNIC and a message will be sent to the listed contacts asking them to ACK (approve) or NAK (No Acknowledgement or disapprove) the modification.

Active content Auto-executable Java, ActiveX, or script files that are embedded in Web pages or email messages.

ACM (address complete message) A BISUP call control message from the receiving exchange to sending exchange indicating the completion of address information.

Acoustic coupler A type of modem which converts digital signals into sound for transmission through telephone lines, and performs the reverse operation when receiving such signals. Acoustic couplers generally have cups for the telephone handset.

Fig. Acoustic coupler

ACPI (advanced configuration and power interface) This power management interface takes the power management out of the BIOS and gives control to the operating system (OS). Typically, a system's BIOS is only able to turn a device off after a certain period of inactivity. With ACPI, the user can instruct the OS to slow down the processor or enter sleep mode. This basically gives the OS, and thus the user, more control of power management. Short for Advanced Configuration and Power Interface, a power management specification developed by Intel, Microsoft, and Toshiba. ACPI, which will be part of the next version of Windows, enables the operating system to control the amount of power given to each device attached to the computer. With ACPI, the operating system can turn off peripheral devices, such as a CD-ROM players, when they're not in use. As another example, ACPI will enable manufacturers to produce computers that automatically power up as soon as you touch the keyboard.

ACPI Hardware Computer hardware with the features necessary to support operating system power management and with the interfaces to those features described using the Description Tables as specified in *Advanced Configuration and Power Interface Specification*

ACPI Machine language ACPI Machine language. Pseudocode for a virtual machine supported by an ACPI-compatible operating system and in which ACPI control methods are written. The AML encoding definition is provided in section 16 of the *Advanced Configuration and Power Interface Specification.*

ACPI name Space A hierarchical tree structure in operating system controlled memory that contains named objects. These objects can be data objects, control method objects, bus and device package objects, and so on. All the information in the ACPI Name Space comes from the Differentiated System Description Table.

ACR allowed cell rate An ABR service parameter, ACR is the current rate in cells/sec at which a source is allowed to send.

ACR (attenuation to crosstalk ratio) One of the factors that limits the distance a signal may be sent through a given media. ACR is the ratio of the power of the received signal, attenuated by the media, over the power of the NEXT crosstalk from the local transmitter, usually expressed in decibels (db). To achieve a desired bit error rate, the received signal power must usually be several times larger than the NEXT power or plus several db. Increasing a marginal ACR may decrease the bit error rate.

Acrobat A platform-independent text and image formatter/viewer from Adobe Systems.

Active channels An Active Channel is what Microsoft calls a Web site that has been enabled for push delivery to Internet Explorer 4.0 browsers. To create a channel, developers write and upload a CDF (channel definition format) file to their Web site; new content is delivered to users automatically when the site is updated. Developers and subscribers can control the update frequency; which channels, subchannels, and items (sections) are subscribed to; and other channel characteristics. Most Active Channels use dynamic HTML (DHTML) and other effects to spice up content and make it more interactive.

Active DBMS A conventional or passive DBMS combined with a means of event detection and condition monitoring. Event handling is often rule-based, as with an expert system.ActiveX A software development kit from Microsoft for development of Internet applications and content.

Active desktop Windows Desktop program that can activate Web pages and ActiveX applications.

Active directory A Microsoft technology based on LDAP that provides a unified view and way to manage all objects on a network. Microsoft created Active Directory as a response to Novell's NDS system that allows administrators to control large networks in a similar manner. Active Directory was first introduced with Windows 2000, and many organizations are moving from the domain model of Windows NT to the Active Directory model of Windows 2000.

Active matrix Flat-panel displays for laptop computers are created by laying diodes over a superfine grid of wires. The diodes are activated by applying current to various points around the grid. Connect enough of these dots and you get an image. Active-matrix displays use transistors to keep their diodes in an on or off state, unlike their passive-matrix cousins, which rely on the diodes' persistence. As a result, active-matrix displays are brighter and produce better color than passive-matrix displays. However, the additional technology required to build active displays also makes them far more expensive.

Active movie A Microsoft technology used for streaming video and audio over the Internet. It is an ActiveX control.

Active object An object that encompasses its own thread of control.

Active open A client-initiated operation that enables a device to establish a TCP link with a server at a fixed IP address.

Active partition That part of the hard disk containing the operating system to be loaded when you start or restart the computer. You can install 2 different operating systems (perhaps DOS and OS/2) on your hard disk, but each must be in its own separate area, or partition. Only one partition can be active at any given time, and to change from the DOS to the non-DOS partition, you may have to use the DOS FDISK command.

Active server pages (ASP) Script extensions contain either Visual Basic or Jscript code. When a browser requests an ASP page, the Web server generates a page with HTML code and sends it back to the browser. So ASP pages are similar to CGI scripts, but they enable Visual Basic programmers to work with familiar tools. This is a page that performs customized "applications" services. A great example is NetLedger.com where individuals or complete business firms can access accounting software that allows all accounting to be maintained in NetLedger's online files. Business transactions (such as billings and collections) can even be managed by the applications server. For now, however, the latest twist on the ASP trend—what Outtask and some analysts are calling the BSP, or business service provider, model—remains immature. The range of business process services being offered in conjunction with hosted applications is narrow, mostly limited to functions such as travel, PC support and payroll. And, while some hosting providers such as Alexandria-based Outtask have begun building mixed portfolios of managed application and business process services from scratch and selling them directly to their customers, many established ASPs are adding the BSP tag to their résumés by forming alliances with the BPO divisions of major consulting and systems integration companies or with leaders in specific areas of outsourcing, such as Automatic Data Processing Inc. for payroll services. Many of those relationships, however, are new. Often, the hosted applications from one vendor and the business services from another are not truly integrated. So the user is often left negotiating and dealing with more than one provider.

Active template library (ATL) A group of routines provided by Microsoft that can be used to help more easily create ASP, ActiveX, and COM objects in C++.

Active timing This is defined as the portion of the Video Signal that carries the actual Video information. Surrounding this region, is the front porch and back porch.Actor In object-oriented programming, an object which exists as a concurrent process.

Active video A video AV standard and open-video architecture that Microsoft Corporation hopes will become the popular standard to replace the Video for Windows (.avi file extension) and Quicktime (.mov file extension) video architecture. Active video attempts to overcome common complaints with its Video for Windows (e.g., limited throughput, poor A/V synchronization, and hardware/software incompatibilities. Also, Active Video will have software MPEG decoding and will cross platforms with Windows, Windows 2000, and Power Macintosh. It will also have an Active Movie filter to play on the Internet via Microsoft's Explorer browser. Whereas Video for Windows was losing out to Apple's Quicktime in popularity, Microsoft's Active Video makes it a closer race between Apple and Microsoft for dominance in the setting of video standards.

Active window The top or front window in a multiple window environment.

Active-matrix screen An LCD display mechanism that uses an individual transistor to control every pixel on the screen. Active-matrix screens are characterized by high contrast, a wide viewing angle, vivid colors, and fast screen refresh rates, and they do not show the streaking or shadowing that is common with cheaper LCD technology.

ActiveX Utilities from Microsoft Corporation that combine older Object Linking and Embedding (OLE) and Component Object Model (COM) utilities. AcitiveX is usually coded in Visual

Basic and is quite confusing since it is an outgrowth of a complex set of OLE and COM technologies. One of the most widespread applications is to give interactive controls (e.g., ask questions, provide answers, perform computations, push buttons, etc.) to users of Internet Explorer on the web. Therein lies a huge risk as well when computers also have windows scripting host (wsh) utilities using ActiveX. WSH files have file extension whs and are similar to PIF files in older 16-bit applications. Prior to WSH applications, users could browse the web and use email without any worries about virus infections as long as security warnings were heeded about file downloads that run in Microsoft Word, Excel, etc. That is no longer the case if WSH utilities are installed. To avoid such risks, users can either rely upon Netscape products for email and web browsing since Netscape products use Java rather than ActiveX software. If users prefer Microsoft Internet Explorer for web browsing and Microsoft Outlook for email, then they may want to consider adding security barriers to WSH risks.

Actual image size The size of the display on the screen is dependent upon the timing signals provided by the video card. The displayable diagonal linear measurement can vary based on the graphic mode being generated and how the monitor responds to the characteristics of the signal.

Actuator The part of a hard drive that the read/ write arms attach to. It is controlled by an electrical signal sent to it that extends or retracts the arms so that they can move across the tracks on the drive platters. Nowadays the movement of these lightweight arms is very fast, appearing like a flicker if you were to view it.

Acuity Sharpness or keenness, especially when used to describe vision.

AD/cycle (application development) A set of SAA-compatible IBM-sponsored products for program development, running on workstations accessing a central repository on a mainframe. The stages cover requirements, analysis and design, production of the application, building and testing, and maintenance. Technologies used include code generators and knowledge based systems, as well as languages and debuggers.

ADA A high-level computer language sponsored by the US Department of Defense. It has a multitasking mechanism, and a number of features useful for software engineering.

Adaline Name given by Widrow to ADAptive LInear NEurons, that is neurons , which learn using the Widrow-Huff Delta Rule.

ADAM (animated dissection of anatomy for medicine) Project that resulted in high quality computer-aided learning modules for schools of medicine.

ADAMO A data management system written at CERN based on the Entity-Relationship model.

Adaptable user interface A toolkit from Oracle allowing applications to be written portably for different windowing systems. It provides one call level interface along with a resource manager and editor across a range of "standard" GUIs, including Macintosh, Windows and the X Window System.

Adapter A printed circuit board that plugs into a computer's expansion bus to provide added capabilities. Common adapters for the PC include display adapters, memory expansion adapters, input/output adapters that provide, serial, parallel, and games peorts, and other devices such as internal modesm, CD-ROMs, or network interface cards. One adapter can often support several different devices; for example, an I/O adapter may support one parallel port, a games or joystick port, and several serial ports. Some PC designs incorporate many of the functions previously performed by these individual adapters on the motherboard.

Adaptive compression Data compression software that continually analyzes and compensates its algorithm, depending on the type and content of the data and the storage medium.

Adaptive differential pulse code modulation A standard that codes for digitized speech. It samples the sound waves 8,000 times a second; the sample representing the difference between two adjacent samples.

Adaptive learning Learning in which a system programs itself by adjusting weights or strengths until it produces the desired output.

ADC (Analog to Digital Convertor) An electronic device that converts analog signals into digital signals. For example, the input port of a sound card can accept analog input from a microphone, and it uses an ADC to convert the analog signal to a digital signal that can be sent along to other parts of your computer.

ADDD (a depository of development documents) A public domain Software Engineering Environment from GMD developed as part of the STONE project.

Additional servers Any name servers, aside from the primary and secondary name servers listed on the Domain Name Registration Agreement, that will be available to resolve a particular domain name to its corresponding Internet Protocol (IP) number(s).

Additive primaries Red, green, and blue are the primary colors of light from which all other colors can be made.

Add-on devices Devices that are traditionallya dded to the base PC system to increase functionality, such as audio, networking, graphics, SCSI controller, and so on. Add-on devices fall into two categories: devices built onto the system board and devices on expansion cards added to the system through a system board connector such as PCI.

Address 1.The precise location in memory or on disk where a piece of information is stored. Every byte in memory and every sector on a disk have their own unique addresses. 2. To reference or manage a storage location. In TCP/IP, an IP address is a 32-bit numeric identifier assigned to a node. The address has two parts, one for the network identifier and the other for the node identifier. All nodes on the same network must share the network address and have unique node address. For networks connected to the Internet, network addresses are assigned by the Internet Activities Board (IAB).Addresses also include IPX addresses -the internal network number and external network number-and the MAC (Media access Control) address assigned to each network card or device.

Address book An address book is a file in which you can store the e-mail addresses of people to whom you frequently write. When you add a person to your address book, you'll typically enter the person's real name and his or her e-mail address. In some e-mail programs, as you type the person's real name in the recipient field of a new message, the program will automatically locate the person's real name and e-mail address and fill it in for you.

Address bus The electronic channel, usually from 20 to 32 separate lines wide, used to transmit the signals that specify locations in memory. The number of lines in the address bus determines the number of memory locations that the processor can access, as each line carries one bit of the address. An address bus of 20 lines (used in early Intel 8086/8088 processors) can access 1MB of memory, one of 24 lines (as in the Intel 80286) can access 16MB, and an address bus of 32 lines (as used by Intel 80386,80486, and later processors, or the Motorola 68020) can access over 4 GB.

Address mask A bit mask used to select bits from an Internet address for subnet address.

Address prefix A string of 0 or more bits up to a maximum of 152 bits that is the lead portion of one or more ATM addresses.

Address resolution Address Resolution is the procedure by which a client associates a LAN destination with the ATM address of another client or the BUS.

Address resolution protocol (ARP) An Ethernet protocol used to translate IP network addresses into Ethernet hardware addresses (also known as Media Access Control (MAC) addresses).

Adjacency The relationship between two communicating neighboring peer nodes.

Adjacent hosts Two hosts are adjacent if they have permanent ARP entries for each other.

Adjunct processor A computer outside a telephone switching system that "talks" to the switch and gives it switching commands.

ADL Assertion (or API) Definition Language. A project for Automatic Interface Test Generation.

Administrative contact/agent The administrative contact/agent is an individual or role account authorized to interact with Network Solutions on behalf of the domain name registrant. The administrative contact/agent should be able to answer non-technical questions about the domain name's registration and the domain name registrant. It is strongly recommended that this contact/agent be the registrant or someone from the registrant's organization.

Administrative domain A collection of managed entities grouped for administrative reasons.

Administrator In the context of Tivoli, a user who is authorized to perform some TME function.

ADO (activex data objects) A Microsoft technology that provides a unified way to access different data sources with a single data model. By providing a single data model, ADO lets you access data in the same way whether it exists in a database, a spreadsheet, and even text files.

ADPCM (adaptive differential pulse code modulation) A reduced bit rate variant of PCM audio encoding . This algorithm encodes the difference between an actual audio sample amplitude and a predicted amplitude and adapts the resolution based on recent differential values.

ADSL (asymmetric digital subscriber line) Modems attached to twisted pair copper wiring that transmit from 1.5 Mbps to 9 Mbps downstream (to the subscriber) and from 16 kbps to 800 kbps upstream, depending on line distance. Asymmetric Digital Subscriber Line is the most popular form of xDSL technology. The key to ADSL is that the upstream and downstream bandwidth is asymmetric, or uneven. In practice, the bandwidth from the provider to the user (downstream) will be the higher speed path. This is in part due to the limitation of the telephone cabling system and the desire to accommodate the typical Internet usage pattern where the majority of data is being sent to the user (programs, graphics, sounds and video) with minimal upload capacity required (keystrokes and mouse clicks). Downstream speeds typically range from 1.5Mbps to 9Mbps. Upstream speeds typically range from 64Kbps to 1.5Mbps.

ADSL lite Is a lower data rate version of ADSL This is the dsl in which the POTS splitter is eliminated at the customer premises and the signal is carried over all of the house wiring which lowers bandwidth due to greater noise impairments.A lower data rate version of Asymmetric Digital Subscriber Line (ADSL) has also been proposed as an extension to ANSI standard T1.413 by the UAWG (Universal ADSL Working Group) led by Microsoft, Intel, and Compaq. This is known as G.lite in the ITU standards committee. It uses the same modulation scheme as ADSL (DMT), but eliminates the POTS splitter at the customer premises. As a result, the ADSL signal is carried over all of the house wiring which results in lower available bandwidth due to greater noise impairments.

ADT (abstract data type) A class of data structures described by means of a set of operations rather than by physical representation, such as a class in object-oriented programming..

ADTF (ACR decrease time factor) This is the time permitted between sending RM-cells before the rate is decreased to ICR (Initial Cell Rate). The ADTF range is .01 to 10.23 sec. with granularity of 10 ms.

Advanced configuration and power interface (ACPI) This power management interface takes the power management out of the BIOS and gives control to the operating system (OS). Typically, a system's BIOS is only able to turn a device off after a certain period of inactivity. With ACPI, the user can instruct the OS to slow down the processor or enter sleep mode. This basically gives the OS, and thus the user, more control of power management.

Advanced development environment (ADE) A toolkit for programmers to use in developing systems management applications in the TME. This requires knowledge of how the underlying object system works.

Advanced graphics port This is a special interface designed to speed up 3d graphics processing by the computer. Video cards must be specifically designed to plug into the AGP connector, and of course, the motherboard must be designed to have said connector. Prior to AGP, 3d video cards were connected to the PCI bus. Basically, AGP allows the video card to have a direct connection to the system memory, allowing 3d instructions to bypass the shared (and thus slower) PCI bus. This speeds up 3d video performance. In addition, the data transfer rate of the AGP bus can be 66MHz or more. That is much higher than the 33MHz speed of PCI. Good news for gamers and 3d artists.

Advanced intelligent network A switched voice and data network consisting of a variety of nework elements. It refers to open interfaced, multi-vendor, telecommunications capabilities that let phone companies create and customize their service offerings.

Advanced intelligent tape (AIT) A tape format initially introduced in 1996. AIT promises low tape tension for longer tape life, very clean tape media, and high capacity and transfer rates. The AIT-1 specification offers 35 GB of native storage per tape and 3MB/second transfer rates; the AIT-2 standard offers 50 GB of native storage with transfer rates of 6MB/second; and AIT-3 boosts that up to 100 GB and 12MB/second. Each AIT tape contains a small memory chip which keeps track of where files are located on the tape, allowing for faster file location than scanning the entire tape until you hit the file you are looking for. AIT competes against DLT at the high-end of the tape drive market.

Advanced power management A software interface (defined by Microsoft and Intel) between hardware-specific power management software (such as that located in a system BIOS) and an operating system power management driver. Replaced by ACPI as the system interface under Microsoft Windows 98 and Windows 2000.

Advanced research projects agency (ARPA) The US government agency that funded the ARPANET, predecessor to the Internet. ARPA is now called DARPA(Defense Advanced Research Projects Agency).

Advanced research projects agency network (ARPANet) A network of interconnected computers that formed the original Internet. The United States military funded the ARPANet, and construction was started in 1968. It was designed to be a redundant network of computers so that no single disruption could break down communications between other units. The ARPANet expanded to universities for research, and soon after the Internet was born.

Advanced run-length limited encoding Abbreviated ARLL. A technique used to store information on a hard disk that increases the capacity of run-lenth limited (RLL) storage by more than 25 %, and increases the data-transfer rate to 9 megabits per second.

Advanced scsi programming interface (ASPI) This was developed by Adaptec so that different devices could be controlled by different SCSI cards, and therefore the SCSI card version would not matter. Basically, if the correct ASPI driver is being used, you can send the same command to any Adaptec SCSI card to make something happen to a device. Most commonly, ASPI is associated with CD-ROM and CD-RW drives.

Advanced technology adapter (ATA) Another name for Integrated Disk Electronics (IDE).

Adversary From an administrator's viewpoint: a hacker or anyone expected to attack your network. A group, organization, or software agent (also known as a malicious agent).

From an attacker's viewpoint: anyone who is responsible for defending the computer resources that the hacker intends to attack. Therefore, attackers (hackers) and defenders (network administrators) are mutual adversaries.

Aegis A CASE tool for project change management, part of the GNU software.

AENOR Asociacion Espanola de Normalizacion y Certificacion. The Spanish standards organisation.

AEP Application environment profile.

Aerodynamics The science and engineering of systems that are capable of flight.

AES Application environment specification: a set of specifications from OSF for programming and user interfaces, aimed at providing a consistent application environment on different hardware platforms. It includes O/S for the operating system (user commands and program interfaces), U/E for the User Environment (Motif), and N/S for Network services.

AFI (authority and format identifier) This identifier is part of the network level address header.

AFIPS American Federation of Information Processing Societies.

AFNOR (association francaise pour la normalisation) The French national standards institute, a member of ISO.

Agent Software that runs on a client computer for use by administrative software running on a server. Agents are typically used to support administrative actions, such as detecting system information or running services.

Aggregation Token A number assigned to an outside link by the border nodes at the ends of the outside link. The same number is associated with all uplinks and induced uplinks associated with the outside link. In the parent and all higher-level peer group, all uplinks with the same aggregation token are aggregated.

AGL Atelier de Genie Logiciel: French for IPSE.

AGOCG (advisory group on computer graphics) Advising UK Higher Education on Computer Graphics, Visualization and Multimedia.

AGTL signaling (assisted gunning transistor logic) AGTL and AGTL+ use the same signaling protocol only at different voltage levels. AGTL+ operates at 1.5V signaling levels, while AGTL operates at 1.25V.

AHFG (ATM-attached host functional group) The group of functions performed by an ATM-attached host that is participating in the MPOA service.

AI Stands for Artificial Intelligence. This is the area of computer science focusing on creating machines that can engage on behaviors that humans consider intelligent. The ability to create intelligent machines has intrigued humans since ancient times, and today with the advent of the computer and 50 years of research into AI programming techniques, the dream of smart machines is becoming a reality. Researchers are creating systems which can mimic human thought, understand speech, beat the best human chess player, and countless other feats never before possible.

AICA Associazione Italiana di Calcolo Automatico.

AIF One format of Macintosh audio (sound) files.

AIFF (audio IFF) A format developed by Apple for storing high-quality sampled sound and musical instrument info; also used by SGI and several professional audio packages.

Ailerons Control surfaces on the trailing edges of the wings of an aircraft— used to manage roll control.

AIMUX (ATM inverse multiplexing) A device that allows multiple T1 or E1 communications facilities to be combined into a single broadband facility for the transmission of ATM cells.

AIR (additive increase rate) An ABR service parameter, AIR controls the rate at which the cell transmission rate increases. It is signaled as AIRF, where AIRF = AIRNrm/PCR.

Air cooling Cooling that involves a heatsink and/or fan. Even though a metal heatsink may make contact with the microprocessor package (or whatever is being cooled), the heatsink ultimately exchanges the heat with air, whether a fan is used or not. Contrast this with water cooling. Air cooling is less efficient than water cooling.

Air gap A type of network security in which a network is secured, at least in part, by keeping it physically separate from other local networks and the Internet. This can be an effective type of security, but it is also limiting in that clients may not be able to get to all resources they need from a single computer.

AIS (alarm indication signal) An all ones signal sent down or up stream by a device when it detects an error condition or receives an error condition or receives an error notification from another unit in the transmission path.

AIT (advanced intelligent tape) A tape format initially introduced in 1996. AIT promises low tape tension for longer tape life, very clean tape media, and high capacity and transfer rates. The AIT-1 specification offers 35 GB of native storage per tape and 3MB/second transfer rates; the AIT-2 standard offers 50 GB of native storage with transfer rates of 6MB/second; and AIT-3 boosts that up to 100 GB and 12MB/second. Each AIT tape contains a small memory chip which keeps track of where files are located on the tape, allowing for faster file location than scanning the entire tape until you hit the file you are looking for. AIT competes against DLT at the high-end of the tape drive market.

AIX An IBM version of the Unix operating system. It will run on PCs with 386 or higher chips and on workstations and mainframes.

Alert Automatic notification of a particular event when it occurs, such as a virus detection.

ALGOL A language developed by the ALGOL committee for scientific applications—acronym for ALGOrithmic Language.

Algorithm A complex mathematical function. Algorithms are use to encrypt and decrypt private information.

Anomaly detection Detects any unacceptable deviation from expected behavior. A profile of expected behavior is defined in advance, either manually or automatically. Software that collects and processes characteristics of system behavior over time and forms a statistically valid sample of such behavior is used to create automatically-developed profiles. Some of these deviations do not require further examination and some do. An anomaly might include:

Users logging on at strange hours or from unfamiliar sites on the network.

Unexplained reboots or changes to system clocks.

Unusual error messages from mailers, daemons, or other servers.

Multiple, failed logon attempts with bad passwords.

Unauthorized use of the su command to gain UNIX root access.

Alias A pointer to one or more users or hosts, typically used for sending mail (in the case of users) or logging in remotely (in the case of hosts).

Aliased nameservers An aliased nameserver is a nameserver that has been labeled as yours (the reseller's) despite the fact it actually belongs to your Web hosting provider. This ensures that domains located on your server are listed as "ns.yourservername.com" instead of "ns.yourprovidersname.com".

Aliasing Visibly jagged steps along angled or object edges, due to sharp tonal contrasts between pixels.

All-points-addressable mode A technique for organizing graphics devices where all points (pixels) on the screen are individually accessible to a running program.

Alpha (alpha test) A term given to a very early version of a hardware or software product which is not yet stable and may lack features. After some testing and some revision, the product will assume beta status. RISC-based 64-bit CPU from DEC (Digital Equipment Corp.) It is designed to run with DOS/Windows, NT and Unix operating systems.

Alpha beta pruning A technique that under certain conditions offers an optimal way to search through data structures called "trees"

Alpha blending This allows two objects to be visually blended together. This is primarily used for 3D atmospheric and environmental effects. It allows such things as "fogging," where an image is rendered behind another translucent image, which creates the effect of looking though fog or looking down through a pool and seeing the bottom. It also allows Depth Cueing, which is the lowering of the intensity of lighting to make an object appear farther away.

Alpha processor The ultimate top-of-the line processor for PCs that uses DEC's 21064 chip. The "Alpha-based" systems such as the DECpc from Digital Equipment Corporation claims it is the fastest system available for Windows 2000.

Alphanumeric A character set which is the union of the set of alphabetic characters and the set of single digit numbers

Alt (alternate) 1. There is an Alt key found on a computer keyboard. The Alt key functions much like a third Ctrl/Shift key in that it alters the value of other characters pressed on the keyboard.

2. The term Alt has also been used to refer to using the Esc key (ASCII 27) to alter the next input.

3. Finally, Alt is used as a prefix for usenet newsgroups that can be created without going through the standard voting procedures, such as alt.pictures.angry.pandas.

ALT (automated loop test system) The operations system that provides a single comprehensive automated test system for testing international customer POTS lines.

Alt key If your keyboard has an alt key, it is used as a shift key; it does nothing on its own. To use it, hold it down, press another key, and release it. To press alt-A, for example, hold the Alt key, press and release the A key, and release the Alt key.simple.

ALT software alternatives To authoring systems that have full CMS utilities. In other words, professors who do not need full CMS features may opt for alternative authoring packages such as hypertext or hypermedia packages that do not have full CMS features.

Altair 8800 The first commercially successful microcomputer, based on the Intel 8080, introduced in 1975 by Micro Instrumentation Telemetry Systems of New Mexico. Over 10,000 were sold, mostly in kit form, and the Altair was packaged with the Microsoft MBASIC interpreter, written by Paul Allen and Bill Gates. The Altair8800 had 256 bytes of memory, received input through a set of switches on the front panel, and displayed output on a row of LEDs.

Alternate routing A mechanism that supports the use of a new path after an attempt to set up a connection along a previously selected path fails.

Alternating current (AC) A type of electrical current that reverses its direction at a regular interval, and can be represented by a sine wave. Alternating current is the type of current typically found in a wall outlet. You plug your TV, computer, refrigerator, etc. into alternating current. These devices then change the alternating current into direct current (DC) so that they can use the current properly.

Alternating current is the reason that we need such complex power supplies, or power bricks, to regulate the flow of current in electronic devices.

ALU (arithmetic logic unit) The part of the CPU that actually does the work of adding, subtracting, multiplying, and dividing, including OR, AND, and NOT operations. The ALU is an execution unit, like the FPU, that is fed with data from the CPU registers.

Alvey A funding programme for collaborative research in the UK.

AM (amplitude modulation) A means of transmitting and receiving radio waves that is based on variances in the amplitude of the radio waves.

Amadeus A PC client for Hyper-G.

Ambient Pertaining to the surrounding atmosphere or environment

Ambiguity The quality of doubtfulness or uncertainty; often subject to multiple interpretations

AMD (advanced microchip devices) A semiconductor manufacturer and is a major competitor of Intel. They manufacture the Athlon, Duron, and K6 CPU chips.

America online The commercial AOL network that "remains the hottest, easiest-to-use and most interesting of the services" according to Mossberg. AOL offers Time Magazine, the Chigago Tribune, and other news and television network options. New services to educators online include an American Federation of Teachers online doctoral program from the Electronic University Network and the Forum on Technology in Education and Training (FORUM-TET).

American standard code for information interchange (ASCII) Pronounced "ass-kee." This is a standard means of representing characters, consisting of 256 characters. The first 128 characters are standardized, and the first 32 of those are control codes, which don't really represent visible characters but rather codes that can be used for text formatting or actions, such as making the computer beep or clearing the screen. After the 32 control codes, the next 96 standardized characters represent numbers, letters (both uppercase and lowercase), and standard punctuation marks. The last 128 characters represent different things on different platforms. ASCII is being largely supplanted by Unicode.

AMI (alternate mark inversion) A line coding format used on T1 facilities that transmits ones by alternate positive and negative pulses.Ami applications of metrics in industry (Assess, Analyze, Metricate, Improve). A method for software project management and process improvement.

Amiga A video computing hardware/software desktop workstation formerly manufactured and marketed by Commodore International based on Motorola microprocessors. Amiga workstations became a widely popular option in conjunction with NewTek's Video Toaster software for home and office videotape productions. Amiga developed its own operating system called Amiga DOS. A major drawback is that as a computer it does not communicate (i.e., its files are not readable) on more popular Apple, PC, and Unix operating systems. For example, it can neither read MS-DOS files into its operating system nor write out MS-DOS files. It is far less of a competitor for digital computers and networking than for analog video computers such as Mac Video. The new Amiga workstations became aggressive low-priced competitors to Silicon Graphics and Sun workstations for 3D animation rendering for broadcast quality video. The Amiga and NewTek workstations compete with Apple AV and SGI competitors, but these options should not be confused with the more extensive concepts of network video servers. CD32, Apple AV, SGI, and Mac). The Amiga OS supported multiple disk types, excluding Macintosh due to the fact that those disks were not constant velocity format. MS-Dos 720k - 1.44k were supported provided the person had a HD drive for the 1.44 capability.

Amoeba A distributed operating system developed by A.Tanenbaum and others at Amsterdam.

Amortized Phasing out something in until it is gradually extinguished, like a mortgage loan.

Amp (ampere) The base unit of electrical current, which is the rate of flow of an electrical charge.

Amplitude modulation (AM) A means of transmitting and receiving radio waves that is based on variances in the amplitude of the radio waves.

Amplitude The size or magnitude of an electrical signal.

AMR (audio modem riser) An Intel specification designed to move the analog I/O functions of sound cards and modems onto a riser card. It allows motherboards to have an I/O slot built into them to make it easier to integrate audio and modem functions onto a motherboard. The specification does not define "an aftermarket standard I/O slot," according to Intel. Basically, the slot is supposed to be filled when you buy a motherboard, with the motherboard manufacturer's choice of modem/audio functions.

Analog Describes any device that represents changing values by a continuously variable physical property such as voltage in a circuit, fluid pressure, liquid level, and son on.An analog device can handle an infinite number of values within its range. By contrast, a digital device can only manage a fixed number of possible values. For example, an ordinary mercury thermometer is an analog device, and can record an infite number of readings over its range. A digital thermometer, on the other hand, can only display temperature in a fixed number of individual steps.A method of signal representation by an infinitely smooth universe of numeric values. Measurements that are characterized as analog include readings of voltage and current. Compare with digital. A relationship of logical similarity between two or more objects.

Analog control An analog control changes value in non-discrete steps. You can tune an analog control to non-distinct values (selecting 107.41234723947392... as the radio station you are tuned to instead of 107.40000000000000...). In some cases, like for volume, analog controls are better. Have you ever used a digital volume control on a new TV, and one setting is too loud while the other is too soft? You just can't get it in between. However, for channel tuning, where values change by fixed steps, a digital control is much better—you just don't need to get in between channel 4 and 5.

Analog display services interface (ADSI) A protocol that allows text messages generated by a remote computer or central office switch to be displayed on a user's telephone or TV set.

Analog technology Technology that uses a stream of continuously changing electrical waves to carry voice or low-speed data.

Analog-to-digital converter ADC or A-D converter. A device that converts continuously varying analog signals into discrete digital signals or numbers.Once analog signals have been converted into digital form, they can be processed, analyzed, stored, displayed and transmitted by computer. The key to analog-to-digital conversion lies in the amount of digital data created from the analog signal. The shorter the time interval between samples, and the more data recorded from that sample, the more closely the digital signal will modern sound boards can sample and playback at up to 44.1 kHz using a 16-bit analog-to-digital converter.

Analysis The part of the software development process concerned with defining the requirements for the product.

Analytic simulation Modeling of systems by using mathematical equations (often differential equations) and programming a computer with them to simulate the behavior of the real system.

Analytical engine Charles Babbage's vision of a programmable mechanical computer.

Anamorphic Unequally scaled in vertical and horizontal dimensions.

Ancestor node A logical group node that has a direct parent relationship to a given node (i.e., it is the parent of that node, or the parent's parent).

Anchor Synonymous with hyperlinks, anchor refers to non-linear links among documents. Or more simply put, it's the word or phrase that can be selected to connect to another page resource.

Anchor color The color on a browser screen that represents the anchor tag (navigation item) colors. The reason so many are blue is that blue is often the default color in browser software. This color can be changed to any combination of red, green and blue. The ability to change these colors at the reader level complicates choice of color at the authoring level.

AND An operation that can be executed on two or more binary strings. The AND operation compares bits from each string. If they are both positive, the operation returns true, or "1"; if not, it returns false, or "0". For example (0 AND 0) = 0, (0 AND 1) = 0, (1 AND 0) = 0, (1 AND 1) = 1. Thus, (0011 AND 1001) = 0001.

ANDF (architecture-neutral distribution format) An emerging OSF standard for software distribution. Programs are compiled into ANDF before distribution, and executables are produced from it for the local target system.

Andrew file system (AFS) A specific instance of a distributed file system (DFS), developed at Carnegie-Mellon University (CMU), allowing multiple file systems to be shared between organizations and treated, at the user interface level, as one giant file system.

Andrew message system A multimedia interface to electronic mail and bulletin boards, developed as part of the Andrew project.

Andrew project A distributed system project for support of educational and research computing at Carnegie Mellon University.

Andrew toolkit A portable user interface toolkit developed as part of the Andrew project, running on the X Window System and distributed with X11R5.

ANI (automatic number identification) A charge number parameter that is normally included in the Initial Address Message to the succeeding carrier for billing purposes.

Animation Time-phased moving graphic images that give the impression of motion such as in motion picture cartoons or videographic movements of objects about the screen. Several frames show a progression of movement, and thereby simulate movement. The best-buy in animation software is Autodesk 3D Studio according to PC Computing, December 1994, p. 204.

Fig. Animation

Animatronics The animation (movement) of something by the use of electronic motors, drives, and controls.

ANM Answer Message: A BISUP call control message from the receiving exchange to the sending exchange indicating answer and that a through connection should be completed in both directions.

Anna A specification language from Stanford University for formally specifying Ada programs. It has a Specification Analyzer and a Consistency Checking System.

Annealing A technique which can be applied to any minimization or learning process based on successive update steps (either random or deterministic) where the update step length is proportional to an arbitrarily set parameter which can play the role of a temperature. Then, in analogy with the annealing of metals, the temperature is made high in the early stages of the process for faster minimization or learning, then is reduced for greater stability.

Annotations Personal notes you can attach to the documents you have saved in your Web browser. The notes are available to you whenever the document is viewed.

Anonymous FTP A File Transfer Protocol (FTP) Is an Internet standard for transferring files between computers. Most FTP transfers require you log in to the system supplying the information by using an authorized username and password. However, a variation known as "anonymous FTP" lets you log in as "anonymous," i.e., you don't need a username or a password.

Anonymous login Access to a system without a login name or password. Strict file restrictions normally limit access.

Anonymous login convention (FTP) Standard username *(anonymous)* and password *(guest)* which allows login within FTP for the purpose of retrieving an unprotected file.

Anonymous posting In a USENET newsgroup, a public message posted via an anonymous server in order to conceal the identity of the original author. This server removes all the information from the message that could identify the sender, and forwards the message to its destination.

ANSI (American national standards institute) In the United States, ANSI serves as a quasi-national standards organisation. It provides "area charters" for groups to write and develop standards in specific fields. These groups include the Institute of Electrical and Electronics Engineers (IEEE) and Electronic Industries Association (EIA).

ANSI/SPARC architecture A layered model of database architecture comprising a physical schema, a conceptual schema, and user views.

Anthropomorphic Having human form, or generally resembling human appearance.

Anti-aliasing A method used to better define higher resolution objects in lower resolution. For example, you would use anti-aliasing if you have two lines that are so close together that at 320x200 they look as if they are one double-width line and you want to represent them better. This is most noticeable when dealing with curves, such as circles. For example, if you look at a circle drawn in a simple paint program at a low resolution, you can see the "steps," or "jaggies"—the points it takes to make the circle. If you raise the resolution you'll notice the "steps" much less. If you use anti-aliasing, different shades of the circle's color are used to "fill in" the gaps caused by low resolution, smoothing out its appearance to the user. Typical uses for anti-aliasing are for smoothing out fonts and straight lines in 3D images. If you are using a system with jagged-looking fonts, chances are that it's not anti-aliasing the fonts.

Anti-virus (AV) scanner Software that scans files to detect and remove viruses. Traditional anti-virus scanners are incapable of dealing with today's most serious content threats, namely active content vandals, including ActiveX, Java, and script vandals.

Anti-virus program An application program you run to detect or eliminate a computer virus or infection. Some anti-virus programs are terminate-and-stay-resident programs that can detect suspicious activity on your computer as it happens, while others must be run periodically as part of your normal housekeeping activities.

Anycast A method available in IPv6 of sending information over a network. It allows a device to send data to the nearest (fastest) of a group of receivers.

AOCE (apple open collaboration environment) A set of software for e-mail, directory services etc.

APA (application portability architecture) DEC's plan for portable applications software.

Apache In early 1995, a group of webmasters decided to get together and expand on the original NCSA HTTP daemon (webserver software), and Apache was born. Today, Apache is the most used webserver on the Internet. Apache is Open Source freeware, and is available for Linux, Windows, and many versions of UNIX.

Ape A graphics package from the Ohio Supercomputer Centre .

Apertos An object-oriented operating system from Sony Computer Science Laboratory.

Aperture grill (slot mask) This form of mask is similar to a shadow mask, but instead of a sheet of metal with holes poked into it it is a series of fine, vertically-aligned metal wires.

API (application program interface) By which an application program accesses operating system.An API can also provide an interface between a high level language and lower level utilities and services which were written without consideration for the calling conventions supported by compiled languages. Netscape Corporation and Microsoft both provide APIs called NSAPI and ISAPI that essentially extend their web servers, and it provides developers a way to put application code actually within the web server. This means that you don't have to start up a separate process each time one of these applications is called. And, since that application is always running, it can maintain connections to the database.

API connection Native ATM Application Program Interface Connection: API connection is a relationship between an API endpoint and other ATM devices that has the following characteristics:

Data communication may occur between the API endpoint and the other ATM devices comprising the API connection·

Each API connection may occur over a duration of time only once; the same set of communicating ATM devices may form a new connection after a prior connection is released·

The API connection may be presently active (able to transfer data), or merely anticipated for the future.

APL A Programming Language developed by Iverson for mathematical applications.

APM (automated power management) Series of techniques used to reduce the power consumption, especially on portable computers, in order to lengthen their autonomy.

APNIC (Asia-Pacific network information center) APNIC is a collaborative effort consisting of national Network Information Centers (NICs) and Internet Service Providers within the Asian-Pacific region. The APNIC acts as a regional Internet Registry, providing the allocation of Internet Protocol (IP) address space to the Asian-Pacific region.

Apollo Apollo Computer, now a division of Hewlett-Packard, also the name of a range of workstations manufactured by this company.

APP Ascend Password Protocol.

Appkit A set of objects used by the application builder for the NeXTstep environment.

Apple Apple Computer Inc, manufacturers of the Macintosh range of Personal Computers.

Fig. Apple Computer Inc.

Apple AV A line of computers that was popular for low-cost analog video computing due to built video capture hardware on the motherboard, a DAV connector, and a scan converter for analog video output to television sets and videotape recorders. The Power Macs have replaced the Apple AVs.

Apple talk remote access (ARA) ARA enables a remote Mac workstation to gain access to an IP network. You can use ARA over a modem or V.120 connection. You can also use synchronous PPP when the calling unit is AppleTalk-enabled Lucent unit. A client can dial in using ARA client software or a PPP dialer that supports AppleTalk.

Applescript It is an English-like language used to write script files which can automate the actions of the computer and the applications which run on it.

Appleshare This is Apple's network system. It is to the Macintosh what FTP is to the PC.

Applet A derivation of "application." You use the Applet tag in HTML code to define calls to Java-based applications within a browser. Thus, any Java program accessible through a Java-enabled browser can be referred to as an applet or Java Applet.

Appletalk A protocol suite developed by Apple Computer in the early 1980s, was developed in conjunction with the Macintosh computer. AppleTalk's purpose was to allow multiple users to share resources, such as files and printers. The devices that supply these resources are called servers, while the devices that make use of these resources (such as a user's Macintosh computer) are referred to as clients. Hence, AppleTalk is one of the early inplementations of a distributed client/server networking system.

Appletalk address resolution protocol (AARP) Provides for the dynamic assignment of node identifiers to nodes within an AppleTalk network.

Appletalk Control Protocol (ATCP) A protocol that enables you to route Apple Talk packets that are encapsulated in Point-to-Point Protocol (PPP).

Appliance server A relatively low-cost computing device used for specific tasks, including Internet connectivity and file and print. Does not have the full capabilities or software of a typical server that is sold for general-purpose office use, but has an extremely high ease-of-use associated with it.

Application A program that really gets some work done. Some programs just organize the computer, get its parts talking to each other, and do other housekeeping chores. Application programs do real-world work, like word processing or accounting.A software program designed to perform a specific task or group of tasks, such as word processing, communications, or database management.

Application extension facility (AEF) A tool kit for systems administrators to use in customizing a TME application to specific needs. This does not require any knowledge of how the underlying object system works.

Application firewall A mechanism that prevents untrusted applications, such as Trojan horses, from accessing and communicating over the Internet.

Application layer The seventh , or highest, layer in the International Organization for Standardization's Open Systems Interconnection (ISO/OSI) model for computer-to-computer communications. This layer uses services provided by the lower layers, but is completely insulated from the details of the network hardware. It describes how application programs interact with the network operating system, including database management, electronic mail, and terminal emulation programs.

Application program interface The complete set of operting system functions that an application program can use to perform tasks such as managing files and displaying information on the computer screen.An API is a complete definition of all the operating system functions available to an application program, and it also describes how the application program should use those functions.In operating systems that support a graphical user interface, the API also defines functions to support windows, icons, pull-down menus, and other components of the interface.

In network operating systems, an API defines a standard method application programs can use to take advantage of all the network features.

Application security Security policies enforced by individual software application, instead of being enforced globally for the entire network.

Application service provider (ASP) A company that provides remote access to applications, typically over the Internet. ASPs are used when an organization finds it more cost effective to have someone else host its applications than to host them itself. The applications served up can be as simple as access to a remote fileserver, or as complex as running an order entry system through your browser. The ASP provides the servers, network access, and applications to be used, typically for a monthly or yearly subscription fee.

Application-level firewall A firewall system that operates on the application layer. This is used to shield private IP addresses by changing the address of outgoing Internet traffic.

Application-specific integrated circuit (ASIC) A IC developed for a specific application, designed by incorporating standard cells from a library, rather than designed from scratch. ASICs can be found in VCRs, microwave ovens, automobiles, and security alarms. Manufacturers use it to consolidate many chips into a single package, reducing system board size and power consumption.

APPN (advanced peer to peer network) IBM network architecture for building dynamic routing across arbitrary network topologies. Intended as an eventual replacement for SNA, IBM's static routed, hierarchical network architecture.

APSE Ada Programming Support Environment.

Apt-get Part of "apt," a package retrieval tool that automatically connects to known Linux package repositories and checks for new packages. It also works out dependencies between packages. Apt-get is used with the Debian Linux distribution.

ARA (appletalk Remote) Access A protocol (and product) that provides system-level support for dial-in (modem) connections to an AppleTalk network. With ARA, you can call your desktop Mac from a PowerBook and remotely access all the available services - files, printers, servers, e-mail, etc.

ARAP Apple Talk Remote Access Protocol .

Arbitration The set of rules used to manage competing demands for a computer resource, such as memory or peripheral devices, made by multiple processes or users.

Arbitrator (1) A software module in Windows that handles the allocation of hardware resources among devices.

(2) Under Windows, the Plug and Play device driver responsible for allocating a specific resource among all drivers that require the resource. For example, VDMAD is a DMA channel arbitrator, and VPICD has services for allocating IRQ lines. Windows 95 provides arbitrators for standard I/O, memory, hardware interrupt, and DMA channel resources.

ARC (previously ARCS) Advanced RISC Computing Specification: the standard hardware architecture of ACE., specifying the baseline hardware requirements to create ACE-compatible systems.

Arcadia A software engineering research project by a consortium of US universities.

Archie A system used on the Internet to locate files available by anonymous ftyp. Archie was written by students and volunteers at McGill University's School of Computer Science in Montreal, Canada, and is available worldwide. Once a week, special programs connect to all the known anonymous ftp sites on the Internet and collect a complete lisint of all th epublicly available files. This listing is kept in an Internet Archive Database, and when you ask Archie to look for a file, only this database is searched rather than the whole Internet; you can then use anonymous ftp to retrieve the file.

Architecture The overall design and construction of all or part of a computer, particularly the processor hardware an the size and ordering sequence of its bytes. Also used to describe the overall design of software.

Archive As a noun, this refers generally to any type of backed-up data. It can refer to tapes, disks, or just simply a group of data that is an old copy of current data. That copy could be one minute old or several years old. As a verb, archive is the act of backing up data or creating an archive.

ARE all routes explorer A specific frame initiated by a source which is sent on all possible routes in Source Route Bridging.

Areal density This typically refers to the amount of data that can be stored on a one-inch square of material. It's usually represented in billions of bits per square inch on a hard drive platter. For example, the first Toshiba 30 GB hard drives that fit into 2.5" form factors had an areal density of 26.7 billion bits. Hard drives with higher areal densities can store more information in an equal space than those with lower areal densities. Hard drive manufacturers are constantly improving areal densities so that they can produce higher capacity drives without making them physically larger.

Argument What you have with your girlfriend when she wants you to stop using your computer so much. Actually, argument refers to the value with which you call a procedure. For example, if you wrote a line of code that said "goto 140" telling your program to go to line 140, the argument is "140." Some procedures will accept multiple arguments, or alternately, require no arguments.

ARIN (American registry for internet numbers) The newly-formed, non-profit organization established to manage the allocation of Internet Protocol (IP) numbers for the areas currently served by the InterNIC's Registration Services: the Americas, the Caribbean, and sub-Saharan Africa. The National Science Foundation (NSF) approved the establishment of ARIN on June 24, 1997.

Arithmetic logic unit (ALU) The part of the CPU that actually does the work of adding, subtracting, multiplying, and dividing, including OR, AND, and NOT operations. The ALU is an execution unit, like the FPU, that is fed with data from the CPU registers.

ARP address resolution protocol Used to dynamically discover the low-level physical network hardware address that corresponds to the high level IP Address for a given host, for instance. ARP is limited to physical network systems that support broadcast packets that can be heard by all hosts on the network.

ARP table A table that Address Resolution Protocol uses to store information for mapping IP addresses to individual machine addresses on a network.

ARPANet (advanced research projects agencynetwork) Formed in 1969 to connect the Department of Defense (DOD) with institutions conducting major defense contract research. The network linked super computers in major research universities with the DOD. This is credited with being the first academic computer network and is considered the "mother" of the Internet. In the 1980s, ARPANet split into two networks called ARPANet and MILNet (for unclassified military research). An interconnection with the DOD Advanced Research Projects Agency (DARPA) led to a set of networks called DARPA Internet that later became referred to as just the Internet.

Array 1. This can be an abbreviation for a group of hard drives functioning as a RAID (Redundant Array of Inexpensive Drives).

2. This also describes a common data structure that holds values in a consecutively numbered group, such as A[1]...[7], where A is an array of 7 different values. There are also multi-dimensional arrays such as A[1,1,1]...A[8,8,8], which can hold many values and still be fairly simply referenced.

Array processor A group of special processors designed to calculate math procedures at very high speeds, often under the control fo another central processor. Some computers use array processors to speed up video operations or for fast floating-point math operations.

Arrow keys The four keys on a computer keyboard that are commonly used to move the cursor around in programs that support such movement. Some keyboards feature 8 arrow keys, which include the four standard directions (up, down, left, right) and the four diagonals.

Article The base component of USENET news; a group of text written and posted to a network news group.

Artifact An unintended, unwanted visual aberration in a video image.

Artifex A CASE environment from ARTIS of Turin for the development of large event-driven distributed systems. It has code-generation and rapid prototyping features.

Artificial intelligence (AI) Is a branch (usually called AI/Expert Systems) of computer science, mathematics, psychology, and systems engineering that attempts to make computer "decision making" more like human decision making and to aid or replace human decision makers with machines. Expert systems attempt to utilize the skills, knowledge, and decision evaluation processes of human experts. For example, computers now aid physicians in diagnosing diseases and computer-guided laser rockets virtually replace human guidance decisions. AI failed to live up to its early expectations when it was believed that AI computers would never fail to win at chess and language translators would soon be put out of work by computers. However, applications of AI have been taking place and computers can now play very good chess to a point where they occasionally beat even the grand masters.

Ascend inverse multiplexing protocol (AIM) An in-band protocol used to manage the interconnection of two remotely located inverse multiplexers. AIM is a feature rich, widely used inverse multiplexing protocol developed and supported by Ascend Communictions. Not to be confused with AOL Instant Messenger.

Ascend tunnel management protocol (ATMP) A vpn protocol. VPNs provide low-cost remote access to private LANs via the Internet. The tunnel to the private corporate network may be from an ISP, enabling mobile nodes to dial-in to a corporate network, or between two corporate networks that use a low-cost Internet connection to access each other.

ASCII (American standard code for information interchange) Computer character set (text and symbols) that enables transfer of text and data between different computing systems. This international standard provides only very plain text without options for font modifications. For example, files from word processors such as Microsoft Word, Word Perfect, and Word Star often cannot be imported to hypertext or hypermedia software without conversion to ASCII code (most word processors will change files to ASCII "text" files). The downside is that nearly all formatting and font variations are lost in ASCII conversions such that imported ASCII text may have to be re-formatted line by line and altered for font preferences. Very few software alternatives have "filters" that import word processor files directly without having to convert to ASCII codes, although many are now adding rich-text format (RTF) utilities. In hypertext authoring, choice of a hypertext software option should include a question concerning whether "filters" are available for avoidance of ASCII text conversions.

Ascii file A file that only contains text characters from the ASCII character set. An ASCII file contains letters, numbers, and punctuation symbols, but does not contain any hidden text-formatting commands. Also known as a text file, and ASCII text file.

Ascii-armored A feature of Pretty Good Privacy (PGP), which "encases" an encrypted message in ASCII, allowing the message to be sent via e-mail as a regular message.

ASDL (abstract-type and scheme-definition language) Developed as part of Esprit project GRASPIN, as a basis for generating language-based editors and environments. It combines an object-oriented type system, syntax-directed translation schemes and a target-language interface.

ASE (advanced software environment) An object-oriented application support system from Nixdorf.

ASIC (application-specific integrated circuit) An ASIC is a circuit designed for a very specific purpose, such as the processors in PDAs or the chips on a motherboard chipset. ASICs contrast with more general-purpose devices such as memory chips or x86 processors that can be used in many different applications.

ASIS ada semantic interface specification An interface between an Ada library and any tool requiring information in it.

ASL The programming-language equivalent for AML. ASL is compiled into AML images. The ASL statements are defined in section 15 of the Advanced Configuration and Power Interface Specification.

ASME (American society of mechanical engineers) Involved in CAD standardisation.

ASN.1 (abstract syntax notation) 1 An ISO/CCITT standard for the description of data. It is intended to facilitate the exchange of data between application programs.

Aspect An IPSE developed by an Alvey project, using Z to specify the object-management system and tool interface.

Aspect ratio The ratio of the horizontal to vertical size of the screen. Some monitors display rectangular pixels which can make the picture or image appear stretched. Software that allows images to be resized and changed with respect to aspect ratios greatly facilitates authoring. Otherwise, images have to be transported to other software for such changes and then transported back in a cumbersome process that makes authors grateful when aspect ratios and image sizes can be modified without such difficulties. Macromedia Director is one of the very few hypermedia authoring systems that has a utility for changing the scale and aspect ratios of imported bitmap pictures as well as rotating and inverting such pictures.

ASPI (advanced scsi programming interface) This was developed by Adaptec so that different devices could be controlled by different SCSI cards, and therefore the SCSI card version would not matter. Basically, if the correct ASPI driver is being used, you can send the same command to any Adaptec SCSI card to make something happen to a device. Most commonly, ASPI is associated with CD-ROM and CD-RW drives.

ASQ (automated software quality) The use of software tools, such as automated testing tools, to improve software quality.

ASQC American Society for Quality Control.

Assembler A program that translates human-readable assembly language programs to machine-readable instructions.

Assembly In the chip making workd , the process of enclosing a device in a plastic or ceramic package.

Assembly language A programming language specific to a microprocessor. It is a very low-level language, where you actually give the processor instructions like "MOV A,B", which moves a value from one register to another. As you might imagine, programming directly in assembly language is quite tedious. Thus, higher level languages, such as C++, Visual Basic, or Java, are normally used and then compiled into assembly language specific to the microprocessor on which the program will be run. The compiler tries to optimize the code during this process (e.g., "MOV A,B" followed by "MOV B,C" might be replaced by "MOV A,C"). Depending on how elegant the optimization is, the code may run faster than if no optimization is used. Today, very small and fast programs can be created by using assembly language (defeating code bloat), but assembly language programming is becoming a dying art.

Assessment The evaluation of the efficiency and effectiveness of technology on attitudes and performance. Tidd (1995) discusses various assessment scales such as the Computer Attitude Scale, the Computer Anxiety Rating Scale, and the Computer Self-Efficacy Scale. Assessment is very difficult because no matter how good the findings are in an empirical study, the relevance of those findings quickly falls away due to constantly emerging technologies that are significantly better than older technologies used in the study.

ASSET (asset source for software engineering technology) A programme to promote software reuse by the DoD.

Assigned cell Cell that provides a service to an upper layer entity or ATM Layer Management entity (ATMM-entity).

Assigned configuration Drivers examine this portion of the device node to determine which resources have been allocated for the device. For Plug and Play cards, the assigned resources for a device can change dynamically or from one system start-up to the next.

Associate Linking a document with the program that created it so that both can be opened with a single command.

Asymmetric encryption Encryption that uses separate keys to encrypt and decrypt messages.

Asymmetrical compression A system that requires more processing capability to compress than to decompress an image. It is typically used for the mass distribution of programs on media such as CD-ROM, where significant expense can be incurred for the production and compression of the program, but the playback system must be low cost. Compare with symmetrical compression.

Asynchronous 1 : not synchronous; not occurring or existing at the same time or having the same period or phase.

2 : of, used in, or being digital communication (as between computers) in which there is no timing requirement for transmission and in which the start of each character is individually signaled by the transmitting device.

Asynchronous communication This method of transferring data does so without a specific timing mechanism between the two communicating parties. The party receiving data isn't expecting more data at any set interval.

Asynchronous communications server A LAN server that enables a network user to dial out of the network and into the public switched telephone network (PSTN), or to access nailed-up lines for asynchronous communications. An asynchronous communications server is also called a dial-in/dial-out server or a modem server.

Asynchronous connection The type of connection a modem makes over a phone line, this connection is not synchronized by a mutual timing signal or clock.

Asynchronous data transmission A type of communication that sends data using flow control rather than a clock to Synchronize data between the source and destination.

Asynchronous digital subscriber line (ADSL) An asymmetric high-speed digital network connection, usually between a home or small business and a telecommunications vendor, providing an always-up direct connection to an Internet Service Provider (ISP).

Asynchronous learning networks ALN networks of education and training modules or courses where students learn in self-paced online pedagogy in contrast to synchronized presentations in traditional classrooms or electronic classrooms. Synchronous education in a scheduled sequence of classes will face serious new competition of asynchronous education distributed on networks where students learn and communicate most any day and most any time of day and study at their own paces. Ideally, faculty or other expert help is available online to both help students and evaluate student work and ideas. In addition, asynchronous courses may schedule synchronous virtual online meetings of subsets of students or entire classes of students. Networked courses may thus be synchronous and asynchronous, although the technical learning components are largely asynchronous.

Asynchronous memory Memory that is not synchronized with the system clock. EDO and FPM are examples of asynchronous memory.

Asynchronous time division multiplexing A multiplexing technique in which a transmission capability is organized in a priori unassigned time slots. The time slots are assigned to cells upon request of each application's instantaneous real need.

Asynchronous transfer mode (ATM) A networking protocol initially designed to move multimedia data around with high reliability and speed. It uses small, fixed-size cells of data that can be more easily controlled and kept at specific service levels than TCP/IP. Some ISPs use ATM as the protocol for their backbones.

AT attachment A disk drive implementation that integrates the controller on the disk drive itself. Also known as IDE. ATA-2 is an extension of ATA that was beefed up to include performance enhancing features such as fast PIO (programmed input/output) and DMA (direct memory access) modes. It also got an improved Identify Drive command. This features lets a hard drive tell the software exactly what its characteristics are, and is the basis for both Plug and Play hard drive technology and compatibility with any new version of the standard that may come. *Fast ATA* supports high speed data transfers specified by ANSI-standardized Programmed Input/Output(PIO) Mode3 and multi-word Direct Memory Access(DMA) Mode 1 protocols. Fast ATA enables the drive to transfer data at speeds as high as 13.3MB/s. *Fast ATA-2* is like Fast ATA, but is a standard that will allow manufacturers to create products that support ANSI PIO Mode 4 and multi-word DMA Mode 2 protocols. With Fast ATA-2, its possible to get data transfers as high as 16.6 MB/s.

AT (attachment packet interface) A hardware and software specification that documents the interface between a host computer and CD-ROM drives using the ATA bus.

AT bus The 16-bit bus started with the IBM-AT (Advanced Technology) systems. It is still the standard interface for most PC expansion cards. It is also known as the ISA (Industry Standard Architecture) bus.

AT command set A set of standard instructions used to activate features on a modem. The code AT is short for ATtention, and precedes most of the modem commands.

AT form factor A PC form factor that describes the way a motherboard fits into a case and works with a power supply. Thus, you match an AT power supply with an AT case and an AT motherboard. Some of the things common to AT motherboards are a large 5-pin DIN socket for plugging a keyboard in, and serial and parallel port interfaces available via riser cards that are not part of the motherboard itself. The AT form factor was succeeded by the ATX form factor.

AT&T US telecom operator.

ATA Short for Advanced Technology Attachment, a disk drive implementation that integrates the controller on the disk drive itself. There are several versions of ATA, all developed by the Small Form Factor (SFF) Committee:

ATA-1: Known also as IDE, supports one or two hard drives, a 16-bit interface and PIO modes 0, 1 and 2.

ATA-2: Supports faster PIO modes (3 and 4) and multiword DMA modes (1 and 2). Also supports logical block addressing (LBA) and block transfers. ATA-2 is marketed as Fast ATA and Enhanced IDE (EIDE).

ATA-3: Minor revision to ATA-2.

Ultra-ATA: Also called Ultra-DMA, ATA-33, and DMA-33, supports multiword DMA mode 3 running at 33 MBps.

ATA/66: A version of ATA proposed by Quantum Corporation, and supported by Intel, that doubles ATA's throughput to 66 MBps.

ATA/100: An updated version of ATA/66 that increases data transfer rates to 100 MBps.

ATA/100 (ultra ata/100) Another extension to the ATA interface that adds a 50% increase in top speed over ATA/66, getting to 100MB/second, up from 66MB/second. This standard also adds some additional error-checking not found in earlier ATA standards. Like Ultra ATA/66, ATA/100 requires an 80-conductor cable to work at full speed.

ATA/133 (ultra ata/133) This refers to what is most probably the final extension to the parallel ATA connection standard. The proposal was created by Maxtor, and allows a top data transfer rate of 133 megabytes per second. Intel didn't support this standard in its chipsets, instead opting to wait for Serial ATA.

ATA/33 (ultra ata/33) An extension to the ATA interface (IDE) that effectively doubles the top data transfer speed of IDE from 16.6MBytes/second up to 33 MBytes/second. Also known as Ultra-IDE.

ATA/66 (ultra ata/66) An extension to the ATA interface (IDE) proposed by Quantum that effectively doubles the data transfer speed of the Ultra ATA/33 interface to 66MBps. To achieve the increase in speed you must use a special 80-conductor cable with 40 data lines and 40 ground lines to keep the signal stable.

ATAPI (at attachment packet interface) This interface is part of EIDE, and it allows a PC to control CD-ROM drives and tape drives across the IDE interface.

AT-commands Set of protocols that allow mobile phones and modems to be controlled.

AtFS (attributed file system) The basis of the Shape VC toolkit. A status model controlling visibility of version objects, locking, and "long transactions" for synchronizing concurrent updates supports cooperative work within projects. The concept of object attributes provides a basis for storing management information with versions and passing this information between individual tools. This mechanism is useful for building integrated environments from a set of unrelated tools.

Athena Project Athena: a distributed system project for support of educational and research computing at MIT. Much of the software developed is now in wider use, especially the X Window System.

Atherton Atherton Technology developed the Software BackPlane CASE framework. Their Atherton Tool Integration Services were the basis for the ATIS standard.

ATIS (a tools integration standard) An object-oriented interface to a set of services that allows the saving, accessing, and managing of information in a common repository. Developed by Atherton Technology and DEC, based on an extended version of the Software BackPlane, now proposed as an industry standard.

ATL (active template library) A group of routines provided by Microsoft that can be used to help more easily create ASP, ActiveX, and COM objects in C++.

Atm adaption layer(AAL) The AAL enables engineers to adapt the asynchronous transfer mode layer to particular services. Lies between the ATM layer and the higher layers and maps or adapts the functions or services of the higher layers onto a common ATM bearer service. ATM

Adobe Type Manager. ATM User-User connection An association established by the ATM Layer to support communication between two or more ATM service users (i.e., between two or more next higher entities or between two or more ATM-entities). The communications over an ATM Layer connection may be either bidirectional or unidirectional. The same Virtual Channel Identifier (VCI) issued for both directions of a connection at an interface.

ATM address Defined in the UNI Specification as 3 formats, each having 20 bytes in length including country, area and end-system identifiers.

ATM (asynchronous transfer mode) A wide-area network technology ; a transfer mode for switching and transmission that efficiently and flexibly organises information into cells. It is asynchronous in the sense that the recurrence of cells depends on the required or instantaneous bit rate. Thus, empty cells do not go unutilised when data is waiting. ATM's powerful flexibility lies in its ability to provide a high-capacity, low-latency switching fabric—for all types of information, including data, video, image and voice — that is protocol , speed and distance independent. Of the plethora of benefits ATM will accrue to its users, probably the most significant is that it represents an enduring, architectural approach due to its inherent scalability. It scales well from small to large systems, from very low to very high transmission speeds (more than 100 Mbps), and from local-area, through metropolitan-area, to wide-area networking environments. This promising technology is not anticipated to be widely used until 1998.

ATM (automatic teller machines) For banks and Asynchronous Transfer Mode switching in networks. The high speed ATM networks allow transmission of video, audio, and data over local and world-wide networks.

ATM forum A group of organizations responsible for determining the ATM standards and its progress within the industry.

ATM layer link A section of an ATM Layer connection between two adjacent active ATM Layer entities (ATM-entities).

ATM link A virtual path link (VPL) or a virtual channel link (VCL).

ATM peer-to-peer connection A virtual channel connection (VCC) or a virtual path connection (VPC).

ATM traffic descriptor A generic list of traffic parameters that can be used to capture the intrinsic traffic characteristics of a requested ATM connection.

ATS (abstract test suite) A set of abstract test cases for testing a particular protocol. An "executable" test suite may be derived from an abstract test suite.

Attachment A file embedded in an e-mail message. It is possible to have one or more attachments embedded in an e-mail message. If you are sending or receiving attachments, you must have an e-mail client that supports MIME encoding, or the attachments will show up in encoded form, which basically looks like a large block of numbers and letters.

Attachment unit interface The portion of the Ethernet standard that specifies how a cable is to be connected to an Ethernet card. AUI specifies a cable connected to a transceiver that plugs into a 15-pin socket on the network adapter.

Attack signature detection Detects patterns corresponding to known attacks. This includes both passive protocol analysis (use of sniffers in promiscuous mode) and signature analysis (interpretation of a specific series of packets or piece of data contained in those packets, that represent a known pattern of attack).

Attenuation The process of the reduction of the power of a signal as it passes through most media. Usually proportional to distance, attenuation is sometimes the factor that limits the distance a signal may be transmitted through a media before it can no longer be received.

ATX (atx form factor) The ATX form factor specification takes the original Baby AT-sized motherboard, rotates it 90 degrees, and calls for a power supply with a side-mounted fan that cools only the power supply, but also the processor and add-in boards. This new approach was designed to lower costs and provide better motherboard placement in an ATX case. In addition, the ATX form factor introduced a large set of I/O ports that are wired directly to the motherboard, and standard support for PS/2 keyboard and mouse connections.

AU The file extension for UNIX audio (sound) files.

AU sounds This is an audio format developed for Sun workstations and often used to distribute sound clips via the Web.

Audio class The class of filters that deals with pulse code modulation or similar digitized data or analog signals. A WDM audio minidriver provides support for audio devices under the WDM audio architecture.

Audio mixing The method of combining multiple streams of audio data into a single stream through some method such as addition and clipping.

Audio modem riser (AMR) An Intel specification designed to move the analog I/O functions of sound cards and modems onto a riser card. It allows motherboards to have an I/O slot built into them to make it easier to integrate audio and modem functions onto a motherboard. The specification does not define "an aftermarket standard I/O slot," according to Intel. Basically, the slot is supposed to be filled when you buy a motherboard, with the motherboard manufacturer's choice of modem/audio functions.

Audio video interleave (AVI) A Microsoft-specified format for saving audio and/or video clips, referred to by Windows as "Video for Windows." You can play the files through the Media Player in Windows or through many popular browser plug-in multimedia players. Files of this type have a .avi extension.

Audio Voice, music, and other sounds recorded and stored in analog or digital form. The term RealAudio refers to a helper-app (plug-in) that allows WWW users to hear audio files in real time. Options for converting written text into audio are given in Text reading.

Audit Systematic examination of system data to ensure conformance with policy, controls, and operational procedures. This is usually followed by a list of recommended changes.

Audit trail A file or database that contains a list of changes made to a specific file. The information includes the name of the file, the date and time of the change, the person making the change, and the text of the change itself.

AUI Interface type between a computer and the LAN.

Authenticate To positively verify the identity of a user, device, or other entity on a network. Usually this is required before access to network resources can be granted.

Authenticated payment program Authenticated payment program from Visa has begun the global rollout of the Authenticated Payment Program. The Program, based on commercial incentives, will vastly improve the payment service for e-merchants, consumers and Visa Members by enhancing convenience, acceptance and security. Consumers will know that they can shop safely and conveniently while preventing fraud on their card, and merchants will know they are dealing with a legitimate cardholder anywhere in the world. The newest authentication technology, 3-D Secure, forms the basis for global interoperability of Authenticated Payments.

Authentication A process of proving the identity of a computer or computer user. For users, it generally involves a user name and password. Computers usually pass a code that identifies that they are part of a network.

Authentication header (AH) A field that immediately follows the IP header in an IP datagram and provides authentication and integrity checking for the datagram.

Authentication server A network server that provides authentication services.

Authentication service A mechanism, analogous to the use of passwords on time-sharing systems, for the secure authentication of the identity of network by servers, and vice versa, without presuming the operating system integrity of either.

Authentication token A hardware or software token used to prove the identity of users in a two-factor authentication system.

Authenticator Same as authentication token.

Authenticode Microsoft's cabinet file signing technology, which uses digital signatures to verify the identity of the author of executable, ActiveX and Java class code and that the code has not been tampered with since being signed. The use of Authenticode protects users who know and trust the author of the code and recognize the certificate as belonging to that author. Hackers can easily subvert this protection by creating certificates with names similar to those that the user trusts.

Authoring Developing (writing of text, recording of audio, importing of video, inserting graphics, etc.) hypertext and hypermedia learning, entertainment, and reference materials. The history and trends in authoring are summarized at.

Authoring software This term refers to software that enables the creation of multimedia or hypertext documents and presentations.

Authoritative A DNS server with all the records for a given domain. (Note that the authorization may not have been granted or delegated to the DNS server.)

Authority The group responsible for administering a DNS domain.

Authority zone The part of a DNS domain for which a name server has responsibility. Authority is sometimes called "knowing the truth" about network name/address translation.

Authorware Macromedia's hypermedia authoring system designed primarily for training and education asynchronous learning courses. Authorware was originally developed for Mac computers and is still the most sophisticated option for Mac users. There is a PC version that faces stiffer competition from high-end authoring systems listed at The main competitor is probably Asymetrix ToolBook in terms of full course development, course management, CD-ROM delivery, and web delivery. For links to Macromecia and applications on the web.

Auto answer A modem indicator light that tells you the modem is ready to pick up the phone, so long as there's a communication program running and prepared to handle the call. The light is often not shining even when the modem is prepared to take a call, so it's not a useful light.

Auto precharge A synchronous DRAM feature that allows the memory chip's circuitry to close a page automatically at the end of a burst.

Auto responder An automated program that acknowledges receipt of an email message (e.g., a Domain Name Registration Agreement, a question, or some other type of electronic correspondence) and creates a tracking number for the email message. The auto responder sends the acknowledgment via email to the requester; the subject line of the email message will contain the tracking number.

Autocad A CAD software package for mechanical engineering marketed by AutoDesk Inc.

Autoexec bat In a DOS system, set of commands executed at each system initialisation (either after power-on or after pressing Control+Alt+Del). This file is restricted to the use of the system administrator.

In a PMF system, the Autouser.bat, executed immediately after the Autoexec.bat, can be accessed and modified by the user.

Automata theory The analytical (mathematical) treatment and study of automated systems

Automatic ring down (ARD) A dedicated point-to-point voice facility between two offices of a trading facility. When the sender picks up the telephone handset, automatically ring the receiver's end for direct connections, without the need to dial.

Automaton An object or being that has a behavior that can be modeled or explained completely by using automata theory.

Autonomous Self governing, or being able to exist independently

Autonomous system Internet TCP/IP terminology for a collection of gateway (routers) that fall under one administrative entity and cooperate using common Interior Gateway Protocol (IGP).

Autonomy The capability of acting in a self-governing manner; being able to exist independently or with some degree of independence.

Auto-parser An automated program that extracts information from the fields in the registration forms. The auto-parser will detect errors or incomplete information in the registration forms. Upon receipt of complete and correct registration forms the auto-parser enters the appropriate data into Network Solutions' domain name database.

Autoresponder Not surprisingly, An Autoresponder automatically responds to anyone that sends mail to it. These are used for a few things, including vacation notices and easy dissemination of information. If you had a vacation autoresponder for instance, you could turn it on when you leave, and anyone that sends mail to your address while you're gone will get an immediate response stating that you are out of town. Businesses use Autoresponders for getting sale information, new product announcements, e-mail brochures and more out to interested customers.

Autouser bat In a pmf system, set of commands accessible by the user in lieu of autoexec.bat.

Availability A measure of how much time a network or a connection is running. Generally the equation is: Time Running / Time Measured (time running divided by time measured). Thus, if you measured something for 20 minutes and it was only up for 19 of them, you'd have 95% availability.

Average selling price (ASP) This term is used in the microchip manufacturing world. Companies like AMD and Intel strive for high ASPs. The ASP is an indication not only of direct profits, but how well a company is keeping up with the technology curve. It is not uncommon for Intel to have an ASP of around US$100 and AMD to be close behind.

AVI (audio video interleaved) Digitized video files (with audio tracks) That satisfy MPC standards for Video for Windows playback. The Media Player (mplayer.exe) file that is included in Windows operating systems runs AVI files. Most PC video capture boards will convert analog video into AVI files. The AVI standard from Microsoft's Video for Windows is giving way to Microsoft's newer Active Video architecture.

AVL Abstract Visualization Language in the Tecate project.

AVS (application visualisation system) A portable modular UNIX-based graphics package supported by a consortium of vendors including Convex, DEC, IBM, HP, SET Technologies, Stardent and WaveTracer.

AWG(American wire gauge)A measure of the thickness of copper, aluminum and other wiring in the U.S. and elsewhere. Copper cabling typically varies from 18 to 26 AWG. The higher the number, the thinner the wire. The thicker the wire, the less suceptible it is to interference. In general, thin wire cannot carry the same amount of electrical current the same distance that thicker wire can.

AWK A pattern scanning and processing language named after its authors: Aho, Weinberger and Kernighan.

AXE A text editor for the X-Window-System.

Axioms Statements that are taken to be true, the foundation of a theory

Azerty Same as QWERTY for a French-style keyboard.

B

B A Formal method of program design.

B2B (business to business) This term is often used to describe websites that sell goods or services to other businesses. Thus, businesses are serving other businesses as opposed to consumers.

B2C (business to consumer) A form of doing business that deals with selling goods and services to the consumer marketplace. Examples of this would be selling consumer electronics, toys, or pet supplies. This contrasts with the business to business model.

Baby AT A motherboard form factor that has the same traits as the standard AT form factor, such as AT power connectors and keyboard input port. However, it is smaller in size, and can be utilized in smaller computer cases.

Back door A usually hidden or secret means for an external user to break into your host, network, application, or data.

Backbone A high-speed line, or series of connections, that forms a major pathway within a network. This term is relative, as a backbone in a small network may be much smaller than non-backbone lines in a large network.

Backbone network A high-speed transmission facility, or an arrangement of such facilities, designed to interconnect lower-speed distribution channels or clusters of dispersed user devices.

Back-end processor A secondary processor that performs one specialized task very effectively, freeing the main processor for other, more important work.

Back-end The final stage in a process or a task not apparent to the user. A common usage is in a compiler. A compiler's back-end generates machine language and performs optimizations specific to the machine's architecture. The term can also be used in the context of Open System Interconnect (OSI) network applications. A standard for layering of protocols (protocol stack) to implement it were was developed in 1978 as a framework for international standards in heterogeneous computer network architecture. The architecture is split between seven layers (lowest to highest):

1. Physical layer
2. Data link layer
3. Network layer
4. Transport layer
5. Session layer
6. Presentation layer
7. Application layer.

Background noise In communications, any unwanted signal that enters a line, channel, or circuit.

Background Unix can run many programs at the same time. If a program runs behind the scenes, with no interaction with you, it runs in the background.

Back orifice A Trojan horse that installs itself as a server on a machine, and allows a user with the BackOrifice client to control the host remotely. Hackers often distribute seemingly harmless executables that also install Back Orifice. Once installed, a hacker can access all files, system passwords, keystrokes, and other confidential information to further compromise the network.

Backplane As opposed to standard cabling schemes where flexible wires are used, a backplane refers to a rigid circuit board that will support higher connection speeds and more logic. For example, many SCSI systems today ship with small SCSI backplanes because the transfer rate of SCSI is getting high enough that standard cables are causing problems when connecting devices. Another example of a backplane is in network connection devices, such as large enterprise scale switches, routers, or PBXs. Some of these devices have a high-speed backplane, and you can plug a group of slower network connection devices into the high-speed backplane.

Back-propagation An important algorithm for learning in feed-forward networks which makes use of a mathematical trick when the network is simulated on a digital computer, yielding in just two traversals of the network (once forward, and once back) both the difference between the desired and actual output, and the derivatives of this difference with respect to the connection weights.

Backside bus A special microprocessor bus that connects the CPU to a Level 2 cache. Typically, a backside bus runs at a faster clock speed than the frontside bus that connects the CPU to main memory. For example, the Pentium Pro microprocessor actually consists of two chips — one contains the CPU and the primary cache, and the second contains the secondary cache. A backside bus connects the two chips at the same clock rate as the CPU itself (at least 200 MHz). In contrast, the frontside bus runs at only a fraction of the CPU clock speed (typically 100 MHz).

Backslash Unix uses a backslash to set off otherwise special characters. In the UNIX shell for example, file in the current directory); \ is an actual backslash, if you want one for some reason. DOS users tend to type backslashes by mistake when Unix would rather see a regular slash(/).

Backup A copy of your important files made for safekeeping in case something happens to the original files; something you should make every day. There are several types of backup methods that can be performed:

Normal backups Backs up all files that have been selected, regardless of the setting of the archive bit and also clears the archive bit to indicate that the files have been backed up. It is also called a *full backup.*

Differential backups Backs up only files that have the archive bit set to show that the file has been modified and leaves the archive bit in its prebackup state. Bascially, they record all the differences that have taken place since the last normal backup.They are often used in combination with normal backups. A nromal backup of all files is performed each weekend to archive all files on the LAN and then a differential backup is performed each night of the week to back all files that have been modified since the weekend. Also, differential backups are commonly used to reduce the amount of time in which backup jobs must run during the week.

Incremental backups Backs up only files that have the archive bit set to show that the file has been modified and clears the archive bit to indicate that the file has been backed up. They are used to further reduce the time interval required to back up networks.

Daily backups Identify files to be backed up by examining the date stamp. If a file has been modified on the same day that the backup is being made, the file will be backed up. These are used to capture changes at intervals shorter than 24 hours.

Backup domain controller (BDC) One or more computers running Windows NT that act as a backup to the primary domain controller (PDC). These machines can authenticate security requests just like the primary domain controller, and will take over for the PDC if it is not available. However, a BDC will remain a BDC until it is manually promoted to a PDC by a domain administrator. With Active Directory Windows no longer requires the sometimes confusing primary and backup domain controllers, just domain controllers instead.

Backup file In Windows 95, a compressed version of the original file and its locations created by Backup.

Backup formats Term denoting the type of format used to backup data. There are several types of backup formats in the backup media markets:4mm and 8mm cartridges, DC-2000 and DC-6000, optical disks, and quarter-inch cartridges.

Backus naur A formal language for syntax specification.

Backward explicit congestion notification (BECN) A bit in the Frame Relay header that is set when the network router detects congestion from the source direction (or "backward," from the packet's point of view).

Backward-compatible Fully compatible with earlier versions of the same application program or computer system.

Bad sector An area on a hard disk or floppy disk that cannot be used to store data, because of a manufacturing defect or accidental damage. One of the tasks an operating system performs is finding, marking, and isolating bad sectors. Almost all hard disks have some bad sectors, often listed in the bad track table, as a result of the manufacturing process, and this is not usually anything to worry about; the operating system will mark them as bad, and you will never even know that they are there.

Bad track table A list of the defective areas on a hard disk, usually determined during final testing of the disk at the factory. Some disk-preparation programs ask you to enter information from this list to reduce the time that a low-level format takes to prepare the disk for use by an operating system.

Bakelite An insulating material used in synthetic goods, including plastics and resins.

Balance The control for the level of sound coming out of the left or right speakers. If you turn the balance control all the way in either direction, you can isolate the sound to the left or right channel, which helps in troubleshooting whether both speakers are connected properly. Other than that, the balance control can fine-tune volume levels to compensate for sound conditions in the room.

Ball grid array (BGA) As opposed to a pin grid array (PGA), a ball grid array is a type of microchip connection methodology. Ball grid array chips typically use a group of solder dots, or balls, arranged in concentric rectangles to connect to a circuit board. BGA chips are often used in mobile applications where PGA chips would take up too much space due to the length of the pins used to connect the chips to the circuit board. More and more designs are moving to BGA form factors.

Ballistics The science and engineering of the motion of projectiles of various types, including bullets, bombs, and rockets.

Bamboo A trusted third-party authentication system from the University of Iowa, similar to Kerberos.

Bandwidth Usually measured in bits-per-second, it is the amount of stuff you can send through a connection. A full page of English text is about 16,000 bits. A fast modem can move about 15,000 bits in one second. Full-motion full-screen video would require roughly 10,000,000 bits per second, depending on compression. Internet Servers are connected to the Internet backbone on a high-speed data link usually on a T-3, T-1 or an ISDN speed links.

A T-3 link can transfer 44.736 M-bits/sec, T-1 can handle 1.5 M bits/sec, while ISDN can only transmit information at a rate of 128 K bits per second. Pugmarks' Servers are linked on high speed T-3 multiple gateway links capable of handling over 10 million hits per day.

Bang(!) In Unix-ese, an exclamation point.The C shell command !!, which repeats the last command, for example, is pronounced "Bang!Bang!"

Bank 1. A slot or group of slots that must be populated with modules of like capacity in order to fulfill the data width requirement of the CPU.

2. A segment of memory on a module, sometimes also referred to as a row. Modules are either single or dual banked

3. An internal logic segment in a memory component. For example, a 64Mb SDRAM has 4 banks.

Bank switching A method of switching between two sets (or banks) of memory chips in a computer, only one of which can be active at a time. Because of the overhead involved in switching between banks, memory-intensive tasks can take much longer to perform using bank-switched memory than when using main memory. Bank-switched memory is often located on an expansion card plugged into an expansion slot on the motherboard.

Banner/ Banner ad A fancy page that's printed between each print job so that you can easily separate jobs from one another. The most common form of advertising found on the Web. The traditional size of a banner ad is 468 by 60 pixels, but there are many other sizes in general use. Banner ads are typically animated GIF graphics or Flash animations that are simply clicked on to go to the website of the advertiser, but can also contain rich media that allows for some degree of interaction with the ad besides a simple click.

Bar (Foobar) FooBar is a derivative of the acronym FUBAR, changed for symmetry. FUBAR stands for Fucked Up Beyond All Recognition. Sometimes used as a whole by programmers to describe data loss, foo and bar are also often used separately when a quick and random name is needed.

Bar codes Alternate standards for marking products or other items for reading by laser beams. They are used extensively for locating items on videodiscs and CDs. The LaserBarCode was the original standard for CAV discs. This was extended to LaserBarCode2 for CLV discs. The Bar Code CD is an audio standard for CD discs.

Barrel An outward bowing of the picture.

Base address An industry-wide specification for the documentation of I/O Ports where the total number of addresses is never mentioned, only the first, or *Base Address*.

Base memory Refer to "Conventional Memory".

Base-10 A number system in which each place represents a power of 10 larger than the place to its right (decimal).

Base-16 A number system in which each place represents a power of 16 larger than the place to its right (hexadecimal).

Base-2 A number system in which each place represents a power of 2 larger than the place to its right (binary).

Base-8 A number system in which each place represents a power of 8 larger than the place to its right (octal).

Baseband Part of the Bluetooth Protocol stack, enabling the physical radio frequency link between Bluetooth units on a piconet.

Baseband system A baseband system transmits signals without converting them to another frequency and is characterized by its support of one frequency of signals. Ethernet-based networks inside campus buildings are transmitted via baseband coaxial cable, with ethernet being the only service supported by the coaxial cable.

BASIC (beginner's all-purpose symbolic instruction code) This programming language was developed in the mid '60s. The language was constructed of simple, English-like commands that were run through an interpreter, line by line, each time the program was "run." This caused BASIC programs to be slow. Nowadays compilers have been developed to speed up BASIC programs, and recent versions of BASIC can do anything that other programming languages can.

Basic input output system (BIOS) A program stored on your motherboard that controls all of the interaction between your components and your Simple access to video, keyboard, hard drive, floppy, CD-ROM, and other devices—that are enough to get an operating system loaded up—are included in the BIOS. Your BIOS is there to get things started for the operating system.

Basic object adapter (BOA) Invokes the performance of a request and returns any results to the client. Also called simply adapter.

Basic rate interface (BRI) BRI is an ISDN interface typically used by smaller sites and customers. This interface consists of a single 16Kbps Data (or"D")channel plus 2 Bearer(or"B") channels for voice and/or data. Aka. Basic Rate Access(BRA).

Bat Filename extension for a batch file.

Batch A group of commands that are executed one at a time.

Batch file An ASCII text file containing operating system commands and possibly other commands supported by the batch processor. The commands in the file are executed one line at a time, just as if you had typed them at the system prompt. You can inlcude program names, operating system commands, batch language commands, and other variables in your batch files. Batch files are used to automate repetitive tasks;almost all DOS users place regulary-used setup commands in a batch file called Autoexec.bat, which executes every time the computer is started.

In DOS, a file that contains one or more commands that are executed together as a set. You create the batch file by using a text editor (like the DOS EDIT command) and run the file by typing its name at the command prompt. A DOS batch file must have the file-name extension .BAT, while an OS/2 batch file has the extension .CMD.

Batch processing An approach to computer utilization that queues noninteractive programs and runs them one after another.

Batch program An ASCII file that contains one or more Windows NT commands. A batch program's filename typically has a .bat or .cmd extension. When you type the filename at the command prompt, the commands are processed sequentially.

Batch scanning Sequential scanning of multiple originals using previously defined, unique settings for each.

Battery A device consisting of one or more cells that can produce a direct current by converting chemical energy to electrical energy. Batteries typically have positive and negative terminals that must be connected for current to flow.

Baud Pronounced bawd. The term is named after J.M.E. Baudot, the inventor of the Baudot telegraph code. In common usage the baud rate of a modem is how many bits it can send or receive per second. Technically, baud is the number of times per second that the carrier signal shifts value - for example a 1200 bit-per-second modem actually runs at 300 baud, but it moves 4 bits per baud (4 x 300= 1200 bits per second).

Baud rate In communications equipment, a measurement of the number of state changes (from 0 to 1 or vice-versa) per second on an asynchronous communications channel.

Baud rate is often mistakenly assumed to correspond to the number of bits transmitted per second, but because in modern high-speed digital communications systems one state change can be made to represent more than 1 data bit, baud rate and bits per second are not always the same. A rate of 300 baud is likely to correspond to 300 bits per second, but at higher baud rates, the number of bits per second transmitted can be higher than the baud rate as one state change can represent more than one data bit. For example, 2400 bits per second can be sent a t 1200 baud if each state change represents tow bits of information. On the PC, the MODE command is used to set the baud rate of a serial device, perhaps a modem or a printer. Both the sending and the receiving devices must be set to the same baud rate, and in times past, mismatched baud rates were one of the most common reasons for communications failures. These days, intelligent modems can lock onto one of a range of rates, and can even change rates in response to changing line conditions during the course of a transmission

Bayesian networks Structures that describe systems in which there is a degree of uncertainty; used in automated decision making.

BBC (broadband bearer capability) A bearer class field that is part of the initial address message.

BBS (bulletin board system) A bulletin board system used to describe message boards that people would dial into directly with modems before the Internet was easily accessible. Instead of dialing into a network where everything is connected, you had your choice of a group of BBSs to dial into, and each one tried to offer the most members, files, and graphics to its members. Typically you paid for access on a monthly basis. More recently, the term describes Internet-based message boards or forums.

BCC (blind carbon copy) When sending an e-mail, if you BCC someone you are sending him or her a copy of your e-mail, but not allowing the recipients in the "To" or "CC" fields of your e-mail client to know that the BCC recipient was sent the message as well. BCC is often used for covert company communications, such as if you are getting irritated at someone and want to let someone else in on it without alerting the party you are irritated about, or if you are sending the CEO of your company a mail telling him or her he or she is wrong about something and want to BCC copies to your friends to gloat over it. Use BCC with caution. One of the most common uses of BCC is when sending mass e-mails; just send the e-mail to yourself and BCC it to the whole group you are sending to. That way, your mailing list is not known to any of the members.

BCD (binary coded decimal) A form of coding of each octet within a cell where each bit has one of two allowable states, 1 or 0.

B-channel The Integrated Services Digital Network (ISDN) channel that carries voice and user data.

BCOB (broadband connection oriented bearer) Information in the SETUP message that indicates the type of service requested by the calling user.

BCOB-A (bearer class a) Indicated by ATM end user in SETUP message for connection-oriented, constant bit rate service. The network may perform internetworking based on AAL information element (IE).

BCOB-C (bearer class c) Indicated by ATM end user in SETUP message for connection-oriented, variable bit rate service. The network may perform internetworking based on AAL information element (IE).

BCOB-X (bearer class x) Indicated by ATM end user in SETUP message for ATM transport service where AAL, traffic type and timing requirements are transparent to the network.

BCP (bulk copy program) A program used to copy databases or parts of databases in Sybase and Microsoft SQL Server environments. It was at first a command line program, but graphical interface programs have been put on top of it to make it more friendly.

BDC (backup domain controller) One or more computers running Windows NT that act as a backup to the primary domain controller (PDC). These machines can authenticate security requests just like the primary domain controller, and will take over for the PDC if it is not available. However, a BDC will remain a BDC until it is manually promoted to a PDC by a domain administrator. With Active Directory Windows no longer requires the sometimes confusing primary and backup domain controllers, just domain controllers instead.

BEA Basic programming Environment for interactive-graphical Applications, from Siemens-Nixdorf.

BECN (backward explicit congestion notification) A Resource Management (RM) cell type generated by the network or the destination, indicating congestion or approaching congestion for traffic flowing in the direction opposite that of the BECN cell.

BEDO Burst EDO is a variant on EDO DRAM in which read or write cycles are batched in bursts of four. Burst EDO bus speeds range from 40MHz to 66MHz, as opposed to the 33MHz bus speeds that can be accomplished using fast page mode or EDO DRAM.

Bedrock A C++ class library for Macintosh user interface portability.

Beep code When you turn on your PC—and all is well—you typically hear a single beep from your computer speaker, signaling that all is OK. If things are wrong—and the computer BIOS senses that things are wrong—a series of beeps will be emitted. This is the beep code. Based on the number of beeps, you can look up the meaning in your motherboard documentation and often diagnose the problem. Obvious things to check are whether your video card, processor, and/or memory are plugged in and seated properly.

Benchmark A repeatable test you use to judge the performance of your network. It attempts to quantify hardware or software performance—usually in terms of speed, reliability, or accuracy. One of the majore problems in determining performance is deciding which of the many benchmarks available actually reflects how you plan to use the system. For best results, you should evaluate performance using the same mix of applications and system commands that you expect to use in your day-to-day work. So in short, The best benchmarks are the ones that closely duplicate the type of work you routinely do on your network.

Benchmarking The process of measuring the performance of hardware or software in a specifically defined and strictly controlled environment. The benchmarking result is usually represented by a time or number rating that corresponds to how quickly certain tasks can be completed. The benchmark must be reproducible, of course, to have any meaning.

Bento A multi-vendor initiative allowing files to contain typed parts, to allow standard access between parts of a compound document independent of the file system.

BeOS An operating system designed by Be, Inc. The original goal of BeOS was to create an OS able to process multiple digital media streams efficiently, with no loss of performance. This contrasts to the design goal of the Windows OS, which had trouble with such operations, especially in older versions. The BeOS was originally designed to work on the PowerPC architecture, and was then ported to he x86 architecture. Be Incorporated, the company that made BeOS, was dissolved in November 2001 and its assets were sold to Palm, Inc.

Beowulf / project A cluster of computers connected to a high-speed private network, running Linux, FreeBSD, or another free OS, and using Beowulf software to function like a single massively parallel computer. All nodes in the system are dedicated to running cluster jobs, and do not function as client machines. A Beowulf cluster is designed for high speed over-reliability. Typically there is only one node that is connected outside of the private network.

This project serves as a repository of information for creating clusters of computers, called Beowulfs, that function as one massively parallel machine. It seeks to further the knowledge of producing a Beowulf cluster and has no centralized management. The Beowulf Project began in 1994 with the creation of a 16-node cluster of machines at a research center operated by NASA, and quickly spread to the creation of other clusters of computers assembled with off-the-shelf hardware that could perform some tasks much faster than a single machine, and for much cheaper than purchasing an expensive supercomputer.

BER (bit error rate) A measure of transmission quality. It is generally shown as a negative exponent, (e.g., 10-7 which means 1 out of 107 bits are in error or 1 out of 10,000,000 bits are in error).

Berkeley internet named domain (BIND) A DNS software package for UNIX/Linux machines. It contains a DNS server, API library, and tools. It is the most widely used DNS server, and most of the DNS servers on the Internet are running BIND. Bind can also refer to the linking of a networking protocol to a network card.

Bernoulli box A high-capacity data storage device featuring a removable cartridge, developed by Iomega Corporation.

Bernoulli numbers The sums of powers of consecutive integers; named after Swiss mathematician Jacques Bernoulli (1654-1705).

BERT (bit error rate test) In the field of DSL, BERT is a test that reflects the ratio of errored bits to the total number transmitted. Usually shown in exponential form10-6 to indicate that one out of a certain number of bits are in error.

Beta A term given to a product that isn't ready for public consumption, but is good enough for a wider testing scope. Many companies publicly release their beta software to a fraction of their users to let them get experience with the new software while the company gets feedback on bugs and features.

Beta software Software that has been released to a cross-section of typical users for testing before the commercial release of the package.

Beta test A phase of Product Delivery allowing users to report bugs in a commercial program. Also, for Device Drivers, a release strategy, where unfinished drivers are released to the public, in the hopes that knowledgeable individuals will dissassemble, repair them, and return their efforts for free.

BGA (ball grid array) As opposed to a pin grid array (PGA), a ball grid array is a type of microchip connection methodology. Ball grid array chips typically use a group of solder dots, or balls, arranged in concentric rectangles to connect to a circuit board. BGA chips are often used in mobile applications where PGA chips would take up too much space due to the length of the pins used to connect the chips to the circuit board. More and more designs are moving to BGA form factors.

BGI (binary gateway interface) Provides a method of running a program from a Web server. Similar to a Common Gateway Interface (CGI). The BGI uses a binary DLL which is loaded into memory when the server starts. While more efficient han a CGI, the BGI must be compiled and is not easily portable to other environments.

BGP (border gateway protocol) The prctocol used by the core routers on the Internet to route TCP/IP packets. BGP replaces the older Exterior Gateway Protocol. Core routers use BGP exchange routing information to determine optimal routing paths and also exchange TCP/IP data packets.

BHLI (broadband high layer information) This is a Q.2931 information element that identifies an application (or session layer protocol of an application).

Bilevel A type of image containing only black and white pixels.

Bilinear filtering Used to smooth flat surfaces by averaging the colors of adjacent pixels, which blurs them and removes blockiness when viewed up close.

Billing contact/agent As used by InterNIC, the billing contact/agent contact is the person or role account designated to receive the invoice for domain name registration fees and renewal (re-registration) fees. The billing contact should be in a position to ensure prompt payment of fees.

Bin A directory that contains programs. Your home directory probably has a subdirectory named bin. The system has directories called /bin and /usr/bin.

Binary Any scheme that uses two different states, components, conditions or conclusions. In mathemathics, the binary or base-2 numbering system uses combinations of the digits 0 and 1 to represent all values. The more familiar decimal system has a base of 10 (0-9).Computers and other digital devices are designed to work with information (internally) in the form of binary numbers, because it is relatively simple to construct electronic circuits that generate two voltage levels ("on" and "off", corresponding to 1 and 0)Unlike computers, people find binary numbers that consist of long strings of 0s and 1s difficult to read, so most people who work at this level use hexadecimal (base-16) numbers instead.

Binary code Binary consists of a string of bits, with bits represented by 1s and 0s, e.g., 0101011100000001. The "bi" refers to base 2 mathematical representation (1s and 0s).

Binary coded decimal (BCD) An ANSI/ISO standard encoding of the digits 0 to 9 using 4 binary bits; the encoding only uses 10 of the available 16 4-bit combinations.

Binary digit A single bit, 1 or 0.

Binary file A file that contains more than plain text (i.e., photos, sounds, spreadsheet, etc.) In contrast to an ASCII file which only contains plain text.

Binary large objects (blob) support The storage and retrieval of "binary large objects" bytes streams of data that may represent images, sound, or video. BLOBs have meaning to client application programs and need not be interpreted by the server.

Binary number system A counting system used in computers consisting of only 1's and 0's (zeros).

Binary search A search technique that splits an ordered list into halves until a result is found. Thus, it splits the list into a top and bottom half, then picks the half that the search term is located in (which can be determined because this search is used on ordered lists) and splits that in half, and so on until the search term is reached. The binary search uses a logarithmic (log2) amount of splits to locate its search term. For example, an ordered list of a million items can be searched in a maximum of 20 splits, a billion can be searched in 30, and so on.

Binary system A machine or abstraction that uses binary codes.

Binary tree An ordered tree where each node has no more than two child nodes. Child nodes are typically distinguished as left and right child nodes.

Binary-coded decimal Abbreviated BCD. A simple system for converting decimal numbers into binary form, where each decimal digit is converted into binary and then stored as a single character. In binary numbers, the largest value that can be stored in a single 8-bit byte is 255, and this obviously represents severe limitation to storing larger numbers. BCD is a way around this limitation that stays within the 8-bit storage format. For example, the decimal number 756 can be broken down so that the numbers 7, 5, and 6 are represented by one byte each. In BCD, each decimal digit occupies a byte, so three bytes are needed for a three-digit decimal number. There is no limit to the size of the stored number; as the number increases in size, so does the amount of storage space set aside to hold it.

BIND (Berkeley internet named domain) A DNS software package for UNIX/Linux machines. It contains a DNS server, API library, and tools. It is the most widely used DNS server, and most of the DNS servers on the Internet are running BIND. Bind can also refer to the linking of a networking protocol to a network card. Bind can also refer to the linking of a networking protocol to a network card.

Bindery The big database where user accounts and other related info are stored on a NetWare server.

Bindings The associatons of network drivers and hardware or you can also describe bindings as a chain of drivers that are linked to a given service. The order of these bindings determines the order in which the computer will search for information via the bindings that are specified.

Binhex Method of encoding binary (or other non-printable character set) for transmission in a text-only media. This is used by the Eudora email client and is also common among MacIntosh programs.

Binomial theorem A theorem giving the procedure by which a binomial expression may be raised to any power without using successive multiplications.

Biometrics The use of unique physical characteristics, such as fingerprints, voice patterns, or retinal scan, to authenticate a user.

BIOS (basic input/output system) In the PC, a set of instructions, stored in read-only memory (ROM), that let your computer's hardware and operating system communicate with application programs and peripheral devices such as hard disks, printers, and video adapters. These instructions are stored in non-volatile memory or as a permanent part of your computer. They are always available at a specific addresses in memory, so all programs can access them to perform their basic I/O functions.

0IBM computers contain a copyrighted BIOS that only their computers can use; however, other companies such as Phoenix, Award, and American Megatrends have developed BIOSes for other manufacturer's computers that emulate or mimic the IBM instructions without using the same code. If you use non-IBM computer, the BIOS company's copyright message and BIOS version number are displayed every time you turn on your computer.

Bios enumerator Responsible in a non-ACPI Plug and Play system for identifying all hardware devices on the motherboard of the computer. The BIOS supports an API that allows all Plug and Play computers to be queried in a common manner.

Bios extensions In the PC, extensions to the main BIOS(basic input/output system) that enable the computer to work with add-on devices such as hard disk controllers and EGA or VGA adapters. The ROM chips containing these extensions do not have to be located on the motherboard; they can also be on expansion boards plugged into the expansion bus. Any BIOS extensions needed to run these expansion boards are loaded automatically when you boot your computer.

Bios parameter block Abbreviated BPB. In the PC, a part of the boot record contained on every formatted disk, that contains information about the disk's physical characteristics. This information includes the version number of the operating system used to format the disk, the number of bytes per sector, the number of sectors per cluster, per track, and per disk, an is provided for use by device drivers.

BIP (bit interleaved parity) A method used at the PHY layer to monitor the error performance of the link. A check bit or word is sent in the link overhead covering the previous block or frame. Bit errors in the payload will be detected and may be reported as maintenance information.

BIS Border Intermediate System.

B-ISDN (broadband integrated services digital network) A high-speed (greater than ISDN primary rate), asynchronous, time division multiplexed transmission facility, or an arrangement of such facilities, designed to provide a wide range of audio, video and date application in the same network.

Bistable multivibrator (flip-flop) A simple element of memory made up of an assembly of logic gates. Based on inputs, the state of a flip-flop can be changed back and forth, affecting the future output of the flip-flop.

BISUP broadband isdn user's part A SS7 protocol which defines the signaling messages to control connections and services.

Bit A unit of measurement that represents one figure or character of data. A bit is the smallest unit of storage in a computer. Since computers actually read 0s and 1s, each is measured as a bit. The letter A consists of 8 bits which amounts to one byte. Bits are often used to measure the capability of a microprocessor to process data, such as 16-bit or 32-bit.

Bit depth How many bits it takes to represent the color in one pixel. The greater the bit depth, the more colors you can potentially display, and the more power it takes to represent a screen full of pixels at that bit depth. Common bit depths are 16 and 32 bits. Bit depth of 1 would only enable 2 colors, bit depth of 2 enables 4 colors, and so on, where the amount of potential colors can be determined by 2^bit_depth.

Bit mapped display A computer display that uses a table of binary bits in memory to represent the image that is projected onto the screen.

Bit rate The amount of bits per second used to encode audio data in an MP3 or other compressed audio file. Bit rate is typically listed in kilobits per second (kbps). Higher bit rates typically mean better sound quality, but that's just one of the factors involved. Typically, bit rates range between 96-256, but any rate is possible.

Bit serial mode A method of transferring binary bits one after another in a sequence or serial stream.

Bit specifications Number of colors or levels of gray that can be displayed at one time. Controlled by the amount of memory in the computer's graphics controller card. An 8-bit controller can display 256 colors or levels of gray; a 16-bit controller, 64,000 colors; and a 24-bit controller, 16.8 million colors.

Bitmap A type of graphics format that specifies a number of pixels and then specifies what color those pixels are. A simplified example: 5 red, 4 green, 3 red, etc. GIF and JPEG files are bitmaps. If an image contains large blocks of solid color, it will take less storage space than an image with a lot of small regions with different colors.

Bitmap font A font where each character is stored as a bitmap graphic. These fonts are not easy to scale to different sizes.

Bitmap Police Character set generated using a method which handles each character as a pixel set. Contrarily, the vectorial polices handle the characters by representing their shape, thus being independent of the actual size.

Bit-mapped graphic A graphic, created using a paint program like MacPaint or PC Paintbrush, composed of a series of dots, or pixels, rather than a set of lines or vectors.

Bitnet An academic computer network that provides interactive electronic mail and file transfer services, using a store-and-forward protocol, based on IBM Network Job Entry protocols. BITNET-II encapsulates the BITNET protocol within IP packets and depends on the Internet to route them. There are three main constituents of the network: BITNET in the

United States and Mexico, NETNORTH in Canada, and EARN in Europe. There are also AsiaNet, in Japan, and connections in South America.

Bits per inch The number of bits (binary digits) that a tape or disk can store per inch of length.

Bits per pixel The number of bits used to represent the color value of each pixel in a digitized image.

Bits per second (bps) This is generally a measure of how fast some device communicates, usually in thousands of bits per second (Kbps) or millions of bits per second (Mbps).

Bitstream A serialized collection of bits; usually used in transfer of bits from one system to another .

Black box Anything that you put input into and get output from, but don't know what's inside or how it works. The black represents the box being opaque so that you cannot see inside.

Black hat A malicious hacker. If a hacker finds a security hole and exploits it or lets others know about it before letting the people affected by the hole know about it, that hacker is described as a black hat hacker. This term comes from cowboy movies, where the bad guy would wear a black hat.

Black list List of known malicious objects (Websites, vandals, script commands, etc.) that should be blocked by default.

Black point A movablc reference point that defines the darkest area in an image, causing all other areas to be adjusted accordingly.

Blind carbon copy (BCC) When sending an e-mail, if you BCC someone you are sending him or her a copy of your e-mail, but not allowing the recipients in the "To" or "CC" fields of your e-mail client to know that the BCC recipient was sent the message as well. BCC is often used for covert company communications, such as if you are getting irritated at someone and want to let someone else in on it without alerting the party you are irritated about, or if you are sending the CEO of your company a mail telling him or her he or she is wrong about something and want to BCC copies to your friends to gloat over it. Use BCC with caution. One of the most common uses of BCC is when sending mass e-mails; just send the e-mail to yourself and BCC it to the whole group you are sending to. That way, your mailing list is not known to any of the members.

B-LLI (broadband low layer information) This is a Q.2931 information element that identifies a layer 2 and a layer 3 protocol used by the application.

Blob (binary large object) A generic term used to describe the handing and storage of long strings of data by middleware. Typically associated with image and video. Refer to Binary Large Object Support.

Block A unit of disk space containing one or more frags.

Block cipher Encryption that breaks information into blocks with a fixed size.

Block diagram A circuit or system drawing concerned with major functions and interconnections between functions.

Block mode A setting in the computer BIOS relating to IDE hard drives. The setting determines the type of Logical Block Addressing that will be used to translate large hard drives properly to the computer BIOS. On most machines with up-to-date BIOSes, you can set this to "Auto" and have hard drives recognized with no further specification on your part. If that doesn't work, you may need to tinker with other settings or use the software provided by the hard drive manufacturer for software translation.

Blog (Slang term for a Weblog) This is a publicly accessible personal journal for an individual. Similar to a personal diary, but shared over the web. The activity of updating a blog is "blogging" and someone who keeps a blog is a "blogger." Blogs are typically updated daily using software that allows people with little or no technical background to update and maintain the blog. Postings on a blog are almost always arranged in chronological order with the most recent additions featured most prominently.

Bluetooth Radio technology that connects electronic devices without using a cable. Data and voice can be exchanged at ranges of up to 10 meters without the need for devices to be lined up together.

Bluetooth sig Bluetooth Special Interest Group. Founded in May 1998 by Ericsson, IBM, Intel, Nokia and Toshiba, the Bluetooth SIG is a forum for the development, promotion and enhancement of Bluetooth technology. The Bluetooth SIG, now led by the Promoter Group (composed of the founding members plus Lucent, Motorola, Microsoft and 3Com) now has some 2000 adopter members.

BMP Bitmap graphics files that are accessible through Windows Paintbrush and most other PC graphics software.

BN becn cell A Resource Management (RM) cell type indicator. A Backwards Explicit Congestion Notification (BECN) RM-cell may be generated by the network or the destination. To do so, BN=1 is set, to indicate the cell is not source-generated, and DIR=1 to indicate the backward flow. Source generated RM-cells are initialized with BN=0.

BN (bridge number) A locally administered bridge ID used in Source Route Bridging to uniquely identify a route between two LANs.

BNC (British naval connector) A connector type for 10Base2 or Thin-Net networks. Shaped like the letter T, it connects coaxial cables. The "T" has two male connectors and one female connector. The female connector can connect to the male connection of an Ethernet card that supports BNC connections, or remain empty. The male connectors link to coaxial cable or a terminator. The BNC part stands for either British Naval Connector, British Nut Connector, or Bayonet Neill-Concelman ... or perhaps it stands for some combination of those terms. Neill and Concelman are the names of the inventors of the BNC Connector.

B-node resolution name One of the four modes of name resolution used on Windows networks. B-node relies exclusively on broadcast messages and is the oldest name resolution mode. A host needing to resolve a name request sends a message to every host within earshot, requesting the address associated with a host name. B-node has two shortcomings:broadcast traffic is undesirable and becomes a significant user of network bandwidths, and TCP/IP routers don't forward broadcast messages, which restricts b-node operation to a single network segment.

Board A hardware component that fits into the expansion slot of a computer unit and expands the capabilities of the computer. A board can enable the computer to communicate with an external hardware device, such as a CD-ROM. Alternate terms are card, expansion card, interface card, interface board.

BOM (beginning of message) An indicator contained in the first cell of an ATM segmented packet.

Bombs Denial of Service attacks, where an email server is bombed with thousands of false email messages, thereby denying it access to the outside world. A number of hacker programs, such as Unabomber, set up unattended automatic email bombing. These programs also make minor changes to the email envelope to conceal its source.

Bookmark A feature of Web browser software that allows you to selectively tag Web sites of interest. As with a traditional bookmark, the feature provides instant connection to the tagged Web page whenever chosen.

Bookreader DEC's CD-ROM-based online documentation browser.

Bookviewer A hypertext documentation system from Oracle based on Oracle Toolkit. It allows the user to create private links and bookmarks, and to make multimedia annotations.

Boolean A type of variable that can store only two values: true and false.

Boolean algebra A system developed by George Boole that deals with the theorems of undefined symbols and axioms concerning those symbols.

Boolean logic A type of mathematical logic named after its designer George Boole. This binary algebraic system is used primarily in switching circuits and database searches. Search engines use logical operators called, Boolean Operators (AND, OR, NOT).

AND: Narrows a keyword search by collecting all terms present in the same document.

NOT: Prevents retrieval of unwanted documents containing a keyword.

OR: which broadens a keyword search by linking related terms.

Boolean operators Fundamental logical operations (for example "and" and "or") expressed in a mathematical form.

Boot An automatic procedure begun when you first turn on or reset your computer, that loads an operating system into memory, usually from hard disk. A set of constructions contained in ROM begin executing, first running a series of power-on self tests (POST) to check that devices such as hard disks are in working order, then locating and loading the operating system, and finally, passing control of the computer over to that operating system.

Boot control Requiring use of a password or other security mechanism to access a PC.

Boot disk A diskette from which you can boot your computer. Normally, your computer boots from a hard disk, but if the hard disk is damaged (for example, by a virus), you can boot the computer from a bootable diskette. For this reason, it's a good idea to make sure you always have a bootable diskette on hand. In Windows 95, you can create a bootable diskette by following these steps:

1. Insert a blank, formatted diskette in the floppy drive.

2. Select Start->Settings->Control Panel.

3. Open Add/Remove Programs.

4. Select the Startup Disk tab and press the Create Disk... button.

A bootable diskette is also called a bootable floppy, boot disk, and startup disk.

Boot drive The drive that the operating system first loads from. (Usually A: or C). Normally, a PC will try to boot from the A: drive (the floppy drive.) If there is no disk in that drive, it will boot from the C: drive (the hard drive.)

Boot partition The volume, formatted for either an NTFS, FAT, of HPFS file system, that contains the Windows NT operating system's files. Windows NT automatically creates the correct configuration and checks this information whenever you start your system.

Boot protocol (bootP) The protocol that defines how a diskless workstation obtains its network address from another host. NeXT workstations also use BOOTP when booted to determine their NetInfo information. Defined in RFC 951 and extended by RFC 2132.

Boot record (master boot record) The first sector on a hard disk or other disk media. When a computer boots up it searches for a master boot record wherever the BIOS tells it to (usually the master hard drive on the first IDE channel, but this can also be checked for in CD/DVD drives and floppy drives) and, based on what the master boot record says, loads up an operating system. Thus, if the master boot record becomes corrupt or is tampered with by a virus, it can cause your computer to be unable to boot.

Boot sector Instructions allowing the hard disk to load the DOS operating system. This record is one of the privileged targets for viruses, because it is executed at each computer power-on.

Bootable disk Any disk capable of loading and starting the operating system, usually alluding to a floppy disk.

Booting Starting up a computer via the power switch, which loads the system software into memory. Restarting the computer via a keystroke combination is called rebooting or a warm boot.

BootP (bootstrap protocol) This protocol is the basis for DHCP. It allows a client computer to receive an IP address from a BootP server without having a static IP address defined beforehand on the client machine.

Bootstrap This either refers to a small piece of intermediate code that will boot up an operating system, or the act of building something without help.

Bootstrapping The process of developing something without reliance on outside help such as investor money. It's referred to often today, and often in the Dot-Com heyday, to describe website designers and entrepreneurs who effectively start their own companies on the Web with only their own investment.

Border gateway protocol (BGP) The protocol used by the core routers on the Internet to route TCP/IP packets. BGP replaces the older Exterior Gateway Protocol. Core routers use BGP exchange routing information to determine optimal routing paths and also exchange TCP/IP data packets.

Border node A logical node that is in a specified peer group, and has at least one link that crosses the peer group boundary.

BOS A data management system written at DESY and used in some HEP programs.

Bot A roBot that usually is a software program that can be good (administering or policing on the network) or bad (causing evil) on the network. Bots commonly are used in real audio chat lines. A WebBot are "smart objects" that can be inserted into web pages to perform tasks that otherwise would require CGI scripting or some other dynamic action programming. WebBots can help set up dynamic chat lines, time image appearances, register and confirm actions, reference annotations, perform calculations, etc. Some HTML editors can be used to create WebBots. Microsoft FrontPage, for example, can be used for:

WebBot Confirmation Field component.

WebBot Include component.

WebBot Scheduled Image component.

WebBot Scheduled Include component.

WebBot Search component.

WebBot Substitution component.

WebBot Table of Contents component.

WebBot Timestamp component.

Bottleneck Part of a system that limits the performance of the system. This term was derived from the neck of a bottle, which limits the flow of liquid due to the smaller circumference of the neck as compared to the wider body of the bottle. Often you will hear of people attempting to find and eliminate the bottlenecks in their computer systems or networks. This is certainly a helpful practice if the bottleneck is slowing things down inordinately, but as soon as you remove one bottleneck from a system remember that something else immediately becomes the bottleneck. For example, if you get a faster processor to speed up your 3D video, the 3D video card may be the bottleneck afterwards.

Boxed processor A microprocessor that is sold singly in a retail box, like something you would buy at a store. This compares to just buying a processor that some OEM takes out of a bulk box of 1,000 processors and throws in a static bag for you to take home. Boxed processors typically come with multi-year warranties directly from the manufacturer.

BPDU (bridge protocol data unit) A message type used by bridges to exchange management and control information.

BPI (bits per inch) The number of bits recorded per linear inch of recording surface.

BPM Business Process Modelling.

BPP bridge port pair (source routing descriptor) Frame header information identifying a bridge/LAN pair of a Source route segment.

BPR Business Process Reengineering.

BPS (bits per second) Basic unit of measure for serial date transmission capacity ; the number of binary digits transmitted over a communications channel in a second. On a classical dial-up line, this speed was 1,200 in the 70s, 4,800 in the 80s. With compression techniques (now common in modems and routers), this speed is multiplied by a factor 2 to 3, thus allowing a throughput approaching 10,000 characters per second (or more than 30 million characters per hour).

BRB Online speak for "Be Right Back".

Breach Successful penetration of network security measures.

Break key The Break Key is used before you log in when you are dialing on a modem to tell Unix that it has guessed wrong about which kind of modem you're using.You may have to press Break two or three times until you get a proper login: message. Some keyboards have a key labeled break. If yours does'nt and you're using a PC with a modem program, try Alt-B or check your modem program's help screen.

Brick and mortar A store or business that either doesn't have a Web presence or has mainly physical locations as opposed to websites. Bricks and mortar are common building materials.

Bridge A piece of network hardware that links two or more network segments. The network topologies do not have to be the same (e.g., you can bridge Ethernet and Token Ring), but the protocols must be (e.g., TCP/IP or IPX/SPX). If the protocols are different on the linked segments, you've got a router, not a bridge. Bridges are used to reduce network traffic, increase cable distance (by acting as a repeater), and also to link dissimilar network topologies that run the same network protocol.

Bridge tap An accidental connection of another local loop to the primary local loop. Generally, it behaves as an open circuit at DC, but becomes a transmission line stub with adverse effects at high frequency. It is generally harmful to DSL connections and should be removed. Extra phone wiring within one's house is a combination of short bridge taps. A POTS splitter isolates the house wiring and provides a direct path for the DSL signal to pass unimpaired to the ATU-R modem.

Brightness Light output measured at the face plate of the CRT; typically measured in foot lamberts (Fl). A minimum brightness level of 20Fl when viewing at full page size is considered acceptable.

Broadband access An ISDN access capable of supporting one or more broadband services.

Broadband network In communications, a technique for transmitting a large amount of information, including voice, data, and video, over long distances. The transmission capacity is divided into several distint channels that can be used concurrently, normally by using frequency-division multiplexing, and these individual channels are protected from each other by guard channels of unused frequencies. A broadband network can operate at speeds of up to 20 megabits per second, and is based on the same technology used by cable television.

Broadband Network transmission capacity that greatly exceeds capacity required for voice transmission over traditional telephone cables. Broadband networks may have dedicated portions for audio, video, and data or they may allow for capacity switching.

Broadband system A broadband system is capable of transmitting many different signals at the same time without interfering with one another. For local area networks, a broadband system is one that handles multiple channels of local area network signals distributed over Cable Television *(catv)* hardware.

Broadcast A method of sending information over a network. With broadcasting, data comes from one source and goes to all other connected sources. This has the side effect of congesting a medium or large network segment very quickly.

Sometimes broadcasting is necessary to locate network resources, but once found, more advanced networking protocols change to point-to-point connections to transmit data. Nowadays, switches and routers often do not pass along broadcast packets, but in the days of shared Ethernet broadcasting could really congest a network.

Broadcast architecture The set of technologies that enable PCs to receive broadcast data.

Broadcast command A command that simultaneously sends data to multiple recipients.

Brouter In networking, a device that combines the attributes of a bridge and a router. A brouter can route one or more specific protocols, such as TCP/IP, and bridge all others.

Brownout A short period of low voltage often caused by an unusually heavy demand for power. It can cause your computer to crash, so invest in an uninterruptable power supply (UPS).

Browser In order to be able to access the Web, you first need to be able to access the internet. You then need software which will let you look at all of the information available on the Web. This is often referred to as browsing and the software that lets you do this is called a browser. In the Math Department, the currently preferred browser on the UNIX machines and Macs is called Netscape, version 2.0.

Browsing The process of requesting the list of computers and services on a network from a browser.

BSD (Berkeley software distribution) Implementation of the UNIX operating system and its utilities developed and distributed by the University of California at Berkeley. BSD is usually preceded by the version number of the distribution, e.g., 4.3 BSD is version 4.3 of the Berkeley UNIX distribution. Many Internet hosts run BSD software, and it is the ancestor of many commercial UNIX implementations.

BSD unix A version of Unix developed and distributed by the University Of California at Berkeley. BSD stands for Berkely Software Distribution.

BSOD (blue/black screen of death) A Windows error message that is shown on a screen with a blue background. In Windows NT/2000/XP, this type of message causes the computer to stop completely, and is usually caused by improperly written hardware drivers or faulty hardware. Other BSODs can occur in different versions of Windows (95/98/Me) as well, but are not always as disastrous. Less frequently, black screens of death (also BSOD) are referred to as well during a complete system crash which may or may not have anything to do with the Windows OS.

BT (burst tolerance) BT applies to ATM connections supporting VBR services and is the limit parameter of the GCRA.

B-TE (broadband terminal equipment) An equipment category for B-ISDN which includes terminal adapters and terminals.

Btrieve An indexed file access method commonly used on NetWare networks.

BTW (by the way) A shorthand term appended to a comment in an online forum or email.

Buffer A temporary location to store or group information in hardware or software. Buffers are used whenever data is received in sizes that may be different than the ideal size for the hardware or software that uses the buffer. For example, a 64-bit processor on a 16-bit bus may have a buffer to hold 16-bit requests until they equal 64-bits. Another use of buffers is to keep hardware from getting overwhelmed with information. In that scenario, you use a large buffer to hold data until a device or program is ready to receive it, instead of just pushing it onto a device that might not be ready. Buffers must be optimized in size to work efficiently for the purpose they are designed.

Buffer overrun Attack where a hacker exploits an unchecked buffer in a program to overwrite the program code. If the hacker overwrites the program code with new executable code, the hacker can change the program's operation. If the hacker enters other data, it usually causes the program to crash.

Buffer underrun A common error where the data stream being fed from the CD-R's cache buffer falls behind the laser doing the writing.

Buffered memory A buffer isolates the memory from the controller to minimize the load on the chip set. It is typically used when the system has a high density of memory and/or when a system has more than 3 memory module sockets.

Bug This is commonly an error in design or programming in a hardware device or piece of software. The effects of a bug may be as harmless as an extra graphic on the screen, or as harmful as a system crash or loss of data. The first computer "bug" was a real bug, a moth, in fact, that was stuck between relays back in an early computer in 1945.

Bug-fix A release of hardware or software that corrects known bugs but does not contain additional new features.

Bulk copy program (BCP) A program used to copy databases or parts of databases in Sybase and Microsoft SQL Server environments. It was at first a command line program, but graphical interface programs have been put on top of it to make it more friendly.

Bulletin board system (BBS) A bulletin board system used to describe message boards that people would dial into directly with modems before the Internet was easily accessible. Instead of dialing into a network where everything is connected, you had your choice of a group of BBSs to dial into, and each one tried to offer the most members, files, and graphics to its members. Typically you paid for access on a monthly basis. More recently, the term describes Internet-based message boards or forums.

Burn Widely used slang that describes the creation of a CD-R disc. During the creation of a CD-R, a laser is used to burn tiny holes inside the disk media.

Burn-in The process of exercising an integrated circuit at elevated voltage and temperature. This process accelerates failures normally seen as "infant mortality" in a chip. (Those chips that would fail early during actual usage will fail during burn-in. Those that pass have a life expectancy much greater than that required for normal usage.)

Burst EDO RAM (BEDO RAM) A type of EDO RAM that can read three consecutive memory locations in three clock cycles—a 1-1-1 burst. This makes BEDO RAM much faster at reading large blocks of data than standard EDO RAM. However, it cannot operate faster than 66MHz, limiting its applications in today's computers. Burst EDO was never more than a niche technology.

Burst mode A data transmission mode in which data is sent faster than normal. There are a number of techniques for implementing burst modes. In a data bus, for example, a burst mode is usually implemented by allowing a device to seize control of the bus and not permitting other devices to interrupt. In RAM, burst modes are implemented by automatically fetching the next memory contents before they are requested. This is essentially the same technique used by disk caches. The one characteristic that all burst modes have in common is that they are temporary and unsustainable. They allow faster data transfer rates than normal, but only for a limited period of time and only under special conditions.

Bus A collection of wires through which data is Transmitted from one part of a computer to another. You can think of a bus as a highway on which data Travels within a computer. When used reference to Personal computers, the term bus usually refers to Internal bus. This is a bus that connects all the internal computer components to the CPU and main memory. There's also an expansion bus that enables expansion boards to access the CPU and memory.

All buses consist of two parts — an address bus and a data bus. The data bus transfers actual data whereas the address bus transfers information about where the data should go.

The size of a bus, known as its width, is important because it determines how much data can be transmitted at one time. For example, a 16-bit bus can transmit 16 bits of data, whereas a 32-bit bus can transmit 32 bits of data.

Every bus has a clock speed measured in MHz. A fast bus allows data to be transferred faster, which makes applications run faster. On PCs, the old ISA bus is being replaced by faster buses such as PCI.

Nearly all PCs made today include a local bus for data that requires especially fast transfer speeds, such as video data. The local bus is a high-speed pathway that connects directly to the processor.

In networking, a bus is a central cable that connects all devices on a local-area network (LAN). It is also called the backbone. The internal pathways (data bus, address bus, and control bus) of wires connecting various parts of a computer. Common standards for buses were Industry Standard Architecture (ISA) 16-bit bus common in AT-compatible PCs, Micro Channel Architecture (MCA) 32-bit buses in IBM PS/2 computers, and Enhanced Industry Standard Architecture (EISA) 32-bit buses that are backward compatible with ISA adapters. An "expansion bus" is an extension of the data bus and address bus that includes slots for adapter boards. It is better than ISA and EISA for hypermedia authoring to also purchase a "local bus" system in 32-bit or higher capacity with eight or more expansion slots for multimedia options. A local bus connects the CPU with peripherals directly so as to improve performance speed. However, in recent years, the VL local buses are not as good as the Peripheral Component Interconnect (PCI) brainchild of Intel. The term "bus" can also apply to standards for connecting electronic components other than computer components. The term CDBus or consumer electronics bus refers to a home or office automation standard such that components connected through power lines, coaxial cable, infrared connections, and telephone lines will be mutually compatible.

BUS (broadcast and unknown server) This server handles data sent by an LE Client to the broadcast MAC address, all multicast traffic, and initial unicast frames which are sent by a LAN Emulation Client.

Bus enumerator In a non-ACPI Plug and Play system, a bus device driver that detects devices located on a specific bus and loads information about devices into the hardware tree.

Bus mastering A technique that allows certain advanced bus architectures to delegate control data transfers between the CPU and associated peripheral devices to an add-in board. This gives greater system bus access and higher data transfer rates than conventional systems.

Bus mouse A mouse that uses the smaller 6-pin connector instead of your computer's serial port. Also referred to as a PS/2 mouse because of its early adoption in the IBM PS/2 series of computers.

Bus speed A measurement, usually in MHz, of how many times data can be transferred over the bus per second.

Bus topology This network topology has computers connected to a strand of network cabling that is connected to network repeaters at one end and terminated at the other. If you break part of the cable or remove the terminator, all machines on that segment lose communication with the network. 10Base2 was a widely used bus topology network in its day.

Business to consumer (B2C) A form of doing business that deals with selling goods and services to the consumer marketplace. Examples of this would be selling consumer electronics, toys, or pet supplies. This contrasts with the business to business model.

Button (bouton) In a graphical user interface, an icon symbolising a button is used to allow the user to select among options, or to confirm an action.

BW bandwidth A numerical measurement of throughput of a system or network.

Byte Eight bits in a row. That is a series of eight pieces of information, each of which can be either 1 or 0. A little higher math tells you that there are 256 different combinations of eight 1s and 0s.(256 is 2 to the 8th power.)There are therefore 256 different values for a byte of information. Most computers use a system of codes called ASCII to determine what each pattern means. The combination 01000001 means A, 01000010 means B, and 00001010 means "end of the line, start a new one."

Bytes per inch (bpi) The number of bytes that a tape or disk can store per inch of length.

Bytes per second (bps) This is generally a measure of how fast some device communicates, usually in thousands of bytes per second (KBps) or millions of bytes per second (MBps).

C

C A programming language developed in the late '70s. It became hugely popular due to the development of UNIX, which was written almost entirely in C. C was written by programmers for programmers, and it lets you write code in sloppy ways that other, more structured languages do not. When you think of programming in C, think of driving a Delorean. It goes really fast, but it's a mess inside.

C beautifier A tool for tidying the syntax of source code.

C sharp An object-oriented programming language from Microsoft based on C/C++ that contains functionality similar to that found in the Java programming language. It is designed to work with Microsoft's .NET platform.

C Shell The C shell is a Unix shell written to look like the C programming language, sort of. It prompts you with %. Its program name is CSH.

C++ An extension to the C language . As a superset of C, it provides additional features for data abstraction and object-oriented programming.

C2 Discretionary Controlled Access Protection . A class of computer system security defined by the US Department of Defence. With C2 systems, information is accessible only to specifically authorised users. C2 functionality is of significant value in commercial applications.

CA (certificate authority) A trusted third-party organization or company that issues digital certificates. The CA guarantees that the holder of the digital certificate is who he or she says he or she is. The issuing party typically confirms the information provided to it by credit card verification.

CA90s Computer Associates's integrated software architecture that attempts to bring order and form to existing CA technology. Its advantage include its lack of hardware bias and the fact that it is not standard-dependent. One of its main components is CA-UNICENTER, selected as System Administration software in France.

Cabinet file (cab file) A compressed file with the extension .cab. Cabinet files are used to store installation files for Microsoft applications, most commonly Windows 9x operating systems and Internet Explorer. Cab files were initially designed to fit large installations onto a group of 1.44 MB floppy disks.

Cable modem The device that you attach a coaxial cable from your cable company directly into that can provide you with high speed Internet access. The cable modem typically has a port on it so that you can connect a network cable between it and your computer to connect you to the cable network. If your cable company supports such access, it is typically at 1.5-

3.0Mbps, about 50-100 times faster than a 56K modem.

Cable select (CSEL) This is basically Plug-and-Play ATA. You plug in your ATA/IDE hard drives, set them to CSEL (Cable Select), and they determine whether they are master or slave automatically, saving you from manual configuration.

CAC (connection admission control) Connection Admission Control is defined as the set of actions taken by the network during the call set-up phase (or during call re-negotiation phase) in order to determine whether a connection request can be accepted or should be rejected (or whether a request for re-allocation can be accommodated).

Cache A special area of memory, managed by a *cache controller*, that improvers performance by storing the contents of frequently accessed memory locations and their addresses. When the processor references a memory address, the cache checks to see if it holds that address. If it does, the information is passed directly to the processor; if not, a normal memory access takes place instead. A cache can speed up operations in a computer whose ram access is slow compared with its processor speed, because the cache memory is always faster than normal RAM.

Cache controller A special-purpose processor, such as the Intel 82385, whose sole task is to manage cache memory. On newer processors, such as the Intel Pentium, cache management is integrated directly into the processor.

Cache memory Generally a small chunk of fast memory that sits between either 1) a smaller, faster chunk of memory and a bigger, slower chunk of memory, or 2) a microprocessor and a bigger, slower chunk of memory. The purpose of cache memory is to provide a bridge from something that's comparatively very fast to something that's comparatively slow. Most microprocessors have built-in cache memory that holds some of the information from main memory. When the processor needs the information it takes it from the speedy cache instead of the slower main memory. Cache memory GREATLY increases the speed of a computer by storing data that is most often accessed.

Cache ram Cache (usually SRAM) stores frequently requested data and instructions. It is a small block of high-speed memory located between the CPU and the main memory. When your computer processor needs data, it will check the Cache first to see if it is there. If the data is not there, it will retrieve it from the slower main memory.

Caching A feature found on many browsers that stores a copy of visited Web pages on the user's hard disk. The next time you visit the site, the page is retrieved from your computer rather than through the Internet.

CACM Communications of the ACM.

CAD (computer aided design) This refers to the use of computers to design things. There are specific CAD programs like AutoCAD that are generally resource-intensive, requiring fast processors, lots of memory, and a big, clear monitor for best results. CAD has enabled people to easily model, create, and walk through or view designs of 3D objects or floor plans from different angles on a computer without actually taking the time to make a physical mock up. This is a huge time saver, and has revolutionized design in general.

CAD/CAM Computer-Aided Design/Computer-Aided Manufacturing. Two highly specialised technical applications of a computer to improve the productivity of the engineer.

CADD (computer aided detector design) A project to develop standards and methods to allow cooperation between HEP detector designers working in different institutes.

Cadre A software engineering vendor in the US.

CAE Common Applications Environment of X/Open , based on POSIX and C.

CAE (computer aided engineering) A technique for using computers to help with all phases of engineering design work. As CAD, but also involving the conceptual and analytical design steps.

CAL The most generic of Computer Aided Learning or Computer Assisted Learning terms. CAL encompasses in-class lecture aids, learning materials for computer labs, electronic books, learning materials available on networks such as the Internet, and any other learning aids that are used with computers or related devices such as compact disc (CD) players connected to television sets.

Calculus A method of dealing mathematically with variables that may be changing continuously with respect to each other.

Call A call is an association between two or more users or between a user and a network entity that is established by the use of network capabilities. This association may have zero or more connections.

Call data record (CDR) Information logged by the private branch exchange (PBX) that tracks who made or received calls from whom, the duration of the call, and other information. CDR is used to bill back telecommunications charges to the appropriate parties.

Callback A process for invoking a method or a desktop command , or for using the gadget library in an application; the means by which dialogs and gadgets respond to user input. For example, when an administrator makes a selection with the mouse, some action is initiated from the user interface to an underlying object representing some system resource or component; that is, the user interface "calls back" to the object to invoke some method or series of methods.

Callback modems Security techniques that collect telephone numbers from authorized users on calls and then dial the users to establish the connections.

Caller ID Caller identification of the phone number of person placing a call to another number. Some states now allow telephone owners to have visual displays of the caller ID.

CALS (computer-aided acquisition and logistics support) A DoD standard for electronic exchange of data with commercial suppliers.

CAMEL Customized Application for Mobile networks Enhanced Logic is a feature of GSM that allows users to roam between networks. CAMEL is a standard that is now starting to be deployed.

Cannon cable (xlr cable) An analog audio cable normally used to connect microphones to professional audio devices. It has three pins and provides a balanced input, as opposed to an unbalanced or single-ended RCA connector.

Capacitance The property of a circuit element that allows it to store an electrical charge.

Capacitor An electronic component that stores up an electrical charge to a certain level and then releases it. A capacitor stores energy between two conducting plates separated by an insulator, or dialectric. Capacitance, or the amount of current that is stored, is measured in farads. You may notice large looking electronic cylinders on your motherboard. These are capacitors, and they are used to provide clean power to your processor. You'll also find larger capacitors in your power supply. CRT televisions and monitors contain many capacitors, that's why you are warned against opening up a CRT device or power supply even when it is off, as there may still be electrical energy in the capacitors.

Capture The NetWare command used to redirect printer output to a network printer. It is usually run in a batch file or login script.

CAQ Computer Aided Quality.

Carbon copy (CC) A method of sending a copy of an e-mail to someone, but implying that the person is not the direct recipient. For example, you send an e-mail with instructions to a group you manage, and CC it to your boss so that he or she knows what's going on but understands that the instructions in the mail were not meant for him or her to carry out. When you carbon copy someone in an e-mail, the recipients in the "To" field of the e-mail are aware of the names in the CC field. If you want to keep names secret from the To and CC recipients, you would use "BCC," or blind carbon copy.

Card A printed circuit board or adapter that you plug into your computer to add support for a specific piece of hardware not normally present on the computer.

Card select number The handle created by the system BIOS or the operating system through the isolation process and assigned as a unique identifier to each Plug and Play card on the ISA bus.

Card services Under Windows, a protected-mode system component that is a VxD linked with the PC Card bus driver. Card Services passes the event notification from socket services to the PC Card bus driver, provides information from the computer's cards to the PC Card bus driver, and sets up the configuration for cards in the adapter sockets.

Cardbus The 32-bit PCMCIA card slot and cards that can work in this slot. Standard PCMCIA, or PC Card, slots were originally 16-bit slots. This caused problems when 100Mbit network cards and fast SCSI cards were used and throughput would not go high enough because the 16-bit slots were too slow.

CARDS Central Archive for Reusable Defense Software of the DoD.

Carrier sense, multiple access with collision detect (CSMA/CD) Different devices on a network may try to communicate at any one time, so access methods need to be established. Using the CSMA/CDcd access method, a device first checks that the cable is free from other carriers and then transmits, while continuing to monitor the presence of another carrier. If a collision is detected, the device stops transmitting and tries later. In a CSMA network with collision detection, all stations have the ability to sense traffic on the network.

Carrier signal In communications, a signal of chosen frequency generated to carry data, often used for long-distance transmissions. The data is added to this carrier signal modulation, and decoded on the receiving end by demodulation.

Cartography Map making.

CAS 2 (cas 2 latency) This implies that two clock cycles are needed to address a column of a memory chip. CAS 2 SDRAM memory is preferable to CAS 3 SDRAM memory, but is often more expensive. DDR memory has CAS 2 and CAS 2.5 for comparison. You can sometimes set the CAS latency of your memory in your computer BIOS.

CAS 3 (cas 3 latency) This implies that three clock cycles are needed to address a column on a memory chip.

CAS Channel Associated Signaling: A form of circuit state signaling in which the circuit state is indicated by one or more bits of signaling status sent repetitively and associated with that specific circuit.

Cas-b4-ras (CBR) CAS before RAS. Column address strobe before row address strobe. A refresh technique in which the DRAM keeps track of the next row it needs to refresh.

Cascaded interrupt An Interrupt Request line reserved by the system (in the IBM PC architecture) for notifying the first interrupt controller that the second has received an interrupt. Used by VGA cards for the Vertical Retrace Interrupt, and the default IRQ setting for most LAN cards.

Cascaded operation An operation in which the first object, originally acting as a server for a client, now becomes a client of a second object on a remote machine, and so on.

Cascading style sheets (CSS) You can use CSS to define one or more styles on a single Web page or group of Web pages. The styles determine how information is displayed in browsers. For example, you could define a style for text that sets the font to Arial and the size to 2, and use that style wherever it is appropriate on your HTML pages. A style can affect one page or a group of them. The vast majority of current browsers support CSS.

CASE (computer-aided software engineering) CASE is an umbrella term for a collection of tools and techniques which are said by their distributors to promise revolutionary gains in analyst and programmer productivity. The two prominent delivered technologies are application generators and PC-based workstations that provide graphics-oriented automation of the front end of the development process.

Case framework A set of products and conventions that allow CASE tools to be integrated into a coherent environment.

Case tools Software tools to help in the application of CASE methods to a software project.

Casemethod An analysis and design method from Oracle, targeted at information management applications.

Case-dependent Software differentiation between upper and lower case characters. Also referred to as case sensitive.

CASSAM Computer Aided Software Support and Maintenance.

CAST Computer Aided Software Testing.

CAT That subset of CAL that entails Computer Aided Teaching. This subset is restricted to software designed for authoring and/or delivery of learning materials in a classroom or on line in a computer network or teleconference in which the instructor is present and using the CAT materials as an aid to his or her teaching.

CATE (computer aided test engineering) CASE methods applied to electronics testing and linked to CAE.

Category 3 cable standard (cat 3) Cat 3 cable is certified to run at up to 16MHz. You can achieve speeds of up to 10Mbps on Cat 3 cable. This cable maxes out with standard 10Mbps Ethernet.

Category 4 cable standard (cat 4) Cat 4 cable is certified to run at up to 20MHz. You can achieve speeds of up to 16Mbps, such as with the 16Mbps token-ring standard.

Category 5 cable standard (cat 5) This was a very common copper wire standard between 1996-2002 and today. It uses an RJ-45 plug and four-pair wire like Cat 3 and Cat 4, but it is certified to run up to 100MHz and is suitable for 100Mbps wiring standards. Higher speeds are possible, and some installers certify Cat 5 wire at 155Mbps or more.

Category 5e cable standard (cat 5 enhanced, cat 5e) A copper wire cable standard that contains four twisted copper wire pairs, like earlier versions such as Cat 3, 4, and 5. It allows connection speeds of 400MHz.

Category 6 cable standard (cat 6) A cable standard for cable that contains four twisted copper wire pairs, just like earlier copper cable standards. It was designed with Gigabit Ethernet in mind, and typically allows transmission speeds of 400-550MHz.

Category 7 cable standard (cat 7) A cable standard for cable that contains four twisted copper wire pairs. It is not yet fully ratified. It typically allows transmission speeds of up to 600MHz.

Cathode ray tube (CRT) One of the main components of most monitors and TVs. A beam of electrons is shot towards the CRT, and as the electrons collide with phosphors on the inside surface they produce light. Today, other technologies are performing better than the heavy and bulky tube monitors. LCD panels, gas plasma panels, and projection units are all in contention, but they still can't compare to the low cost of a CRT monitor or TV.

Cause An international (mainly North American) nonprofit association for managing and using information technology in higher education.

CAV (constant angular velocity) Playback in magnetic and laser discs where the disc rotates at a constant speed. Relative to CLV variable speeds, the CAV approach results in varying data retrieval times that depend upon where the read/write head is located relative to the disc spindle. Authors of CAV disc products try to locate commonly accessed files closer to spindle. In videodiscs, CAV discs hold only 30 minutes of video on each side of a 12-inch disc. However, CAV facilitates searching for individual frames.

CBDS (connectionless broadband data service) A connectionless service similar to Bellcore's SMDS defined by European Telecommunications Standards Institute (ETSI).

CBIOS (compatiblity basic input/output system) Firmware service routines built into the IBM PS/2 series of computers with Micro Channel Architecture (MCA), generally considered to be a super-set of the original IBM PC BIOS.

CBR (constant bit rate) An ATM service category which supports a constant or guaranteed rate to transport services such as video or voice as well as circuit emulation which requires rigorous timing control and performance parameters.

CBT (computer-based training) In which the computer becomes a tutor for asynchronous learning that adjusts to each student's learning pace. CBT that contains artificial intelligence for adapting training requirements and options to different aptitudes and skills of individual students is referred to in military training as Intelligent CBT (ICBT) to distinguish ICBT from traditional CBT that does not automatically adapt to skills and needs of different learners.

CCD (charge coupled device) A semiconductor device capable of both photodetection and memory, which converts light to electronic impulses. One- and two-dimensional CCD arrays are used in scanners to perform the first stage in converting an image into digital data. They are particularly attractive because they can step the signals from each detector across the array in response to a clock signal, permitting each scan line to be read through a single electrical connection.

CCI Common Client Interface for Mosaic.

CCITT (comité consultatif internationale de téléphonie et de télégraphie) An organization ,based in Geneva, that develops world-wide data communications standards. CCITT is part of the ITU (International Telecommunications Union). Three main sets of standards have been established: CCITT Groups 1-4 standards apply to facsimile transmissions; the ccitt v series of standards apply to modems and error detection and correction methods; and the CCITT x series standards apply to local area networks.

CCITT Group III The original standard for compression and decompression of facsimile.

Group IV The optimised standard for black-and-white office documents. Neither Group III nor Group IV handles color. Both are required to reduce bandwidth and storage demand.

CCITT x series A set of recommended standards issued by CCITT to standardize protocols and equipment used in public and private computer networks, including the transmission speeds, the interfaces to and between networks, and the operation of user hardware.

CCL (common command language) A standard for bibliographic information retrieval systems.

CCR (current cell rate) The Current Cell Rate is an RM-cell field set by the source to its current ACR when it generates a forward RM-cell. This field may be used to facilitate the calculation of ER, and may not be changed by network elements. CCR is formatted as a rate.

CD compact disc A "small" injection-molded optical disc containing digitized information that has been recorded with a laser device and must be read on a laser device. The term "small" generally refers to a disc that is 8 cm or 12 cm

(4.72 inches) in diameter as opposed to videodiscs that typically are much larger in diameter. Also, videodiscs usually are restricted to analog inputs from videotape whereas CDs rely on inputs from computer tape or other digitized platforms. Although there are several types of CDs for audio, television, and computer playback, the CD-Audio and CD-ROM discs have overwhelming shares of the market. CD-ROM discs now hold approximately 680 Mb (i.e., 680 million characters) although compression techniques make it possible to record CDs from even larger computer files. Usually CDs have slower access speeds than magnetic hard drives, but speeds are improving and playback of video is now possible on both CD-ROM and CD-I players. Although the best known CDs once were those that contain only audio recordings, there is a rapidly growing market for various types of CDs that contain computer files and/or files that can be read on special devices connected to television sets.

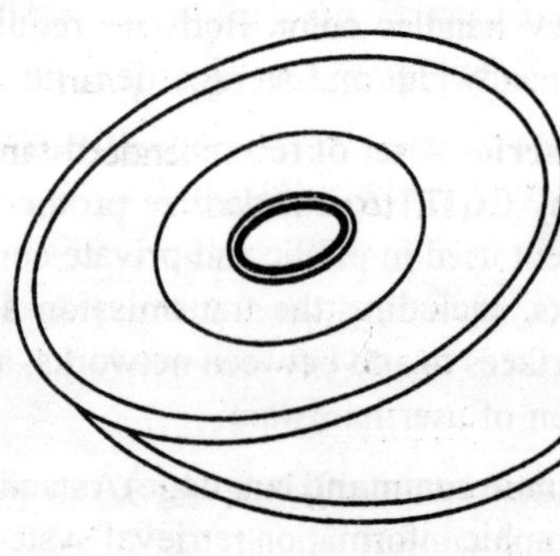

Fig. CD Compact disc

Cd rom drive A device used for loading large programs from CD ROM and sharing interrupts with LAN cards. Newer CD ROM players allow you to replace a Hard Disk with a CD ROM drive and search endlessly for device drivers when upgrading to Win95.

CD+G Audio CD plus still-image graphics such as with Photo CD. Although these are commonly displayed on television screens, they are less interactive than CD-I, CD-VIS, CD-R, CD-Karaoke, CD-3DO, CD-MM, and CD-TV.

CD32 The 32-bit multimedia CD system that plays on Amiga Computers from Commodore Corporation. These CDs are used for CD movies, games, and educational material on Amiga Computers. The future of the CD32 is clouded by the 1994 declaration of bankruptcy by Commodore Corporation.

CD-3DO A type of compact disc designed originally to compete against CD-I and CD-MM for interactive television set entertainment and, possibly, education. Large companies such as Panasonic, Sanyo, and others are producing playback machines for TV sets. The 3DO video games lost out completely to competitors like Matsushita, Philips, Sony, and Victor who agreed upon a competing CD-Karaoke standard. Prospects once seemed high that this would emerge a winner.

CDA (compound document architecture) DEC's set of standards for compound document creation, storage, retrieval, interchange and manipulation.

Cd-audio A CD that contains only audio playback. These were invented by Philips and Sony and have become extremely popular in the music recording industry. In order for these discs to be compatible with consumer playback machines, most discs are recorded according to the CD-Digital Audio "Reebok" standard.

CD-DVD digital video (or versatile) disc Combines the best features of CD-ROM size and data storage with capacity for video storage beyond that of videodiscs. DVD is so revolutionary that in the next decade it will probably replace VHS videotapes and CD-ROMs and videodiscs.

CD-erasable An alternate term for CD-RW compact discs that can be erased and written over with new and/or updated computer files. The key feature of CD-RW is that these CDs will play on newer CD-ROM drives. This was not the case with older CD-Erasable discs. An older type of CD rewriting technology unveiled by Sony Corporation in 1993 that will allow for erasing and recording over CD discs that could not be played back on CD-ROM drives.

Although some companies have sold rewritable CDs for some time, the playback hardware has not become a standard like CD-ROM playback drives. In 1997, however, virtually all vendors of CD recording hardware offer a CD-RW drive that will play and record discs that will play on CD-ROM drives. This technology brings the world of CDs closer to the world of videotapes and floppy discs. However, unlike floppy discs holding 1.44 Mb of data, the CDs will hold 650 Mb of data. This makes the recording and revision of multimedia files in a cheap storage medium (possibly less than one dollar) a feasible option.

CDIF (case data interchange format) An emerging standard.for interchange of data between CASE tools.

CD-karaoke The video CD format that JVC and Philips initially agreed upon that eventually became the standard Video CD format agreed upon by major vendors such as Matushita, Philips, Sony, and Victor of Japan. Initially, vendors were trying to develop CDs for television sets that each had a different standard analogous to having different track gauges for different railroads. The agreed upon video standard in 1993 at last makes it possible to cross platforms in CDs for television.

CDM (content data model) An SGML-based DoD specification for interactive manuals.

CDMA (code division multiple access) A 2G digital wireless technology that allows multiple calls to share a radio frequency 1.23MHz wide in the 800MHz-1.9GHz band without causing interference. This is accomplished by assigning each call a unique code and varying its signal by that code to allow only the caller and receiver with that code to communicate with each other. The original CDMA standard allows transmission of up to 14.4Kbps per channel, with up to 8 channels being able to be utilized at once for 115Kbps speeds.

CDMA/TDMA Code Division Multiple Access and Time Division Multiple Access Dual-mode cellular telephones that aid in the receiving of fax and computer network data on computers and PDAs.

CDMA2000 The multiplexed version of the IMT-2000 standard developed by the ITU, and it's part of 3G wireless technology. It increases wireless data transmission speeds of the original CDMA standard to 144Kbps using a single channel and 2Mbps by utilizing 16 channels.

CD-MM Older Sony CDs that compete with CD-VIS, CD-I, and CD-3DO discs that also play back visual as well has audio entertainment and learning materials in a hypermedia format on a television set. These will be replaced with newer players for CD-DVD. CD-MM discs required special players that connected to a television much like a VCR machine. They compete with CD-I discs but are not the same size and will not play on CD-I players. Only discs developed by Sony Corporation will run on CD-MM players. Various CD-MM games, encyclopedias, hypermedia art books, and other consumer products are available on CD-I discs in department stores and video stores. Whereas CD-I and CD-ROM discs may be recorded on CD-R blanks in home recording devices, it is less likely that CD-MM discs will ever be produced outside professional studios. Users will thus be limited by what Sony develops and promotes. In 1993, Sony agreed to a new CD-format that is more in line with other players in the market. With the initial market shock of CD-3DO, the future of CD-I and CD-MM is seriously in doubt.

CDPD (cellular digital packet data) Technology that facilitates more traffic on existing cellular networks. CDPD hardware is required for sending e-mail to PDAs.

CD-R or CD-RW A term used for machines (drives) that will record CD laser discs that will read on standard CD-ROM drives. CD "encoding" depicts the recording (burning or transfer of files) to a CD, whereas CD "decoding" depicts the reading of those files.

The term CD-Erasable in the early 1990s depicted recording of erasable CDs that could not be read only in special drives rather than CD-ROM drives. The first CD-RW drive on the market (in March 1997) is from RICOH for $595. Now CD-RW is the latest thing in erasable CDs. In times past, CD-R depicted a recordable CD blank disc also known as a CD-WORM disc. CD-R is now an obsolete term since, in 1997, CD-RW discs also known as CD-RW or CD-Rewritable discs made "read only memory" a thing of the past. Of course it is always possible to file protect and computer files in any type of storage so that they cannot be overwritten. In 1997, virtually all the manufacturers of CD-RW recording machines for CD-ROMs will offer CD-Erasable drives that will likely replace most CD-R technology up to 1997. Laser recording machines typically connect to a computer's SCSI or IDE controller. High-end desktop computers now come with CD-R or CD-RW recorders and players all in the same drive. Recording CDs of any type is often referred to as "burning" or "baking." A CD recorder will not record every type of CD. Virtually all of them record CD-ROM discs and some will record CD-I discs.

CD-ROM extended architecture (cd-rom/xa) An extension to the CD-ROM format, developed by Microsoft, Phillips and Sony, that allows for the storage of audio and visual information on compact disk, so that you can play the audio at the same time you view the visual data. CD-ROM/XA is compatible with the High Sierra specification also known as ISO standard 9660.

CDSL (consumer digital subscriber line) Is a proprietary technology trademarked by Rockwell International. EtherLoop EtherLoop is currently a proprietary technology from Nortel, short for Ethernet Local Loop. EtherLoop uses the advanced signal modulation techniques of DSL and combines them with the half-duplex "burst" packet nature of Ethernet. EtherLoop modems will only generate hi-frequency signals when there is something to send. The rest of the time, they will use only a low-frequency (ISDN-speed) management signal. EtherLoop can measure the ambient noise between packets. This will allow the ability to avoid interference on a packet-by-packet basis by shifting frequencies as necessary. Since EtherLoop will be half-duplex, it is capable of generating the same bandwidth rate in either the upstream or downstream direction, but not simultaneously. Nortel is initially planning for speeds ranging between 1.5Mbps and 10Mbps depending on line quality and distance limitations.

Cd-stand alone Reference to audio/video players that stand alone in the sense of not needing a computer. The term generally refers to set-top video boxes for network television or to CD players such as CD-3DO, CD-I, CD-MM, CD-TV, CD-VIS, etc.

CDV (cell delay variation) CDV is a component of cell transfer delay, induced by buffering and cell scheduling. Peak-to-peak CDV is a QoS delay parameter associated with CBR and VBR services. The peak-to- peak CDV is the ((1-a) quantile of the CTD) minus the fixed CTD that could be experienced by any delivered cell on a connection during the entire connection holding time. The parameter "a" is the probability of a cell arriving late.

CD-VIS The Memorex MD-2500 Visual Information System CD player marketed by Radio Shack that competes with CD-MM, CD-I, and CD-3DO discs that also play back visual as well has audio interactive entertainment on television sets. The Memorex MD-2500 requires no host computer to perform interactive operations from a remote control. Compton's Multimedia Encyclopedia disc and some other discs are available, but the market share of CD-VIS never became great enough to attract widespread authorship of VIS discs. At present there are very few titles and interest in CD-VIS relative to CD-I and CD-3DO is waning.

CDVT (cell delay variation tolerance) ATM layer functions may alter the traffic characteristics of ATM connections by introducing Cell Delay Variation. When cells from two or more ATM connections are multiplexed, cells of a given ATM connection may be delayed while cells of another ATM connection are being inserted at the output of the multiplexer. Similarly, some cells may be delayed while physical layer overhead or OAM cells are inserted. Consequently, some ran domness may affect the inter-arrival time between consecutive cells of a connection as monitored at the UNI. The upper bound on the "clumping" measure is the CDVT.

Cell A coverage area around a specific transmitter. that communicates with cellular telephones and enables phone calls to the same or other cells. If a cellular phone user is traveling while calling, he or she may be switched from transmitter to transmitter while moving from one cell to another.

Cell broadcast Technology designed for the simultaneous delivery of short messages to multiple mobile users within a specified region. This is one to many version of SMS.

Cell header ATM Layer protocol control information.

Cell loss priority (CLP) A two-bit field in the ATM header that defines the priority of the cell, for congestion avoidance and data loss routines.

Cellphone (cellular telephone) A mobile, wireless telephone that communicates with a local transmitter using a short-wave analog or digital transmission. Cellular phone coverage is limited to areas where a cellular phone can adequately communicate with a nearby transmission tower.

Cells in frames Cells In Frames is a protocol established by the CIF Alliance which specifies how to transport ATM protocol over Ethernet, Token Ring and other frame protocols. CIF uses software at the workstation instead of a new hardware Network Interface Card to do QOS scheduling and ABR flow control.

Cellular automata A collection or array of objects that are programmed identically to interact with one another

Cellular neural networks (CNN) A neural network topology that uses multidimensional array structures comprised of cells that work together in localized groups.

Central office A circuit switch that terminates all the local access lines in a particular geographic servicing area; a physical building where the local switching equipment is found. xDSL lines running from a subscriber's home connect at their serving central office.

Central processing unit (CPU) The brains of the computer. When most people think of processors, they think of Intel, AMD, Motorola, or IBM. The Pentium 4 and Athlon are popular CPUs. The CPU's first instruction is to check the system BIOS and do what the BIOS tells it. The CPU is designed to run a group of instructions, or instruction set. CPU instructions can consist of adding together numbers, subtracting, fetching information from memory, and numerous other simple functions. The computer's operating system feeds the CPU instructions after the BIOS locates the operating system and puts it into main memory.

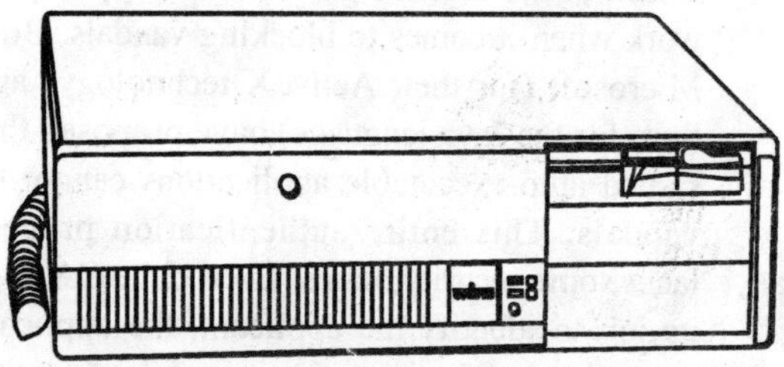

Fig. CPU

Centronics parallel interface A standard 36-pin interface in the PC world for the exchange of information between the PC and a peripheral such as a printer, originally developed by the printer manufacturer Centronics,Inc. The standard defines 8 parallel data lines, plus additional lines for status and control information.

CER (cell error ratio) The ratio of errored cells in a transmission in relation to the total cells sent in a transmission. The measurement is taken over a time interval and is desirable to be measured on an in-service circuit.

CERN (conseil europeen pour la recherche nucleaire) In English, that's the European Council for Nuclear Research. CERN, not Al Gore, is credited with creating the World Wide Web as we know it. In late 1990, Tim Berners-Lee of CERN thought up the Web as a way to quickly share information between physicists all over the world. Berners-Lee and Robert Cailliau wrote the first Web browser, running under the NeXTStep OS, and the first webserver. The two created and gave meaning to the terms: URL, HTTP, and HTML.

Certificate The digital equivalent of credentials. A certificate contains the sender's public key and verifies the sender's identity. Certificates provide a safe method of distributing public keys because they can be validated and signed by a trusted certificate authority. Certificates are used in a VPN during the key exchange process to ensure that the keys are actually exchanged between two known parties.

Checking for digital signatures simply does not work when it comes to blocking vandals. Both Microsoft (for their ActiveX technology) and Sun (for the Java language) have proposed that signed auto-executable applications cannot be vandals. This entire authentication process lacks some security basics. Even if the CA does its job to identify the applicant, the applicant can still provide the authority a false identity. More importantly, absolutely nothing is done to check if the application is hostile.

Certificate authority (CA) A trusted third-party organization or company that issues digital certificates. The CA guarantees that the holder of the digital certificate is who he or she says he or she is. The issuing party typically confirms the information provided to it by credit card verification.

Certificate revocation list (CRL) List of invalidated certificates revoked or otherwise invalidated by a Certificate Authority (CA). Theft of a private key, change of employment, expiration, and other reasons can all lead to a certificate being revoked.

Certified novell administrator (CNA) The title of an individual who has passed tests on networking using Novell products. This certification is aimed at network administrators who oversee the day-to-day operations of maintaining Novell NetWare networks that are already installed.

Certified novell engineer (CNE) A certification similar to the CNA but requiring the passing of more tests. It is aimed at people interested in installing and planning the rollout of Novell NetWare- based networks, with day-to-day operations just a part of the certification.

CES (circuit emulation service) The ATM Forum circuit emulation service interoperability specification specifies interoperability agreements for supporting Constant Bit Rate (CBR) traffic over ATM networks that comply with the other ATM Forum interoperability agreements. Specifically, this specification supports emulation of existing TDM circuits over ATM networks.

CF (compactflash) A 50-pin connection standard used in some PDAs, digital cameras, hardware MP3 players, and other small hardware devices. It was initially designed to offer PCMCIA-ATA standard access to Flash memory in a smaller form factor than PCMCIA at 43 mm by 36 mm and thicknesses of 3.3 mm (Type I) or 5.5 mm (Type II), but the standard has been expanded to support other peripherals, such as CF modems, CF network cards, and other types of I/O devices with the CompactFlash+ standard.

CFI CAD Framework Initiative. A consortium working on interface standards for integrating CAD tools and data.

CFM (cubic feet per minute) A measure of airflow, and you can use it to compare the efficiency of fans designed to cool computers or computer components. Higher CFM rates are better.

CFML (cold fusion markup language) For creation of dynamic and interactive Web pages. Along with the usual Hypertext Markup Language (HTML) tags that determine page layout and appearance, the page creator uses CFML tags to bring in content based on the results of a database query or user input. CMFL is a proprietary language developed for use with ColdFusion, a product from Allaire.

CGA (color/graphics adapter) A video adapter introduced by IBM in 1981 that provided low-resolution text and graphics. CGA provided several different text and graphics modes, including 40- or 80-column by 25 line 16-color text mode, and graphics modes of 640 horizontal pixels by 200 vertical pixels with 2 colors, or 320 horizontal pixels by 200 vertical pixels with 4 colors.

CGA Stands for **color graphics adapter** IBM's first microcomputer color standard. CGA allowed a maximum of four colors at a resolution of 320 x 200 or two colors at 640 x 200.

CGI (common gateway interface) Is one of the most popular UNIX-based programs/devices that supply interfaces between browsers and servers on the Internet. A standard for running external programs from a World-Wide Web HTTP server. CGI specifies how to pass dynamic components to the executing program as part of the HTTP request. For example, it will allow answers typed into an HTML form on the client computer to be tabulated and stored in a database on the server-side computer. Commonly, the server-side CGI program will generate some HTML which will be passed back to the client's browser. For example, it might report to the client user that the form is not filled out properly or report the invoice total of an order. CGI allows the returned HTML (or other document type) to depend in any arbitrary way on the request. The CGI program can, for example, access information in a database and format the results as HTML. CGI is not a programming language. There are various "CGI" scripting programs. Perl is a common choice for writing CGI scripts. in UNIX code. Some HTTP servers require CGI programs to reside in a special directory, often "/cgi-bin" but better servers provide ways to distinguish CGI programs so they can be kept in the same directories as the HTML files to which they are related. In order to improve performance, Netscape devised NSAPI and Microsoft developed the ISAPI standard which allow CGI-like tasks to run as part of the host server process, thus avoiding the overhead of creating a new process to handle each CGI invocation.

Cgi-bin The most common directory to store CGI programs on a web server. The "bin" part of "cgi-bin" is an abbreviation of "binary", dating back to when programs were referred to as "binaries".

CGM (computer graphics metafile) International standard for 16-bit color graphics. CGM files cross platforms between PCs and Macs and can be generated in most graphics, paintbrush, and draw software.

Chad The piece of paper that is removed from a punch card when holes are punched into it. Problems with chads that don't punch through were seen quite a bit when punch cards were the main storage media of early computers, and then again in the U.S. presidential elections in 2000, where punch cards were used to register votes.

Challenge handshake authentication protocol (CHAP) An access control protocol that dynamically encrypts the user's ID and password. The logon procedure in the user's machine obtains a key from the CHAP server, which it uses to encrypt the username and password before transmitting it.

Change and configuration management service (CCMS) Management by subscription. Allows applications to create abstract, architecture- and platform-independent profiles that describe configuration settings for the resources and services they manage.

Change management A consistent set of techniques that aid in evolution, composition and policy management of the design and implementation of an object or system.

Channel associated signalling (CAS) Signalling bits are transmitted in-band, along with the digitized voice itself.

Channel service unit/data service unit (csu/dsu or dsu/csu) A piece of hardware that you use to translate the digital data frames of a T1 line into a 10BaseT connection where Internet connectivity is concerned. If the T1 lines are used for voice connections, a CSU/DSU is required to translate the digital frames into signals that your office phone switch can interpret. Basically, the phone network/Internet consists of a bunch of CSU/DSUs talking to one another. When you lease a T1 line, your provider typically supplies you with a CSU/DSU, often with a setup cost. A synonym for CSU/DSU is DSU/CSU.

Channel Transmission line that can carry the sound of a separate MIDI instrument. Each MIDI port allows up to 16 separate channels for sending or receiving data. Each channel can function as a separate instrument in an ensemble, each using its own patch and responding independently to continuous controllers.

Channel has another meaning on the World Wide Web.

Chaos theory A branch of mathematics dealing with differential equations having solutions which are very sensitive to initial conditions.

Character A single letter, number, or symbol. This term applies to data typed into a computer, shown on computer screens, or printed (or written) on paper.

Character matrix The total number of Horizontal and Vertical spaces required per character.

Characters per second (CPS) The amount of text characters printed in a second. This term was used more when daisy wheel and dot matrix printers were common. Nowadays, printers are rated more by pages per minute (ppm), as the amount of characters printed are irrelevant to modern printers that work on a page-by-page basis. Although inkjet printers still go line by line like dot matrix printers, they are much faster, and it's easier to compare page printing speeds.

Charge coupled device (CCD) Photosensitive CCDs are used in scanners, digital cameras, and video cameras. The CCD basically reads the image by storing a group of charges based on the image to which it is exposed. These charges are analog charges, as opposed to simple digital on/off charges. Thus, you can grab degrees of light and color to transfer a visual image into a group of electrical charges, and then to your computer screen, video tape, or printer.

Chassis The physical framework of the computer system that houses modules, wiring, and power supplies.

Chat In computer terms, this is a synchronous exchange of typed information that is viewed by two or more people over a computer network. (verb: to chat) To participate in the synchronous exchange of information with one or more people over a computer network. Normally, you type in a remark, send it, and see it appear onscreen. Likewise, others can see the information at the same time and submit their own remarks.

Chat lines (chat rooms) Real time internet conversations (written or oral) that transpire in real (synchronous) time as opposed to conferencing (e.g., message board posting and topic classification." There are many sources for free chat software downloads. One such source is at http://www.chat.yahoo.com/.

Check bits Extra data bits provided by a module to support ECC.

Checksum A number computed by glomming together all the characters from an entire file in a special mathematical way. If you are afraid that a file is going to change, perhaps getting messed up by being transmitted across noisy lines, you can calculate a checksum before and after transmitting it. If you get the same checksum, the file probably did'nt change.

Cheops A satellite-based batch data dissemination project between CERN and member state institutes.

Chief information officer (CIO) An executive title, usually at a medium or large-sized company. The person that bears this title is in charge of the flow of information in and out of the company, and also guides the technology used in information systems. The CIO's focus, as opposed to the CTO, is more on internal technology use and the IT department. A CIO is more concerned with keeping systems running day-to-day and uptime. CIOs are typically more managerial than CTOs.

Chief technology officer (CTO) An executive title related to CIO, usually at a medium or large-sized company. The CTO is, however, more focused on the use of technology in products developed by the company and technology delivered to external customers. CTOs are typically more technical than CIOs.

Child node A node at the next lower level of the hierarchy which is contained in the peer group represented by the logical group node currently referenced. This could be a logical group node, or a physical node.

Child peer group A child peer group of a peer group is any one containing a child node of a logical group node in that peer group. A child peer group of a logical group node is the one containing the child node of that logical group node.

Child version A version of a version.

Chip (microprocessor) Short for microchip. This term is commonly used to describe the CPU. More specifically, it refers to the part of the CPU that actually does the work, since many CPUs now contain L1 and L2 caches on-chip.

Chip scale package A type of ball grid array in which the package is roughly the size of the die.

Chipkill A technology developed by IBM for servers and other systems that demand high availability. It allows a computer motherboard and BIOS to detect problems with the computer's memory and selectively disable problematic parts of the memory. Depending on the technology used, this technology may or may not require specialized memory chips.

Chipping Just as software can contain unexpected functions, it is also possible to implement similar functions in hardware. Today's chips contain millions of integrated circuits that can easily be configured by the manufacturer so that they also contain some unexpected functions. They could be built so that they fail after a certain time, blow up after they receive a signal on a specific frequency, or send radio signals that allow identification of their exact location - the number of possible scenarios exceeds, by far, the scope of this paper. The main problem with chipping is that the specific (adapted) chip be installed in the place that is useful for the Information Warrior. The easiest solution is to built the additional features into all the chips manufactured in the country that is interested in this type of IW.

Chipset The chips that control the functions and features on a motherboard. The chipset determines how much memory you can put into a motherboard and what processors you can use with it. Of course, there are physical connectors on your motherboard that limit these things as well, but motherboard manufacturers use the chipset as a basis for what type of connectors they can put on a motherboard.

Chkdsk (check disk) A Microsoft program that checks your hard drive for logical errors as opposed to physical defects. This program is supported in DOS and all versions of Windows. Windows NT/2000/XP uses it as its main disk checking program. DOS and Windows replaced this program with the friendlier scandisk.exe, but chkdsk.exe is still available and is still the main disk checking program for NTFS partitions.

Choices An object-oriented operating system from University of Illinois.

Chorus A distributed operating system developed at INRIA

Chromatic dispersion The natural distortion of pulses of light as they move through an optical network; it results in data corruption.

CHRP (common hardware reference platform) Architecture in processors for Power PCs. This term has been replaced by "PowerPC Reference Platform" and is IBM's open system standard intended to ensure compatibility among PowerPC-based systems built by different companies.

CI(congestion indicator) This is a field in a RM-cell, and is used to cause the source to decrease its ACR. The source sets CI=0 when it sends an RM-cell. Setting CI=1 is typically how destinations indicate that EFCI has been received on a previous data cell.

CICS (customer information control system) Not to be confused with CISC, CICS is online transaction processing application server software originally written by IBM for mainframes for dealing with customer information and transaction processing in the enterprise. Now versions of CICS are available for UNIX and x86 platforms as well.

CIE coordinates The CIE Coordinates for any color are obtained from a CIE Color Chart.

CIE The "commission internationale de l'eclairage". An organization that has established a number of widely-used color definitions.

CIL (component integration laboratories) An effort to create a common framework for interoperability between applications on desktop platforms, formed by Apple, IBM, Novell, Oracle, Taligent, WordPerfect, and Xerox.

CIM object manager A key component of the WBEM architecture. A central message of WBEM is uniform data representation encapsulated in object-oriented fashion in the CIM. CIMOM provides a collection point and manipulation point for these objects. Formerly HMOM.

CIP (carrier identification parameter) A 3 or 4 digit code in the initial address message identifying the carrier to be used for the connection.

CIP (common indexing protocol) For use by directory services when passing indexing information: under study by an IETF working group.

Cipher A set of rules for transforming a message from plain text to encrypted text. The cipher is a part of the encryption scheme.This can also refer to ciphertext.

Ciphertext Information that has been encrypted into seemingly meaningless text.

CIR (committed information rate) This term is used by ISPs to represent an amount of data that you should, on the average, be able to draw through your connection to the ISP's servers. This is measured in kilobits or megabits per second.

Circuit breaker A device that interrupts the flow of electricity if an excessive level of current is detected. It's a better design than the fuse, as it can just be reset (instead of replaced) to turn the electrical flow back on.

Circuit Most commonly, this describes an electrical device with a defined path of electrical current that can receive input voltages in a 0 range and a 1 range, and responds with an output voltage that is also in a 0 or 1 range based on the logic inside of the circuit. If the circuit has a 0 range of 0-1 volts and a 1 range of 4-5 volts and receives a 0.5 volt input, it will act as if it has received a "0" input. Ranges are necessary because voltages are never exact. When thinking about the logic behind a circuit, it is easiest to think of the inputs and outputs simply as a 0 or 1 instead of a range of voltages.

Circuit switching A type of communication system that established a connection, or circuit, between the two devices before communicating and does not discount until all data is sent.

Circuit-switched A type of network connection which establishes a continuous electrical connection between calling and called users for their exclusive use until the connection is released. Ericsson PBX is a circuit-switched network.

CIS (case integration services) A committee formed to discuss CASE tool integration standards related to ATIS.

CISC (complex instruction set computer) Microchips that support a large amount of instructions of varying length. On the other side of the coin, you have RISC chips that use a smaller instruction set of more regular length. The battle between RISC and CISC rages on, but when it comes down to it, either way has its advantages and disadvantages. With CISC you can implement often-used strings of instructions into single instructions that could give you an advantage over the numerous small instructions used in RISC. However, the unpredictability of the length of a CISC instruction typically limits CISC from blowing RISC away.

CIX (commercial internet exchange) A non-profit trade association of Public Data Internetwork service providers.

CL (connectionless service) A service which allows the transfer of information among service subscribers without the need for end-to- end establishment procedures.

Clarinet A commercial news service dedicated to a wide range of topics that provides tailored news reports via the Internet. You can access ClariNet news within Usenet newsgroups.

Class (classe) Often confused with object, a class defines an entity in the application to be programmed by specifying its data structure and the procedures that can operate on the data.

Class A language developed by the Andrew Project Andrew-Project: one of the first attempts to add object-oriented object-oriented features to C.

Class For hardware, the manner in which devices and buses are grouped for purposes of installing and managing device drivers and allocating resources. The hardware tree is organized by device class, and the operating system uses class installers to install drivers for all hardware classes.

Class a certification An FCC certification for computer equipment, including mainframe and mini computers destined for use in an industrial, commercial, or office setting, rather than for personal use at home. The Class A commercial certification is less restrictive than the Class B certification.

Class A IP A group of IP addresses where the first number remains the same, and the last three can vary. It could be represented by w.x.y.z, where the x, y, and z can be any number from 0-255, and the w represents the first static part of the IP address (e.g., 10.x.y.z). Thus, the number of possible combinations within the Class A address are 256256256 = 16,777,216. Of course, some of the addresses, like those ending in .0 and .255, are not used, so the actual number of usable addresses in a Class A is somewhat less than that. The subnet mask of a class A IP address is 255.0.0.0. Thus, only the last three digits of the IP address are used to determine where traffic gets routed within the Class A. There are 254 class A groups in existence.

Class B IP A group of IP addresses where the first two numbers remain the same and the last two can vary. It could be represented by w.x.y.z, where the y and z can be any number from 0-255, and the w and x represent the first static part of the IP address (e.g., 10.251.y.z). Thus, the number of possible combinations within the Class B address are 256256 = 65,536. Of course, some of the addresses, like those ending in .0 and .255, are not used, so the actual number of usable addresses in a Class B is somewhat less than that. The subnet mask of a class B IP address is 255.255.0.0. Thus, only the last two digits of the IP address are used to determine where traffic gets routed within the Class B. There are about 65,000 class B groups in existence.

Class C IP A group of IP addresses where the first three numbers remain the same and the last one can vary. It could be represented by w.x.y.z, where the z can be any number from 0-255, and the w, x, and y represent the first static part of the IP address (e.g., 10.251.37.z). Thus, the number of possible combinations is 256. Of course, some of the addresses, like those ending in .0 and .255, are not used, so the actual number of usable addresses in a Class C is 254. The subnet mask of a class C IP address is 255.255.255.0. Thus, only the last digit of the IP address is used to determine where traffic gets routed within the Class C. There are about 16.7 million class C groups in existence.

Class driver A driver that provides system-required, hardware-independent support for a given class of physical devices. Such a driver communicates with a corresponding hardware-dependent port driver, using a set of system-defined device control requests, possibly with additional driver-defined device control requests. Under WDM, the class driver creates a device object to represent each adapter registered by minidrivers. The class driver is responsible for multiprocessor and interrupt synchronization.

Class library A library of reusable classes Classfor use with an object-oriented object-oriented programming system

Classless internet domain routing (CIDR) A protocol that allows for variable-length addresses that allows for more- and less-specific routing information. This replaces the old class A, class B, class C routing scheme.

Class-relation method A design technique based on the concepts of object-oriented object-oriented programming and the Entity-Relationship Entity-Relationshipmodel from the French company Softeam.

Clean The file system /f is guaranteed to have a static, stable structure. Only unmounted filesystems or read-only file systems are clean by definition.

Cleanroom A software development approach aimed at producing software with the minimum number of errors.

Clear to send Signal sent by a modem to a computer indicating that the modem is ready to accept data and to forward them to the telephone line.

Clear-text password The plain text version of an encrypted password.

Click The action of pressing on the button of a mouse or other input device. The press of the button when the cursor or pointer is in certain locations will cause the operating system or program you are running to react accordingly.

Clickable image Any image that has instructions embedded in it so that clicking on it initiates some kind of action or result. On a web page, a clickable image is any image that has a URL embedded in it.

Click-to-type A system GUIs use to control which window you are working in. When you want to move to a different window, move the mouse and click in the new window to tell the GUI you want to use that window.

Client A general term that can mean a few things. In the client/server architecture, a client consists of any machine connected to a network that exchanges data with a server, and can also refer to the person using the machine. In addition, the term client refers to any software that is used on a client machine to exchange data with software running on a server, such as an e-mail client. When you send and receive e-mail you use an e-mail client that connects to an e-mail server.

Client stub An ORB interface that provides for the collection, transmission, marshaling and unmarshaling.

Client-server Client server technology came about when computers began to cost less. Mainframes are very expensive, and didn't give users much personal freedom. The client/server model promised to change that scenario, and it's much more popular today. Basically, a client computer with its own memory and hard drive communicates with a server whenever it needs data from the server. The client can run by itself without the server and communicate with different servers as it needs to.

Client/server relationship A client application is one that resides on a user's computer, but sends requests to a remote system to execute a designated procedure using arguments supplied by the user. The computer that initiates the request is the client and the computer responding to the request is the server. Many network services follow a client and server protocol.

Client-server architecture An information-passing scheme that works as follows: a client program, such as Mosaic, sends a request to a server. The server takes the request, disconnects from the client and processes the request. When the request is processed, the server reconnects to the client program and the information is transferred to the client. This architecture differs from traditional Internet databases where the client connects to the server and runs the program from the remote site. Note: in an X-11 environment, the meanings of client and server are reversed.

Clip art Graphics/artwork distributed for use in word processors, Web pages, or desktop publishing. Graphic designers often use clip art as a shortcut to developing images from scratch. Some clip art is in the public domain, but much of it is copyrighted and restricted to certain uses. Take care to understand the copyright, or lack thereof, when you use clip art.

Clipboard A holding device that contains the most recently copied or cut text or image such that contents of the clipboard can be pasted one or more times into other parts of the document at hand or other documents. It is usually possible to cross between different software options such as between Windows programs.

Clipper chip The Clipper Chip is a cryptographic device being promoted by the U.S. government. Its purported advantage is that it provides a standard for securing private voice communication. With Clipper, however, the government has the opportunity to obtain decryption keys that are held in escrow by two government agencies. Although the Clipper proposal requires legal authorization to obtain these keys, the history of illegal domestic surveillance by Federal agencies makes the existence of this "back-door" decryption channel a cause for concern.

Clipping The conversion of all tones lighter than a specified grey level to white, or darker than a specified grey level to black, causing loss of detail. This also applies to individual channels in a color image.

Clock Function allowing the computer to maintain date and time, and to calculate the elapsed time between two events.

Clock cycle Think of a clock cycle as one tick of the second hand (but generally at a much higher speed). Computer clocks run voltage through a tiny crystal that oscillates at a predictable speed to give a meaningful timing method to the computer. One clock cycle doesn't necessarily mean that the processor does one operation. Today's high-end processors often complete more than one operation per clock cycle, and other times, in the worst cases, it will take several clock cycles to complete one operation.

Clock rate The number of pulses emitted from a computer's clock in one second. It determines the rate at which logical or arithmetic gating is performed in a synchronous computer.

Clock speed The speed in MHz of a microprocessor. It is one way of gauging the performance of a microprocessor; however, different processor architectures dictate that a higher clock speed in one architecture does not always mean better performance over a lower clock speed in another architecture.

Clock/calendar board An internal time-of-day and month-year calendar that is kept up-to-date by a small battery-backup system. This allows the computer to update the time even when turned off.

Clock-mulitplying A mechanism used in certain chips that allows the chip to process data and instructions internally at a different speed from that used for external operations.

Clone Hardware that is identical in function to an original.

Clone Copy A clone NetInfo server is an exact copy of a master NetInfo server in the same subdomain.

Closed security environment An environment where the configuration ensures sufficient access to protect applications and devices from malicious code.

CLP (cell loss priority) This bit in the ATM cell header indicates two levels of priority for ATM cells. CLP=0 cells are higher priority than CLP=1 cells. CLP=1 cells may be discarded during periods of congestion to preserve the CLR of CLP=0 cells.

CLP Constraint Logic Programming.

CLR (cell loss ratio) CLR is a negotiated QoS parameter and acceptable values are network specific. The objective is to minimize CLR provided the end-system adapts the traffic to the changing ATM layer transfer characteristics. The Cell Loss Ratio is defined for a connection as: Lost Cells/Total Transmitted Cells. The CLR parameter is the value of CLR that the network agrees to offer as an objective over the lifetime of the connection. It is expressed as an order of magnitude, having a range of 10-1 to 10-15 and unspecified.

Cluster The smallest unit of hard disk space that DOS can allocate to a file, consisting of one or more contiguous sectors. The number of sectors contained in a cluster depends on the hard disk type.

Clustering Clustering is a technology using two or more computers that function together as a single entity for fault tolerance and load balancing. This can increase reliability and uptime in a client/server environment. One computer will sense when another computer is failing or getting bogged down and will take over full operation or just some of its tasks, depending on whether it's a complete fail-over design or just load balancing.

CLV (constant linear velocity) In terms of disk drives, this means that the rate of data being read off of the disk stays the same from center to outer edge. To accomplish this, the drive motor speeds up and slows down as data is read from different areas of the disk—the linear velocity remains constant. An 8x CD-ROM drive that operates at CLV will read data at 8x anywhere on the disk, from the center to the outer edge. That means that data is written closer together towards the center of the disk and further apart towards the edge.

Clx The Common Lisp interface to the X-Window-System, equivalent to Xlib.

CM Configuration Management.

CMC (computer mediated communication) A very broad term that encompasses chat lines, virtual communities, and other forms of communication.

CMIP (common management interface protocol) An ITU-TSS standard for the message formats and procedures used to exchange management information in order to operate, administer maintain and provision a network.

CML (chemical markup language) A means for interchanging chemical information, based on SGML.

CMOS Abbreviation of complementary metal oxide semiconductor. Pronounced see-moss, CMOS is a widely used type of semiconductor. CMOS semiconductors use both NMOS (negative polarity) and PMOS (positive polarity) circuits. Since only one of the circuit types is on at any given time, CMOS chips require less power than chips using just one type of transistor. This makes them particularly attractive for use in battery-powered devices, such as portable computers. Personal computers also contain a small amount of battery-powered CMOS memory to hold the date, time, and system setup parameters.

CMR (cell misinsertion rate) The ratio of cells received at an endpoint that were not originally transmitted by the source end in relation to the total number of cells properly transmitted.

CMTS (cable modem termination system) Central device for connecting the cable TV network to a data network like the internet. Normally placed in the headend of the cable TV system.

CMVC Configuration Management Version Control from IBM.

CMYK (cyan-magenta-yellow-black) An alternate color scheme to the RGB color scheme. Combinations of cyan, magenta, yellow, and black are used to represent colors. The CMYK scheme is used mainly in print, such as magazines. Combining cyan, magenta, and yellow produces black, but that black is not always pure enough, thus, the addition of the K, for pure black. Color inkjet printers use CMYK to represent images. The best printers have separate black instead of wasting all the colors to print a faux brownish black.

CNA (certified novell administrator) The title of an individual who has passed tests on networking using Novell products. This certification is aimed at network administrators who oversee the day-to-day operations of maintaining Novell networks that are already installed.

CNE (certified novell engineer) A certification similar to the CNA but requiring the passing of more tests. It is aimed at people interested in installing and planning the rollout of Novell NetWare- based networks, with day-to-day operations just a part of the certification.

CNI (coalition for networked information) Promotes the creation of and access to information resources in networked environments in order to enrich scholarship and enhance intellectual productivity.

CNR (complex node representation) A collection of nodal state parameters that provide detailed state information associated with a logical node.

COAST (cache on a stick) Coast modules are used to upgrade a motherboard's L2 cache and Tag memory on some socket 7 and older motherboards.

Coaxial cable A high-capacity cable used in networking. It contains an inner copper conductor surrounded by plastic insulation, and an outer braided copper or foil shield. Coax is used for broadband and baseband communications networks, and is usually free from external interference, and it permits very high transmission rates over long distances.

COB (chip on board) A system in which semiconductor dice are mounted directly on a PC board and connected with bonded wires or solder bumps. The dice are usually mechanically protected with epoxy.

COBOL (common business-oriented language) A programming language developed in the '60s by several computer companies and the U.S. Department of Defense. COBOL is still used today for programming business applications, and COBOL programmers were a major source of the Year 2000 headache. In fact, many of them came out of retirement to fix the mess they made, whether voluntarily or by direction, to save a couple of valuable bits of data back when bits cost big money.

COD (connection oriented data) Data requiring sequential delivery of its component PDUs to assure correct functioning of its supported application, (e.g., voice or video).

Code A series of instructions that make up a program.

Code division multiple access (CDMA) A2G digital wireless technology that allows multiple calls to share a radio frequency 1.23MHz wide in the 800MHz-1.9GHz band without causing interference. This is accomplished by assigning each call a unique code and varying its signal by that code to allow only the caller and receiver with that code to communicate with each other. The original CDMA standard allows transmission of up to 14.4Kbps per channel, with up to 8 channels being able to be utilized at once for 115Kbps speeds.

Code generator A code generator is part of a compiler. It takes intermediate code and translates it into the final workable code in the target language.

Code management A source code management system helps program developers keep track of version history, releases, parallel versions etc. There are several in popular use.

Codec 1. Short for compressor/decompressor, a codec is any technology for compressing and decompressing data. Codecs can be implemented in software, hardware, or a combination of both. Some popular codecs for computer video include MPEG, Indeo and Cinepak.

2. In telecommunications, (short for coder/decoder) a device that encodes or decodes a signal. For example, telephone companies use codecs to convert binary signals transmitted on their digital networks to analog signals converted on their analog networks.

3. The translation of a binary value into a voltage that can be transmitted over a wire.

Codecenter A proprietary software development environment for C programs, offering an integrated toolkit for developing, testing, debugging and maintainance (formerly Saber-C)

Cognitech A French software house specialising in Artificial Intelligence.

Cognitive Pertaining to the concepts of knowing or perceiving.

Cold boot A cold reboot (also known as a hard reboot) is when power to a computer is cycled (turned on and off) or a special reset signal to the processor is triggered (from a front panel switch of some sort). This restarts the computer without first performing the usual shut-down procedure. (With many operating systems, especially those with disc caches, after a hard reboot the system may well be in an "unclean" state, and require that checks and repairs to on-disc file system structures be performed before normal operation can begin.) It may be caused by power failure, be done by accident, or be done deliberately as a last resort because nothing else to retrieve the system from a "hung" state works.

Coldfusion A server side extension developed by Allaire that allows documents similar to HTML, usually with the .cfm extension, to be parsed and run on a webserver. ColdFusion allows Web designers to embed database calls into HTML-like documents, and is designed to provide easier access to database servers than by using standard CGI calls.

Collaboration A joint effort that network technology has facilitated with email, FTP, and more advanced means of sharing ideas, documents, and data. Writing has become more of a collaborative effort since the dawn of the WWW. The WWW takes authors beyond the telephone by enabling them to speak to one another (audio), (videoconferencing), and visualize documents and data.

Collabrashare Collaboration groupware from Netscape Corporation. Netscape Collabra provides enterprise group discussions based on Internet standards, letting the groups share and track information efficiently. Collabra makes it easy to share information and create a knowledge base that people can access at any time. You can eliminate unnecessary meetings and save valuable time by discussing important issues in a public or private discussion forum. Netscape Collabra extends open Internet standards to create a powerful collaboration tool for the corporation, and it seamlessly integrates with Netscape Collabra Server.

Collage A synchronous collaborative data analysis tool for use over the Internet.

Collar A derivative instruments investing term where an investor puts a "collar" around investment risk, usually by selling a put option (an option to purchase) and purchasing a call option (an option to sell) around an investment. Amgen and Oracle sold put warrants on their own common stock and then used the proceeds to purchase calls on the same stock. This process is called a "costless collar" and is used to express a bullish view of the stock by management.

Collection A group of objects, with or without any particular relationships other than belonging to a named group.

Collision What happens on a piece of networking equipment, usually a shared hub, that is being asked to transfer more data than it can handle. Collisions occur when a client on the network tries to transfer data and has to retry because the device is busy and the data figuratively "collides" with other data on the network.

Collocation The act of placing elements or objects in a specific order.

Co-located hosting This hosting option gives webmasters complete control over their server. You are responsible for providing the physical hardware and network administration; the hosting company will provide you with the rack space and Internet connection.

Co-location (CoLo or Co-Lo) The practice of having your webservers, or other servers, hosted at another location by another company. Often, companies will co-locate their webservers at an ISP that handles the bandwidth, power, cooling, and, to varying degrees, the care and maintenance of the webservers.

Color balance The ability of the monitor to show and maintain the same color when switching or varying the intensity of the screen.

Color cast An overall color imbalance in an image, as if viewed through a colored filter.

Colorimeter A light-sensitive device for measuring colors by filtering their red, green, and blue components, as in the human eye.

Column address strobe (CAS) An electrical signal that determines which column is read or written to on a DRAM chip. You must combine a column address strobe with a row address strobe to define a location on a DRAM chip.

Column Part of the memory array. A bit can be stored where a column and a row intersect.

Com (.com) The top level domain originally intended for "commercial" entities. One of the worldwide top level domain, in which any person or organization may register a domain name.

COM (component object model) A Microsoft specification that describes methods of communication between components. For example, if you were to drag an item over a window, the item and window would have some rules of communication that they would follow. Those rules are described in the Component Object Model.

COM (continuation of message) An indicator used by the ATM Adaptation Layer to indicate that a particular ATM cell is a continuation of a higher layer information packet which has been segmented.

Com port In DOS, the device name used to denote a serial communications port. In versions of DOS after 3.3 four COM ports are supported, COM1, COM2, COM3, and COM4. Also refers to,Component Object Model; the core of OLE. Defines how OLE objects and their clients interact within processes or across process boundaries.

COM (component object module) In DOS systems, the name of a serial communications port. DOS supports four serial ports: COM1, COM2, COM3, and COM4. However, most software uses system interrupts to access the serial ports, and there are only two IRQ lines reserved. This means that the four COM ports share the same two IRQ lines. Typically, COM1 and COM3 use IRQ4, while COM2 and COM4 use IRQ3. So in general, if you have two devices, one of which is attached to COM1 and the other to COM3, you cannot use them simultaneously.

COM1, COM2, etc Most serial ports and internal modems on DOS/WIN PCs can be configured to either COM1 or COM2 in order to accommodate the situation where both may exist. The DOS MODE command is used to change the output direction to such serial devices as modems.

COMIS a COMpilation and interpretation system A FORTRAN FORTRANinterpreter use by the PAW PAW

COMMA Common Object-oriented Object-oriented Methodology Metamodel Architecture from OPEN

Comma separated values (CSV) A file extension used for a flat text data file consisting of items of data separated by commas. Each line of data is separated by a carriage return.

Command A word you type to get Unix to do something. Actually, the UNIX shell listens to the commands you type and tries to execute them. some commands are things the shell knows how to do. Other commands are seperate programs, stored in files on the disk. When you type a command, press Enter or Return at the end of the line.

Command line Commands you type to run an application. You can type commands at an MS-DOS prompt or in the Run dialog box in the Program Manager of Windows. Interfaces in which you type commands rather than choose them from a menu are often called command line interfaces. MS-DOS has a command line interface while the Macintosh does not.

Command line interface (CLI) A line-based (as opposed to a screen-based) interface between the user and an application.

Command processor Also called command interpreter. The command processor is that part of the operating system that displays the command prompt on the screen, interprets and executes all the commands and file names that you enter, and displays error messages when appropriate. It also contains the *environment* a memory area that holds values for important system definitions or defaults that are used by the system, and which can be changed by the user.

Command prompt Any blinking cursor waiting, or prompting, for user input. In DOS the C: prompt greets you on most systems—this is a type of command prompt. As well, if you use any version of Windows you can get to a DOS-looking window that allows you to type in commands. UNIX can also greet you with a command prompt. For novice users a command prompt can be confusing, as it's unclear what to do next; but for experts a command prompt is a necessity at times.

Command.com The command processor for MS-DOS based systems. It provides the C> prompt, and it interprest the usesr's English commands and performs the operation requested.

Committed information rate (CIR) This term is used by ISPs to represent an amount of data that you should, on the average, be able to draw through your connection to the ISP's servers. This is measured in kilobits or megabits per second.

COmmon business-oriented language (COBOL) A programming language developed in the '60s by several computer companies and the U.S. Department of Defense. COBOL is still used today for programming business applications, and COBOL programmers were a major source of the Year 2000 headache. In fact, many of them came out of retirement to fix the mess they made, whether voluntarily or by direction, to save a couple of valuable bits of data back when bits cost big money.

Common channel signalling (CCS) Signalling bits are transmitted out-of-band, in a separate channel from the digitized voice. Typically a number of voice channels have their signalling combined together into a single signalling channel.

Common desktop environment (CDE) A common windowing scheme, based on the X11 Motif system, used both in Solaris and HP-UX, to provide a similar look and feel for users.

Common gateway interface (CGI) CGI scripts are commonly used to customize results at a Web site. Generally, when the visitor performs fills in a form or clicks a link, the server executes a script that uses information that the visitor entered.

In order to do this, the server executes a program using input provided by an outsider. This opens a security hole whereby an attacker can "feed" a CGI script with input that lets the attacker hack the site.

Furthermore, some CGI scripts record information, such as a record of the contents of the current visitor's virtual shopping basket, in temporary files. If the administrator configures the script incorrectly, the information can be written among the data files making up the Web site itself, thus enabling an informed attacker to retrieve the information later using a Web browser.

Common information model Describes the WBEM data representation schema that is now a DMTF-sponsored industry standard. CIM evolved from HMMS (HyperMedia Management Schema).

Common internet file system (CIFS) The name for Microsoft's version of a networked file system.

Common object request broker architecture (CORBA) A standard that allows programs or objects to communicate even though they may have been written by different vendors. CORBA is defined by a group of 800 companies called the Object Management Group, a non-profit consortium that produces and maintains computer industry specifications for interoperable enterprise applications. Microsoft has been a member of OMG since 1992 and has released competing technologies, first with OLE and more recently with DCOM.

Common peer group The lowest level peer group in which a set of nodes is represented. A node is represented in a peer group either directly or through one of its ancestors.

Communication endpoint An object associated with a set of attributes which are specified at the communication creation time.

Communication port Logical address for channeling communication using a specific protocol. Each communication port is associated with a protocol and a physical port.

Communication protocol For computers engaged in telecommunications, the protocol (i.e., the setting and standards) must be the same for both devices when receiving and transmitting information. A communications program can be used to ensure that the baud rate, duplex, parity, data bits, and stop bits are correctly set.

Communicator PDA type equipment integrated with or attached to a mobile phone, for example Nokia Communicator 99110. Ericsson MC218.

Comnet A simulation tool from CACI for analysing wide-area voice or data networks, based on SIMSCRIPT.

Compact disc file system Controls access to the contents of CD-ROM drives.

Compact disc read only media (CD-ROM) CD-ROM media is read-only media that holds about 650 MB of data. It's generally accepted as the easiest way to distribute software. CD-ROM drives can also read audio CDs even though they are in a different format than standard CD-ROM media.

Compact disc recordable (CD-R) CD-R drives record up to 650 MB of data onto specialized CD-R media. The media is more expensive compared to the mass-produced CDs that software is generally distributed on, but cheap for the amount of data you can store on it. CD-R media is a WORM technology. You can Write to it Once and Read Many times, but you can't erase anything you've written.

Compact disk CD. A non-magnetic, polished, optical disk used to store large amounts of digital information. Digital information is tored ont he CD as a series of microscopic pits and smooth areas that have different reflective properties. A beam of laser light shines on the disk so that the reflections can be detected and converted into digital data.

Compact flash A small flash memory module. The memory chips are enclosed in a plastic case and retain data after they are removed from the system. The most common uses for these are in pagers, handheld computers, cell phones, digital cameras, and audio players.

Compactflash (CF) A 50-pin connection standard used in some PDAs, digital cameras, hardware MP3 players, and other small hardware devices. It was initially designed to offer PCMCIA-ATA standard access to Flash memory in a smaller form factor than PCMCIA at 43 mm by 36 mm and thicknesses of 3.3 mm (Type I) or 5.5 mm (Type II), but the standard has been expanded to support other peripherals, such as CF modems, CF network cards, and other types of I/O devices with the CompactFlash+ standard.

Compactflash+ (CF+) An extension to the CompactFlash standard that allows for use of devices other than plain storage Flash memory and microdrives. With CompactFlash+, devices such as CompactFlash network adapters and modems are now possible.

Compatibility mode An asynchronous, host-to-peripheral parallel port channel defined in the IEEE 1284-1944 standard. Compatible with existing peripherals that attach to the Centronics-style PC parallel port.

Compatible ID An ID used by the Plug and Play Manager to locate an INF to install a device if there was no match on the hardware IDs for the device.

Compiled A program that is translated from human-readable code to binary code that a central processing unit (CPU) can understand.

Compiled executable code The binary code that a central processing unit (CPU) can understand; the product of the compilation process.

Compiler A compiler translates a computer program from one language into another, catching any errors in syntax along the way.Most commonly, you translate some high level language, such as C++ or COBOL, into optimized machine language. This form of compilation puts your programs into a form that your computer (specifically your microprocessor) can understand without any translation, thus speeding them up greatly over programs that must be interpreted as they are run.

Complementary metal-oxide semiconductor (CMOS) A method of constructing transistors which produces microchips that run with relatively low power consumption compared to other methods. Most of the chips found in a modern PC are built using CMOS technology.

Complex instruction set computer (CISC) Microchips that support a large amount of instructions of varying length. On the other side of the coin, you have RISC chips that use a smaller instruction set of more regular length. The battle between RISC and CISC rages on, but when it comes down to it, either way has its advantages and disadvantages. With CISC you can implement often-used strings of instructions into single instructions that could give you an advantage over the numerous small instructions used in RISC. However, the unpredictability of the length of a CISC instruction typically limits CISC from blowing RISC away.

Component Instrumentation A specification for DMI related to the service layer.

Component object model (COM) A Microsoft specification that describes methods of communication between components. For example, if you were to drag an item over a window, the item and window would have some rules of communication that they would follow. Those rules are described in the Component Object Model.

Composite video A signal that combines the luminance, chrominance, and synchronized video information onto a single line. This has been the most prevalent NTSC video format.

Compressed files Files whose file size has been reduced using a compression method. Files are often compressed before sending them across a network, in order to ease network congestion and save server disk space. Different compression systems use different algorithms. Among the compression types are: ZIP, GZIP, ARC, ARJ, LZH, TAR, and RAR.

Compressed files are often used to hide vandals and viruses.

Compressed video A digital video image or segment that has been processed using a variety of computer algorithms and other techniques to reduce the amount of data required to accurately represent the content and thus the space required to store the content.

Compression ratio A comparison of the amount of space saved by data compression. A compression ratio of 2:1 ("two to one") results in a doubling of the storage capacity.

Compression Takes something large and makes it smaller. Compression generally comes in two forms: lossy and lossless. Lossy compression is best used on graphics files and sound files, where loss of quality is acceptable in many situations. Lossy compression crunches down the data at a much higher ratio, at the expense of having an image or a sound that isn't quite the same as before it was compressed. In the best scenario the data takes up less space, but the person viewing the graphic or listening to the sound file will not be able to notice. Lossless compression squeezes data down so that at some later date it can be uncompressed and returned to its exact structure. Lossless compression is best used on data files and programs.

Compuserve A commercial network that has some of the "richest offerings available, but it has been the slowest to change and can be much costlier than the other services. It has a wide choice of bulletin boards, U.S. News and World Reports magazine, and Navigator to the Internet. News services are relatively cheap, but modem line costs are somewhat expensive.

Computation bound A condition where the speed of operation of the processor actually limits the speed of program execution. The processor is limited by the number of arithmetic operations it must perform.

Computer An electronic system that can store and process information under program control. A computer is the part of the system that contains a processing unit that does the thinking. Sometimes people refer to the computer as the entire package; the processing unit, keyboard, screen, disk drives_the works. You may need to know if you have a computer on your desk or if you have a terminal connected to a computer somewhere else. If you are using a PC with a program such as kermit or procomm as a terminal to communicate with a computer running Unix, when we talk about the "computer", we mean the Unix machine.

Computer aided design (CAD) This refers to the use of computers to design things. There are specific CAD programs like AutoCAD that are generally resource-intensive, requiring fast processors, lots of memory, and a big, clear monitor for best results. CAD has enabled people to easily model, create, and walk through or view designs of 3D objects or floor plans from different angles on a computer without actually taking the time to make a physical mock up. This is a huge time saver, and has revolutionized design in general.

Computer associates (CA) A major independent software vendor established in 1976. It had its initial public offering in December 1981. CA has assumed the role of receive of troubled software companies. In 1987, having already acquired 16 companies in five years, CA hit full stride. During the next two years, it purchased Uccel, Applied Data Research and Cullinet. They then purchased Legent in 1995. CA has been able to trim fat from the acquired companies and then pump the acquired products through its distribution channels.

Computer emergency response team (CERT) The CERT Coordination Center is the organization that grew from the computer emergency response team formed by the Defense Advanced Research Projects Agency (DARPA) in November 1988 in response to the needs identified during the Internet worm incident. The CERT charter is to work with the Internet community to facilitate its response to computer security events involving Internet hosts, to take proactive steps to raise the community's awareness of computer security issues, and to conduct research targeted at improving the security of existing systems.

Computer fraud Intended misrepresentation, alteration or disclosure of data in order to perform an operation for personal gain.

Computer graphics adapter (CGA) A video standard that allowed a resolution of 320x200 with a whopping four colors. It was replaced byEGA. You can get 16 colors on CGA if you go down to 160x100resolution. This is the first real graphics standard for IBM PC-compatible computers.

Computer model A computer model is a recreation of a static scene, be it a house or a complex CAD design.

Computer peripheral A device that is connected to a computer to support its operation; for example, a keyboard or a disk drive unit

Computer search service (CSS) A fee-based service, offers access to more than 500 databases, primarily in the sciences and social sciences, from which the Library can create customized bibliographies.

Computer simulation A prediction of the outcome of events by using actual data and attempting to mimic the environment on a computer. Computer simulations are used often in predicting the weather.

Computer telephony integration (CTI) Simply put, this represents the integration of a computer and telephone. Its serious uses include phone registration, fax-back systems, and other systems that record or supply information by simple touch-tone telephone access. A basic use of this technology would be using your computer/modem as an auto- dialer so you don't have to push the buttons on your phone.

Computer-assisted tomography The use of computers in assisting with the management of X-ray images.

COMx Serial communication interface identification (COM1 or COM2 for example). It is an internal software address used for transmitting data between a PC/DOS computer and an external device.

Concatenate The act of combining two string into a single, longer string.

Concatenated stripe Allows multiple disk partitions to be treated as a single large partition by the kernel.

Conceptualization A creative process that is directed at envisaging a structure or collection of relationships within components of a complex system.

Concrete class In object-oriented programming, a class suitable to be instantiated.(as opposed to an abstract class).

Concurrency control Concurrency control deals with the issues involved with allowing multiple people simultaneous access to shared entities, be they objects, data records, or some other representation. It is very important to have a recovery system such that if bad data is entered in a shared environment the databases can be recovered. It is important understand transactions, which are collections of actions that potentially modify records. More than one record may be involved, especially in double entry bookkeeping. An example of a transaction is a transfer of funds between two bank accounts. Concurrency controls are related to transactions controls, but they are not the same since transactions controls apply to single-person as well as multiple-person access. Transactions controls are intended to assure that updated transactions are allowable and orderly. Transactions in relational databases are often commands in a two phase commit system. A "two phase commit" transactions control is the process by which a relational database ensures that distributed transactions are performed in an orderly manner. In this system, transactions may be terminated by either committing them or rolling them back.

Concurrent clean A functional language functional-language for the Macintosh from the University of Nijmegen.

Concurrent engineering An approach where all aspects of a product's life-cycle are considered as early as possible in the design, manufacturing and maintenance process.

Concurrent Pertaining to simultaneous activities, for example simultaneous execution of many computer programs.

Conditional A JavaScript statement that performs an action if a particular condition is true, usually using the if statement.

Conditional statement In programming, this is a type of command that controls the flow of a program based on whether certain conditions are met. The statement is normally set up in the form: IF (specific condition is met) THEN (do this action) ELSE (do this if the condition is not met). The "Else" statement or condition does not usually have to be listed specifically. It can be implied that if there is no type of Else statement then program flow continues normally if the condition is not met. Conditions can range from simple (x equals 3) to more complex conditions (x is not less than or equal to the number of characters in a string).

Confidentiality The quality of not disclosing or providing unauthorized individuals, entities, or processes with access to information. Breaches of confidentiality can be deliberate or accidental. The premeditated distribution of a customer database may be a calculated act of sabotage. On the other hand, replying to all recipients of an email may leak confidential plans that are just as damaging, even if unintentional.

Config.SYS The configuration file for DOS systems. Whenever a DOS computer boots up, it reads the CONFIG.SYS file (if it exists) and executes any commands in it. The most common commands are BUFFERS= and FILES=, which enable you to specify the buffer size and the number of files that can be open simultaneously. In addition, you can enter commands that install drivers for devices.

Configuration control Management of changes to a system's hardware or software settings in order to ensure that a system is safe from improper or unauthorized changes.

Configuration file A file, created by an application program or by the operationg system, containing configuration information specific to your own computing environment. Application program config. files may have a file-name extension of CPG or SET; Window's config. files use the INI file-name extension.

Configuration management The process of identifying, defining, recording and reporting the configuration items in a system and the change requests. Controlling the releases and change of the items throughout the life-cycle life-cycle.

Configuration manager The Windows Plug and Play system component that drives the process of locating devices, setting up their nodes in the hardware tree, and running the resource allocation process. Each of the three phases of configuration management—boot time, real mode, and protected mode—have their own configuration managers.

Configuration This is a general-purpose computer term that can refer to the way you have your computer set up. It is also used to describe the total combination of hardware components that make up a computer system and the software settings that allow various hardware components of a computer system to communicate with one another.

Configure The act of changing software or hardware actions by changing the settings.

Connection and streaming architecture Kernel-mode streaming in WDM.

Connection In switched virtual connection (SVC) environments the LAN Emulation Management entities set up connections between each other using UNI signaling.

Connectionless The model of interconnection in which communication takes place without first establishing a connection. Establishing a connection. Sometimes called datagram. Examples; LANs, Internet IP, OSI, CLNP, UDP, ordinary postcards.

Connection-oriented The model of interconnection in which communication proceeds through three well-defined phase: connection establishment, data transfer, connection release. Example: X.2.5, Internet TCP and OSI TP4, registered letters.

Connectivity In networking, the degree to which any given computer or application program can cooperate with other network components, either hardware or software, purchased from other vendors.

Console game A game designed to be played on a game console.

Console operator In NetWare, the user working at the file server's console.

Console This term can be used generally to describe a computer, a terminal, or, more recently, a dedicated gaming system.

Constant angular velocity (CAV) A method of reading (or writing) data from (or to) a spinning disk. As data is read from the disk, the drive motor always spins at the same speed. For example, CD- drives that work at CAV will read data at 12x towards the center, which has less space to record data, and 20x towards the larger data track on the edge, where the disk is moving faster.

Constant linear velocity (CLV) In terms of disk drives, this means that the rate of data being read off of the disk stays the same from center to outer edge. To accomplish this, the drive motor speeds up and slows down as data is read from different areas of the disk—the linear velocity remains constant. An 8x CD-ROM drive that operates at CLV will read data at 8x anywhere on the disk, from the center to the outer edge. That means that data is written closer together towards the center of the disk and further apart towards the edge.

Constructor A function provided by a class in C++ to instantiate an object.

Consultative committee on international telegraphy and telephony (CCITT) A committee, sponsored by the United Nations, that defines network standards, including X.400 and X.500. This committee has been recently renamed to International Telecommunications Unions/ Telecommunications Standardization Sector (ITU/TSS).

Contact form (contact template) The electronic form used to register a new domain name contact/agent or modify information for an existing contact. Formerly referred to as the contact template.

Contact/agent Contacts/Agents are individuals or groups who represent the registrant on matters related to the registrant's domain name. There are three types of contacts/agents: administrative, technical, or billing. The entity listed as the administrative, technical, or billing contact/agent should be the entity best able to answer questions about that particular aspect of the domain name's registration, and should be authorize to represent the domain name registrant. A contact/agent may be a single person or may be a group or organization where several individuals act in a role (e.g., Internet Service Provider (ISP) Support Center).

Container class A class class whose instances are collections of other objects. Examples include stacks, queues, lists and arrays.

Content inspection protocol client (CIPC) The CIPC is a protocol and server specific component of the CR . Also referred to as the Data Source.

Content inspector (CI) Scan engine that inspects the content of files and email. It is a generic component that can be installed. anywhere on the network. The same CI can be used for different protocols and server types. You can add CIs for load balancing as traffic increases.

Content redirector (CR) Intelligent software unit that determines whether to redirect content to a CI and reroutes inspected content to its intended destination. It immediately performs a preliminary inspection to block files that you do not want under any circumstances and to allow files from sources that you trust. Each CR contains a Policy Manager that is managed by eConsole .

Content scrambling system (CSS) This is a method of scrambling DVD movie content so that DVD movies will not be played on unlicensed DVD player hardware. CSS is part of a complex group of technologies, including Macrovision and DVD Region control, developed to attempt to control the viewing and copying of DVD movies. A side effect of CSS is that no DVD movie playing software was developed for Linux, and thus the DeCSS program was created—its legality is still being fought out in the court systems in various countries.

Content security The ability to specify the content of a communication as an element of security policy, in contrast to defining the security policy based on header information only. Effective Content Security requires that a content inspector be able to open and read the contents of the communication.

Content vectoring protocol (CVP) An OPSEC API that enables VPN-1 and CheckPoint's FireWall-1 to send the contents of a file to a third party Content Security application. This ensures that transmitted files are not dangerous to the network.

Context . The environment in which a process runs, including it's set of register values within the CPU, the current stack values, which instruction is being executed, and the allowable memory access boundaries. A *context switch* is a sudden change in these, for example, a function call which modifies the stack, registers, and instruction pointer simultaneously, or a CPU's switch from executing one process to another, which produces similar effects.

Context sensitive help . Information about where you are in the application, which is not where you want to be. Often describes how to use the mouse and the menus to select things you don't want (required in User Friendly software).

Continuity RIMM Modules that are used to fill all unused RIMM sockets in a system. Continuity-RIMMs do not use any active components; instead, they are used to continue the channel so that the signal can be properly terminated at the motherboard.

Contrast ratio (CR) This ratio is equivalent to the brightness of the white level divided by the brightness of the black level of a display. A higher contrast ratio makes it easier to distinguish dark colors from one another. Early LCD screens had low contrast ratios compared to CRT monitors and were criticized for this, as many 3D games involved skulking about dark areas where contrast made a huge difference in seeing what was going on.

Control code Special nonprinting codes that cause electronic equipment to perform specific actions.

Control connections A Control VCC links the LEC to the LECS. Control VCCs also link the LEC to the LES and carry LE_ARP traffic and control frames. The control VCCs never carry data frames.

Control key The key on the keyboard labelled control or ctrl. It is used as a shift key. It does nothing of it's own. To use it hold it down, press another key, and release it. To press Cntrl-D, for example, hold the Ctrl key, press and release the ctrl key.

Control method A definition of how an ACPI-compatible operating system can perform a simple hardware task. For example, the operating system invokes control methods to read the temperature of a thermal zone. Control methods are written in an encoded language called AML.

Control panel Windows family containing management tools.

Control program for microprocessors (CP/M) CP/M was THE operating system before IBM created the PC. IBM was shopping for an OS for the PC, ended up going with Microsoft, and Bill Gates created DOS. CP/M is not really used on anything but fossils at this point.

Controller A device that controls the transfer of data from a computer to a peripheral device and vice versa. For example, disk drives, display screens, keyboards, and printers all require controllers. In personal computers, the controllers are often single chips. When you purchase a computer, it comes with all the necessary controllers for standard components, such as the display screen, keyboard, and disk drives. If you attach additional devices, however, you may need to insert new controllers that come on expansion boards.

Controllers must be designed to communicate with the computer's expansion bus. There are three standard bus architectures for PCs — the AT bus, PCI (Peripheral Component Interconnect), and SCSI. When you purchase a controller, therefore, you must ensure that it conforms to the bus architecture that your computer uses.

Controllerless modem Also host-based controller. A modem that consists of a DSP without the usual microcontroller. The host CPU provides the AT command interpreter, modem-control functions, and v.42 bis implementation. Compare with software modem.

Conventional memory On DOS systems, conventional memory refers to the portion of memory that is available to standard DOS programs. DOS systems have an address space of 1MB (megabyte), but the top 384K (called high memory) is reserved for system use. This leaves 640K of conventional memory. Everything above 1MB is either extended or expanded memory.

Convergence The ability of the three electron beams (red, green, and blue) in a CRT monitor to meet at a single point and produce one dot. If a monitor is mis-converging, you will notice shadows of blue or red around any white images. Often, this will occur in only some parts of the screen. Some CRT monitors have convergence controls, but most do not, making it impossible to correct this condition without opening it up, which isn't a good idea due to how CRT monitors hold electrical energy.

Cookies Applets that enable a web site to collect information about each user for later reference. Web Browsers like Netscape Navigator set aside a small amount of space on the user's hard drive to record detected preferences. Cookies perform storage on the client side that might otherwise have to be stored in a generic-state or database server on the server side. Cookies can be used to collect information for consumer profile databases. Browsers can be set to refuse cookies.

Cooperative multitasking A form of multitasking in which all running applications must work together to share system resources.

Cooperative processing The process by which a single application is partitioned between two or more hardware platforms. Each segment of the application can communicate with the others. Physical connectivity can occur via a direct channel connection, a local-area network node, a peer-to-peer communication link or a master/slave link. The application software can exist in a distributed processing environment, but this is not a requirement.

COOTS Conference on Object-Oriented Technologies and Systems.

Copeland The name given to Apple's troubled operating OS 8 System 8.0 for Mac and PowerPC computers. New features were to include OpenDoc object programming support, advanced security, TCP/IP support, and IPX support. Although it was expected to be released in 1996, Copeland was once again delayed for purposes of adding competitive features, especially networking utilities. In early 1997, Mac OS 8 (Copeland) development was purportedly in a state of chaos after losing some important engineers and the director of OS 8 development. The development was sidetracked when Apple purchased Steve Job's NEXTStep and announced that NEXTStep would become the core of future Mac and PowerMac operating systems. Apple's hopes are riding heavily upon the evolution of a new operating system called Rhapsody that is a revolutinary operating system based upon NEXTStep technology.

Copper barrier An assumption that limits the amount of data that can be sent through a single copper wire as used in DVI connections, and thus why there are two types of DVI wiring. The assumed limit was approximately 165MHz when the DVI standard was put together.

Copper distributed data interface (CDDI) A high-speed networking standard whose underlying medium is copper or telephone cable. The topology is dual-attached, counter-rotating Token Ring.

Coprocessor Electronic component that relieves the microprocessor of some important tasks. Increased performance can often be achieved through the use of coprocessors. For example, a math coprocessor performs many of the math operations outside the microprocessor. A coprocessor may also speed graphics computations.

Copyrights The legal rules and regulations concerning the copying and redistribution of documents.

CORBA common object request broker architecture Is in competition with Microsoft's OLE/DCOM object-oriented Middleware technology for business applicaions. CORBA is most popular in communications Middleware using an Object Request Broker ORB. CORBA evolved out of TCP/IP. DCOM is bundled with the Windows 2000 operating system but has lackluster support for other operating systems. CORBA is more flexible with other operating systems. Both CORBA and OLE/DCOM are designed to distribute objects or assembly of appplications from discreet, self-contained components. Both are appealing in the fast growing technology of "object middleware." Object middleware has corporate appeal due to the ability to provide highly abstracted object-oriented programming interfaces. Microsoft added new terminology in this area. For example, COM depicts a Component Object Model to describe the base model used for building components. The term DCOM is the Distributed form of COM. ActiveX (formerly OCX) is the packaging technology for controls and supercedes prior Visual Basic Controls known as VBX. OLE no longer means object linking and embedding. OLE now refers to a collection of technologies. CORBA allows users to connect disparate systems and form object architectures. XML will allow users to transmit structured information within, between and out of those systems, and to represent information in a universal way in and across architectures. Both technologies are platform-, vendor- and language-independent. The conceptual fit is perfect.

Core An old fashioned term for "memory." A long time ago(in the '60s and '70s), most memory consists of thousands of tiny, metal donuts, called cores, strung on arrays of teeny-tiny wires.Some UNIX enthusiasts still refer to memory as "core." In UNIX systems this term is commonly used in reference to memory, and the crash dump "core" files you will find if you do something naughty in UNIX. The term goes back to when memory chips were actually magnetic coils, or core memory.

CORE chemistry online retrieval experiment A project to publish American Chemical Society journals electronically.

Core dump In UNIX systems, when a program crashes it "dumps" out an image of the memory and registers so that you may go through and see what caused the problem. This is almost as useful as the Netware and Windows NT memory dumps. However, if the problem is important enough and persistent enough, the dump gives knowledgeable developers/admins something to look at in order to try to fix the bugs in the system.

Corresponding entities Peer entities with a lower layer connection among them.

COS corporation for open systems An international consortium of computer users and vendors, set up to provide ways of testing OSI OSI implementations.

COSE common open software environment An initiative by Hewlett-Packard, Sun, IBM, Novell, Univel and SCO to move towards consistency and interopability between Unix suppliers.

Cosine A trigonometric function of an angle, defined as the ratio of the length of the adjacent side of a right-angled triangle divided by the length of its hypotenuse.

COSS Common Object Services Specification in CORBA CORBA.

COST A set of software tools for SGML SGML documents.

Cost plus 1. The ultimate goal of every government contractor.

2. The foundation of the USA's military-industrial complex.

3. A type of contract where all Research & Development expenses are charged to the government, whatever they are, in addition to fees.

Cost-risk analysis Assessment of the cost of adding data protection features to a network versus the cost of losing or compromising the data.

COTS (commercial off the shelf) A government purchasing term requiring commercial availability of products bought on contract. An attempt to avoid "cost-plus contract" minded defense contractors from making custom systems that only they can maintain.

Counter measure Any action, device, procedure, technique, or other measure that minimizes the security weaknesses of a system.

Counterfeiting The act of knowingly producing non-genuine objects, especially in relation to currency

Country code A standard two-letter abbreviation for the name of a country. It is used with domain names with locations outside the United States. For example, "ca" in "domainmart.com.ca" refers to Canada. For a complete list of countgry codes.

CP/M (control program for microprocessors.) CP/M was THE operating system before IBM created the PC. IBM was shopping for an OS for the PC, ended up going with Microsoft, and Bill Gates created DOS. CP/M is not really used on anything but fossils at this point.

CPCS (common part convergence sublayer) The portion of the convergence sublayer of an AAL that remains the same regardless of the traffic type.

CPCS-SDU (common part convergence sublayer-service data unit) Protocol data unit to be delivered to the receiving AAL layer by the destination CP convergence sublayer.

CPE (customer premises equipment) End user equipment that resides on the customer's premise which may not be owned by the local exchange carrier.

CPI (capabilities and preferences information) Is the generic term used to describe the information relating to a particular device, the network it operates on and the user's preferences as to content reception. This information is stored on CC/PP server.

CPM (cost per thousand) The practice of calculating a cost per 1000 ad displays. It is used by programs that pay on an impression basis — with the CPM rate being the amount you earn for every 1000 times an advertisement is displayed. CPM can also be calculated for pay-per-sale, pay-per-lead and pay-per-click programs by using this formula.

CPN (calling party number) A parameter of the initial address message that identifies the calling number and is sent to the destination carrier.

CPS (characters per second) The amount of text characters printed in a second. This term was used more when daisy wheel and dot matrix printers were common. Nowadays, printers are rated more by pages per minute (ppm), as the amount of characters printed are irrelevant to modern printers that work on a page-by-page basis. Although inkjet printers still go line by line like dot matrix printers, they are much faster, and it's easier to compare page printing speeds.

CPSR (computer professionals for social responsibility) A US non-profit organisation concerned with the effects of computers on society.

CPU (central processing unit) Think of this as the brains of the computer. When most people think of processors, they think of Intel, AMD, Motorola, or IBM. The Pentium 4 and Athlon are popular CPUs. The CPU's first instruction is to check the system BIOS and do what the BIOS tells it. The CPU is designed to run a group of instructions, or instruction set. CPU instructions can consist of adding together numbers, subtracting, fetching information from memory, and numerous other simple functions. The computer's operating system feeds the CPU instructions after the BIOS locates the operating system and puts it into main memory. That encompasses a computer's RAM, processing, and control circuitry, including the arithmetic-logic (ALU) unit. Both the ALU and the control units are wholly contained on the microprocessing chip whereas the primary storage is on the mother board or the expansion bus. For test comparisons of Intel Pentium, PowerPC, and Mips R4X00, and DEC Alpha, Montgomery ranks Pentium and Mips highest in terms of file servers. He ranks Pentium higher on most graphics and business applications criteria except for price since PowerPC is a cheaper alternative. There are, of course, other considerations. The PowerPC currently performs better than Pentium in terms of temperature, speed, and price, but all these advantages are expected to disappear when Intel introduces its upgrade versions of the Pentium. The PowerPC, however, will not perform as well using DOS and Windows operating systems.

CPU cache Fast Static RAM that provides 0 wait state (next clock cycle) access to memory for the CPU. The number of wait states is calculated by the reciprocal of the clock speed, e.g. 1/33MHz = .000 000 030 S or 30+ NanoSeconds. For a Pentium 100, 1/100MHz = .000 000 010 S or 10 nS. However, advertising standards require 100 MHz Pentiums to claim 0 wait state caches when implemented with 15 nS SRAMS.

CPU terminator A card that ensures that electrical signals on a CPU bus are terminated properly in multiprocessor systems where not all CPU slots are filled with CPUs. Some multiprocessor systems require that all processor slots be full so that the processor bus is terminated properly. If you have a four-processor system but only one processor, you will need three CPU terminators to ensure proper bus termination.

Cracker This is the common term used to describe a malicious hacker, though it also can refer to code breakers. Crackers get into all kinds of mischief, including breaking or "cracking" copy protection on software programs, breaking into systems and causing harm, changing data, or stealing. Hackers largely regard crackers as a less educated group of individuals who cannot truly create their own work, and simply steal other people's work to cause mischief or for personal gain, not to promote understanding.

Crankback A mechanism for partially releasing a connection setup in progress which has encountered a failure. This mechanism allows PNNI to perform alternate routing.

Crash An unexpected program halt, sometimes due to hardware failure, but most often due to a software error, from which there is no recovery.

CRAY cray research inc Manufacturers of a range of large powerful mainframes.

CRC (cyclic redundancy check) A test to see whether data has been transferred properly over a modem or to and from disk media. The sender of the data adds a check number to the end of the data being sent, and the receiver applies the same check to the data and compares the number it gets with the check number. If they don't match, the data can be requested again.

CREASE Catalog of Resources for Education in Ada and Software Engineering. A database maintained by AdaIC.

Credentials package A cryptographically sealed data package containing information about the principal, method, object, location, and authorization of a request.

CRF cell relay function This is the basic function that an ATM network performs in order to provide a cell relay service to ATM end-stations.

CRF connection related function A term used by Traffic Management to reference a point in a network or a network element where per connection functions are occurring. This is the point where policing at the VCC or VPC level may occur.

Crimp tool A special tool used to attach connectors to cables.

Critical mass The scale or volume at which processes become self-perpetuating. In Web publishing, it is said that after achieving a certain amount of material and resources, it will create a self-sustaining chain reaction.

CRM (customer relationship management) System based upon information technology. Central to CRM are databases customer relationships in sufficient detail so that management, salespeople, people providing service, and perhaps the customer directly could access information, match customer needs with product plans and offerings, remind customers of service requirements, know what other products a customer had purchased, and so forthNew Offering from PwC Division touts consistent CRM PwC ConsultingTM, a division of financial services organization PricewaterhouseCoopers, has released CRM ACCEL — a complete multi-channel CRM program designed to help companies reduce the cost of serving customers while increasing revenue

Crontab A UNIX/Linux command that allows you to view (crontab -l) or make changes (crontab -e) to the list of jobs scheduled to be run by the cron daemon.

Cross platform A term given to software that can be used on multiple hardware platforms, such as the x86 PC, the Macintosh, or Sun's Solaris systems. One such piece of software is Java.

Cross software Software developed on one kind of computer for use on another (usually because the other computer does not have itself adequate facilities for software development).

Crossover cable An Ethernet cable using RJ-45 connectors, where one end of the cable has the order of the second two pairs of the 8 wires (green and orange) swapped. Instead of wires 1, 2, 3, and 6 going straight through, you have 1 going to 3, 2 going to 6, 3 going to 1, and 6 going to 2. (Thanks to DN for pointing that out.) You can use a crossover cable to directly connect two 10BaseT or 100BaseT network cards, basically making a network of two computers for easy file transfer or configuration of network printers or other devices. As well, crossover cables are often used to connect 10BaseT and 100BaseT hubs together.

Cross-platform The ability of a software package or an electronic "book" to run in more than one operating system such as Icon Author and TIE crossings between Windows, Unix, and DOS operating systems. Some will only play back on cross-platforms but cannot be used to author in the platform of choice. Apple Media Kit and ScriptX authoring will run in DOS, Mac, Unix, and other operating systems, but neither option can be used for authoring in DOS or Windows. Insight into Multimedia and TIE can be used to playback in UNIX but authoring can only be undertaken in Windows. Hardware that crosses platforms in emulation (such as playing back Windows software in emulation on a Mac computer) frequently does not work well with complex authoring systems such as CBT ToolBook or Quest options that only perform well in Windows. Often very expensive options are priced for cross-platform capabilities that are limited in terms of authoring features present in software that will not cross platforms. GainMomentum authoring package from Sybase crosses platforms between UNIX, Windows, and Windows 2000. However, in spite of its very high price this package does not contain many of the wonderful authoring features found in Windows-only CBT ToolBook that is less than 10% of the cost of GainMomentum. Only a small proportion (less than 20%) of the hypermedia authoring options have cross-platform capabilities, but it is becoming a priority of many vendors to upgrade their products with cross-platform capabilities.

CRS (cell relay service) A carrier service which supports the receipt and transmission of ATM cells between end users in compliance with ATM standards and implementation specifications.

CRT (cathode ray tube) One of the main components of most monitors and TVs. A beam of electrons is shot towards the CRT, and as the electrons collide with phosphors on the inside surface they produce light. Today, other technologies are performing better than the heavy and bulky tube monitors. LCD panels, gas plasma panels, and projection units are all in contention, but they still can't compare to the low cost of a CRT monitor or TV.

Cryptanalysis Analysis of a cryptographic system and its values in order to uncover sensitive data or confidential variables.

Cryptographic application programming interface (CAPI) Standard interface that enables applications to communicate directly with ISDN equipment.

Cryptographic hash function A process that computes a value (hashword) from a particular data unit. If data unit is later changed, the hashword will no longer match the data.

Cryptographic token interface (cryptoki) Pronounced crypto-key, it is the API that holds cryptographic information and perform cryptographic functions for PKCS#11.

Cryptography The study of the principles, means, and methods for rendering plain text unintelligible, and for converting encrypted messages into intelligible form.

Cryptology The study of hidden, disguised, or encrypted communications.

Cryptolope The combination of "cryptographic" security encription with "envelopes" of domain. Cryptolopes enable publishers on the WWW to securely distribute content with copyright protections and security over payments for copyrighted material usage.

Cryptosystem A system or mechanism that is used to automate the processes of encryption and decryption.

CS convergence sublayer The general procedures and functions that convert between ATM and non-ATM formats. This describes the functions of the upper half of the AAL layer. This is also used to describe the conversion functions between non-ATM protocols such as frame relay or SMDS and ATM protocols above the AAL layer.

CSCW computer supported cooperative work (also known as Groupware) Software tools and technology to support groups of people working together on a project, often at different sites.

CSD Circuit Switched Cellular Data.

CSel (cable select) This is basically Plug-and-Play ATA. You plug in your ATA/IDE hard drives, set them to CSEL (Cable Select), and they determine whether they are master or slave automatically, saving you from manual configuration.

CSMA/CD (carrier sense multiple access with collision) detection A local-area network access technique in which multiple stations connected to the same channel can sense transmission activity on that channel and defer the initiation of transmission while the channel is active. Sometimes called contention access.

CSNET (computer+science network) A large computer network, mostly in the U.S. but with international connections. CSNET sited include universities, research labs, and some commercial companies. Now merged with BITNET to form CREN.

CSU (channel service unit) An interface for digital leased lines which performs loopback testing and line conditioning.

CSU/DSU (channel service unit/data service unit) A piece of hardware that you use to translate the digital data frames of a T1 line into a 10BaseT connection where Internet connectivity is concerned. If the T1 lines are used for voice connections, a CSU/DSU is required to translate the digital frames into signals that your office phone switch can interpret. Basically, the phone network/Internet consists of a bunch of CSU/DSUs talking to one another. When you lease a T1 line, your provider typically supplies you with a CSU/DSU, often with a setup cost. A synonym for CSU/DSU is DSU/CSU.

CSV (comma separated values) A file extension used for a flat text data file consisting of items of data separated by commas. Each line of data is separated by a carriage return.

CT (conformance test) Testing to determine whether an implementation complies with the specifications of a standard and exhibits the behaviors mandated by that standard.

CTD (cell transfer delay) This is defined as the elapsed time between a cell exit event at the measurement point 1 (e.g., at the source UNI) and the corresponding cell entry event at measurement point 2 (e.g., the destination UNI) for a particular connection. The cell transfer delay between two measurement points is the sum of the total inter-ATM node transmission delay and the total ATM node processing delay.

CTI (computer telephony integration) Simply put, this represents the integration of a computer and telephone. Its serious uses include phone registration, fax-back systems, and other systems that record or supply information by simple touch-tone telephone access. A basic use of this technology would be using your computer/modem as an auto- dialer so you don't have to push the buttons on your phone.

CTIA Cellular Telecommunications Industries Association.

CTO (chief technology officer) An executive title related to CIO, usually at a medium or large-sized company. The CTO is, however, more focused on the use of technology in products developed by the company and technology delivered to external customers. CTOs are typically more technical than CIOs.

Ctrl (control key) A key on a computer keyboard that typically adds 64 bits to the ASCII value of a key being pressed. Based on the program that is running, it can have different effects. It was added to create more key combinations besides just using the Shift key. In selection of items, holding down the Ctrl key will typically allow you to select or de-select a single item from a group without affecting the rest of your selection.

Current job The job most recently started or stopped. When you use the jobs command to list jobs, the current job is marked with a plus sign(+).

Curses A set of subroutines in UNIX for handling navigation on a terminal screen using the cursor.

Cursor This is often represented by a blinking line or square on your computer screen. The cursor is there to let you know where information will be displayed when you type on a keyboard. Many program manuals make reference to the cursor and describe where it should be placed so that you can enter information into software properly. You can use the pointer to place the cursor.

Customer information control system (CICS) Not to be confused with CISC, CICS is online transaction processing application server software originally written by IBM for mainframes for dealing with customer information and transaction processing in the enterprise. Now versions of CICS are available for UNIX and x86 platforms as well.

Customer premise equipment Simply put customer premise equipment is the equipment that big company's that provide broadband services use;i.e., voice ports,channel banks, PBX's,Integrated Access Mulitplexers,etc. This is as opposed to subscriber premise equipment.

Customer relationship management (CRM) A class of enterprise software that enables a large company to manage all contact (or "touches") that it has with its customers. It would track, for example, calls to tech support, faxes, e-mails, direct mail, telephone contacts, and any other contact that a company would have with a customer and vice-versa. This information can be used for analysis of customer relationships, and gives salespeople an understanding of what to say when calling up a customer.

CWIS (campus wide information system) Bulletin board services that can be accessed on the Internet. These are available on most college campuses and provide bulletin board information on campus calendars, e-mail directories on the campus, employment opportunities, campus events, course catalogs, etc.

Cxt core AMD added a feature to its K6-2 processor, running at 400MHz, called write combining, that queues up memory requests until there is a sufficient amount to fill the bus. So, AMD refers to processors with this technology as having the CXT Core.

Cybercafe A shop, cafe, or meeting place where users can rent a computer for a short time to access the Internet.

Cybermall A term commonly used to describe an electronic site shared by a number of commercial interests.

Cybernetics A unified approach to understanding the behavior of machines and animals developed by Norbert Wiener.

Cyberpunk Cyberpunk was originally a cultural sub-genre of science fiction taking place in a not-so-distant, dystopian, over-industrialized society. The term grew out of the work of William Gibson and Bruce Sterling and has evolved into a cultural label encompassing many different kinds of human, machine, and punk attitudes. It includes clothing and lifestyle choices as well.

Cyberspace A term coined by William Gibson in his fantasy novel "Neuromancer" to refer to a near-future computer network where users mentally travel through matrices of data. The term is now used to describe the Internet and the other computer networks.

Cyborg A person who is partially flesh and bone, but has one or more robotic appendages electronically linked to his or her nerves. Often, a cyborg is said to be half human and half machine. For example, the "Terminator" character is a robot covered with human tissue—this is not a true cyborg. As well, a human with an artificial limb that is removable is not a cyborg. For a true cyborg it is hard to tell internally where the human ends and the robotic parts begin, and hard to separate one from the other. The Borg characters from Star Trek could be said to be true cyborgs, as they have a series of implants that truly merge flesh and machine.

Cyclic redundancy check (CRC) A test to see whether data has been transferred properly over a modem or to and from disk media. The sender of the data adds a check number to the end of the data being sent, and the receiver applies the same check to the data and compares the number it gets with the check number. If they don't match, the data can be requested again.

Cycloids Pertaining to circles, in either a static way or in a way that involves movement.

Cylinder This term is somewhat synonymous with the tracks on a hard disk drive. However, instead of a single track, a cylinder refers to the location of all the drive read and write heads, typically accessing multiple platters. Thus, when these tracks are mentally pictured, they are stacked up like a cylinder. Since all the heads are locked together, a specific cylinder number is equivalent to a track number on a specific platter, but refers to all platters at once.

D

DA (destination address) Information sent in the forward direction indicating the address of the called station or customer.

DAA (distributed application architecture) Under design by Hewlett-Packard and Sun. A distributed object management environment that will allow applications to be developed independent of operating system, network or windowing system.

DAB/DAR Digital Audio Broadcast and Digital Audio Radio broadcasting in digital formats via satellites and fiber optic cable.

DAC (digital to analog convertor) An electronic device that converts digital signals into analog signals. You can find DACs in a variety of devices, including sound cards. The DAC would be used to convert digital signals from your computer into analog signals that can be sent to your speakers—assuming you use standard analog speakers.

Daemon Disk And Execution Monitor programs that are not initially executed but lie in wait for certain contingencies to occur. Daemons are extremely common in UNIX operating systems. The slightly revised form Demon refers to the program itself whereas Daemon refers to an operating system process.

Daisy chain In computer terminology, this refers to connecting one device (historically SCSI, but now USB or FireWire as well) to another device, instead of directly to a computer. In fact, you can daisy chain several SCSI devices to one another, and only one of them needs to be connected to a computer with a SCSI interface for them all to be controlled by it.

Daisy wheel printer A printer that uses a wheel with all the characters on it to produce output. The wheel spins to the desired character and makes an imprint, then spins to go to the next character. It sounds like a little machine gun. These printers generally aren't used much anymore due to the decreased cost of other printers that can produce graphics as well as text. The one good thing about a daisy-wheel printer is that the text is generally very crisp, but even that advantage is nullified now with laser printers that can produce very crisp characters as well.

DAO (disc at Once) This is a single-session method of writing data to a CD-R/RW disc that creates a disc in a format suitable for commercial duplication. Basically, the entire disc is written at once in contrast to Track at Once.

Dark fiber Fiber optic wiring that has been installed but has not been turned on yet. Often, companies that lay fiber optic cabling will lay extra cable, since the laying of miles of cable is a very costly and time consuming procedure.

This dark fiber will lay dormant until the company needs extra capacity, or until it leases it to another company that needs the capacity. Then the company "lights it up" by sending optical data over the fiber.

DARPA Defense Advanced Research Project Agency of the US Department of Defense,.responsible for the development of new technology, including ARPANET ARPANET.

DASD (direct access storage device) IBM nomenclature for a storage peripheral that can respond directly to random requests for information; usually denotes a disk drive.

DASE Distributed Application Support Environment.

DAT (digital audio tape) Used for recording computer disc files onto a cheap backup and storage medium. DAT tapes are contained in small cartridges that are the cheapest means of storing vast amounts of data. For example, a cartridge smaller than the palm of an adult hand can hold two or more gigabyes of data. Popular manufacturers of DAT backup tape drives include Sony and Hewlett-Packard.

Data Information in a form suitable for processing by a computer, such as the digital representation of text, numbers, graphic images, or sounds.

Data area In DOS, that part of a floppy disk or hard disk that is available for use after the boot record, partition table, root directory, and file allocation table have been established by the formatting program. This area is the largest part of a disk and is where programs and data files are located.

Data bits In asynchronous transmissions, the bits that actually comprise the data; usually 7 or 8 data bits make up the data word.

Data bus A group of parallel conductors (circuit traces) found on the motherboard that is used by the CPU to send and receive data from all the devices in the computer. Also called the external data bus.

Data center Any computing environment where there is a service agreement between the people managing the computing resources and the users. A company computer network is a data center, but so is a network at an ISP. Additionally, data center has come to mean a website or network with its resources dedicated to providing information on a particular subject.

Data compression (compression) Takes something large and makes it smaller. Compression generally comes in two forms: lossy and lossless. Lossy compression is best used on graphics files and sound files, where loss of quality is acceptable in many situations. Lossy compression crunches down the data at a much higher ratio, at the expense of having an image or a sound that isn't quite the same as before it was compressed. In the best scenario the data takes up less space, but the person viewing the graphic or listening to the sound file will not be able to notice. Lossless compression squeezes data down so that at some later date it can be uncompressed and returned to its exact structure. Lossless compression is best used on data files and programs.

Data connections Data VCCs connect the LECs to each other and to the Broadcast and Unknown Server. These carry Ethernet/IEEE 802.3 or IEEE 802.5 data frames as well as flush messages.

Data conversion The translation of data from one format to another. Often when data are moved from one system to another, some form of data conversion is required to convert the data to a format the receiving system can interpret. Sometimes it is necessary to have an intermediate format.

Data definition language A language enabling the structure and instances of a database to be defined in a human- and machine-readable form.

Data dictionary A repository of information about data, such as its meaning, relationships to other data, origin, usage and format. The dictionary assists company management, database administrators, systems analysts and lication programmers in effectively planning, controlling and evaluating the collections, storage and use of data. A data dictionary manages data categories such as alias, data elements, data records, data structure, data store, data models, data flows, data relationships, processes, functions, dynamics, size, frequency, resource consumption and other user-defined attributes.

Data driven attack Encoding seemingly innocuous data with malicious content, which causes damage when executed by a user or a process.

Data encoding scheme The method used by a disk controller to store digital information onto a hard disk or floppy disk. Common encoding schemes used in the PC world include *modified frequency modulation* (MFM) encoding, *run-length limited* (RLL) encoding, and *advanced run-length limited* (ARLL) encoding.

Data encryption standard (DES) A standard method of encryptiong and decrypting data, developed by the U.S. National Bureau of Standards.

DES is a block of cipher that works by a combination of transposition and substitution, and was developed after years of work at IBM, rigorously tested by the National Security Agency, and finally accepted as being free of any mathematical or statistical weaknesses. This meaning, that it is impossible to break the system using statistical frequency tables or to work the algorithm backwards using standard mathematical methods. DES has remained unbroken despite years of use; it completely randomizes the information so that it is impossible to determine the encryption key even if some of the original text is known. DES is used by the federal government and most banks and money-transfer systems to protect all sensitive computer information.

Data entry A job function where the employee is expected to enter data into a computer. Typically, the only technical skill you need for such jobs is typing. Some people use data entry positions to springboard into low-end technical support and head on towards more technical jobs.

Data exposure The widespread connectivity which organizations provide to their employees has vastly improved productivity and profitability for most companies. However, more organizations are finding out every day that this connectivity is not without risk. Just as email connectivity allows employees to quickly access the information they need, it also allows them to transmit unauthorized confidential information worldwide at wire speed. Organizations are liable for what their employees do, and email is an uncontrolled route, which is often used for illegal or unproductive activities. Employees use company email to reveal confidential projects, business strategies, private customer information, and to conduct businesses on the side. Apart from tying up valuable bandwidth, these activities often expose organizations to legal liabilities.

Lawsuits related to sexual harassment, discrimination, violated non-disclosure agreements, and negligence due to inappropriate use of email cost companies over $500 million a year.

Data flow diagram A graphical notation used to describe how data flows between processes in a system. An important tool of most structured analysis techniques.

Data frames Logical, structured packets in which data can be placed. The Data Link layer Packages raw bits from the physical layer into data frames. The exact format of frame used by network depends on the topology.

Data integrity Ability to know the level of protection against data modification or destruction.

Data link layer The OSI layer that is responsible for data transfer across a single physical connection, or series of bridged connections, between two network entities.

Data marshaling, data unmarshaling The conversion of data back and forth between some local format and a common interchange format.

Data mining Sorting through data to identify patterns and establish relationships. Data mining parameters include:

Association - looking for patterns where one event is connected to another event.

Sequence or path analysis-looking for patterns where one event leads to another later event.

Classification - looking for new patterns (May result in a change in the way the data is organized).

Clustering - finding and visually documenting groups of facts not previously known.

Forecasting - discovering patterns in data that can lead to reasonable predictions about the future.

Data mode A set of data structures with manipulation and validation operators for general purpose usage. Examples are the Entity-Relationship model.

Data model The logical data structure developed during the logical database design process is a data model or entity model . It is also a description of the structural properties that define all entities represented in a database and all the relationships that exist among them.

Data packet In networking, a unit of information transmitted as a discrete entity from one node on the netwok to another. More specifically, in packet-switching networks, a packet is a transmission unit of a fixed maximum length that contains a header, a set of data, and error control information.

Data partitioning A technique applied to databases (but not restricted to them) which organizes data objects into related groups.

Data rate The speed of a data transfer process, normally expressed in bits per second or bytes per second.

Data reduction technique An approach to simplifying data, e.g. summarization.

Data set ready (DSR) Signal emitted by a modem indicating that it is ready to exchange signals with the computer.

Data terminal equipment (DTE) In communications, any device, such as a terminal or a computer, connected to a communications channel or public network.

Data terminal ready (DTR) A hardware signal defined by the RS-232-C standard to indicate that the computer is ready to accept a transmission.

Data transfer rate The data transfer rate determines how fast a drive or other peripheral can transfer data with its controller. The data transfer rate is a key measurement in drive performance.

Data type The type of data that is being used in a computer program. Different types of data take up different amounts of space. Some common data types are integer, float (for floating point numbers), or string (for a text string). If a procedure is expecting one data type and it gets another, you could get an error message or a crash, but that depends specifically on the programming language being used.

Data warehouse A database, frequently very large, that can access all of a company's information. While the warehouse can be distributed over several computers and may contain several databases and information from numerous sources in a variety of formats, it should be accessible through a server. Thus, access to the warehouse is transparent to the user, who can use simple commands to retrieve and analyze all the information. The data warehouse also contains data about how the warehouse is organized, where the information can be found, and any connections between data. Frequently used for decision support within an organization, the data warehouse also allows the organization to organize its data, coordinate updates, and see relationships between information gathered from different parts of the organization.

Data mining is the discovery and modeling of hidden patterns in large amounts of data. It is usually case-based, in that the parameters can be statistically modeled. Technically, data mining is statistical analysis, but on a complex scale. IBM invented data mining and holds some of the patents. One of the goals of data mining is to allow the user to discover patterns and build models automatically, without knowing exactly what she's looking for.

The models are both descriptive and prospective. They address why things happened and what is likely to happen next. A user can pose "what-if" questions to a data-mining model that can not be queried directly from the database or warehouse. Examples include: "What is the expected lifetime value of every customer account," "Which customers are likely to open a second account," or "Will this customer cancel our service if we introduce higher fees?" (Questions like this assume a Natural Language front end.)

Text mining is a subset of data mining which applies the same rules and logic, but is directed at gleaning information from large bodies of text rather than numerical data. The information technologies associated with making data mining a functional process are neural networks, genetic algorithms, fuzzy logic, and rule induction. Data mining is becoming more prevalent as businesses, governments and organizations look for ways to leverage the existing mountains of information they already have.

Database A file created by a database manager that contains a collection of information organized into records, each of which contains labeled categories (called fields).

Database administrator (DBA) A person whose job it is to manage databases. A DBA's tasks may include assigning security privileges to the databases, creating and designing databases, and controlling the importing and exporting of data between databases and external sources. The creation and design of databases is a science. You can increase or decrease performance greatly by designing a database properly or improperly.

Datagram A packet of information medium and associated delivery information, such as the destination address, that is routed through a packet-switching network.

Data-link layer The second of seven layers of the International Standards Organization's Open Systems Interconnection (ISO/OSI) model for computer-to-computer communications. The data-link layer validates the integrity of the flow of data from one node to another by synchronizing blocks of data, and by controlling the flow of data.

Dataviews Graphical user interface development software from V.I.Corporation, aimed at constructing platform-independent interactive views of dynamic data.

Daughter board (daughter board) A circuit board that plugs into a larger circuit board, or motherboard. Often processors are contained on daughterboards, along with cache memory. For example, Intel's Pentium II (and pre-FC-PGA Pentium III) processors shipped on a daughter board that plugs into the Slot 1 on the motherboard.

DAV (digital audio video) Connectors such as those found on the Apple AV that allow the flow of digitized video to bypass the computer's main bus.

Db (decibel) A logarithmic measure of sound intensity. It is equal to 10 times the common logarithm of the ratio of sound intensity to a reference intensity. A rating of 85 dB is loud, and prolonged exposure to those sound levels could damage hearing.

DB (data bus) connector Any of several types of cable connectors used for parallel or serial cables. The number after DB represents how many pins the connector has;i.e., DB-25 has twenty-five pins.

DB/DC database/data communication This acronym refers to IBM's collection of transaction managers and database managers, e.g., Customer Information Control System, Information Management System, Database-2 and SQL/DS.

DB-25 The name for the connector used for parallel ports on PCs. It has 25 pins, as you would expect.

DBMS Database Management System. A complete software facility for building, maintaining and generating reports from a database. It has evolved along three generic forms :

Hierarchical DBMS (1960s) - records were organised in a pyramid-like structure, with each record linked to a parent.

Network DBMS(1970s) - records could have many parents, with embedded pointers indicating the physical location of all related records in a file relational DBMS (1980s) - records were conceptually held in tables, similar in concept to a spreadsheet. Relationships between the data entities were kept separate from itself. Data manipulation created new tables, called views.

Dbx The "companding" compression and expansion of audio signals to reduce noise distortions of stereo television broadcasts.

DC (direct current) A type of electrical current that moves in one direction at a constant rate, such as a standard 9 volt battery. Batteries provide direct current.

DCC (data country code) This specifies the country in which an address is registered. The codes are given in ISO 3166. The length of this field is two octets. The digits of the data country code are encoded in Binary Coded Decimal (BCD) syntax. The codes will be left justified and padded on the right with the hexadecimal value "F" to fill the two octets.

DCC (digital compact cassette) Format that improves sound quality relative to traditional analog formats of audio cassettes. Analog cassettes can be played on DCC tape decks such that the purchase of a DCC tape deck does not preclude listening to analog tapes.

DCE (distributed computing environment) DCE is the Open Software Foundation's solution to the problems of interconnectivity in a heterogeneous computing environment, standards and security. The DCE is composed of two sets of services : fundamental services from Digital Equipment Corp., Hewlett-Packard, the Massachusetts Institute of Technology, and Siemens, and data-sharing services from Microsoft, Sun Microsystems and Transarc. DCE integrates remote procedure calls, presentation services, a naming directory, security, threads (sequential flow of control similar to task) , time services (to synchronise clocks in a DCE) and a distributed file system.

DCF Document Composition Facility.

DCI (display control interface) A device-driver specification from Intel and Microsoft intended to speed up video playback in Microsoft Windows. Multimedia applications and programs that manage digital video benefit from the usage of DCI.

DCOM (distributed component object model) Yet another Microsoft technology. It is a version of the COM that is designed to work across networks and, specifically, the Internet.

DCS (desktop color separation) An image format consisting of four separate CMYK PostScript files at full resolution, together with a fifth EPS master for placement in documents.

DDE (dynamic data exchange) A method of exchanging data between applications on MacOS, Windows, and OS/2 operating systems. DDE is similar to OLE, but predates it. It enables multiple applications to have access to the same data, such as a word processor having data from a spreadsheet pasted into it. Changes made in either application to the data are reflected in the main document.

DDIF (digital document interchange format) A CDA specification for representing compound documents in revisable format; a DEC standard for document encoding.

DDN (defense data network) A global communications network serving the US Department of Defense composed of MILNET, other portions of the Internet, and classified networks which are not part of the Internet. The DDN is used to connect military installations and is managed by the Defense Information Systems Agency (DISA).

DDR Double data rate is a type of SDRAM in which data is sent on both the rising and falling edges of clock cycles in a data burst. It is usually referred to as DDR as opposed to DDR SDRAM.

DDR SDRAM (double data rate SDRAM) A standard that is used to boost conventional SDRAM memory up to speeds of 200MHz and beyond.Standard SDRAM tops out around 150-166MHz, and DDR SDRAM starts at 200MHz by effectively doubling the speed of 100MHz SDRAM by sending two bits of data per clock cycle. A new standard called DDR II will push DDR SDRAM over 400MHz effective speeds, where standard DDR trails off.

DDS (digital data storage) A storage standard used with medium cost tape media and tape drives, used mainly for small businesses and departmental backups. DDS tapes are the same size and form factor as DAT tapes used to store music digitally on tape media, but DDS media is more robust and more expensive. There are four different DDS standards: DDS-1 through DDS-4. The four standards allow for backup of 2 GB, 4 GB, 12 GB, and 20 GB worth of uncompressed (native) storage respectively. Storage sizes are typically listed as double for compressed data. DDS media is good for up to 10 years, but should not be used for more than 100 backups or it may become unreliable. DDS tapes are falling to the wayside as DLT, AIT, and other standards offer higher reliability. Sony and HP have both announced that they will not be supporting DDS-5, which pushes DDS data storage up to 40 GB of native storage per tape.

DDTS Distributed Defect Tracking System.

Deactivation The process of removing a domain name from the zone files for the top level domains. When a domain name is deactivated, the Domain Name System (DNS) will no longer have the information needed to resolve the domain name to its corresponding Internet Protocol (IP) number(s), effectively disabling the domain name as a tool for locating the related computers or organizations. InterNIC refers to this status as being "On Hold." The domain name record, however, remains in InterNIC' domain name database.

Debit accounts A payment system for InterNIC' customers who regularly register large numbers of domain names, e.g., Internet Service Providers (ISPs). Customers establish a debit account with a minimum deposit, and then as they receive invoices they contact InterNIC' debit accounts section and request that the invoices be paid from the available account funds.

Debug The act of diagnosing, fixing, or removing bugs from a computer programs. It can also be used to describe the fixing of bugs in HTML or other computer-based texts that are not necessarily programs. The first computer "bug" was an actual moth, and debugging that computer involved physically removing the moth from the system, as it was impeding electrical flow.

Debugger A program that searches other programs for bugs. In addition to identifying definite or possible bugs, debuggers can usually step through programs one operation at a time. Debuggers are associated with a particular programming language, and are typically packaged as part of a programming language or set of programming tools.

Debugging Executing a program, one statement at a time, to identify and fix errors.

DEC alpha A 64-bit microprocessor from Digital Equipment Corporation, introduced in 1992. It is a superscalar design, which allows the processor to execute more than one instruction per clock cycle.

Decibel (Db) A logarithmic measure of sound intensity. It is equal to 10 times the common logarithm of the ratio of sound intensity to a reference intensity. A rating of 85 dB is loud, and prolonged exposure to those sound levels could damage hearing.

Decimal system A number system in which each place represents a power of 10 larger than the place to its right (base-10).

Decision trees Classifiers in which a sequence of tests are made to decide the class label to assign to an unknown data item; the sequence of tests can be visualized as having a tree structure.

Decnet The network marketed by DEC to connect its computers together.

Decoder A circuit or device that restores a coded signal to its original form based on knowledge of the process used to code the signal.

Decoding Decoding is the process by which attachments are returned to their original form after having been subjected to encoding for transmission over the Internet. If the sender of the file has used a form of decoding appropriate to your computer and e-mail program, the decoding will occur automatically. If this is not the case, you may be able to set up a helper application for this purpose. If you receive a file that needs special decoding, you can sometimes identify the required form of decoding by the three letter extension at the end of the file's name.

Decompression The expansion of compressed image files.

Decrement To decrease the value of a variable by one. In java Script, this can be done with the decrement operator,++.

Decryption Decryption is the process of converting encrypted data back into its original form, so it can be understood.

DeCSS A program that was developed to allow Linux to read DVD movies scrambled with the Content Scrambling System. The writers of the program reverse engineered the CSS scrambling method that the MPAA (Motion Picture Association of America) uses to prevent playing of DVD movies on unlicensed DVD players. DeCSS also allows DVD data to be decoded and translated into other formats. However, you can copy DVD movies without using DeCSS, as DVD content does not have to be decoded to be copied.

Dedicated hosting A hosting feature that allows a Web site to have its own server. This is more flexible than shared hosting , as webmasters typically have full control over the back end of the server, including choice of OS. Administration, however, is still handled by the hosting company.

Dedicated line A telephone or data line that is always available. For example, a leased telephone line can be dedicated for computer data communications. This line is not used by other computers or individuals, is available 24 hours a day, and is never disconnected.

Default gateway The default host is used by internal computers as a gateway to communicate with the Internet.

Demilitarized zone (DMZ) A network isolated from the trusted or secure network by a firewall. Network administrators often isolate public resources, such as Web or email servers in the DMZ to prevent an intruder from attacking the internal network.

Denial of service (DoS) Flooding an IP address with useless traffic in order to cause legitimate connection attempts to fail. DoS attacks do not reveal sensitive data to the attacker, however, they can cause untold damage to reputation as well as lost business.

Default node representation A single value for each nodal state parameter giving the presumed value between any entry or exit to the logical node and the nucleus.

Default route A routing table entry which is used to direct packets addressed to networks not explicitly listed in the routing table.

Default The fallback value. If nothing else is specified the default value will be used. If you install a program it generally installs with the default settings unless you override the pre-programmed settings with your preferences.

Default value (valeur par defaut) Implicitly used value, when no explicit value has been used by the user.

Defense advanced research projects agency (DARPA) The central research and development organization for the United States Department of Defense. It manages and directs selected basic and applied research and development projects for the Department, and pursues research and technology where risk and payoff are both very high and where success may provide dramatic advances for traditional military roles and missions and dual-use applications.

Deferred procedure call Method used in Windows NT® and Windows 2000 for event scheduling.

Deformations Mechanical systems where a structure is physically misshapen, e.g., dented.

Defragment When you defragment a hard drive you use a software utility to arrange the order of your files so that each file is represented in a physically continuous segment. Defragmentation can improve your hard drive performance because it can read any particular file in a continuous stream instead of jumping here and there around a hard drive to locate each file segment.

Defragmenter Any uitility program that rewrites all the parts of a file into contiguous clusters on a hard disk.

Degauss To remove magnetism from a device. The term is usually used in reference to color monitors and other display devices that use a Cathode Ray Tube (CRT). These devices aim electrons onto the display screen by creating magnetic fields inside the CRT. External magnetic forces — such as the earth's natural magnetism or a magnet placed close to the monitor — can magnetize the shadow mask, causing distorted images and colors. To remove this external magnetic forces, most monitors automatically degauss the CRT whenever you turn on the monitor. In addition, many monitors have a manual degauss button that performs a more thorough degaussing of the CRT. You can also use an external degausser that degausses the monitor from the outside. Since it may be impossible to remove the external magnetic force, degaussing works by re-aligning the magnetic fields inside the CRT to compensate for the external magnetism.

Degrade To reduce quality or performance of a system.

Deletion The process of removing a domain name and its corresponding record from the Domain Name System (DNS) and InterNIC' domain name database. A deleted domain name cannot be used to locate computers on the Internet and will be made available for other parties to register on a first-come, first-served basis. A domain name may be deleted at the request of the domain name registrant, as a result of non-payment of fee, or due to circumstances particular to individual cases.

Delimited The separation of data elements in a text file by a character or combination of characters. The character that separates the elements is the delimiter. The most common form of delimited file is tab delimited, as tab characters are not often used within data elements, and are easily understood by most operating systems and character formats.

Delimiter A text character that marks the beginning and/or end of a unit of data or separates different data components. For example, periods are used as delimiters in domain names, hyphens and parentheses are used in phone numbers and social security numbers, and blank spaces and commas are used in written text. In HTML the opening delimiter of an element or tag is the less than symbol, <, and the closing delimiter is greater than symbol, >.

Dell computer US PC manufacturer, among the 5 largest in this business.

Delphi An object-oriented object-oriented development system from Borland.

Delta project A European Economic Community (EEC) funded project of the Commission of European Communities. With a budget of over $100 million, this is probably the world's largest attempt to apply modern technologies to distance training and education. Partners in the project include major universities, telecommunications companies, and business firms of all sizes across the EEC. Collis and de Vries (1994) report on 27 major projects with over 300 sub-projects in network education and multimedia development.

Delta The information which differentiates a version version from members of its immediate family.

Delta-4 Definition and Design of an open Dependable Distributed system architecture. An Esprit Esprit project investigating the achievement of dependability in open distributed systems, including real-time real-time systems.

Deltase A distributed processing environment concerned with fault-tolerant and process-control applications from the Esprit Esprit Delta-4 Delta-4 project.

Demand paging A common form of virtual memory management where pages of information are read into memory from disk only when required by the program.

Demilitarized zone (DMZ) A part of a network that is protected by a firewall, but may be accessed by external Internet clients. The DMZ generally contains servers such as SMTP servers, remote access machines. or webservers. Client machines and internal servers that do not need to be accessed by Internet clients are kept in a more protected segment of the network than the DMZ. Alternately, DMZ can be used to refer to the media layer where route peering is done among multiple administrative regions with their own traffic policies.

Demodulation This is the process of converting analog information (like over phone lines) into digital information (like in a computer).

Demographics The study of the statistical data pertaining to a population

Demon (daemon) A term mainly used regarding UNIX processes. A daemon (or demon) is a process that starts and does nothing until it is called by another process or a certain condition is met. This is similar to a TSR program.

Demultiplexer (demux) A logic circuit that takes a single input and sends it to one of several outputs. In networking, it is used to describe a device that receives a transmission of several signals over a single line and can properly decode the single line signal into multiple signals.

Demultiplexing A function performed by a layer entity that identifies and separates SDUs from a single connection to more than one connection.

Denial of service (DoS) A type of network attack that attempts to render a network or Internet resource useless to users, typically by sending large amounts of repeated requests for data. The target may be e-mail services or an IRC server, or it could be access to a particular website. The methods of attack vary, but the end result is that a resource is artificially slowed down or unavailable to legitimate users.

Density Density is a brightness control to lighten or darken a printout to more closely reflect its screen appearance and to compensate for deficiencies in toner or paper quality.

Densitometer A measuring instrument that registers the density of transparent or reflective materials. Colors are read as tonal information.

Deploy To distribute Content Security clients to desktops throughout a network.

Deregulation The lowering of restrictions, rules, or regulations pertaining to an activity or operation (often commercial).

DES (data encryption standard) An encryption method developed by IBM in 1977. It uses a private 56-bit key that is applied to each 64- bit block of data. The sender and receiver must each know the private key. Anything encrypted by DES encryption has 72,000,000,000,000,000 (or 72 quadrillion) possible keys. DES encryption has been broken, but it took over 14,000 computers operating in succession to crank through codes until the proper key was found.

DES (destination end station) An ATM termination point which is the destination for ATM messages of a connection and is used as a reference point for ABR services.

Descreening Removal of halftone dot patterns during or after scanning printed matter by defocusing the image. This avoids moire patterning and color shifts during subsequent halftone reprinting.

Design Design is usually considered to be the phase of software development following analysis, and concerned with how the problem is to be solved.

Design recovery A subset of reverse engineering reverse-engineering in which domain knowledge, external information, and deduction of fuzzy reasoning are added to the observations of the subject system to identify meaningful higher level abstraction beyond those obtained directly by examining the system itself.

Desktop A display of one or more icons representing system resources.

Desktop case A computer case designed to sit on your desktop. It's wider than it is tall and sturdy enough to put a heavy CRT monitor on top of it.

Desktop commands (DTC) Commands used in the Advanced Development Environment (ADE) to manipulate a dialog / instance.

Desktop management interface (DMI) A system that allows computers to send distress signals to a main system on a network. It is a means to detect problems before they crash the computer irrecoverably.

Desktop management task force (DMTF) This motley crew was assembled to create the DMI standard.

Desktop manager A user interface to system services, usually icon and menu based like the Macintosh Finder, enabling the user to run applications and use a filing system without directly using the command language of the operating system.

Desktop publishing A fancy type of word processing. A desktop publishing program lets you do typesetting and is useful for preparing books, newsletters, and the like. The most common Unix desktop publishing programs are Interleaf and FrameMaker.

Desktop search Search utilities that search for words, phrases, characters, pictures, and even multimedia files on your personal computer. Popular alternatives are from Google (GDS) , Yahoo, and Microsoft.

Destructor A function provided by a class in C++ to delete an object.

DESX 120-bit encryption (DES extended) A Data Encryption Standard (DES) with over 72,000,000,000,000,000 (72 quadrillion) possible encryption keys. For each given message, the key is chosen at random from among this enormous number of keys.

Developer A person who creates computer programs, and may specialize in one or more methods of creating computer programs, Web pages, or programming languages, such as Java, C++, or Fortran, for example.

Development The process of analysis, design, coding and testing software.

Device Any circuit that performs a specific function, such as a parallel port.

Device bay An industry specification that defines a mechanism for both peripheral devices and system bays that allows adding and upgrading PC peripheral devices without opening the chassis.

Device bay interface specification A specification originally designed to provide a simple and generic way of interfacing computers and their components.Device Bay devices are about the size of a VCR tape, and would have interfaced via USB or FireWire, making it easy to plug a new hard drive or other device into the front of your PC. However, Device Bay never took off, as it was expected in 1998 but never arrived.

Device driver This is basically synonymous with the term "driver." It's a piece of software that tells an operating system specifically how to communicate with a device. For high speed devices such as 3D graphics cards, using an up-to-date device driver is important to guarantee performance and stability.

Device ID A unique ASCII string for the device created by enumerators to identify a hardware device and used to cross-reference data about the device stored in the registry. Distinguishes each logical device and bus from all others on the system.

Device node The basic data structure for a given device, built by the Configuration Manager. Device nodes are built into memory at system startup for each device and enumerator. Each device node contains information about the device, such as currently assigned resources.

Device object A kernel-mode-only object type used to represent a physical, logical, or virtual device whose driver has been loaded into the system.

Device-dependence The requirement that a specific hardware component be present for a program to work.

Device-independent bitmap A file format designed to ensure that bitmap graphics created using one application can be loaded and displayed in another application exactly the way they appeared in the originating application.

DFD Data-Flow-Diagram.

DFS (distributed file system) A Microsoft technology introduced in Windows 2000 that allows multiple servers and shared directories on a network to appear as a single network drive, thus helping to ease the annoying problem of running out of drive letters in complex environments. With DFS, you can have your users' H: drive, for example, be a collection of network resources instead of just a single share.

DGL data generation language A tool for generating test data for hardware or software systems.

DHCP (dynamic host configuration protocol) A method of automatically assigning a TCP/IP address to a client. A DHCP server is used to dole out a TCP/IP address from a pool of TCP/IP addresses to a client that supports DHCP. When you connect to your ISP over a modem or broadband you are typically assigned a dynamic (non-static) TCP/IP address via DHCP. The big advantage to DHCP is that you don't need to manually assign a TCP/IP address to a client—the DHCP server takes care of that. After an amount of time passes where the client does not contact the server, the server puts the TCP/IP address of the client back into the pool to be assigned to that client or any other client hat requests a TCP/IP address. The disadvantage of DHCP for the DHCP client is that the client is not guaranteed to have a particular TCP/IP address at any given time. For that you want a static IP address.

DHTML (dynamic html) This was independently defined by Microsoft and Netscape and implemented in version 4 of their browsers to allow for more dynamic and user-interactive Web pages, and better positioning of Web elements. Both the Netscape and Microsoft versions of dynamic HTML include some support for Cascading Style Sheets, which is a real standard defined by the World Wide Web Consortium.

Diagnostics A procedure or program that is run internally to test a piece of software or hardware and ensure that it is operating properly. For example, if R2-D2 of Star Wars decided to start running into walls, C3PO would probably make him run diagnostics on himself to try to figure out what his problem was.

Diagonal linear measurement "Official" screen size is the diagonal measurement of the CRT before its mounted in the monitor cabinet. Some monitor CRT category sizes are 14", 15", 17", 19", and 21".

Dial-back A remote access connection to a company network using a modem and telephone line.

Dial-back authentication A safety measure where a host modem dials back to a predefined number to resume contact and continue authentication.

Dial-in An Internet account that connects a PC directly to the Internet. These accounts use a software application to connect to an Internet Service Provider (ISP) and establish a TCP/IP link to the Internet. To access a dial-in connection, a PC needs either a modem to connect via a regular phone line or a terminal adapter (TA) to connect via an ISDN phone line.

Dialog A two-way communication link between an administrator and one or more TME resources.

Dialog box Rectangle displayed on the screen after selecting certain menu options. Dialog boxes propose complementary options in relation with the requested operation.

Dialog editing library (DEL) A library of C functions that permits dynamic, persistent creation and editing of dialog descriptors at run-time.

Dialog specification language (DSL) Provides the dialog layout and interaction for handling application output and input.

Dialup A method of connecting to the Internet via the regular phone system through a modem, rather than one through an internal network (LAN) or permanent leased telephone line. This is the most likely way you would connect to the Internet from home if you have not made any special arrangement with your local telephone company or your Internet Service Provider (ISP). For alternative connections, you might want to consult with your ISP first.

Dial-up connection The most popular form of Net connection for the home user, this is a connection from your computer to a host computer over standard telephone lines.

Dial-up line A communication connection from your computer to a host computer over standard phone lines. Unlike a dedicated line, you must dial the host computer in order to establish a connection. Dial-up line is currently the most popular form of Net connection for the home user.

Dial-up networking A component in Windows 95 that enables you to connect your computer to a network via a modem. If your computer is not connected to a LAN and you want to connect to the Internet, you need to configure Dial-Up Networking (DUN) to dial a Point of Presence (POP) and log into your Internet Service Provider (ISP). Your ISP will need to provide certain information, such as the gateway address and your computer's IP address. You access DUN through the My Computer icon. You can configure a different profile (called a connectoid) for each different online service you use. Once configured, you can copy a connectoid shortcut to your desktop so that all you need to do to make a connection is double-click the connectoid icon.

DIB (dual independent bus) The bus architecture between Intel's Pentium II processor, memory, and L2 cache. One bus connects the processor to L2 cache and a second connects the processor to main memory. Having two buses instead of one increases performance over single-bus architectures. In addition, the speed of the external L2 cache can scale up independently from the speed of the system bus.This allows for faster cache access. The final feature of the DIB architecture is a pipeline on the cache to the processor bus that allows multiple simultaneous cache requests.

Dichroic mirror A special type of interference filter, which reflects a specific part of the spectrum, whilst transmitting the rest. Used in scanners to split a beam of light into RGB components.

Die An individual rectangular pattern on a wafer that contains circuitry to perform a specific function. Die are encapsulated to form the black chips that are then placed on a module.

Die size Simply put, this is the two dimensional (length by width) measurement of a microprocessor. The thickness of the processor is not considered. Typical die sizes range between 20-500 square millimeters with most consumer processors from Intel and AMD around the 80-200 square mm mark. Smaller die size allows more chips to be created with a given amount of raw materials.

Dielectric A material that exhibits insulating properties, as opposed to conducting properties.

Diesel generator A diesel-powered generator used by hosting companies as a back-up source to generate electricity in the event of a power outage.

Difference engine A mechanical calculator designed by Charles Babbage that automated the production of mathematical tables by using the method of differences.

Differential analyzer A computer constructed in the early 1930s by Vannevar Bush at Massachusetts Institute of Technology (MIT); it solved differential equations by mechanical integration.

Differential SCSI This type of SCSI is used to connect devices that are far apart or that may suffer from interference. Standard SCSI cabling is limited to 6 meters; differential SCSI supports distances of up to 25 meters away from the SCSI host adapter.

Diffie-hellman key agreement An approach that allows two parties to use unencrypted text to agree on a key for symmetric encryption without compromising the key itself.

Digest Scrambled data unit created by a one-way hash function and used in a digital signature to identify a document and ensure the integrity of its data.

Digital (DEC) digital equipment corporation Maynard, California. Third worldwide computer manufacturer, recentered on processors business, and more especially the 64-bit Alpha chip.

Digital A system that defines data in a discrete, non-fluctuating (i.e., non-analogue), numerical method. Similar to a binary system.

Digital audio Analog sound waves stored in a digital form; each digital audio file can be decomposed into a series of samples.

Digital audio tape (DAT) This type of magnetic tape, introduced by Sony, at one point threatened to supplant the normal audio cassette with a better quality alternative. Unfortunately, it never really took off due to foolish licensing issues that kept its price very high.However, the small tapes took off big in the computer industry. You can get DAT drives today that hold up to 40 GB of data compressed with DDS-4. Audio DAT tapes are not compatible with data drives.

Digital certificates Certificates used in authentication that contain encrypted digital identification information.

Digital control A control that doesn't directly cause a physical change in something, but rather sends a signal that a processor interprets. The processor then makes the change. An example of a digital control would be a television set with buttons instead of knobs.

Digital cross-connect system (DCS) Pronounced "dax;" a digital version of or replacement for the analog data center patch panels.

Digital data storage (DDS) A storage standard used with medium cost tape media and tape drives, used mainly for small businesses and departmental backups. DDS tapes are the same size and form factor as DAT tapes used to store music digitally on tape media, but DDS media is more robust and more expensive. There are four different DDS standards: DDS-1 through DDS-4. The four standards allow for backup of 2 GB, 4 GB, 12 GB, and 20 GB worth of uncompressed (native) storage respectively. Storage sizes are typically listed as double for compressed data. DDS media is good for up to 10 years, but should not be used for more than 100 backups or it may become unreliable. DDS tapes are falling to the wayside as DLT, AIT, and other standards offer higher reliability. Sony and HP have both announced that they will not be supporting DDS-5, which pushes DDS data storage up to 40 GB of native storage per tape.

Digital divide Imaginary line separating those who can access digital information from those who cannot.

Digital envelope A type of security that uses two layers of encryption to protect a message. First, the message itself is encoded using symmetric encryption. Next, then the key to decode the message is encrypted using public-key encryption. By only using public-key encryption on the key, overhead is reduced, thereby overcoming one of the problems of public-key encryption, i.e., that it is slower than symmetric encryption.

Digital library Distributed access to collections of digital information

Digital light processing (DLP) A video projection technology that uses hundreds of thousands of rotating mirrors to project high quality, high definition images. DLP was originally developed by Texas Instruments.

Digital linear tape (DLT) A technology designed by DEC and sold to Quantum used for backing up huge amounts of data (up to 35 GB per tape without compression, 70 GB with compression). The drives are very expensive and so is the media, but they are bulletproof.

Digital millennium copyright act (DMCA) A controversial reform of the U.S. copyright laws that is the first attempt to update those laws for the age of digital technology. It covers circumvention of copyright protections, fair use of copyrighted materials, and protection of ISPs from liability—as long as they follow certain practices. However, DMCA also prohibits circumventing of access controls and copyrights, and bans devices which do such circumvention. The problems with this arise when computer scientists, security analysts, users, etc., are unable to test supposedly secure products for lax security, and if they do find lax security they are unable to tell anyone or they could face prosecution. The first major DMCA case involved a Russian programmer whose company created software that allowed the bypassing of eBook security by Adobe. This allowed legitimate users to back up their eBooks and use them in different formats, which is legal by fair use standards; but it also allowed illegitimate users to potentially make pirated copies of the eBooks, which the DMCA prohibits.

Digital private network signalling system (DPNSS) A Common Channel Signalling (CCS) protocol used in telecommunications networks.

Digital signal level 0 (DS-0) The signal used to carry a standard analog or digital phone line connection. 24 DS-0 connections can be carried on a T1 line. The speed of the line is either 64Kbps, or 56Kbps if the eighth bit is used for signaling information.

Digital signal level 1 (DS-1) Synonym for T1.

Digital signal level 2 (DS-2) Synonym for T2.

Digital signal level 3 (DS-3) Synonym for T3.

Digital signal level 4 (DS-4) Synonym for T4.

Digital signal level 5 (DS-5) Synonym for T5.

Digital signal processor (DSP) A DSP is a microprocessor designed to work with analog signals such as video or audio that have been digitally encoded. The DSP then takes these digital representations and performs operations on them. DSPs are used in video, sound, and modem technology. Intel's MMX instruction set was the first attempt to make x86 processors (specifically the Pentium processor line) more capable of DSP operations. This follows Intel's theory of putting all the processor work onto its processors. However, DSP chips are still used in many devices for PCs, as they can keep the CPU from being bogged down.

Digital signature A form of electronic signature that works with a public and private key encryption system and a certificate authority. To sign an electronic document with a digital signature, you use digital signature software to select the document and enter an authorization code that is unique to your digital signature. The signature consists of a string of characters and the signer's name, title, company, certificate serial number, and the name of the certificate authority.

Digital subscriber line (DSL) A form of high-speed Internet access currently competing with cable modems. DSL works over standard copper phone lines. In fact, most DSL service is limited to only copper lines, where fiber optics and Digital Loop Connects will actually cause problems in rolling out DSL to entire areas. DSL is still preferred by many technical users as it is a direct connection that is theoretically not bogged down by other users in the area like cable modems can be.

Digital subscriber loop (DSL) The enabling of high-speed digital data transfer over standard telephone cables and systems in conjunction with normal telephone speech data.

Digital television (DTV) Standard television signals are in analog format. Some HDTV systems (such as Japan's early efforts) use analog signals as well. Digital Television refers to the standard of transmitting and receiving television signals using purely digital transmission.

Digital This implies a value represented by a group of discrete steps. Some claim that digital representations of images and sound are more accurate; others that the translation of analog sounds and pictures into digital representations causes loss in realism. The bonus to digital reproduction is that if done well enough and designed to correct errors, digital reproduction can sound good over a long period of time. Records and tapes are analog, CDs are digital. Play a CD a million times and it should sound the same. Play a record a million times and it will degrade due to the weight of the stylus changing the physical record over time and the inherent friction involved in analog systems.

Digital to analog convertor (DAC) An electronic device that converts digital signals into analog signals. You can find DACs in a variety of devices, including sound cards. The DAC would be used to convert digital signals from your computer into analog signals that can be sent to your speakers—assuming you use standard analog speakers.

Digital variable/versatile/video disc (DVD) This is much like a CD-ROM except that it stores over 7 times as much data in its simplest form. DVD is the successor to CD-ROM technology. DVD discs are the same size physically as CD-ROM discs, but hold between 4.7-18 GB of data using dual-layer and double-sided discs. The first wave of DVD drives were read-only devices, but newer versions (such as DVD-R/+R/-RW/+RW/-RAM) are beginning to work with write-once and rewriteable media.

Digital video interface (DVI) A connection standard for linking a video card and a display that requires a digital signal, such as an LCD panel. Analog video signals can also be used with the DVI interface. It has 24 pins, 12 for each channel. A single channel can handle 1600x1200 resolution at 60Hz. Dual channels can do 2048x1536 or even higher resolutions.

Digital watermarks Special data structures permanently embedded into a program or other file type, which contain information about the author and the program.

Digital-to-analog converter DAC or D-A converter. a device that converts discrete digital information into a continuously varying analog signal.

Digitizers A purely graphical input device - i.e., a computer-aided design/computer-aided manufacturing system device used in computer-aided engineering for converting locations into storable electronic impulses - with a surface on which a location or point is selected and then automatically converted into a digital X-Y co-ordinate suitable for transmission to a computer.

DII dynamic invocation interface An OMG specification.

Dijkstra's algorithm An algorithm that is sometimes used to calculate routes given a link and nodal state topology database.

Dill The abbreviated way to say "DLL," which is a Windows file extension that stands for dynamic link library.

DIMM (dual in-line memory module) A circuit board with memory chips on it, very much like a SIMM except that it is larger and contains more pins. DIMMs are 64-bit memory devices, so you just need a single DIMM for a processor with a 64-bit memory path to work properly; or you can potentially double up DIMMs for a 128-bit memory interface if your motherboard supports it. Most memory today is sold on DIMMs.

Din connector A German standard used mostly for audio applications. DIN connectors are used for keyboards, PS/2 style mice, MIDI, and Apple printer attachments. DIN connectors are round.

DIN (deutsche institut fuer normung) The German standardisation body, a member of ISO.

Diode An electronic device with two electrodes/ terminals, one called the cathode and the other the anode, and a single PN junction (which uses part P-type and part N-type semiconductor material). The diode will conduct current in only one direction, and only when the cathode voltage is positive relative to the anode voltage by a specified amount. The specific voltage depends on which semiconductor materials the PN junction is manufactured from. Diodes are often used as a rectifier to convert AC power to DC, but they have many uses.

Diode tube An obsolete form of diode that was made of metal elements in a sealed and evacuated glass tube.

DIP document image processing Storage, management and retrieval of images.

DIP dual in-line package Standard format for integrated circuits manufacturing, in which silicon-engraved microcircuits are embedded in a rectangular plastic or ceramic container, and connected on each long side of the circuit through pins directed towards the bottom.

DIP switch dual in-line package Case on a computer board that contains small switches for configuring hardware components. A given board can be configured in a way that is compatible with the entire system of other peripheral hardware.

Dip switch One or more switches that are housed in a rectangular box on a circuit board. The switches are binary in nature, either on or off for each switch. Dip switches were more common on old ISA cards, and are often used in place of groups of jumpers. Nowadays Plug-and-Play and the abundance of Flash memory for saving settings have all but eliminated these nasty things in consumer PCs.

DIR This is a field in an RM-cell which indicates the direction of the RM- cell with respect to the data flow with which it is associated. The source sets DIR=0 and the destination sets DIR=1.

Direct access storage device(DASD) A storage device such as a hard disk, whose data can be accessed directly, without having to read all the preceding data.

Direct connection A permanent communication connection between your computer system (either a single CPU or a LAN) and the Internet. This is also called a leased line connection because you are leasing the telephone connection from the phone company. A direct connection is in contrast to a SLIP/PPP or dial-up connection.

Direct current A type of electrical current that moves in one direction at a constant rate, such as a standard 9 volt battery. Batteries provide direct current.

Direct memory access (DMA) A method of transferring information directly from a mass-storage device such as a hard disk or from an adapter card in memory (or vice versa), without the information passing through the processor. because the processor is not involved in the transfer, direct memory access is usually very fast. DMA transfers are controlled by a special chip known as a DMA controller; 8237A is used in most PCs. Generally, most PCs use two of these chips to provide 8 DMA channels numbered 0 through 7; channel 4 is used to connect-or cascade-the two controllers together. Channels 0 thru- 3 are 8-bit channels, and can manage up to 64K of data in a single DMA operation; channels 5 thru 7 transfer data 16 bits at a time and can manage up to 128K of data. Channel 3 is reserved for the floppy disk drive controller, and channel 5 is used by the hard-disk controller in PS/2 systems.

Direct rambus dram (DRDRAM) One possible future successor to SDRAM, and competitor to DDR SDRAM. DRDRAM (also now simply called RDRAM) was originally developed by Rambus, Inc. This RAM architecture is capable of speeds starting at 266, 356, and 400MHz, and transfers data on the up and down ticks of a clock cycle, where standard SDRAM tops out at about 200MHz. You may see RDRAM referred to at 532, 712, and 800MHz, but that is actually 2662, 3562, and 400MHz2, where the 2 denotes transfer on the up and down tick of the clock. Intel picked RDRAM to be the future of RAM for PCs, but RDRAM ran into many stumbling blocks due to the complexity of manufacturing it. RDRAM was used in the popular Nintendo 64 game machine for its high-speed capabilities and low pin count, necessary for the intense 3D rendering being done on a low complexity system. RDRAM started out using a 16- bit bus, while SDRAM and DDR have 64-bit buses. Thus, 100MHz SDRAM has half the throughput of RDRAM at 400MHz (10064 = 6,400Mbits/second; 400216 = 12,800Mbits/second). However, newer RDRAM uses a 32-bit bus and is clocked up to 533MHz2. Still, it never achieved dominance in the PC market.

Direct set A set of host interfaces which can establish direct layer two communications for unicast (not needed in MPOA).

Direct x A set of APIs developed by Microsoft that enables programmers to write programs that access hardware features of a computer without knowing exactly what hardware will be installed on the machine where the program eventually runs. DirectX achieves this by creating an intermediate layer that translates generic hardware commands into specific commands for particular pieces of hardware. In particular, DirectX lets multimedia applications take advantage of hardware acceleration features supported by graphics accelerators. DirectX 2, released in 1996, supports the Direct3D architecture. DirectX 5, released in 1998, adds new layers to the DirectX API. In addition to the low-level layer that communicates directly with multimedia hardware, DirectX 5 also includes a Media layer that enables programmers to manipulate multimedia objects and streams. DirectX 5 also supports USB and IEEE 1394 buses, AGP, and MMX.

Directdraw A set of APIs introduced for Windows 95 and NT that allow programmers to directly access the video controller, allowing for faster graphics response.

Direction buttons Buttons on a program with a graphical user interface that provide a way of navigating through information or documents.

Directive (Security.) Specific actions to be taken and directions to be followed in implementing a policy. Adherence to directives is mandatory for users.

Directory service A standard database that provides distributed, scalable, client/server-based repositories of data that are read much more frequently than they are modified. Users and applications can use directory access protocols (DAPs) to access these directories.

Directory The name for a logical container for files. Directories were devised to organize files. Without directories, all the files on your hard drive would be in one big listing. When you request a list of files from a computer, you generally only see the files within one directory. Directories can contain files and/or other directories. Nowadays, most operating systems are calling directories "folders," but we know what they really are.

Direct-to-plate Direct exposure of image data onto printing plates, without the intermediate use of film.

Direct-to-press Elimination of intermediate film and printing plates by the direct transfer of image data to printing cylinders in the press.

Dirty Not clean. A filesystem is dirty if it is in use or if there is no guarantee that the file system structure is static.

DISA Data Interchange Standards Association (USA).

Disabilities products A variety of hardware and software options for users having certain types of disabilities.

Disc at once (DAO) This is a single-session method of writing data to a CD-R/RW disc that creates a disc in a format suitable for commercial duplication. Basically, the entire disc is written at once in contrast to Track at Once.

Disclaimer A message that is attached to outgoing email in order to reduce legal liability. As a result of recent litigation, the ability to add and customize email disclaimers has become an element of network security policy.

Discussion group A section within USENET dedicated to a particular topic or interest. Discussion groups are also known as newsgroups.

Disintermediation A change in business practice whereby consumers elect to cut out intermediary agencies and deal directly with a provider or vendor.

Disk Also known as DASD, it is a round flat thing on which information is recorded in much the same way as you record stuff on a cassette tape.

Disk cache An area of computer memory where datat is temporarily stored on its way to or from a disk. A disk cache program can significantly speed up most disk operations. DOS contains the disk cache driver SMARTDRV.SYS, and OS/2 provides CACHE if you are using the high performance file system, or DISKCACHE if you are using the file allocation table system. Disk cache programs are also available from other third party sources.

Disk controller The electronic circuitry that controls and manages the operation of floppy or hard disks installed in the computer.

Disk defragmenter Arranges the blocks of information for a file into adjacent blocks on your hard drive, which may significantly improve the file access times.

Disk drive A peripheral storage device that reads and writes magnetic or optical disks. Three common types of disk drives are :floppy-disk drive, hard-disk drives, and compact disc drives.

Disk duplexing (RAID 1) There are two forms of RAID 1: disk duplexing and disk mirroring. Disk mirroring involves two hard drives that are on the same drive controller. The same data is written to both drives, so write operations are slower because you must write data to two drives. Read operations are the same speed, as if you only had one drive. Disk duplexing is much like disk mirroring, but each drive is on a separate controller. This speeds up the normally slow write operations and also adds an additional level of redundancy, in case one of your controller cards dies. With RAID 1 you get half the space you paid for because you're writing twice as much data.

Disk ISO controller Also HDC. A special-purpose chip and circuitry that directs and controls reading from and writing to a computer's disk drive.

Disk mirroring There are two forms of RAID 1: disk duplexing and disk mirroring. Disk mirroring involves two hard drives that are on the same drive controller. The same data is written to both drives, so write operations are slower because you must write data to two drives. Read operations are the same speed, as if you only had one drive. Disk duplexing is much like disk mirroring, but each drive is on a separate controller. This speeds up the normally slow write operations and also adds an additional level of redundancy, in case one of your controller cards dies. With RAID 1 you get half the space you paid for because you're writing twice as much data.

Disk operating system (DOS) This OS is what got it all started for PCs. It was produced by Microsoft and was a 16-bit command line (non-GUI) operating system, designed to run on 16-bit chips. It was still used for years on 32-bit chips. Today you can find a similar command line interface in all Windows products for quick and easy mouse-less file manipulation by running the "cmd" command.

Disk optimizer A utility program that rearranges files and directories on a disk for optimum performance.

Disk striping (raid 0) Also known as disk striping, this form of RAID combines two or more hard drives into a single logical drive. Any data is written in blocks first to one drive, then the next, and so on. A RAID 0 configuration sacrifices redundancy for raw speed. The more drives you use the faster your logical drive will be. The space available on the logical drive is the sum of space on all of the drives used, assuming that all drives are the same size. If drives are of disparate sizes, RAID 0 generally only uses a piece of the drive equal to the smallest drive. Of course, if one drive dies, you lose all of the information on the entire RAID. Use RAID 0 with care.

Disk striping with parity (raid 5) A RAID 5 configuration utilizes three or more hard drives and stripes the data across them, much like RAID 0. The difference is that parity information is striped across the drives as well, so if you lose any one drive the information can be reconstructed from the parity information. For example, with three drives the first stripe is data (on drive 1), data (on drive 2), parity (on drive 3); then data, parity, data; then parity, data, data. This pattern continues. If one drive fails, you get a mix of parity and data on the remaining two drives, and you can reconstruct all of the data. Of course, before the data is reconstructed the RAID operates in "degraded mode" and is slow. To reconstruct the data you must remove the failed drive and replace it with another, or use a "hot spare." During reconstruction the array continues to be slow. Once the RAID is reconstructed performance returns to normal levels. RAID 5 performance is similar to RAID 0 performance, but a bit slower due to the parity information. Performance increases, like RAID 0, when more drives are added. With RAID 5 you get most of the space that you've paid for, minus one drive's worth. A common option with RAID 5 is the hot spare, where a drive sits idle until needed. If you lose a drive, the hot spare takes over and the RAID is rebuilt automatically. Of course you still get the performance penalty during the rebuilding stage, but it can be set to happen automatically.

Disk suite A product from Sun Microsystems that allows the kernel to treat multiple distinct disk partitions as larger logical partitions (up to one terabyte per logical partition). It also allows for mirroring data, or storing data on multiple partitions simultaneously.

Disk-at-once recording *Single-session recording* mode, where all the data to be included on a disk is written in one pass. You must write in this mode to have your CD mass-produced by a stamping house.

Diskette This term is synonymous with floppy disk. You may also hear the long version, floppy diskette. Nowadays most people just say "disk."

Display adapter The thing inside your computer that lets it talk to the screen.

Display data channel The Plug and Play baseline for monitors. The communications channel between a monitor and the display adapter to which it is connected. This channel provides a method for the monitor to convey its identity to the display adapter.

Display postscript An extended form of PostScript PostScript permitting its interactive use with bitmap displays.

Display Unit such as CRT or LCD allowing the user to read information produced by the computer.

Distance learning The form of education where the instructor and students are separated by either location or time (or both), usually mediated by some electronic communication mechanism

Distance vector multicast routing protocol (DVMRP) A non-hierarchical, non-scaling multicast routing protocol.

Distributed component object model (DCOM) Yet another Microsoft technology. It is a version of the COM that is designed to work across networks and, specifically, the Internet.

Distributed computing environment (DCE) An OSF product. A windowing environment similar to Motif.

Distributed database A database whose objects (tables, views, columns and files) reside on more than one system in a network, and can be accessed or updated from any system in the network.

Distributed denial of service (DDoS) attack A Denial of Service attack launched against a site from multiple sources. This magnifies the intensity of the attack and helps cloak the attacker's identity. Generally the attacker places client software on a number of unsuspecting remote computers, then later uses these computers to launch an attack. A DDoS attack is more effective than a simple DoS attack and is more difficult to prevent.

Distributed file system (DFS) A Microsoft technology introduced in Windows 2000 that allows multiple servers and shared directories on a network to appear as a single network drive, thus helping to ease the annoying problem of running out of drive letters in complex environments. With DFS, you can have your users' H: drive, for example, be a collection of network resources instead of just a single share.

Distributed network computing Distributed Network Computing where a network computer can perform computing functions in another computer on the same network. In the early days of the Internet, Telnet could be used for remote computing. In modern times, the trend is toward database access and computing among networked computers.

Development tools for data enabled frameworks are starting to emerge. New standards are also starting to emerge like CORBA's IIOP, Sun's

RMI, amd Microsoft's DCOM. RMI is part of the Java programming language library which enables a Java program running on one computer to access the objects and methods of another Java program running on a different computer. Some vendors are also having their own proprietary extensions as well. IIOP is built upon CORBA technology. DCOM is Microsoft Corporation's standard for distrubuted network computing.

Distributed processing A computer system in which processing is performed by several separate computers linked by a communications network. The term often refers to any computer system supported by a network, but more properly refers to a system in which each computer is chosen to handle a specific workload, and the network supports the system as a whole.

Distributed systems Computer systems comprised of many individual computers that are interconnected and act in concert to complete operations

Distribution office support systems (DISOSS) The IBM SNA electronic mail routing architecture for their mainframes. A distributed electronic mail system.

Dither A technique used to blend pixels to cause them to appear as an intermediate color that is not displayable due to color depth limitations. It is most often used to blur ugly banding that occurs when a computer image is generated with large shade changes on low color displays, graphics generated for display on low color displays, or when making complex graphic files into simple standards such as the GIF standard, which only supports 256 colors.

Diversely routed A network is diversely routed if there are multiple routes from point A to point B.

Divx This was supposed to be a standard that would offer competition to DVD movies, and allow people to purchase Divx discs that would only be enabled for a couple of days of viewing, eliminating the hassle of returning videotapes or DVD movies after you rent them. Divx ultimately failed due to consumer disinterest. More recently, the Divx name has also served as a slang term for a form of video compression based on MPEG-4.

DL/I The data manipulation language of IMS.

DLG (digital line graph) A format for map files.

DLL (dynamic link library) A file of functions, compiled, linked, and saved separately from the processes that use them. Functions in DLLs can be used by more than one running process. The operating system maps the DLLs into the process's address space when the process is started up or while it is running. Dynamic link libraries are stored in files with the .DLL file extension.

DLM (distributed lock manager) On distributed VMS systems.

DLP projector (digital light processing projector) A display device that can project an image onto a wall or projection screen. This type of projector competes with LCD projectors, and instead of tiny embedded LCD screens it uses microchips covered with microscopic mirrors that are used to reflect light. It's possible to have a DLP projector with three separate DLP chips, similar to an LCD projector with three separate small LCD panels, but some DLP projectors use a color wheel in conjunction with a single DLP chip to produce the red, green, and blue spectrum.

DLT (digital linear tape) A technology designed by DEC and sold to Quantum used for backing up huge amounts of data (up to 35 GB per tape without compression, 70 GB with compression). The drives are very expensive.

DMA (direct memory access) Hardware devices attached to PCs (ranging from keyboards to sound cards) can be designed to send their instructions to and from main memory in one of two ways. The default is to ask the CPU to do the work. The more efficient way is to allocate one of the PC's DMA channels to send instructions directly to memory. This leaves the CPU free to do more important things. Like IRQs, DMA channels are limited in number, and you can't allocate one channel to more than one device. Most users come in contact with DMA when they install a sound card that—if they're lucky—picks the right channel during setup.

Dmax The point of maximum density in an image or an original.

DMCA (digital millennium copyright act) A controversial reform of the U.S. copyright laws that is the first attempt to update those laws for the age of digital technology. It covers circumvention of copyright protections, fair use of copyrighted materials, and protection of ISPs from liability—as long as they follow certain practices. However, DMCA also prohibits circumventing of access controls and copyrights, and bans devices which do such circumvention. The problems with this arise when computer scientists, security analysts, users, etc., are unable to test supposedly secure products for lax security, and if they do find lax security they are unable to tell anyone or they could face prosecution. The first major DMCA case involved a Russian programmer whose company created software that allowed the bypassing of eBook security by Adobe. This allowed legitimate users to back up their eBooks and use them in different formats, which is legal by fair use standards; but it also allowed illegitimate users to potentially make pirated copies of the eBooks, which the DMCA prohibits.

DME distributed management environment From the Open Software Foundation, DME will result in architectures and services that will simplify systems management applications across multiple platforms. DME includes such tasks as backup/restore, printing services, software installations, software distribution and user management. A more global initiative allows organisations to have a consistent approach to managing their systems.

Dmf A special format for 3.5" floppy disks that permits storing 1.68 MB of data on a standard 1.44-MB disk. This enables Microsoft to provide more software on fewer disks. For example, with a product like Office 95, users will have to install eight fewer disks as a result of DMF disk compression.

DMI (desktop management interface) A standard method of identifying PC hardware and software components automatically, without input from the user. A framework created by the Distributed Management Task Force (DMTF). DMTF specifications define industry-standard interfaces for instrumentation providers and management applications.

DMI pool The set of data about a computer and its components, including partition data for your hard drive. When a PC boots it will display the message, "Verifying DMI Pool," and if it will not boot past this it typically means your motherboard is not able to access your hard drive properly. This can be caused by a wrong BIOS setting for your hard drive or a non-bootable floppy disk if your floppy drive is set to boot first.

Dmin The point of minimum density in an image or an original.

DMS Document Management System.

DMTF (desktop management task force) This crew was assembled to create the DMI standard.

DMZ (demilitarized Zone) A part of a network that is protected by a firewall, but may be accessed by external Internet clients. The DMZ generally contains servers such as SMTP servers, remote access machines. or webservers. Client machines and internal servers that do not need to be accessed by Internet clients are kept in a more protected segment of the network than the DMZ. Alternately, DMZ can be used to refer to the media layer where route peering is done among multiple administrative regions with their own traffic policies.

DNS (domain name service) This service maps TCP/IP numbers, such as 123.12.4.245, to a more easily remembered name, such as www.geek.com. Thus, when you type www.geek.com into your browser, it goes out to the DNS server specified by your ISP and asks for a matching TCP/IP address.If the browser finds a DNS entry for the name you typed in, you see the appropriate website. If not, it lets you know. Every domain name that is actually being used for a website has a corresponding TCP/IP address. When you set up a site you have your ISP add a DNS entry to its DNS servers. This entry gets replicated across the Internet in a matter of hours, and, once fully replicated, you can reach your website from any Internet connection.

DNS entry The DNS routing tables are filled with DNS entries that map TCP/IP addresses to more easily recognized names. If your browser says it can't find a particular DNS entry, here are some possible reasons: you may not be able to communicate with your DNS server, the site may not be responding, or your connection is broken. If a DNS server really doesn't have the entry, there may be nothing mapped to that particular domain name address. If the domain name was just set up, the entry may not have fully replicated to your DNS server. Remember, people can own a domain name and not have an entry for it on any DNS server if they are not paying an ISP to host it.

DNS record types The domain name record types are:

A Address, specifying the IP address.

CNAME Canonical name, an alias pointing to the true name of the host. Requires its right hand side to have an A record.

HINFO Host information, detailed information about the specific host, such as location or operating system version.

LOC Location, specifies the geographical location of the host.

MX Mail exchange, specifies that the host on the left side will accept mail for the host on the right hand side at the priority shown (lower is preferred).

NS Name server, specifies a host that will act as a domain name server for the specified domain.

PTR Pointer, used to provide reverse lookups.

RP Responsible person, the contact information for the specified domain.

SOA Start of authority, the meta information for the specified zone. Contains email information, a serial number, and the time to live values. The specific format is defined in RFC 2181.

TXT Text, a comment on the record. Otherwise ignored.

WKS Well-known services, lists those services for a host. Allows for mnemonics (http, smtp, telnet) instead of specifying port numbers (80, 25,21).

DNS server A server that uses DNS to translate domain names into IP addresses.

DNS spoofing The practice of assuming the DNS name of another system in order to masquerade on the Internet as someone else. For example, www.cleancontent.com might return the address of a server that appears to be correct, but actually is www.infectedfiles.com.

This is usually accomplished by compromising a DNS server for a valid domain, or corrupting the victim network's name service cache.

Dock To insert a portable computer into a base unit. Cold docking means the computer must begin from a power-off state and restart before docking. Hot docking means the computer can be docked while running at full power.

Docking station A device into which a laptop connects to gain functionality it has sacrificed for portability. Most laptops have a proprietary connector on the back. Many docking stations have all the ports that you wished your laptop had, but doesn't. Ultra- light laptops don't have many ports because there is no room for them and they add weight. So to compromise, you buy a docking station that has all the ports you need for when you want your tiny laptop to act like a desktop machine. Some companies use docking stations to free users from having to plug and unplug their network and power connections each time they bring the laptop into the office.

DOCSIS (data-over-cable service interface specification) This is a standard for cable modems that was ratified by the ITU in March 1998. Before DOCSIS, cable modems made by one brand would not necessarily work on all cable systems. It supports data delivery up to 27Mbps.

Document examiner A high-performance hypertext hypertext system by Symbolics that provides on-line access to their user documentation.

Document style semantics and specification language An ISO standard under preparation, addressing the semantics of high-quality composition in a manner independent of particular formatting systems or processes. DSSSL is intended as a complementary standard to SGML SGML for the specification of semantics.

Document When used in reference to the World Wide Web, a document is any file containing text, media or hyperlinks that can be transferred from an HTTP server to a client program.

Document window This is the Web browser's scrollable window in which HTML documents can be viewed.

Documentation Literature in a human-readable form that is referred to in support of using a computer or computer system

Dod Networking Model A four-layer conceptual model describing how communication should take place between computer systems. The four layers are Process/Application, Host-to-Host, Internet, and Networking Access. DOD is the acronym for Department of Defense, the government agency that provided the original funding for the development of the TCP/IP protocol suite.

DOE distributed object environment A distributed object-oriented object-oriented application framework from SunSoft.

DOI digital object identifier A system of unique and persistent identifiers devised by the Association of American Publishers. The DOI is intended to mark digital objects in electronic commerce so that a user of the object can contact the current provider to get additional information or complete a transaction.

Dolby-NR (dolby-noise reduction) System invented by Ray Dolby. There are various levels of quality, which in rank order from lowest to highest quality include Dolby B (good), Dolby C (better), Dolby S (best), and Dolby SR (professional). DSB Dolby surround digital systems are even higher quality systems used in movie soundtracks and videodiscs. HDTV will also include DSD. A sound enforcement system first used in the movie *THX 1138* by George Lucas is now known as the THX system. The THX-licensed speakers use a professional Dolby process for commercial and home theater systems.

Domain This term describes the Internet's addressing scheme, and also a security construct in Windows operating systems. For the Internet, domains are represented by domain names such as Geek.com or UGeek.org. These domains are mapped to TCP/IP addresses by DNS servers so that browsers can find websites. Under Windows, domains are groups of server and client machines that exist in the same security structure. You can also define security relationships based on how domains interact with each other. Windows NT 4 domains include a primary domain controller and optionally one or more backup domain controllers to manage security. Windows 2000 domains have domain controllers that share responsibilities more equally, eliminating the primary and backup distinction.

Domain controller Primary server within a domain and primary storage point for domain-wide security information.

Domain distributed operating multi access interactive network The proprietary network protocol used by Apollo Apollo workstations.

Domain level A level in a NetInfo domain hierarchy.

Domain name A Domain Name is much like a trademark or a license. It allows people to find your website by name instead of by number. It also allows customers to have a much more professional look because their website can be. There can only be one of any Domain name in the world. If http://www.myweb.com is already registered by another company, then you must find a name that is not yet registered. Domain names can be only 63 charecters long in total. This includes the .com at the end but does not include the http://www at the beginning. It is the 'unique name' that identifies an Internet site. Domain Names always have two or more parts, separated by dots. The part on the left is the most specific, and the part on the right is the most general. A given machine may have more than one Domain Name but a given Domain Name points to only one machine. For example, the domain names:Domain Name Service (DNS) A UDP protocol for resolving names to IP addresses and vice versa. This leads to a hierarchical host naming structure which gives each computer on a network a unique name.

Domain name disputes Disputes that arise over conflicting positions as to who has the right to register a specific domain name. Disputes often occur when a domain name that is the same, or similar to, a valid registered trademark is registered by a party that is not the owner of the registered trademark. A central factor in domain name disputes is the fact that domain names at the same level of the hierarchy must be unique. You might want to consult InterNIC' Domain Name Dispute Policy.

Domain name registration agreement The legally binding contract between InterNIC, the registrar for com, net, org, and edu, domains, and the individual or organization applying for a domain name. The Domain Name Registration Agreement must be completed and submitted electronically to register a new domain name with InterNIC. The Domain Name Registration Agreement is also the form used to update and modify information in a domain name record.

Domain name system (DNS) A local database that translates domain names to Internet Protocol (IP) addresses. It is much easier for humans to remember and use names than IP numbers, which are what computers need to find each other on the Internet. Individual Internet computers around the globe maintain their specific portion of this database, and the data held in each portion of the database is made available to all computers and users on the Internet. The DNS comprises computers, data files, software, and people working together.

When you enter [www.DomainMart.com] in your browser, the local DNS server finds a match and connects your to the site. Most people who access the internet from home use an Internet Service Provider (ISP). The ISP typically assigns Internet Protocol (IP) numbers dynamically to these users. That is, they have a different IP number each time they log on to the internet. This allows a provider to use a limited number of addresses for all of their users as the ISPs total subscriber base is never logged in at once.

To be able to register a domain name, your ISP must assign you a static IP number (one that never changes). This is usually an additional cost. Of course, you still need a computer system that will host your domain. Most ISPs offer domain hosting.

Domain names The name by which a domain is known to the network.

The errors are due to clocking information and overhead in managing the multiplexing of the channels on the fiber. Usually, all of the machines on a given Network will have the same extension as the right-hand portion of their Domain Names. It is also possible for a Domain Name to exist but not be connected to an actual machine. This is often done so that a group or business can have an Internet e-mail address without having to establish a real Internet site. In these cases, some real Internet machine must handle the mail on behalf of the listed Domain Name.

DOMF (distributed object management facilit)y An OMG compliant object management system; part of DOE.

Domino Lotus product suite that integrates a store and forward database, email, and Web access.

Dongle The slang term for an external hardware device with some memory inside it that attaches to your computer and dangles off of it (thus the term dongle). Often, companies that sell expensive software packages use dongles as proof that a computer actually has a license to use the software that is being used—the software checks to see if a dongle is installed. If not, it may refuse to run, or run with limited functionality.

Doping A step used in the production of semiconductor materials where charged particles are embedded into the device so as to tailor its operational characteristics.

DORIS 3-10 GeV Center of mass electron-positron storage ring/collider at DESY.

DOS MS DOS Microsoft Disk Operating System introduced by Microsoft Corporation in 1981. It became the operating system standard for PCs around the world and still serves as the foundation of the popular Microsoft Windows extended operating system. The ability to operate from DOS on low-capacity PCs having only 640K of random access memory (RAM) has become the limitation in modern times for DOS to remain a standard for higher speed and higher RAM computers. DOS has not been upgraded for newer 32-bit processors and will eventually fade as the newer 32-bit, 64-bit, and higher capacity PCs spread across world markets.

Dot bomb This is a derogatory slang term for the era of the Dot Com website when many companies were funded with unrealistic expectations and questionable business plans, causing a virtual bomb to go off in the economy as most of the companies eventually collapsed.

Dot com (.com) This literally refers to the suffix of a domain name intended to be used for websites associated with companies. Figuratively, "Dot Com" is used often by investors to describe companies, such as Geek.com, which are mainly Internet-based. This contrasts to brick and mortar.

Dot matrix printer This type of printer prints out little dots that can form graphics or characters. It was popular a while back because the only other choice was a daisy- wheel printer that didn't print any graphics. These printers are generally loud, producing a high-pitched buzzing sound, and they don't produce very good graphics. You'll still find them in bank machines, cash registers, and applications that require a physical imprint on paper (to create a carbon copy), but most people don't want anything to do with them.

Dot or "." The top of the hierarchy or root in the Domain Name System (DNS).

Dot pitch The smaller the better, as it relates to CRT monitors. The dot pitch is a measure of distance between phosphor dots of the same color on a CRT monitor. A high dot pitch generally produces a blurred and unclear picture. Smaller dot pitches produce a sharper, crisper image that stands up to close examination. There is contention on how the dot pitch should be measured: horizontally, vertically, or diagonally, resulting in some monitor makers reporting the lowest rating as their official dot pitch. Take the measure of dot pitch with a grain of salt.

Dots per inch (DPI) Most often this term is used to describe printer or scanner resolution. If a printer is said to print at 300 dpi, it will be capable of printing 300 dots horizontally and 300 dots vertically over a square inch. Thus, if you have a printer with a higher dpi value, you should have a crisper image. The same holds true for scanners—a higher dpi theoretically relates to a higher quality scan. Besides scanners and printers, dpi is often discussed when referring to flat panel displays. As flat panel technology increases you get a higher dpi value, and thus can display a larger image in a smaller space without losing any detail. The goal in printers, scanners, and displays is to keep dpi values high enough so that the user is displayed a high-quality image and cannot see the individual dots (or pixels) that make up the image.

Dotted decimal notation The convention for writing 32-bit IP Addresses as a set of four 8-bit numbers written in base 10 with periods separating them.

Double buffering A method of smoothing onscreen animation using two buffers to hold images. By rendering both images offscreen, the computer can then display a smoother and less flickery animation by switching from one buffer to the next and back and forth instead of fetching the image and waiting for it to be drawn each time in the same single buffer, which may cause some flickering.

Double data rate sdram (DDR SDRAM) A standard that is used to boost conventional SDRAM memory up to speeds of 200MHz and beyond.Standard SDRAM tops out around 150-166MHz, and DDR SDRAM starts at 200MHz by effectively doubling the speed of 100MHz SDRAM by sending two bits of data per clock cycle. A new standard called DDR II will push DDR SDRAM over 400MHz effective speeds, where standard DDR trails off.

Double-clicking "Double-clicking with a mouse" means moving the mouse until the cursor is on the thing you want to use and then quickly pressing and releasing mouse button twice. It takes some practice to get the two clicks fast enough but not too fast.If your mouse has several buttons, use the leftmost button unless you are instructed otherwise.

Double-layer supertwist nematic (DSTN) This is a form of passive matrix LCD screen. It is an improved version of the standard supertwist nematic passive matrix LCD screen where the display is divided into two sections and addressed separately to deal with slow switching speeds that result in poor visibility.

Download Transferring files or objects from a server to a client. The most common protocols used for downloading are FTP and HTTP. Although transferring files is a common occurrence on the Internet, it poses less of a threat than email and Web surfing because it is an activity usually undertaken by experienced users. However, by trusting a product's description to be factual, a user can inadvertently download a program that, upon execution, does something unexpected.

Down-sampling The reduction in resolution of an image, necessitating a loss in detail.

Downsizing The process of moving computing work to a smaller computer. More generally, it is often applied to applications that might otherwise have been implemented on a big computer, being brought up on a small computer.

Downstream frequency The frequency used for transmitting data from the Cable Modem Termination System to the cable modem. Normally in the 42/65-850 MHz range depending on the actual cable plant capabilities.

Downstream The downloading (receiving) of data from the Internet to a client machine. Downstream speeds are typically much greater than upstream speeds in high speed consumer Internet connections such as cable modems and ADSL.

DPI (dpdots Per Inch) Most often this term is used to describe printer or scanner resolution. If a printer is said to print at 300 dpi, it will be capable of printing 300 dots horizontally and 300 dots vertically over a square inch. Thus, if you have a printer with a higher dpi value, you should have a crisper image. The same holds true for scanners—a higher dpi theoretically relates to a higher quality scan. Besides scanners and printers, dpi is often discussed when referring to flat panel displays. As flat panel technology increases you get a higher dpi value, and thus can display a larger image in a smaller space without losing any detail. The goal in printers, scanners, and displays is to keep dpi values high enough so that the user is displayed a high-quality image and cannot see the individual dots (or pixels) that make up the image.

DPMA (dynamic power management architecture) This architecture allows computers to have a variety of advanced power management features.

DPS Display PostScript Display-PostScript.

DQO Data Quality Objectives.

Dr. Watson This is diagnostic software that runs automatically in Windows NT/2000/XP and can be turned on in Windows98/Me. Dr. Watson takes over when a program crashes and writes a snapshot of information about the crash to disk.

Drafts Drafts are unfinished messages. Your e-mail program allows you to store a not-yet-ready-post message as a draft, and provides a folder for this purpose. This is a handy feature, since it's often a good idea to make sure that a message really says what you want it to say before you send it, especially when the letter is important.

Drag-and-drop The action of dragging an item with the mouse from one location to another, and releasing the mouse button at the destination.

Dragging "Dragging the mouse" means moving the mouse until the cursor is on the thing you want to drag, pressing and holding the mouse button, moving the mouse until the thing is where you want to drag it to (with the button still down), and then releasing the mouse button. If your mouse has several buttons, use the leftmost button unless you are instructed otherwise.

Dragon An Esprit project aimed at providing effective support to reuse in real-time distributed Ada applications.

DRAM (dynamic random access memory) This is the most common form of computer memory. It needs to be continually refreshed in order to properly hold data, thus the term "dynamic." If the power goes off, DRAM loses all of its data, thus making it a bad choice for long-term storage of data. The bonus to DRAM is that it's very fast, much faster than Flash memory or other non-dynamic memory.

DRDRAM (direct rambus DRAM) One possible future successor to SDRAM, and competitor to DDR SDRAM. DRDRAM (also now simply called RDRAM) was originally developed by Rambus, Inc. This RAM architecture is capable of speeds starting at 266, 356, and 400MHz, and transfers data on the up and down ticks of a clock cycle, where standard SDRAM tops out at about 200MHz. You may see RDRAM referred to at 532, 712, and 800MHz, but that is actually 2662, 3562, and 400MHz2, where the 2 denotes transfer on the up and down tick of the clock. Intel picked RDRAM to be the future of RAM for PCs, but RDRAM ran into many stumbling blocks due to the complexity of manufacturing it. RDRAM was used in the popular Nintendo 64 game machine for its high-speed capabilities and low pin count, necessary for the intense 3D rendering being done on a low complexity system. RDRAM started out using a 16- bit bus, while SDRAM and DDR have 64-bit buses. Thus, 100MHz SDRAM has half the throughput of RDRAM at 400MHz (10064 = 6,400Mbits/second; 400216 = 12,800Mbits/second). However, newer RDRAM uses a 32-bit bus and is clocked up to 533MHz2. Still, it never achieved dominance in the PC market.

Drive bay This is usually a 5.25" wide 1" tall hole in a computer case suitable for the installation of some sort of drive. Some are exposed so that a removable drive (e.g., floppy, CD-ROM) can fit. Some are not exposed and are meant for hard drives that users don't need access to.

Driver A driver is software that works to communicate between an operating system and a peripheral. Think of it as a translator. If you use a crappy driver, your OS won't understand your video card and may become unstable and crash. Hardware manufacturers constantly update drivers to make them faster and more stable. Operating systems typically come with a set of drivers, but peripherals newer than your operating system typically require new drivers which must be installed via CD-ROM, floppy, or downloaded from the Web. Each device has its own set of specialized commands that only its driver knows. In contrast, most programs access devices by using generic commands. The driver, therefore, accepts generic commands from a program and then translates them into specialized commands for the device.

Driver stack Device objects that forward IRPs to other device objects. Stacking always occurs from the bottom up and is torn down from the top.

Dropdown menu A type of menu that appears as a text box with an arrow pointing down in part of the box. It allows a user to click on it, and a list of choices appear below the menu. After the information drops down, one of the items can be selected. It's possible that the information appears above the menu if there is not space below it.

Drum scanner Early drum scanners separated scans into CMYK data, recording these directly onto film held on a second rotating drum.

Drum The part of a laser printer onto which the laser produces an electrostatic image. The drum is then rolled in toner and that toner is transferred to paper with pressure and heat. Most drums are coated with selenium for its electrical properties. Selenium is a nonmetallic element in the sulfur family, and it allows the drum to hold a charge and attract toner.

Dry camera A digital camera that records images directly to a disk or other medium that can be read directly into computers without having to develop imaging film with "wet" developer chemicals. Various vendors have relatively inexpensive dry cameras whereas these same vendors like Nikon, Kodak, Logitech, and Dycam have superior and very expensive models that have much higher imaging quality. Apple, Stormware, and other vendors have only the lower priced modes. Photographs can be scanned readers that plug into the back PCs, although the later versions will also plug directly into a PCMCIA slot for downloading into a computer. An example of the latter option is Nikon's Coolpix model.

DS (distributed single layer test method) An abstract test method in which the upper tester is located within the system under test and the point of control and observation (PCO) is located at the upper service boundary of the Implementation Under Test (IUT) - for testing one protocol layer. Test events are specified in terms of the abstract service primitives (ASP) at the upper tester above the IUT and ASPs and/or protocol data units (PDU) at the lower tester PCO.

DS/DD (double-sided double-density) Usually refers to 360k 5.25" floppy disks, or 720k 3.5" disks. These disks are obsolete and not recommended for new PCs, which can use the high-density disks.

DS-0 (digital signal level 0) The signal used to carry a standard analog or digital phone line connection. 24 DS-0 connections can be carried on a T1 line. The speed of the line is either 64Kbps, or 56Kbps if the eighth bit is used for signaling information.

DS-1 (digital signal Level 1) The North American Digital Hierarchy signaling standard for transmission at 1.544 Mbps. This standard supports 24 simultaneous DS-0 signals. The term is often used interchangeably with T1 carrier although DS-1 signals may be exchanged over other transmission systems.

DS-2 (digital signal level 2) The North American Digital Hierarchy signaling standard for transmission of 6.312 Mbps that is used by T2 carrier which supports 96 calls.

DS3 (digital signal 3) Is an international transmission standard that uses pulse-code modulation and time-division multiplexing to achieve a data rate of 44.736 Mbps and provide full T3 connectivity; it is often used for ATM formats. E3 is the European counterpart that has a rate of 34.368 Mbps.

DS3 PLCP (physical layer convergence protocol) An alternate method used by older T carrier equipment to locate ATM cell boundaries. This method has recently been moved to an informative appendix of the ATM DS3 specification and has been replaced by the HEC method.

DSE (distributed single-layer embedded) An abstract test method in which the upper tester is located within the system under test and there is a point of control and observation at the upper service boundary of the Implementation Under Test (IUT) for testing a protocol layer, or sublayer, which is part of a multi-protocol IUT.

DSL (digital subscriber line) Technology for transmitting data up to 50 times faster than present analog modem and ISDN alternatives. Telephone companies are hoping that DSL service will keep telephone lines competitive with cable modems and other competitive alternatives to present telephone transmission services. Telephone companies are considering two dominant DSL technologies: Asymmetric Digital Subscriber Line (ADSL, ASL) and High Rate Digital Subscriber Line (HDSL). ADSL technology will deliver higher downstream speeds (6 Mbps) than upstream speeds (640 kbps).

ADSL or ASL differs from DSL in that there is an asymmetry in transmission speeds into (download) and out of (upload) your computer. In ASL, the upload speeds are much slower than the download speeds. However, ASL connections are being pushed heavily into the huge home market, whereas DLS is being touted for the business firm market.

DSP (digital signal processor) A DSP is a microprocessor designed to work with analog signals such as video or audio that have been digitally encoded. The DSP then takes these digital representations and performs operations on them. DSPs are used in video, sound, and modem technology. Intel's MMX instruction set was the first attempt to make x86 processors (specifically the Pentium processor line) more capable of DSP operations. This follows Intel's theory of putting all the processor work onto its processors. However, DSP chips are still used in many devices for PCs, as they can keep the CPU from being bogged down.

DSS (digital satellite systems) Such as those introduced by Hughes Communications and USSB United States Satellite Broadcasting, Inc. The term for commercial satellite dishes used for this system is DirectTV which will compete actively with full-service cable TV. Since 120 channel capacity is expected on small 18-inch home satellite dishes, it becomes much more feasible to bring remote education into homes, schools, and offices.

DSTN (double-layer supertwist nematic) This is a form of passive matrix LCD screen. It is an improved version of the standard supertwist nematic passive matrix LCD screen where the display is divided into two sections and addressed separately to deal with slow switching speeds that result in poor visibility.

DSU/CSU (channel service unit/data service unit) A piece of hardware that you use to translate the digital data frames of a T1 line into a 10BaseT connection where Internet connectivity is concerned. If the T1 lines are used for voice connections, a CSU/DSU is required to translate the digital frames into signals that your office phone switch can interpret. Basically, the phone network/Internet consists of a bunch of CSU/DSUs talking to one another. When you lease a T1 line, your provider typically supplies you with a CSU/DSU, often with a setup cost. A synonym for CSU/DSU is DSU/CSU.

DTD (document type definition) A document type definition (DTD) that follows the rules of the Standard Generalized Markup Language (SGML). A DTD is a specification that accompanies a document and identifies what the funny little codes (or markup) are that separate paragraphs, identify topic headings, and so forth and how each is to be processed. For example, the most common DTD in web documents is HTML. DTD is vital to extracting SGML and XML from web documents and databases that are not marked up with SGML or XML.

Dtl (designated transit list) A list of nodes and optional link IDs that completely specify a path across a single PNNI peer group.

DTP (desk top publishering) A PC Term that describes a program that enables you to design, create and print a variety of projects such as letterheads, birthday cards, calendars, business cards, invitations etc. that would have previously only been possible by using the services of an outside printers business.

DTS digital surround (digital theater systems - digital surround) A form of encoding and decoding surround sound first used in 1993 in the film Jurassic Park. It features 6 discrete channels of audio, with 5 standard speaker channels and one subwoofer channel. DTS can work along with THX speaker certification and placement, or it can work separately.

DTV (digital television) Standard television signals are in analog format. Some HDTV systems use analog signals as well. Digital Television refers to the standard of transmitting and receiving television signals using purely digital transmission.

Dual banked A memory module with two banks or rows.

Dual boot A system that can boot to two different operating systems. Some OSes, such as Windows NT/2000/XP and versions of Linux, allow for dual booting when installed. Of course, you can also use other methods, such as commercial programs that install a special boot partition that is capable of launching operating systems from other partitions. You can also boot to many more than two operating systems on the same machine.

Dual homed This refers to a computer with two network cards. Such configurations are often used to function as routers in a situation where two networks are connected but dedicated router hardware is not available or is too costly. One common example would be a home computer user who wishes to share Internet access to other computers in a home network. One network card would connect to a cable modem or DSL, and the other would connect to the rest of the home network while some Internet sharing software is used to make the computer function as a router. For corporate use, a dual homed machine can be used for redundancy or increased networking transfer capacity.

Dual independent bus (DIB) The bus architecture between Intel's Pentium II processor, memory, and L2 cache. One bus connects the processor to L2 cache and a second connects the processor to main memory. Having two buses instead of one increases performance over single-bus architectures. In addition, the speed of the external L2 cache can scale up independently from the speed of the system bus.This allows for faster cache access. The final feature of the DIB architecture is a pipeline on the cache to the processor bus that allows multiple simultaneous cache requests.

Dual in-line memory module (DIMM) A circuit board with memory chips on it, very much like a SIMM except that it is larger and contains more pins. DIMMs are 64-bit memory devices, so you just need a single DIMM for a processor with a 64-bit memory path to work properly; or you can potentially double up DIMMs for a 128-bit memory interface if your motherboard supports it. Most memory today is sold on DIMMs.

Dual in-line package (DIP) A standard housing constructed of hard plastic commonly used to hold an integrated circuit. The circuit's leads are connected to two parallel rows of pins designed to fit snugly into a socket; these pins may also be soldered directly to a printed -circuit board.

Dual-band Characterizes a handset that is able to operate on two different frequencies.

Dualscan A passive matrix LCD screen that uses a better method of displaying graphics, producing a sharper, more vivid image than standard passive matrix screens.

Dumb terminal A workstation consisting of keyboard and monitor, used to put data into the computer or receive information from the computer. Dumb terminals were originally developed to be connected to computers running a multi-user operating systems so that users could communicate directly with them. All processing is done at and by the computer, not the dumb terminal. IN contrast, a smart terminal contains processing circuits which can receive data from the host computer and later carry out independent processing operations.

Dump Back-up of data.

Duplex A telecommunications term that describes part of the communications between a local modem and a remote computer. In full duplex mode, the remote computer is set up to return the characters that are sent to it so that they can be displayed on your screen. In half duplex mode, the remote computer does not return the characters sent to it.

DVD (digital versatile disc or digital video disc) A new type of CD-ROM that holds a minimum of 4.7GB (gigabytes), enough for a full-length movie. Many experts believe that DVD disks, called DVD-ROMs, will eventually replace CD-ROMs, as well as VHS video cassettes and laser discs. The DVD specification supports disks with capacities of from 4.7GB to 17GB and access rates of 600 KBps to 1.3 MBps. One of the best features of DVD drives is that they are backward-compatible with CD-ROMs. This means that DVD players can play old CD-ROMs, CD-I disks, and video CDs, as well as new DVD-ROMs. Newer DVD players, called second-generation or DVD-2 drives, can also read CD-R and CD-RW disks. DVD uses MPEG-2 to compress video data.

DVD+RW This standard reads standard DVD-ROM discs, and reads and writes to DVD+RW media.

DVD-R This standard is to DVD-ROM like CD-R is to CD-ROM. It uses 4.7 GB disks that can only be written to once, and which then can be read by standard DVD-ROM drives. Apple embraced this standard early, and it is already an entrenched standard that Gateway is also supporting.

DVD-RAM The DVD-RAM standard uses media that can be written and read multiple times, like RAM chips. The first DVD-RAM media held 2.6 GB worth of data per side, and had to be manually flipped over to access the other side. Updates to the standard allowed full 4.7 GB DVD capacity. DVD-RAM drives can read standard DVD disks, but need a special caddy to hold the disks. DVD-RAM media is shaped like the caddy and cannot be inserted into standard DVD drives. DVD-RAM is on the way out.

DVI (digital video interactive) Video compression hardware and standard developed by the Moving Pictures Experts Group (MPEG) before MPEG video boards hit the market. DVI is a form of compressed full-motion video for computer file storage. Full-motion video at over 30 frames per second takes up so much digitized storage that video must be compressed to make it more useful in hypermedia. DVI was an early compression option that required special and somewhat expensive DVI hardware installation inside the computer of both authors and users (readers) of hypermedia materials. New technology allows for video compression without such expensive hardware. MPEG hardware for video coded compression and decompression seems to be taking over the recent market share lead over DVI largely due to quality of the MPEG and options emerging after DVI. At present, it is not clear whether MPEG or DVI/Indeo will emerge as the international standard with greatest market acceptance.

DXF Drawing Interchange Format used for Macintosh graphic files. The standard file-exchange format for 3-D and CAD programs.

DXI (data exchange interface) A variable length frame-based ATM interface between a DTE and a special ATM CSU/DSU. The ATM CSU/DSU converts between the variable-length DXI frames and the fixed-length ATM cells.

Dye sublimation A printing process using small heating elements to evaporate pigments from a carrier film, depositing these smoothly onto a substrate.

Dylan An object-oriented object-oriented dynamic language.

Dynamic Type of RAM (random access memory). To keep data in the DRAM, this data needs to be "refreshed" (recharged). The electric charge fades out of a DRAM like air seeps out of a balloon. Because of this change, it is called "dynamic."

Dynamic data exchange (DDE) A method of exchanging data between applications on MacOS, Windows, and OS/2 operating systems. DDE is similar to OLE, but predates it. It enables multiple applications to have access to the same data, such as a word processor having data from a spreadsheet pasted into it. Changes made in either application to the data are reflected in the main document.

Dynamic detection The process by which a system can detect that a new device has been added or removed from the PC. This process allows the operating system and applications to immediately begin using the added devices or stop using the removed devices without rebooting the system.

Dynamic host configuration protocol (DHCP) A method of automatically assigning a TCP/IP address to a client. A DHCP server is used to dole out a TCP/IP address from a pool of TCP/IP addresses to a client that supports DHCP. When you connect to your ISP over a modem or broadband you are typically assigned a dynamic (non-static) TCP/IP address via DHCP. The big advantage to DHCP is that you don't need to manually assign a TCP/IP address to a client—the DHCP server takes care of that. After an amount of time passes where the client does not contact the server, the server puts the TCP/IP address of the client back into the pool to be assigned to that client or any other client hat requests a TCP/IP address. The disadvantage of DHCP for the DHCP client is that the client is not guaranteed to have a particular TCP/IP address at any given time.

Dynamic HTML (DHTML) This was independently defined by Microsoft and Netscape and implemented in version 4 of their browsers to allow for more dynamic and user-interactive Web pages, and better positioning of Web elements. Both the Netscape and Microsoft versions of dynamic HTML include some support for Cascading Style Sheets, which is a real standard defined by the World Wide Web Consortium.

Dynamic invocation interface (DII) Used by a client to dynamically build a request to be sent to a server.

Dynamic IP address An IP address that is allocated by the network each time a computer or other device logs on. This is common in systems with dial-up connections.

Dynamic link library (DLL) A library of procedures that programs can call on. The DLL produces output related to the supplied input. DLLs can be somewhat of a black box, as you don't really need to know what's inside them, just what they do.

Dynamic links Logical connections between two objects that can be modified if the objects themselves move or change state.

Dynamic power management architecture (DPMA) This architecture allows computers to have a variety of advanced power management features.

Dynamic programming language A programming language where programs can dynamically change in structure as they are run.

Dynamic random access memory (DRAM) This is the most common form of computer memory. It needs to be continually refreshed in order to properly hold data, thus the term "dynamic." If the power goes off, DRAM loses all of its data, thus making it a bad choice for long-term storage of data. The bonus to DRAM is that it's very fast, much faster than Flash memory or other non-dynamic memory.

Dynamic ur A URL that results from the search of a database-driven Web site or the URL of a Web site that runs a script. In contrast to static URLs, in which the contents of the Web page do not change unless the changes are coded into the HTML, dynamic URLs are generated from specific queries to a site's database. The page is merely a template to display the results of the query. Most of the content comes from the database that is associated with the site. Instead of changing information in the HTML code, the data is changed in the database.

E

E.164 A public network addressing standard utilizing up to a maximum of 15 digits. ATM uses E.164 addressing for public network addressing.

E1 Also known as CEPT1, The 2.048 Mbps rate used by European CEPT carrier to transmit 30 64 kbps digital channels for voice or data calls, plus a 64 kbps signaling channel and a 64 kbps channel for framing and maintenance.

E3 Also known as CEPT3, The 34.368 Mbps rate used by European CEPT carrier to transmit 16 CEPT1s plus overhead.

EAPLS European Association for Programming Languages and Systems.

EARN European Academic Research Network.

East A Eureka Eureka project developing a software engineering platform.

EAX (environmental audio) A hardware and software audio standard developed by Creative Labs. It was originally used in SoundBlaster sound boards, and is supported by other companies as well now. EAX offers 3D positional audio and allows the manipulation of sounds so that they can seem to be heard in different listening environments.

EBCDIC (extended binary coded decimal interchange code) A way of encoding 256 characters in binary, much like ASCII, but used mainly on mainframes. Most of the time EBCDIC is only mentioned in translations between EBCDIC and ASCII.

EBIOS (enhanced bios) This translates between the partition table limitations of a standard computer BIOS and the IDE limitations to provide up to 8 GB of storage space using the IDE interface. Your computer's BIOS has maximums of 1024 cylinders, 256 heads, and 63 sectors (8 GB). The IDE interface has a maximum of 65,536 cylinders, 16 heads, and 256 sectors (128 GB). Put these maximums together (1024 cylinders, 16 heads, and 63 sectors) and you've got a measly 504 MB of data to work with. The EBIOS translates these limitations in such a way that you can actually achieve the BIOS max of 8 GB on one IDE device. Newer IDE standards have since been developed to up the top hard drive size to 128 GB and beyond.

E-books Short for electronic books; books available for downloading onto an e-book reader.

E-Business A term that is easily confused with E-Commerce. E-Business may be an umbrella term that refers to any type of business transaction on the Internet. Some writers, however, may use the term in a more restricted context such as a business-to-business (B2B) transaction as opposed to a business-to-consumer (B2C) transaction. For example, a B2B transaction might be a business firm's online banking transaction. E-Commerce refers more to the B2C context where a firm sells goods on the internet and makes collections via some payment scheme such as online credit card transactions.

EC (electronic commerce) Managing business transactions using networking and electronic means.

ECC (error checking and correcting) This generally refers to memory chips or motherboards that support the checking for, and possibly correcting of, memory errors in full-parity memory chips. ECC memory uses some extra memory on the memory chips for parity information, and checks to see whether a memory error has occurred. If a minor (one-bit) memory error occurs, the ECC logic will handle it. With full-parity memory (one step below ECC), you will be alerted of a memory error and your system will stop. With non-parity memory you will experience random results, usually crashing, and possible data corruption. If a two-bit or larger error occurs in ECC memory, your system will be halted—similar to what happens with parity memory when any error is encountered. Many caches built into computer microprocessors now have ECC features.

ECFA (European committee for future accelerators) This body, whose principal role is to take care of Europe's requirements for future particle accelerators, has also looked at particle physics data handling on a European-wide basis.

Echo Return response between a host server and a terminal computer. It is generally coded to be "on" or "off." If echo is "on" (full duplex), the host will send back every character the user types in. If echo is "off" (half duplex), the host will not send back the characters, and the user's local computer or terminal writes each character to the screen directly. This can be confusing to new users if the state of the echo parameter is different on the host computer and the user's computer.

ECHT European Conference on Hypertext Hypertext.

ECIP2 An Esprit Esprit Project on the definition of a specification language at the requirement level.

ECIS European Committee for Interoperable Systems.

ECM Enterprise Component Modelling.

ECMA (European computer manufacturers association) Develops standards for submission to International Standards Organisation.

ECO Engineering Change Order.

Ecommerce The process of conducting business over the Internet. Normally encryption is used to ensure the security of financial transactions.

Econsole Management console that lets you monitor and manage Content Security policies from anywhere on or off the network.

ECRC (electronic commerce resource centers) A network of US government sponsored centers that provide support to government and industry in developing and implementing strategies for business process improvement, implementing enabling technologies, and migrating to electronic commerce

Eden An object-oriented distributed operating system based on an RPC RPC mechanism .

EDGAR Electronic Data Gathering, Analysis, and Retrieval database of the Securities and Exchange Commission (SEC). EDGAR contains the digitized versions of many corporate filings, including 10Q quarterly and 10K annual financial reports of registered corporations and mutual funds. The EDGAR database is one probably the most widely used database by investors and financial analysts. The drawback is that many of the filings are very long, sometimes exceeding 300 pages. Searching is usually tedious and requires considerable financial searching and accounting skills. Until filings are marked up in XBRL, the searching EDGAR will be tedious.

Currently, there are some corporate Web sites to aid in searching for EDGAR data. One of the best known is EDGAR Online at EDGAR Online uses enhanced parsing technologies to quickly extract the popular data most often sought after by investors. Added services include email alerts, multiple file formates, and spreadsheet downloads. One of EDGAR Online's most popular services is a sales lead geration product called Wealth ID. This provides personal wealth information about individuals who file SEC Form 144 regarding sales of restricted stock.

Edge connector Metal tabs on the edge of a printed circuit board (PCB). The edge contacts are the interface between the PCB and the socket that allow the system to communicate with the memory module.

Edge device A physical device which is capable of forwarding packets between legacy interworking interfaces (e.g., Ethernet, Token Ring, etc.) and ATM interfaces based on data-link and network layer information but which does not participate in the running of any network layer routing protocol. An Edge Device obtains forwarding descriptions using the route distribution protocol.

Edge effect A term used in the semiconductor industry. Square chips are made on silicon wafers that are round. Because of this, there is a certain amount of silicon at the edge of the round wafers on which full chips cannot be constructed.

EDGE Enhanced Data for GSM Evolution is an ETSI standard. It is a higher bandwidth version of GSM, allowing for transmission speeds of up to 384Kb per second, that makes use of existing GSM infrastructure.

EDH Electronic Document Handling.

EDI The abbreviation for Electronic Data Interchange or Electronic Data Invoicing. The EDI system allows linked computers to conduct business transactions such as ordering and invoicing over telecommunications networks. The technology dates back to the 1970s when the first attempts at setting uniform standards commenced. However, EDI in telecommunications never lived up to its expectations largely due to high fees of Value Added Network (VAN) providers that, prior to the Internet usage, charged both monthly and transaction fees. In the late 1990s, EDI became less costly (as low as 10% of former VAN costs) when business applications exploded on the Internet and in intranets. The ultimate goal of EDI is to have standardized computer forms for business transactions and networking of nearly all aspects business transactions. This would greatly simplify use of networks to conduct business, accounting for transactions, and auditing.

EDIF Electronic Design Interchange Format.

EDIFACT Electronic Data Interchange for Administration, Commerce and Transportation. An EDI standards development group.

EDM Engineering Data Management.

EDMS Electronic Document Management System.

EDO (extended data out) An asynchronous DRAM operating mode that improves access times compared to fast page mode (FPM) DRAMs.

EDO Memory Short for Extended Data Output Dynamic Random Access Memory, a type of DRAM that is faster than conventional DRAM. Unlike conventional DRAM which can only access one block of data at a time, EDO RAM can start fetching the next block of memory at the same time that it sends the previous block to the CPU.

EDO RAM (extended data out RAM) The successor to standard fast page DRAM. It's a conceptually faster RAM chip that has small bits of SRAM cache built into it. It still runs at slow DRAM speeds (<= 50 MHz), and thus is no longer used. At one time, it was a popular memory format and offered enhanced memory performance.

EDUCOM A group of cooperating colleges and universities dedicated to advancing computer and network communications technology in education. EDUCOM coordinates newsletters and other publishing efforts along with conferences and related activities.

Eduquest A revitalized system of multimedia hardware and software packages from IBM Corporation. The system primarily targets the K-12 education system in the United States. The new system is designed to be more powerful with networked PCs and a variety of Plug and Play adapters for auxiliary components.

EEMA European Electronic Messaging Association.

EEPROM Acronym for "electrically erasable programmable read-only memory" an EEPROM is a special type of PROM that can be erased by exposing it to an electrical charge. Like other types of PROM, EEPROM retains its contents even when the power is turned off. Also like other types of ROM, EEPROM is not as fast as RAM. EEPROM is similar to flash memory (sometimes called flash EEPROM). The principal difference is that EEPROM requires data to be written or erased one byte at a time whereas flash memory allows data to be written or erased in blocks. This makes flash memory faster.

EFCI (explicit forward congestion indication) EFCI is an indication in the ATM cell header. A network element in an impending-congested state or a congested state may set EFCI so that this indication may be examined by the destination end-system. For example, the end-system may use this indication to implement a protocol that adaptively lowers the cell rate of the connection during congestion or impending congestion. A network element that is not in a congestion state or an impending congestion state will not modify the value of this indication. Impending congestion is the state when a network equipment is operating around its engineered capacity level.

EFF (electronic frontier foundation) An organisation working on civil rights issues in networkin.

EFS (error free seconds) A unit used to specify the error performance of T carrier systems, usually expressed as EFS per hour, day, or week. This method gives a better indication of the distribution of bit errors than a simple bit error rate (BER). Also refer to EGA (enhanced graphics adapter) The standard that came after CGA and before VGA. It allowed resolutions up to 640x350 pixels and 16 colors from a palette of 64. It was soon replaced by VGA. EGA images look squished because the aspect ratio of 640x350 is not flattering compared to the more standard 640x480 resolution of VGA that corresponded exactly to the 4:3 aspect ratio of most computer monitors.

EGP (exterior gateway protocol) A reachability routing protocol used by gateways in a two-level internet. EGP is used in the Internet core system.

EHTS (emacs hypertext System) An experimental multiuser hypertext hypertext system from the University of Aalborg. It consists of a text editor (based on Epoch Epoch and GNU GNU Emacs Emacs and written in elisp) and a graphical browser browser (based on XView XView and written in C) running under the X Window System X-Window-System and OpenWindows OpenWindows Both tools use HyperBase HyperBase as database.

EIA Electronic Industries Association, in charge of defining norms in the USA.

EICAR European Institute of Computer Research. A non-profit organization.

EIDE (enhanced integrated development environment) Also called EIDE, is a term that Western Digital coined in 1994 to represent a particular set of extensions it devised to the original AT Attachment standard. At that time, the official ATA standard was rather limiting, and work was progressing towards the new

ATA-2 standard. Western Digital decided that it did not want to wait for the new standard, and also that it could better position itself as a market leader by creating a new feature set for (then) future drives.

EISA (extended industry standard architecture) This is the 32-bit extension of the 16-bit ISA expansion slot. It was generally used only in server machines, and it never caught on for consumers because 32- bit VL-Bus and PCI were more accessible. However, for server machines, EISA beat out VL-Bus and PCI because you could have numerous EISA slots in one machine without any complex wiring. Some server boxes had as many as 14 EISA slots. VL-Bus and PCI initially supported fewer than four slots, and that was a problem if you wanted to install 7 network adapters and 5 RAID cards. EISA made it possible. Nowadays PCI is much more robust, and VL-Bus has long since fallen by the wayside.

ELAN (emulated local area network) A logical network initiated by using the mechanisms defined by LAN Emulation. This could include ATM and legacy attached end stations.

Electrically erasable programmable read-only memory (EEPROM) A memory chip that maintains its contents without electrical power, and whose contents can be erased and reprogrammed either within the computer or from an external source. EEPROMs are used where the application requires stable storage without power, but where the chip may have to be reprogrammed.

Electromagnetic A piece of metal that becomes magnetic only when electricity is applied to it; in general, the more electricity applied to metal, the stronger its magnetism.

Electromagnetic field (EMF) A form of radiation given off by all electrical devices. Most notably for computer users, CRT computer monitors used to give off potentially dangerous amounts of EMF radiation, especially from the sides and rear. This radiation was blamed for causing miscarriages and even cancer. Newer monitors are heavily shielded and give off much lower levels of radiation, especially through the front, where users typically sit.

Electromagnetic interferece (EMI) Any electromagnetic radiation released by an electronic device that disrupts the operation or performance of any other device. embedded controller The general class of microcontrollers used to support OEM-specific implementations, mainly in mobile environments. The embedded controller performs complex low-level functions through a simple interface to the host microprocessor(s). embedded controller interface ACPI defines a standard hardware and software communications interface between an operating system driver and an embedded controller—for example, Smart Battery and AML code. This allows any operating system to provide a standard driver that can directly communicate with an embedded controller in the system, thus allowing other drivers to communicate with and use the resources of system embedded controllers.

Electromagnetic relays Switches that have a high current carrying capacity, which are opened and closed by an electromagnet.

Electromagnetic spectrum A range of frequencies over which electromagnetic radiation can be generated, transmitted, and received.

Electromigration This is when metal atoms wander into the dividing layers on a microprocessor. It is caused by the combination of electricity and heat. Processors are designed to run within certain heat and electrical specifications, and if run at higher heat and/or electrical specifications, electromigration may occur. If this occurs to a great degree and enough metal atoms wander off of the lines in a processor, they may permanently ruin the processor by thinning a connection so that it does not work effectively, or even making an electrical connection where one is not intended to be. Overclocking and raising voltage supplied to a processor increases the risk of electromigration.

Electronic classroom A large or small classroom filled with multimedia devices. The usual context is that of a lecture hall where the instructor has fingertip control of multimedia aids such as computer images, video tape images, videodisc images, audio, CD-ROM players, Internet connections, cameras that transfer images to large screens, etc. Some electronic classrooms have student response hardware such as response pads or even computer terminals. Usually, however, the electronic classroom is not viewed in the same context as a computer/ multimedia lab or a language lab. In a lab setting the student usually works alone or in small teams in front of computers. In an electronic classroom, the instructor is usually focusing the attention of the entire class upon the same learning media. However, labs can be equipped with central screens so that combinations of instructor-focused materials can be combined with individual learning. Large lecture halls can also be equipped with students who combine large lectures with "studio classroom learning.

Electronic jamming In the old days (and even today) electronic jamming was used to block communications channels at the enemy's equipment so that they can't receive any information. The next step is not to block their traffic, but instead overwhelm them with incorrect information. This type of disinformation can also be combined with the possibilities described in the section "soft war".

Electronic mail A system allowing computer users to exchange messages via a network.

Electronic signature Any form of electronic identifier, including a digital signature.

Electronically erasable prom (EEPROM) This type of storage is not as fast as DRAM, but maintains data through power loss. It is very similar to Flash memory, except EEPROMs are normally written to one byte at a time, while Flash memory is written to in blocks.

Electrostatic discharge (ESD) The dissipation of electricity. (In layman's terms, a "shock.") ESD can easily destroy semiconductor products, even when the discharge is to small to be felt.

Element A single member of an array, referred to with an index.

EMACS (Editor macros) A popular and powerful text editor used primarily on Linux/UNIX systems. It was written around 1975 in the MIT labs by Richard Stallman. EMACS is often compared with VI, another popular Linux/UNIX text editor.

E-mail alias An E-mail aliase account is sometimes called a forwarding account. This type of e-mail allows you to appear to have an address on one domain, yet behind the scenes the mail is forwarded on to your real e-mail account.

Email forwarding A process to redirect your incoming mail to a specific mailbox. For example, if you have a number of email addresses, forwarding all your email to a single mailbox makes keeping tracking of them much easier, as you only need to check one mailbox, rather than checking all of them individually. Consult your ISP for fees.

E-mail Electronic mail transmitted between millions of users connected on networks worldwide. Messages are exchanged instantaneously, usually at zero marginal cost to users, thereby saving greatly on national or international telephone and express mail fees. Messages may be stored in computer files and processed at a user's convenience. Precautionary advice is given under ActiveX.

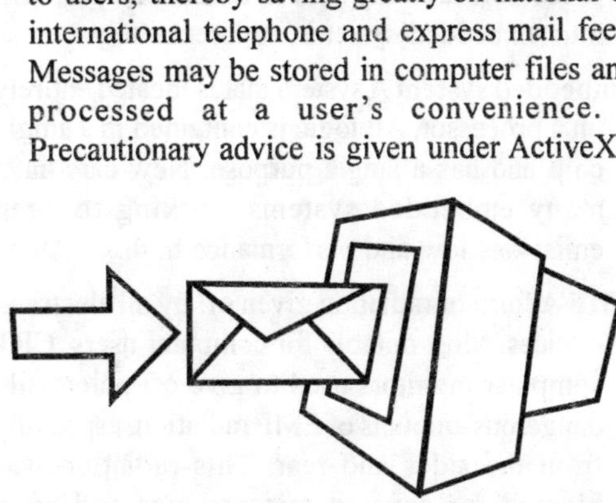

Fig. E-mail

Email policy Policies that address issues, such as:

Which users are entitled to send or receive email.

What files and text can be included in email.

To and from what addresses.

How HTML formatted mail is handled.

Content inspection of attachments to prevent vandals and viruses from infecting the network.

Embedded computers Computers that do not have human user orientated I/O devices; they are directly contained within other machines

Embedded memory This is memory that is built directly onto a processor. For example, a graphics chip may have embedded memory instead of using separate memory chips. Use of embedded memory in PCs and PC components nowadays is fairly rare, as attaching a large amount of memory to a chip reduces yields and increases costs.

Embedded object Microsoft Office programs enable different document types to be embedded within a document using the OLE standard. DDE links between applications can also be used to embed an object.

Embedded processor A microprocessor used in an embedded system. Typically these processors are smaller, consume less power, and utilize a surface mount form factor, as opposed to more standard consumer processors. Embedded processors are only sold to consumers pre-built into embedded systems, not separately.

Embedded system A system that is located entirely on a processor. All logic is contained in a single chip and has a single purpose. New cars have many embedded systems working to keep emissions low and performance high.

EMF A form of radiation given off by all electrical devices. Most notably for computer users, CRT computer monitors used to give off potentially dangerous amounts of EMF radiation, especially from the sides and rear. This radiation was blamed for causing miscarriages and even cancer. Newer monitors are heavily shielded and give off much lower levels of radiation, especially through the front, where users typically sit.

EMI (electromagnetic interference) Equipment used in high speed data systems, including ATM, that generate and transmit many signals in the radio frequency portion of the electromagnetic spectrum. Interference to other equipment or radio services may result if sufficient power from these signals escape the equipment enclosures or transmission media. National and international regulatory agencies (FCC, CISPR, etc.) set limits for these emissions. Class A is for industrial use and Class B is for residential use.

EML (element management layer) An abstraction of the functions provided by systems that manage each network element on an individual basis.

Emoticon A picture built out of ASCII characters, often sideways, used in human-to-human electronic communications, such as e-mail, chat, and IRC. The use of emoticons is intended to compensate for the lack of evocative, emotional content in computer text. The most popular type of emoticon is the smiley face.

Emoticons These are groups of text characters that, when viewed sideways, look like facial expressions. For example, the most common one is the happy face :) — a colon and a close parenthesis. There are many, many more, such as the semicolon wink ;) or the colon-p :P that looks like you are sticking your tongue out. The purpose of emoticons is to convey a feeling in a text-based message that may or may not be obvious to the reader. They are typically used in informal communications, especially when using sarcasm or trying to add extra feeling to the message.

EMS (element management system) A management system that provides functions at the element Management Layer.

Emulation Refers to the ability of a program or device to imitate another program or device. Many printers, for example, are designed to emulate Hewlett-Packard LaserJet printers because so much software is written for HP printers. By emulating an HP printer, a printer can work with any software written for a real HP printer. Emulation tricks the software into believing that a device is really some other device. Communications software packages often include terminal emulation drivers. This enables your PC to emulate a particular type of terminal so that you can log on to a mainframe. It is also possible for a computer to emulate another type of computer. For example, there are programs that enable an Apple Macintosh to emulate a PC.

Emulator This is usually a program that performs the same operation of another program or a piece of hardware. For example, there are programs that allow a PC to act like a Commodore 64, a Nintendo Entertainment System, or even a Macintosh. These emulators are often developed by talented programmers just to prove that something can be done.

Encapsulated postscript (EPS) The file format of the PostScript page description language. The EPS standard is device independent, so that images can easily be transferred between different applications, and they can be sized and output to different printers without any loss of image quality or distortion.

Encapsulation The ability to provide users with a well-defined interface to a set of functions in a way which hides their internal workings. In object-oriented object-oriented programming, the technique of keeping together data structures and the methods method(procedures) which act on them.

Enciphered Encrypted or encoded; a mathematical process that disguises the content of messages transmitted

Encoded files Files with data that has been changed from 8-bits to 7-bits to enable it to travel over SMTP.

Encryption can be used to verify the identity of a sender by adding an encrypted block of data (signature) to the end of a message. When decrypted, the block matches the contents of the message itself. Encryption can also be used for privacy by encrypting the entire message.

Encoding Encoding translates an attachment to a form that eases its transmission over the Internet. When an encoded file is received, it must be decoded. There are a variety of encoding schemes, including MIME, Base 64, UUEncode on the PC, and Binhex on the Macintosh.

Encrypt The act of making data unreadable in an orderly fashion so that it can be decrypted later.

Encrypted email A number of encryption schemes can be used to encrypt email. Regardless of the scheme used, encryption interferes with content inspection, which cannot take place as long as the email is encrypted. In order to protect against malicious content in encrypted email, a network wide desktop protection scheme must be used to ensure that the content is inspected the moment it is decrypted. Regularly scheduled Mail scans of all public and private folders on MS Exchange and Lotus Notes/Domino Servers can also prevent malicious encrypted email from using these servers to replicate throughout your organization.

Encrypted password A password that has been "jumbled" to protect it from being discovered and used by someone other than the person to whom it belongs. Encrypted passwords generally have an equivalent "clear-text password." InterNIC' Guardian plan allows the use of encrypted passwords, which help to ensure that modification of a domain name record, contact record, or host record can only be completed by an authorized source.

Encrypting file system (EFS) A feature of the Windows 2000 operating system that allows any file or folder to be stored in encrypted form and decrypted only by an individual user or an authorized recovery agent.

Encryption algorithm A mathematical algorithm, such as DES , for encrypting and decrypting data.

Encryption Encryption is the process of converting data into "unreadable code" is so that unauthorized people cannot understand the content. Encryption may be used to make stored data private (e.g., data that is stored on a potentially vulnerable hard disk), or to allow a nonsecure communications channel to serve as a private communications channel. Encryption is sometimes described as the process of converting plaintext into ciphertext. To decipher the message, the receiver of the encrypted data must have the proper decryption key.

End of input Usually the Cntrl-D character.

End station These devices (e.g., hosts or PCs) enable the communication between ATM end stations and end stations on "legacy" LAN or among ATM end stations.

End user license agreement (EULA) The contract found in most software packages that describes the rights to which the user of the software is entitled. Typically, it will explain how many people can use the software, whether it can be used on multiple machines, and whether it is transferable.

End user Refers to the person who uses the application program to produce their own results.

End-effector The end piece of a robotic arm that can receive various types of grippers and tools

Energy star Norm defined by the EPA (US Environment Protection Agency) for computer manufacturers aiming at reducing electrical consumption.

Engine This is the working part of a database or application.

Enhanced bios (EBIOS) This translates between the partition table limitations of a standard computer BIOS and the IDE limitations to provide up to 8 GB of storage space using the IDE interface. Your computer's BIOS has maximums of 1024 cylinders, 256 heads, and 63 sectors (8 GB). The IDE interface has a maximum of 65,536 cylinders, 16 heads, and 256 sectors (128 GB). Put these maximums together (1024 cylinders, 16 heads, and 63 sectors) and you've got a measly 504 MB of data to work with. The EBIOS translates these limitations in such a way that you can actually achieve the BIOS max of 8 GB on one IDE device. Newer IDE standards have since been developed to up the top hard drive size to 128 GB and beyond.

Enhanced expanded memory specification (EEMS) A revised version of the original Lotus-Intel-Microsoft Expanded Memory Specification (LIM EMS), that lets DOS applications use more than 640KB of memory space.

Enhanced graphics adapter (EGA) A video adapter standard that provides medium-resolution text and graphics, introduced by IBM in 1984. EGA can display 16 colors at the same time from a choice of 64, with a horizontal resolution of 640 pixels and a vertical resolution of 350 pixels.

Enhanced ide (EIDE) This standard allowed for two IDE channels that can each support two devices in peaceful coexistence. It also allowed for hard drives up to 8 GB in size and CD-ROM devices.

Enhanced metafile (EMF) A temporary file created by an operating system before data is sent to a printer. The EMFs are created so that control is returned to the program that is printing more quickly. Then the EMF is sent to the print spooler to be converted into language that the printer can understand. Think of the EMF as a quick and dirty scratch file the OS creates so that programs don't have to talk to the (usually slow) printer directly and thus tie up your computer.

Enhanced parallel port (EPP) An enhanced version of the parallel port specification for PCs. Nowadays most parallel ports (and printers) support EPP mode, and EPP mode should be used for maximum performance when frequent bidirectional communications are necessary through the parallel port. However, it is probably better just to go with USB instead.

Enhanced small device interface (ESDI) A popular hard disk, floppy disk, and tape drive interface standard, capable of a data transfer rate of 10 to 20 megabits per second. ESDI is most often used with large hard disks. enhanced television Combines standard television with HTML information related to programs.

Enstructions The computer knows how to execute, or it can contain a shell script (a list of Unix shell commands) that Unix knows how to execute.

Enter key In a Unix shell, pressing Enter means that you have just typed a command and you want Unix to do it. In a text editor, pressing Enter means you want to begin a new line. The Enter key and the Return key usually do the same thing(your keyboard may have one, the other, or both).

Enterprise information system A system of client and server computers that can be used to manage all of the tasks required to manage and run a large organization.

Enterprise mail exchange (EMX) A product by SoftSwitch, Inc., that acts as a protocol converter for electronic mail between the Unix/ SMTP, IBM 3090/DISSOS, and cc.

Enterprise resource planning (ERP) The daunting task of planning and organizing business functions in the enterprise. It also refers to a class of software designed to help organizations do this. Often the installation of this type of software can be a complex task, taking many months and many millions of dollars. ERP software can help companies manage everything from sales and marketing to human resources.

Enterprise The entirety of an organization that uses computers. Typically it refers to very large corporations, or software or hardware solutions designed for large organizations. Enterprise companies usually have numerous locations and hundreds, if not thousands, of users to support—a scenario which requires an entirely different type of IT system and management than a small to mid-sized company.

Entity-relationship diagram A type of diagram used in the Entity-Relationship Entity-Relationship model.

Entry-level system A computer system that meets the basic requirements for a specific task. As computers become both cheaper and more capable, the definition of an entry-level system changes. Also, application developers continue to create new and more complex programs, which in turn demand more capability from the hardware. enumeration The process by which logical devices and buses, and their available resources, are identified by Plug and Play during system setup. enumerator A Plug and Play device driver that detects devices below its own device node, creates unique device IDs, and reports to Configuration Manager during startup. For example, a SCSI adapter provides a SCSI enumerator that detects devices on the SCSI bus.

Environment Normally this is your surroundings. Inside your computer, the environment is the settings of a group of variables. Think of it as the surroundings or boundaries set for a process or program running inside your computer.

EOM (end of message) An indicator used in the AAL that identifies the last ATM cell containing information from a data packet that has been segmented.

E-OTD (enhanced observed time difference) Is a mobile location system that uses different between time of arrival, at the handset and at a nearby locator, of a signal transmitted by the mobile network to pin-point the devices position.

EPCS (experimental physics control systems) A group of the European Physical Society, focussing on all aspects of controls, especially informatics, in experimental physics, including accelerators and experiments.

EPG (electronic program guide) Tthat displays scheduled shows on screen such as TV Guide On Screen.

Ephemeris A record showing positions of astronomical objects and artificial satellites in a time-ordered sequence.

EPIC (explicitly parallel instruction computing) This is Intel and Hewlett-Packard's invention, designed to be used on Intel's Itanium processor. It is a method for arranging instructions so that they are ordered to be explicitly parallel. That is, multiple instructions can easily be executed at once, assuming that the hardware supports it. Intel's IA-64 architecture, including Itanium processors, is designed to get the most out of instructions arranged in this manner.

EPOC Operating system specifically designed for mobile devices by Symbian, a consortium formedof Psion, Ericsson, Matsushita, Nokia and Motorola. It is best known for its implementation on Psion PDAs and Ericsson R380 mobile phones.

EPP (enhanced parallel port) An enhanced version of the parallel port specification for PCs. Nowadays most parallel ports (and printers) support EPP mode, and EPP mode should be used for maximum performance when frequent bidirectional communications are necessary through the parallel port. However, it is probably better just to go with USB instead.

EPROM (erasable programmable read-only memory and pronounced ee-prom) EPROM is a special type of memory that retains its contents until it is exposed to ultraviolet light. The ultraviolet light clears its contents, making it possible to reprogram the memory. To write to and erase an EPROM, you need a special device called a PROM programmer or PROM burner. An EPROM differs from a PROM in that a PROM can be written to only once and cannot be erased. EPROMs are used widely in personal computers because they enable the manufacturer to change the contents of the PROM before the computer is actually shipped. This means that bugs can be removed and new versions installed shortly before delivery.

EPS (encapsulated postscript) An EPS file usually has two parts: a PostScript (text) description that tells a PostScript printer how to output the resolution-independent image, and (optionally) a bit-mapped PICT image for on-screen previews. (EPS files without a PICT preview is usually displayed as a gray rectangle.) EPS files generally can't be edited, even by the program that created them (Illustrator files are exceptions).

ER (explicit rate) The Explicit Rate is an RM-cell field used to limit the source ACR to a specific value. It is initially set by the source to a requested rate (such as PCR). It may be subsequently reduced by any network element in the path to a value that the element can sustain. ER is formatted as a rate.

Erasable programmable read only memory (EPROM) This is normally read-only memory that retains its information until it is exposed to ultraviolet light. You can often tell a chip is an EPROM by the small window on it that lets ultraviolet light though to program the EPROM.

ERC An extended entity-relationship entity-relationship model .

ERCIM European Research Consortium on Informatics and Mathematics. An association of European research organizations promoting cooperative research on key issues in information technology.

ERCS Extended Reference Concrete Syntaxes for SGML, to support East Asian and other non-English languages.

ERD Entity-relationship diagram.

Ergonomic Being of suitable geometry and structure to permit effective or optimal human user interaction with machines.

Eric An index to educational journal articles and documents collected by national clearing houses for educational information. It provides summaries of the articles and documents, and contains citations back to 1966.

ERP (enterprise resource planning) The daunting task of planning and organizing business functions in the enterprise. It also refers to a class of software designed to help organizations do this. Often the installation of this type of software can be a complex task, taking many months and many millions of dollars. ERP software can help companies manage everything from sales and marketing to human resources.

Errata Minor errors in microprocessor design that are corrected with a new stepping of the processor. The difference between errata and a serious defect is really based on how many people or systems are seriously affected by the issue. It is standard practice for the first volume production of microprocessors to contain errata that is fixed in later generations. Most early errata are worked around by chipsets, BIOS, and drivers.

Error This occurs in a program when it encounters a situation that it was not programmed to deal with. If errors are trapped properly, they can be dealt with by the program itself. If not, they will be dealt with by the operating system on which the program is running.

Error checking and correcting (ECC) This generally refers to memory chips or motherboards that support the checking for, and possibly correcting of, memory errors in full-parity memory chips. ECC memory uses some extra memory on the memory chips for parity information, and checks to see whether a memory error has occurred. If a minor (one-bit) memory error occurs, the ECC logic will handle it. With full-parity memory (one step below ECC), you will be alerted of a memory error and your system will stop. With non-parity memory you will experience random results, usually crashing, and possible data corruption. If a two-bit or larger error occurs in ECC memory, your system will be halted—similar to what happens with parity memory when any error is encountered. Many caches built into computer microprocessors now have ECC features.

Error codes At InterNIC, standard codes that are used to indicate common errors in the Domain Name Registration Agreement, the contact forms, or the host form that prevent the processing of the Domain Name Registration Agreement or forms.

Error control Strategy implemented in software, hardware or procedures for detecting and possibly correcting the errors happening in a communication system.

Error correction A method used to correct erroneous data produced during data transmission, transfer, or storage.

Error detection and correction A mechanism used during a file transfer to determine whether transmission errors have occurred, and to correct those errors, if possible. Some programs or transmission protocols request a retransmission of the affected block of data if such an error is detected. More complex protocols attempt to both detect and correct transmission errors.

Error rate In many cases, it may be acceptable if an input device generates a certain number of errors. This is often referred to as the error rate and the acceptable level will vary according to the input device being used and the business application. Optical character recognition, for example, is generally considered a comparatively unreliable means of entering data. At present, a typical OCR software package will have an error rate of between five and ten per cent.

ES end system A system where an ATM connection is terminated or initiated. An originating end system initiates the ATM connection, and terminating end system terminates the ATM connection. OAM cells may be generated and received.

Escape key The key labeled Escape or Esc. What this key does depends on the program you are using. The vi editor uses it to switch from input mode to command mode.

ESCD Setup data that is stored in a Plug-and-Play-compatible system BIOS. It consists of the system resource requirements of legacy (non-PNP) devices, and the last working configuration of Plug-and-Play-compliant devices. Plug-and-Play devices that have ESCD entries will use the same resources each time the system boots—as long as no new hardware has been added. This ensures a stable configuration. Plug-and-Play OSes such as Windows 95 and its successors have access to the ESCD, as you would guess if you've ever had to manually change device configurations in Windows (by using the "Device Manager").

ESD Electro Static Discharge and is defined as a sudden flow of electricity between two objects at different electrical potentials. ESD is a primary cause of integrated circuit damage or failure.

ESD testing One kind of test that hardware usually has to pass to prove it is suitable for sale and use. The hardware must still work after is has been subjected to some level of electrostatic discharge. Some organizations have their own ESD requirements which hardware must meet before it will be considered for purchase.

Different countries have different legal regulations about levels of ESD. The best way to help prevent ESD is either to use a wrist strap, or a grounding mat. However most users do not have access to such items therefore you can follow the below guidelines to help prevent ESD as much as possible.

Clothes - Insure what you are not wearing an item that conducts a lot of Electrical Charge, such as a wool sweater. Also it is generally a good idea to remove all jewelry as well.

Weather - When working on your computer insure there is not an electrical storm outside which increases the potential of ESD.

Cords - Insure everything is removed from the back of the computer (power cord, mouse, keyboard, etc).

Zero Potential - Insure you and the computer are at Zero Potential by continuously touching the un-painted metal chassis (computer frame) or the Power supply.

Standing - When working inside the computer it is highly recommended that you stand at all times.

Surface - It is always best to stand on a wooden surface. Avoid working on a computer in carpeted areas.

ESF (extended superframe) A DS1 framing format in which 24 DS0 times lots plus a coded framing bit are organized into a frame which is repeated 24 times to form a superframe.

ESI (end system identifier) This identifier distinguishes multiple nodes at the same level in case the lower level peer group is partitioned.

Esoteric Relating to a specialized field of endeavor that is characterized by its restricted size.

Estelle A formal description technique developed for OSI protocol specification.

Ethernet A LANcabling technology that uses CSMA/CD delivery. Ethernet runs over many different media, ranging from thick cable (10Base5) to twisted-pair wire (10BaseT). Ethernet has been standardized by the International Electrical and Electronics Engineers (IEEE) organization. The three most common Ethernet cabling standards are:

Thick Ethernet (10Base5) This is the original Ethernet cabling which used a thick, half -inch diameter coaxial cable. It operates in baseband mode with a bandwidth of 10Mbps. The maximum cable length of a segment is 500 meters. The IEEE label 10Base5 summarizes these characteristics:10-Mbps bandwidth, baseband operation, and 500 meter segments.Thick Ethernet uses MAUs(multistation access units), N-type, and AUI (attachment unit interface) connectors.

Thin Ethernet (10Base2) Is a CSMA/CD network with these features: 10-Mbps bandwidth, baseband operation, and segment lengths of approximately 200 meters(the exact limit is 185 meters). The coaxial cable used is considerably thinner than thicknet coax. Thin Ethernet uses BNC (bayonet) and T connectors.

Ethernet address The hardware address that identifies the Ethernet network interface card inside a computer. Also called the physical address. No two Ethernet addresses are identical. event set A uniquely identified set that represents a group of items about which a client can be notified.

Ethernet sniffing The use of software to monitor the Ethernet interface for packets of interest. When the software identifies a packet that fits specific criteria, such as a password, it logs it to a file.

ETSI European Telecommunications Standards Institute: The primary telecommunications standards organization.

Euclidean geometry The study of points, lines, angles, polygons, and curves confined to a plane.

EULA (end user license agreement) The contract found in most software packages that describes the rights to which the user of the software is entitled. Typically, it will explain how many people can use the software, whether it can be used on multiple machines, and whether it is transferable.

Eureka A European technological development programme.

Event A condition, often the result of a user's action, that can be detected by a script.

Event handler A special type of function that executes automatically when a particular user-enabled, system-enabled, or code-generated event occurs.

Event integration facility (EIF) Defines and forwards management events from existing applications to the Enterprise Console, and provides facilities to process the events.

Eworld A commercial world-wide network launched by Apple Corporation to compete with Interchange, CompuServe, Prodigy, and America Online. Key features of eWorld include its ease of use and graphical interface. The major limitation is that its use is restricted to Mac operating systems.

Exabyte (EB) 1 Quadrillion bytes or 1,152,921,504,606,846,976 bytes.

Excel Microsoft spreadsheet.

Exception An indication that some event of particular interest has occurred, such as an error in a procedure, an authorization failure or any other unanticipated event. Generally, an indication that a request was not performed successfully.

Executable file A file in a format that the computer can directly execute. Unlike source files, executable files cannot be read by humans. To transform a source file into an executable file, you need to pass it through a compiler or assembler. In DOS systems, executable files have either a .COM or .EXE extension and are called COM files and EXE files, respectively.

Execution flow The section of code that the application executes, depending on branching decisions.

Execution unit The part of a microprocessor pipeline that actually follows and runs the instructions that are sent to the CPU after the instructions are decoded.

Exit border node The node that will progress a call over an outside link. This is the last node within a peer group to see this call.

Exodus A package from White Pines allowing the Macintosh to be used as an X server X-server.

Expandability The ability of a system to accommodate expansion. In hardware, this may include the addition of more memory, more or larger disk drives, and new adapters, and in software may include the ability of a network to add users, nodes, or connections to other networks.

Expanded memory A DOS mechanism by which applications can access more than the 640KB of memory normally available to them.

The Expanded Memory Specification LIM 4.0 is the standard method of accessing expanded memory, and lets programs running on any of the Intel 8086 family of processors access as much as 32MB of expanded memory. The expanded memory manager creates a block of addresses into which data (held in memory above the 1 MB limit) is swapped in and out as needed by the program. In other words,a 64K segment of addressable memory creates a small window through which segments of expanded memory can be seen, but only one segment at a time.

Expanded memory manager(EMM) A device driver that supports the software portion of the expanded memory specification in an IBM-compatible computer.

Expansion bus A group of control lines that provide a buffered interface to devices located either on the system board or on cards that are plugged into expansion connectors. Common expansion buses included on the system board are USB, PC Card, and PCI.

Expansion card This is generally a printed circuit board that can be plugged into a computer, and is designed to increase the functionality of that computer.

Expansion slots One of the connectors on the expansion bus that gives an adapter access to the system bus. The amount of additional adapters that one may add is determined by how many expansion slots are inside your computer.

Expansion unit An external housing available with certain portable computers designed to contain additional expansion slots and maintain a connection to the main expansion bus in the computer's system unit.

Expert system An intelligent computer program that contains a knowledge base, specialized software, and a set of algorithms or rules that infer new facts from knowledge and from incoming data.

Explicitly parallel instruction computing (EPIC) This is Intel and Hewlett-Packard's invention, designed to be used on Intel's Itanium processor. It is a method for arranging instructions so that they are ordered to be explicitly parallel. That is, multiple instructions can easily be executed at once, assuming that the hardware supports it. Intel's IA-64 architecture, including Itanium processors, is designed to get the most out of instructions arranged in this manner.

Exploit A means of gaining access to a computer system, typically through a known bug in a program or operating system. Many webservers on the Internet that are not up to date with security patches are vulnerable to exploits, and the effects of these exploits are seen when malicious worms run rampant and spread to unpatched systems.

Export When you export data you are taking that data from a program, or file and saving it in another that is generally easier to manipulate or pull into a different program. An example would be pulling data from a SQL database and saving it as text so that you can use it in a mailmerge. Thus, the exporting frees the mailmerge program from having to understand the complex SQL format—it just needs to understand the exported text file.

Express author A front end to Asymetrix Multimedia ToolBook that performs automatic scripting to both speed authoring and aid ToolBook novices. This front end is mainly an aid to beginning authors who do not plan to become ToolBook experts.

Expression A combination of variables, constants, and operators that can be evaluated to a single value.

Extended ASCII character set The second part of the ASCII character set from decimal code 128 to decimal code 255. This part of the ASCII character set is not standard, and will contain different characters on different types of computer. ECP Extended capabilities port. An asynchronous, 8-bit-wide parallel channel defined by IEEE 1284-1944 that provides PC-to-peripheral and peripheral-to-PC data transfers.

Extended binary coded decimal interchange code (EBCDIC) A way of encoding 256 characters in binary, much like ASCII, but used mainly on mainframes. Most of the time EBCDIC is only mentioned in translations between EBCDIC and ASCII.

Extended data out RAM (EDO RAM) The successor to standard fast page DRAM. It's a conceptually faster RAM chip that has small bits of SRAM cache built into it. It still runs at slow DRAM speeds (<= 50 MHz), and thus is no longer used. At one time, it was a popular memory format and offered enhanced memory performance.

Extended DOS partition A further optional division of a hard disk, after the primary DOS partition, that functions as one or more additional logical drives. A logical drive is simply an area of a larger disk that acts as though it were a separate disk with its own drive letter. Creating an extended partition allows you to install a second operationg system, such as OS/2; and in early DOS versions it is the only way to use disk space above 32MB. NOTE:DOS partitions are created and changed using the FDISK command.

Extended industry standard architecture (EISA) A PC bus standard that extends the traditional AT-bus to 32 bits and allows more than one processor to share the bus.

Extended markup language (XML) A superset of HyperText Markup Language (HTML) and another language in the Standardized General Markup Language (SGML) family, used for instances of programs (such as clients or servers) to exchange information.

Extended memory Memory above and beyond the standard 1MB (megabyte) of main memory that DOS supports. Extended memory is only available in PCs with an Intel 80286 or later microprocessor. Two types of memory can be added to a PC to increase memory beyond 1MB: expanded memory and extended memory. Expanded memory conforms to a published standard called EMS that enables DOS programs to take advantage of it. Extended memory, on the other hand, is not configured in any special manner and is therefore unavailable to most DOS programs. However, MS-Windows and OS/2 can use extended memory.

Extended memory manager a device driver that supports the software portion of the extended memory specification in an IBM-compatible computer.

Extended memory specification (XMS) A standard developed by Microsoft, Intel, Lotus, and AST Research that has become the preferred way of accessing extended memory in the PC.

Extended partition A type of partition that is an extension of a primary partition. It's possible to have many extended partitions on a hard drive.

Extended system configuration data (ESCD) Setup data that is stored in a Plug-and-Play-compatible system BIOS. It consists of the system resource requirements of legacy (non-PNP) devices, and the last working configuration of Plug-and-Play-compliant devices. Plug-and- Play devices that have ESCD entries will use the same resources each time the system boots—as long as no new hardware has been added. This ensures a stable configuration. Plug-and-Play OSes such as Windows 95 and its successors have access to the ESCD, as you would guess if you've ever had to manually change device configurations in Windows (by using the "Device Manager").

Extensible database A DBMS that allows access to data from remote sources as if it were part of the database.

Extensible markup language (XML) A standard created by the W3C. It is a language with many similarities to HTML. What XML adds is the ability to define custom tags, such as , and define the meaning of those tags within the XML document itself—thus the term "extensible."

You can extend the XML language easily. XML is becoming more and more common as more browsers and webservers support it. It is also a very flexible way to exchange data over the Web and interpret and use data from other websites.

Extension (file extension) DOS, Windows, and, to a lesser extent, UNIX and Linux use the last three characters of a filename, after a period, to signify what type of file a file is, such as text, movie, sound, etc. The MacOS has a file system that contains an identifier for file types that is invisible when looking at the filename, and allows you to call files whatever you want without a messy extension on the end. Some common examples are: .exe (executable file), .bat (batch file), .wav (wave sound file), and .txt (text file).

Exterior Denotes that an item (e.g., link, node, or reachable address) is outside of a PNNI routing domain.

Exterior link A link which crosses the boundary of the PNNI routing domain. The PNNI protocol does not run over an exterior link.

Exterior reachable address An address that can be reached through a PNNI routing domain, but which is not located in that PNNI routing domain.

Exterior route A route which traverses an exterior link.

External command A command the shell does'nt actually know how to do. Instead, a program is stored in a file with the same name as the command. If you type the ed command, for example, Unix runs the program contained by a file named ed.

External firewall A firewall between a company and the outside world (Internet). Certain data (for example, mail and news) can flow unimpeded, but interactive sessions or scripts cannot affect data in either inbound or outbound directions.

External modem A modem that resides in a self-contained box outside the computer system. Contrast with an internal modem, which resides on a printed circuit board inserted into the computer. External modems tend to be slightly more expensive than internal modems. Many experts consider them superior because they contain lights that indicate how the modem is functioning. In addition, they can easily be moved from one computer to another. However, they do use up one COM port.

External viewer A program used for presenting graphics, audio and video files. Programs that allow the viewing of GIF and JPEG files and the hearing of AU files fall into this category.

Extranet A term depicting networks on the Internet dedicated to business communications between a vendor and its suppliers, customers, or dealers. The term originated from network pioneer Robert Metcalfe. Using the common format of the World Wide Web, companies, their suppliers, customers, or suppliers exchange data electronically rather than sending paper-based information back and forth. It is viewed as an Internet alternative to Electronic Data Interchange comprised of dedicated lines and software rather than the Internet. Extranets are a lower cost alternative to EDI.

Extremely low-frequency emission(ELF) Radiation emitted by a computer monitor and other very common household electrical appliances such as televisions, hair dryers, electric blankets and food processors. ELF emissions fall into the range from 5Hz to 2000Hz, and decline with the square of the distance from the source. Emissions are not constant around a monitor; they are higher from the sides and rear, and weakest from the front of the screen. Low-emission models are available, and laptop computers with an LCD display do not emit any ELF fields.

F

Fab This is short for fabrication plant. A fab is a factory that takes raw silicon wafers and creates chips with them. Often, fabs are categorized by what process they use. For example, the Intel Pentium chip with MMX was produced in a fab with a 0.35 micron process. Fabrication plants cost billions of dollars to build and are outdated within years. However, they can have a decent life producing volume products after they are no longer considered high-end.

Fabless This term refers to a company that produces chips but doesn't own a fabrication plant, or fab. These companies are starting to become more and more successful at creating chips and renting out other companies' excess fab space to produce their chips. In fact, some fabrication plant owners specifically target such fabless companies to offer their fab space for rent.

Fabrication plant A fab is a factory that takes raw silicon wafers and creates chips with them. Often, fabs are categorized by what process they use. For example, the Intel Pentium chip with MMX was produced in a fab with a 0.35 micron process. Fabrication plants cost billions of dollars to build and are outdated within years. However, they can have a decent life producing volume products after they are no longer considered high-end.

Facsimile (fax) Almost always referred to as fax, this is the term for the electronic transmission of printed documents over a phone line. Usually transmission occurs between fax machines, but you can also use a computer with a fax modem, or a dedicated fax card.

Failover When one device stops working and another device automatically takes its place, typically after a set amount of time has lapsed since the first device stopped responding. Basically, the work done by the device figuratively fails over onto the other device.

Fairness As related to Generic Flow Control (GFC), fairness is defined as meeting all the agreed quality of service (QOS) requirements, by controlling the order of service for all active connections.

Fan A device designed to move air by sucking air into one side and pushing it out the other. Fans are a necessary part of most computing devices because microprocessors heat up when run at high frequencies. Fans move the hot air away and allow the microprocessors to be cooled off. Fans are also used in power supplies to keep them cool.

FAQ (frequently asked questions) A document that lists the most common questions about something (with the answers, of course). A simple way to find information on a complex topic is to do an Internet search for _topic_ FAQ, where _topic_ represents the topic for which you are looking.

Fast file system (FFS) The first major revision to the Unix file system, providing faster read access and faster (delayed, asynchronous) write access through a disk cache and better file system layout on disk.

Fast-SCSI Plain vanilla fast-SCSI never really existed, but was sometimes used as slang for Fast SCSI 2. This version of SCSI transfers data at 10 megabytes per second. The connections all contain 50 pins.

Fast-wide SCSI 2 This version of SCSI upped the pin count to 68, effectively doubling the signal speed of Fast-SCSI 2 to 20 megabytes per second.

FAT (file allocation table) This is one way to index the contents of storage media, such as your hard drive. The operating system looks here to know where on the drive files are located. There are different flavors of FAT: the standard DOS flavor is called FAT-16; Windows 95 OSR2 and newer versions additionally supported FAT-32, which allows for larger hard drive partitions.

FAT 32 A new version of the file allocation table (FAT) available in Windows 95 OSR 2 and Windows 98. FAT32 increases the number of bits used to address clusters and also reduces the size of each cluster. The result is that it can support larger disks (up to 2 terabytes) and better storage efficiency (less slack space).

Fat client Today's fast PCs are fat clients. They've got lots of memory and big hard drives. They store information and typically run programs locally off of their hard drives. Fat clients usually work in client/server environments, where they can take on some of the processing workload and leave the servers free to serve data. Fat clients are much more customizable and powerful than thin clients, but they are harder to manage and control. For example, users can't install AOL software on a thin client.

Fat-16 The original DOS File Allocation system. It uses a table to tell the OS where on a hard drive or other storage media each file is located. Due to the 16-bit nature of FAT-16, it is limited to hard drive partitions that are 2 GB in size.

Fatal error An operating system or application program error from which there is no hope of recovery without rebooting (and thus losing any unsaved work.).

Fatmen A distributed file and tape management system for HEP data.

Fault tolerance A design method that ensures continued system operation in the event of individual failures by providing redundant elements. At the component level, designers include redundant chips and circuits and add the capability to bypass faults automatically. At the computer system level, they replicate any elements likely to fail, such as processors and large disk drives. Fault-tolerant operations often require backup or UPS power systems in the event of a main power failure, and may imply the duplication of entire computer systems in remote locations to protect against vandalism, acts of war, or natural disaster.

Favorite A method of storing and organizing selected URLs in Internet Explorer.

Fax Devices for transmitting and receiving photocopies over telephone lines. Text and graphics may be printed on paper or stored in computer files. Text is received as a graphic and must be translated by specialized software to be stored as text files for word processors.

Fax machine This is generally a single purpose device that can send and receive facsimiles. The machine is normally able to scan in a document and transmit it over a phone line to another fax machine. Also, it can receive faxes from other machines and print them out.

Fax modem A device you can attach to a personal computer that enables you to transmit and receive electronic documents as faxes. A fax modem is like a regular modem except that it is designed to transmit documents to a fax machine or to another fax modem. Some, but not all, fax modems do double duty as regular modems. As with regular modems, fax modems can be either internal or external. Internal fax modems are often called fax boards.

FBGA Fine pitch ball grid array is a die package with a fine pitch ball arrangement on the underside of the package (larger than CSP).

FC feedback control Feedback controls are defined as the set of actions taken by the network and by the end-systems to regulate the traffic submitted on ATM connections according to the state of network elements.

FC-AL (fiber channel-arbitrated loop) A fast, serial-based standard meant to replace the parallel SCSI standard. It is primarily used in high cost server systems, and to connect storage devices to servers. It is software-compatible with SCSI and can handle 126 devices per port. FC-AL connections can run as far as 10 kilometers using optical cabling, or 30 meters with standard copper cabling.

FCC certification Approval by the FCC that a specific computer model meets its standards for radio frequency interference emissions. There are two levels of certification. Class A certification is for computers used in commercial settings, such as mainframes and minicomputers. Class B certification is for computers used in the home and in home offices, such as PCs,laptops, and portables.

FCC (federal communications commission) A U.S. government regulatory body for radio, television, all interstate telecommunications services, and all international services that originate inside the U.S. All computer equipment must be certified by the FCC before it can be offered for sale in the U.S. to ensure that it meets the legal limits for conductive and radio frequency emissions, which could otherwise interfere with commercial broadcasts.

FC-PGA (flip chip-plastic grid array) This is Intel's newer packaging of the Socket 370 design. It features a different electrical setup than Socket 370, but is physically compatible. Thus, old Socket 370 motherboards will not be compatible with new FC-PGA chips, but new FC- PGA motherboards may be able to handle Socket 370 processors. It is not clear why Intel made the electrical change. The physical changes put the core closer to the surface, allowing better cooling as the processor core comes in closer contact to the heatsink.

FCS (frame check sequence) Any mathematical formula which derives a numeric value based on the bit pattern of a transmitted block of information and uses that value at the receiving end to determine the existence of any transmission errors.

FDD (floppy disk drive) This commonly refers to a 3.5 inch disk drive that uses 1.44 MB 3.5 inch floppy disks. However, the term can be used to apply to any drive that uses floppy disk media.

FDDI (fiber distributed data interface) An American National Standards Institute standard for 100 Mbps fiber-optic local area networks. Incorporates token processing and supports circuit-switched voice and packetized data. Components include: PMD (Physical Layer Medium Dependent), which deals with physical connections including fiber links, cables and connectors.; PHY (Physical Layer Protocol) which includes the encoding/decoding of packets and data clocking; MAC (Media Access Control) which includes parameters for token passing, addressing, packed sizes and framing; and SMT (Station Management) which governs management of the physical network.

FDisk The program Microsoft operating systems MS-DOS and non-NT versions of Windows use to create partitions on hard drives. Technically, the program is called fdisk.exe. It uses a text-based interface. Windows 95b first added support for FAT-32 partitions into fdisk. Before that it only supported partitions up to 2 GB using FAT-16. This is also a slang term for wiping a drive out completely.

Feature A feature is something that a piece of hardware or software is designed to do. Many things that appear to be bugs are actually features. Often, a hardware or software developer will have to make a trade-off in functionality that causes some undesirable effects. If the developer is aware of this and accepts it, it is not a bug but a feature.

FEBE (far end block error) A maintenance signal transmitted in the PHY overhead that a bit error(s) has been detected at the PHY layer at the far end of the link. This is used to monitor bit error performance of the link.

FEC (forward error correction) A technique for detection and correction of errors in a digital data stream.

Feed-forward A multilayer perceptron perceptron network in which the outputs from all neurons go to following but not preceding layers, so there are no feedback loops.

Female connector Any cable connector with receptacles designed to receive the pins on the male part of the connector.

Femtosecond (FS) One quadrillionth of a second (1/1,000,000,000,000,000 seconds).

Ferroelectric RAM (FRAM) Initially developed by Ramtron, this is a type of non-volatile RAM that compares favorably to Flash memory in access/read/write speeds, but is harder to produce than Flash or DRAM in high densities. FRAM is used in some portable devices, but hasn't really caught on compared to other memory technologies.

FFT Fast Fourier Transform.

FG (functional group) A collection of functions related in such a way that they will be provided by a single logical component. Examples include the Route Server Functional Group (RSFG), the IASG (Internetwork Address Sub-Group), Coordination Functional Group (ICFG), the Edge Device Functional Group (EDFG) and the ATM attached host Behavior Functional Group (AHFG).

Fiber channel-arbitrated loop (FC-AL) A fast, serial-based standard meant to replace the parallel SCSI standard. It is primarily used in high cost server systems, and to connect storage devices to servers. It is software-compatible with SCSI and can handle 126 devices per port. FC-AL connections can run as far as 10 kilometers using optical cabling, or 30 meters with standard copper cabling.

Fiber distributed data interface (FDDI) This is a fiber optic interface that allows data to travel extreme distances (many miles/kilometers) without signal loss. It is far superior to copper wire for data integrity as well. FDDI is often used to connect Internet, LAN, or WAN backbones together due to these properties.

Fiber optic A method of physical data transmission that is a newer alternative to sending electrical signals over copper wires. The way it works is by pulsing light down a strand of glass. These pulses represent binary code—so far that's no better than copper. The advantage is that a single strand of fiber optic can carry thousands and thousands of different frequencies at once without data loss.

Fiber optic cable A transmission technology that sends pulses of light along specially manufactured optical fibers. Each fiber consists of a core, thinner than a human hair, surrounded by a sheath with a much lower refractive index. Light signals introduced at one end of the cable are conducted along the cable as the signals are reflected from the sheath. Fiber optic cable is lighter and smaller than traditional copper cable, is immune to electrical interference, and has better signal-transmitting qualities. However, it is more expensive than traditional cables and more difficult to repair.

Fibre channel The British spelling of "fiber", i.e., "fibre" is used to describe this standard. Fibre Channel uses fiber-optic cable to connect computers or peripherals. It is much more expensive than standard copper cabling, and thus has been a niche product with lots of potential. Today it is used sparingly to connect RAID systems to computers, or to connect drives together within high-end RAID systems.

Field programmable gate array (FPGA) A microchip that can be made with thousands of programmable logic gates. Good features of FPGAs include short development times and low production costs. FPGAs are often used for prototype or custom designs, including DSP and logic emulation.

Field searching A strategy in which a search is limited to a particular field; in a search engine, a search may be limited to a particular domain name or date, narrowing the scope of searchable items and helping to eliminate the chance of retrieving irrelevant data.

Field-replacable unit (FRU) A hardware component that can be replaced in the field, as opposed to at the factory.

FIFO buffer (first in first out buffer) An area of memory that holds information in the order in which it was received until the computer has time to use it.

File The base unit data on a hard drive from the perspective of the user viewing the hard drive through an operating system. Computer programs may be one or several files. Additionally, a file may be split (fragmented) into several pieces on a hard drive, but still appear as a single unit to the user.

File allocation table (FAT) A table maintained by the DOS or OS/2 operating systems that lists all of the clusters available on a disk. The FAT includes the location of each cluster, as well as whether it is in use, available for use, or damaged in soem way and therefore unavailable.

Because files are not necessarily stored in consecutive clusters on a disk, but can be scattered all over the disk, the FAT also keeps track of which pieces belong to which file. OS/2 supports a compatible version of the DOSFAT, sometimes known as the SuperFAT, which adds 32-bit capabilities to increase speed, access to OS/2 extended attributes, and a free space bitmap which results in much reduced allocation times.

File compression program An application program that shrinks program or data files, so that they occupy less disk space. The file must then be extracted or decompressed before you can use it. Many of the most popular file compression programs are shareware, like PKZIP,LHA, and StuffIt for the Macintosh, although utility packages like PC Tools from Central Point Software also contain file compression programs.

File extension DOS, Windows, and, to a lesser extent, UNIX and Linux use the last three characters of a filename, after a period, to signify what type of file a file is, such as text, movie, sound, etc. The MacOS has a file system that contains an identifier for file types that is invisible when looking at the filename, and allows you to call files whatever you want without a messy extension on the end. Some common examples are: .exe (executable file), .bat (batch file), .wav (wave sound file), and .txt (text file).

File format Applications save files in a certain way. They organize the data in a way that makes sense for the information they are saving and to programs that work with that type of file. There are many standard file formats, such as GIF and JPG. These are graphical formats and are in common use.

File fragmentation The storage of a file in several noncontiguous areas of a disk, rather than as one single unit. When you store a file on a disk, DOS looks for the first available free cluster on the disk, and stores the file there. If the file is too large for one cluster, the operationg system looks for the next free cluster, and stores the next part of the file there. These clusters may not be next to one another, and may be widely scattered over the disk. This fragmentation can slow down data retrieval if the problem becomes severe, but by using a defragmenter, you can restore that lost performance. The defragmenter program removes file fragmentation by rewriting all files and directories into contiguous areas of your disk.

File permissions When you place files on a UNIX system you can assign the files various levels of permission, specifying who can access them, and what type of access they can have.

File recovery The process of recovering deleted or damaged files from a disk. In many operating systems, a deleted file still exists on disk until the space it occupies is overwritten with something else. A file can be deleted accidentally, or can become inaccessible when part of the file's control information is lost. There are many utility packages that offer file recovery programs (i.e., Norton Utilities for Symantec, PC Tools from Central Point Softwar).

File server Any computer that allows other computers to access files stored on its hard drive or other storage media. The file server also controls who can and cannot access these files. Most other types of servers, including database and webservers, are just glorified file servers. Webservers serve up Web pages, but Web pages are files. Database servers serve up data, but that data is contained in files. However, the distinction is that file servers typically allow access to the files in their raw format, such as through a file management program or command, while webservers and database servers may not allow that form of access.

File sharing In networking, the sharing of files via the network file server. Shared files can be read, reviewed, and updated by more than one individual. Access to the file or files is often regulated by password protection, account or security clearance, or file locking, to prevent simulataneous changes from being made by more than one person at a time.

File system A hierarchical structure of data on one or more disks or partitions. The actual structural details depend on the file system type. Common Internet File System (CIFS), distributed file system (DFS), Fast File System (FFS), Hierarchical File System (HFS), Institutional File System (IFS), Network File System (NFS), and Unix File System (UFS).

File transfer protocol (FTP) filters (1) Components that provide the basic building blocks for processing data.

(2) Under the WDM Stream architecture, also known as a functional device or multimedia processing driver. Each filter's capability is described in part by a number of connection points called pins. Each pin can consume, produce, or both consume and produce a data stream such as digital audio. Specialized tasks can be solved by connecting filters by way of their pins into a topology—for example, to play filtered and mixed audio.

(3) Under WDM, a filter is implemented as a kernel-mode entity that is a device object implemented by a kernel driver.

(4) Under Microsoft DirectShow, a filter is a user-mode entity that is an instance of a COM object, usually implemented by a DLL.

File transfer The ability to transfer text, graphics, software, spreadsheets, audio files, and video files over vast distances on computer networks such as the Internet. For example, the entire works of Shakespeare can be downloaded from Dartmouth College and government documents may be transferred from the Library of Congress.

Filespec A contraction of file specification, commonly used to denote the complete drive letter, path name, directory name, and file name needed to access a specific file.

Film recorder Used in reference to color transparency recording devices, and sometimes also to imagesetters.

Filter queries Queries used to select subsets from a data collection, e.g., all documents with a creation date later than 01/01/2000.

FIMS Form Interface Management System.

Finger An Internet tool for locating people on other sites. Finger can also be used to give access to non-personal information, but the most common use is to see if a person has an account at a particular site. The most famous finger site was a Coke machine at Carnegie-Mellon University that students had wired to the Internet. They could then finger the machine and find out how many bottles remained and how long they had been in the machine so they wouldn't walk all the way there and find an empty machine or warm soda.

Finger gateway A source listing of graphics images that have been placed around the world on the Internet.

Firewall A method of preventing unauthorized access to a computer system, often found on networked computers.

A firewall is designed to provide normal service to authorized users, while at the same time preventing those unauthorized users from gaining access to the system; in reality, they almost always add some level of inconvenience to legal users, and their ability to control illegal access may be questionable.

A system designed to prevent unauthorized access to or from a private network. Firewalls can be implemented in both hardware and software, or a combination of both. Firewalls are frequently used to prevent unauthorized Internet users from accessing private networks connected to the Internet, especially intranets. All messages entering or leaving the intranet pass through the firewall, which examines each message and blocks those that do not meet the specified security criteria.

There are several types of firewall techniques:

Packet filter: Looks at each packet entering or leaving the network and accepts or rejects it based on user-defined rules. Packet filtering is fairly effective and transparent to users, but it is difficult to configure. In addition, it is susceptible to IP spoofing.

Application gateway: Applies security mechanisms when a TCP or UDP connection is established. Once the connection has been made, packets can flow between the hosts without further checking.

Proxy server: Intercepts all messages entering and leaving the network. The proxy server effectively hides the true network addresses.

In practice, many firewalls use two or more of these techniques in concert. A firewall is considered a first line of defense in protecting private information. For greater security, data can be encrypted.

Firewall policy A set of rules ranked in numerical order.

FireWire A serial connection technology that promises to speed data at 200-800Mbps and up. Digital video camera manufacturers and Apple have embraced this connection standard. It is also available on PCs, but adoption is not as widespread.

Firing tables Precalculated tables that can give an artillery gunner the correct allowances for wind conditions and distance by dictating the elevation and deflection of a gun.

Firmware The software that is embedded onto a piece of hardware in order to control that hardware. Generally, firmware can be upgraded and is placed on an EEPROM. Sometimes if a new driver for a piece of hardware is released, new firmware will also be released that is required to get the full functionality or performance of the driver. In other cases, firmware will have some bugs or undesirable features, and can be upgraded to work out the problems. Of course, the rest of the hardware cannot be upgraded without replacing pieces of it, so manufacturers try to store as many critical function controls as they can in the firmware in case they need to change them. For them, if a bug is found it is the difference between recalling a product and simply telling their affected customers to upgrade the firmware.

First in, first out (FIFO) A method used to process information in which the first item in the list is processed first. FIFO is commonly used when printing a set of documents; the first document received in the queue is the first document to be printed.

First person shooter (FPS) This describes a video game that is played from the first person perspective, i.e., looking out of the eyes of the main character. As well, to achieve the "shooter" aspect, the main character usually has some type of weapon, and to achieve your goals you must kill off enemies. The first meaningful game of this genre was Castle Wolfenstein 3D, and other popular examples include the Doom, Quake, and Unreal series.

Fixed Disk A disk that used to be broken but that now works.

Fixed-frequency monitor A monitor designed to receive an input signal at just one frequency. This is in contrast to a multisynch monitor, which can detect and adjust to a variety of different input signals.

Flame This refers to harsh or chastising e-mail or other Internet communication. Flames are sent to you when you make someone angry, usually in a chat room, Usenet newsgroup, or other message board. If you don't follow proper netiquette, chances are you will get flamed. Used as a verb, flame is the act of sending a harsh communication.

Flame war A prolonged series of flames in a USENET newsgroup, which may have begun as a creative exchange or views but which quickly degenerates into personal attacks and crude name-calling.

Flash A popular piece of animation software developed by Macromedia. Flash is widely used on the Web because it requires little bandwidth, therefore making it friendly to users with low or high-speed connections.

Flash bios . An user-upgradable memory device (required *not* to have the usual BIOS identification code and therefore undetectable by memory managers) that is mapped into a PC's upper memory and conflicts with programs that the memory manager loades over top of it. Used to implement Plug-n-Play and other quickly changing specifications.

Flash card A small flash memory module. The memory chips are enclosed in a plastic case and retain data after they are removed from the system. The most common uses for these are in laptops, pagers, handheld computers, cell phones, digital cameras, and audio players. There are several different form factors of flash cards, including Compact Flash, SmartMedia, PCMCIA, and Small Form Factor Flash Card.

Flash memory A special form of non-volatile EEPROM that can be erased at signal levels normally found inside the PC, so that you can reprogram the contents with whatever you like without pulling the chips out of your computer. Also, once a flash memory has been programmed, you can remove the expansion board it is mounted on and plug it into another computer if you wish.

Flash ROM A rewriteable ROM that doesn't lose its info when the power turns off.

Flat file A database that contains a single table and can be easily represented using plain text. This type of database contrasts with a relational database, which can contain any number of tables that are linked together. Often, to keep things simple when transferring data between organizations, people will request a flat file. Common flat file text formats include tab-delimited and CSV.

Flat panel display (FPD) A type of display that has much less depth than a standard CRT-based display. Types of FPDs include gas plasma displays and LCD screens.

Flat screen This typically refers to a CRT monitor that is made more flat than a standard tube by using more than one electron gun. It is most useful to professionals who rely on the precision of their monitors. It is also better for the standard user because a straight light across the monitor looks straight and not curved. This can also refer to flat panels and projection screens, which are also flat.

Flat shading The most basic shading technique, in which the entire object is only one color. This causes the image to appear blocky.

Flatbed scanner Any scanning device that incorporates a flat transparent plate, on which original images are placed for scanning. The scanning process is linear rather than rotational.

FLC/FLI File extensions for animations conforming to Autodesk formats. With appropriate changes in the win.ini file, most PC computers will play back these animations without having Autodesk software installed.

Flicker Lit condition of the display caused by mismatch of phosphor and Vertical refresh when the phosphor begins to decay prior to being refreshed giving the display the appearance of "flashing".

Flip chip-plastic grid array (FC-PGA) This is Intel's newer packaging of the Socket 370 design. It features a different electrical setup than Socket 370, but is physically compatible. Thus, old Socket 370 motherboards will not be compatible with new FC-PGA chips, but new FC- PGA motherboards may be able to handle Socket 370 processors. It is not clear why Intel made the electrical change. The physical changes put the core closer to the surface, allowing better cooling as the processor core comes in closer contact to the heatsink.

Flip-flop (bistable multivibrator) A simple element of memory made up of an assembly of logic gates. Based on inputs, the state of a flip-flop can be changed back and forth, affecting the future output of the flip-flop.

Floating point A three-part representation of a number that contains a decimal point. The number is represented first by the sign, then the number itself, then decimal position. Some examples of floating point numbers are 4.23423412, 1234.1234234, or 4.00. Floating point numbers offer a specific amount of precision, often 8-bit, 16-bit, 32-bit, or 64-bit. This precision controls how accurately floating point results are represented and calculated during arithmetic operations between floating point numbers. For a simple example, if you have a low level of precision and you divide 1 by 3, you will get 0.33. With a higher level of precision you would see that it is 0.333333333333, and so forth. Thus, your calculation is inaccurate by 0.003333333333 (which is 0.333333333333 - 0.33). A small inaccuracy such as that may not matter if you are pumping out frame rates on a 3D game, but if you are building an airplane's engine you might want to make sure your design program handles a proper amount of precision for the job you are doing. When writing software, larger floating point precision takes more space to store, and may be slower depending on the hardware you are running on.

Floating point operation (FLOP) This describes a single manipulation of a floating point number in a microprocessor. One measure of the speed of a microprocessor is how many FLOPs can be accomplished in a second.

Floating point unit (FPU) The part of a microprocessor that is designed to handle floating point calculations. Often the efficiency of this part of the processor will decide whether a processor is successful or not. Cyrix M-II chips and AMD K6-2 chips had weak floating point units when compared to Intel Pentium III processors, thus limiting their success. AMD's Athlon chip had a strong floating point unit, and it was very successful against the Pentium III. Floating point performance matters a lot in games and complex data manipulations, thus the "pro" or "Geek" segment of the market that drives system buys and recommends components.

Floating-point calculation a calculation of numbers whose decimal point is not fixed but moves or floats to provide the best degree of accuracy. Floating-point calculations can be implemented in software, or they can be performed much faster by a separate floating-point processor.

Floating-point processor A special chip that handles sophisticated calculations, such as those used in spreadsheets, CAD, and scientific programs.

Floppy disk Any type of disk media which is not rigid. Often it's contained in hard cases, which can lead to confusion in identification. Commonly, the term is used to describe 1.44 MB 3.5 inch diskettes, but it applies to any media. Zip disks, for example, are floppy in nature if removed from their casing.

Fig. Floppy disk

Floppy disk controller A special-purpose chip and associated circuitry that directs and controls reading from and writing to a computer's disk drive.

Flowcharts Techniques for graphically describing the sequencing and structure of program source code.

Fluid dynamics The science and engineering of the motion of gases and liquids

Flush protocol The flush protocol is provided to ensure the correct order of delivery of unicast data frames.

FM (frequency modulation) A method of sending and distinguishing radio signals by modifying the frequency of the radio wave.

FM synthesis (frequency modulation synthesis) A method of creating music using frequencies to represent instruments. As you can imagine, this does not create beautiful and complex music, but flat, lifeless electronic sounds. It was useful—and often used—in early video games before wavetable synthesis became widespread.

FMV (full motion video) Depicting video at 30 or more fps.

Focus Sharpness of a pixel or series of pixels on the CRT face plate. Also measured as the spot size.

Folder A term coined to be synonymous and more accessible than "directory." Now the terms are basically synonymous, but folder tends to imply a more graphical interface for managing files.

Font As it relates to computers today, a font is a specific style of displaying characters (a typeface), often scalable to a variety of sizes. "Arial" is a font, for example. This differs from the traditional definition of font, where each style and size was its own font (i.e., "9 point Arial" as opposed to simply "Arial").

Foobar FooBar is a derivative of the acronym FUBAR, changed for symmetry. FUBAR stands for Fucked Up Beyond All Recognition. Sometimes used as a whole by programmers to describe data loss, foo and bar are also often used separately when a quick and random name is needed.

Footprint This refers to the general size of something, whether physical or virtual. The footprints of small Internet appliances are compared against those of larger PCs, as are smaller LCD screens vs. CRT screens. Different operating systems and programs have their own footprints in the amount of bytes they typically take up on a hard drive, or the amount of physical memory they consume while running.

Foreground In an operating system, a process that runs in the foreground is runnign at a higher level of priority than a background task. Only multitasking operating systems support true foreground and background processing; however, some applications programs can mimic background and foreground processing; many word processors will print a document while still accepting input from the keyboard.

Foreign address An address that does not match any of a given node's summary addresses.

Foresight A software product from Nu Thena providing graphical modelling tools for high level system design and simulation.

Fork When Unix starts a new process, it does so by cloning an existing process. The cloning process is known in Unix-ese as forking.

Form factor Typically this refers to the compatibility among PC motherboards, cases, and power supplies. A motherboard, case, and power supply with the same form factor can be used together. Some examples of form factors are AT, ATX, Baby AT, or NLX. Some cases, power supplies, and even motherboards will work in multiple form factors. This is commonly seen in older computer cases that will work with AT or ATX motherboards.

Formal methods Several formal approaches to program specification have been developed, such as those based on VDM or Z. They can be used to develop software with high reliability, for safety-critical or high-volume applications.

Formal standards Specifications or styles that are approved by vendor-independent standards bodies, such as the American National Standards Institute, the International Standards Organisation, the Institute of Electrical and Electronics Engineers, and the National Institute for Standards and Technology.

Format After partitioning your hard drive, it must be formatted so that it can be used by the operating system. Formatting basically makes your hard disk ready for initial use. The same procedure must be done to removable media such as floppy disks. Some types of formatting wipe out the whole disk, while others just set up the framework for data to be written using a type of quick format. Another type of formatting is a SCSI low-level format. This type of format makes a drive ready to be used by a SCSI controller. When you format a drive you typically lose all information on that drive.

Formatting 1)To apply the page-layout commands and font specifications to a document and produce the final printed output.

2) The process of initializing a new, blank floppy disk or hard disk so that it can be used to store information.

FORML Formal Object Role Modeling Language.

Fortran A high-level programming language, a bit more advanced than BASIC but not quite as complex as C. This language refuses to die because it is so huge in the scientific research community. It's not a tough language to learn, and it's fairly powerful. About 60% of scientific programming is still done in Fortran.

FORTRAN Formula Translator Developed in 1954 by IBM, it is a high-level programming language, most widely used for scientific and engineering applications because it has excellent mathematical functions. Many programmers consider it to sacrifice "elegance" for speed of numerical manipulations.

Forum A feature of online services and bulletin boards that allows subscribers to post messages for others to read, and to reply to messages posted by other users.

Forward delta The delta delta which, when combined with a version version, creates a child version.

Forward engineering The traditional process of moving from high-level abstractions and logical, implementation-independent designs to the physical implementation of a system.

Forward explicit congestion notification (FECN) A bit in the Frame Relay / header that is set when the network router has detected congestion in the destination direction (or "foreward," from the packet's point of view).

Foundry A synonym for semiconductor fabrication plant. A foundry is the actual location that produces microprocessors. The term foundry initially referred to a location where metal was poured into molds, but in technology speak it refers to the place where microprocessors are molded.

Fourth generation language A high-level language, usually non-procedural, to allow users inexperienced in programming to develop database applications.

FPA Function Point Analysis.

FPD (flat panel display) A type of display that has much less depth than a standard CRT-based display. Types of FPDs include gas plasma displays and LCD screens.

FPGA (field programmable gate array) A microchip that can be made with thousands of programmable logic gates. Good features of FPGAs include short development times and low production costs. FPGAs are often used for prototype or custom designs, including DSP and logic emulation.

FPM (fast page mode) A feature used to support faster sequential access to DRAM by allowing multiple accesses to the currently open row to be made after supplying the row address just once.

FPO (for position only) A low resolution image placed in a document to indicate where the final version is to be positioned.

FPS (frames per second) In video. Typical "full-motion" video in television and movies is 30 fps, but in digitized video such high fps rates are not yet common. Apple's QuickTime and Microsoft's Video for Windows typically run at 12 to 18 fps.

FPU (floating point unit) The part of a microprocessor that is designed to handle floating point calculations. Often the efficiency of this part of the processor will decide whether a processor is successful or not. Cyrix M-II chips and AMD K6-2 chips had weak floating point units when compared to Intel Pentium III processors, thus limiting their success. AMD's Athlon chip had a strong floating point unit, and it was very successful against the Pentium III. Floating point performance matters a lot in games and complex data manipulations, thus the "pro" or "Geek" segment of the market that drives system buys and recommends components.

FQDN (fully qualified domain name) The official name assigned to an individual computer. Organizations register names, such as "example.com", then assign unique names to their computers, such as "mail.example.com".

Fractional T1 This term refers to using a theoretical "piece" of a T1 line, such as 128Kbps', 256Kbps', or 512Kbps' worth of the 1.5Mbps T1 line. Many ISPs offer fractional T1 as a lower-cost alternative to a full T1 and a higher-cost alternative to ISDN. However, if you check the prices it's almost always worth it to go for full T1. The phone company has to install a full T1 connection anyway, and you'll just be paying a bit more a month. Basically, since a T1 is only four wires the full line is installed and the ISP will only allow traffic up to the limit for which you are paying.

Fragment A piece of a file. When a file is written to a hard drive it is sometimes written in multiple fragments because there is no contiguous space available that is large enough to store the file.

Fragmentation This occurs when a hard drive writes a file in multiple segments instead of in a physically contiguous area. A higher level of fragmentation means that most files are fragmented, and many files contain lots of fragments. A low level of fragmentation implies that more files are in one piece, and that if files are fragmented they are only in a few fragments. For example, say you have two files, file A and file B and you write them both to a hard drive. A low level of fragmentation may be represented by: AAAABBBB. A high level of fragmentation may be represented by: AABBABABA. Fragmentation is caused by deletion of small files, and then trying to fit larger files into the leftover spaces. Over time it is a common occurrence that is unavoidable in most file systems.

Frame A single screen-sized image that can be displayed in sequence with other slightly different images to create animated drawings. A video frame consists of two interlaced fields of either 525 lines (NTSC) or 625 lines (PAL/SECAM), running at 30 frames per second (NTSC) or 25 frames per second (PAL/SECAM). Film runs at 24 frames per second.

Frame relay An International Telegraph and Telephone Consultative Committee (CCITT) recommendation (I.122) and American National Standards Institute standard (T1S1). Frame relay is an ISDN (Integrated Services Digital Network) packet-mode bearer service that defines a user-to-network interface. The two main benefits are bandwidth on demand and integrated access. The standard currently addresses data communications speeds up to 2 Mbps over permanent virtual circuits. By reducing the network functions performed, frame relay takes advantage of more robust physical facilities to improve throughput.

Frame-grabbing system A combination of hardware and software, designed to capture individual frames from video clips for further digital manipulation, or consecutive replay on computer platforms.

Framemaker Commercial publishing software available on a wide variety of workstations and addressing technical and scientific needs.

Frames per second (FPS) This term relates to video or 3D games, and is the amount of single full screen (or full window) pictures (or frames) that are displayed each second to generate what appears to be a moving image. Typical digital video displays at around 30 FPS. Higher frame rates are not really necessary, as the human eye cannot typically handle more than about 30 FPS. Some games will average 30 FPS or higher and look choppy. Usually this is due to intense scenes that cause the action to dip below 30 FPS for short periods of time. Rates of over 100 FPS in games are common nowadays with less complex 3D action games, but do not necessarily add to the experience of playing a game.

Fraud The nature of the Internet makes it unusually susceptible to fraud. In order to combat fraud, organizations need to take measures to verify the source and integrity of data transmitted over the Internet. This includes the use of both certificates and anti-spoofing techniques.

Free list A list of unallocated blocks and inodes kept in the superblock.

Free memory An area of memory not currently in use.

Free text search This type of search allows you to give a fragment of a word and have it found in any part of that word. For example, doing a free text search for "the" could return "Thesis," "Blithe," and "Diphtheria."

FreeBSD (free Berkeley software/standard distribution) A UNIX-like operating system that runs on the Intel x86 platform and is based on an OS developed at University of California at Berkeley. It is now a no-cost operating system, and the source can be downloaded and modified.

Freedom of information act (FOIA) Permits individuals to gain access to records and documents that are in the possession of the government.

Freehep An organisation offering a repository of software and related information for high energy physics applications.

Freenets Bulletin board services that are funded by individuals and organizations dedicated to making information freely available on networks. They operate much like public libraries through the National Public Telecommunication Network (NPTN.). Users can connect through modems or through Internet terminals.

Freeware A form of software distribution where the author retains copyright of the software, but makes the program available to others at no cost. Freeware is often distributed on bulletin boards, or through user groups. The program may not be resold or distributed by others for profit.

Freon Hydrocarbon-based gases used as refrigerants and as pressurants in aerosols.

Frequency bands Ranges of signal frequencies that are of particular interest in a given application.

Frequency modulation encoding (FM) A method of storing digital information on a disk or tape. FM encoding is inefficient in its use of disk space and has largely been replaced by more efficient methods liek modified frequency modulating(MFM) encoding, and the more complex method of run length limited (RLL) encoding and advanced run length limited (ARLL) encoding.

Frequently asked questions (FAQ) A document that lists the most common questions about something (with the answers, of course). A simple way to find information on a complex topic is to do an Internet search for _topic_ FAQ, where _topic_ represents the topic for which you are looking.

Fresco An object-oriented object-oriented API API for graphical user interfaces, under development by the X consortium X-consortium as an open, multi-vendor standard.

Front side bus (FSB) The speed of the bus connecting the microprocessor, its chipset, and connected main memory. In architectures where the processor interacts directly with main memory, the definition of a singular front side bus is less clear. In such a case you would have to specify two FSB speeds, one for the connection to main memory and one for the connection to the processor chipset.

Front-end processor A specialized processor that manipulates data before passing it on to the main processor. In large computer-to-computer communications, a front-end processor is often used to manage all aspects of communications, leaving the main computer free to handle the data processing.

Front-end The part of a program or process that the user interfaces with and controls.

FrontPage A popular site design and management tool developed by Microsoft.

FRS (frame-relay service) A connection oriented service that is capable of carrying up to 4096 bytes per frame.

FRTT (fixed round-trip time) This is the sum of the fixed and propagation delays from the source to the furthest destination and back.

FS (femptosecond) One quadrillionth of a second (1/1,000,000,000,000,000 seconds).

FSAA (full screen anti-aliasing) A method used by 3D graphics cards to provide anti-aliasing to all objects in a 3D environment. This acts to smooth out the jagged appearance of edges on some 3Dobjects. Different graphics cards have different implementations of FSAA, and image quality varies greatly.

FSB (front side bus) The speed of the bus connecting the microprocessor, its chipset, and connected main memory. In architectures where the processor interacts directly with main memory, the definition of a singular front side bus is less clear. In such a case you would have to specify two FSB speeds, one for the connection to main memory and one for the connection to the processor chipset.

FSM Finite State Machine.

FS-VDSL (full-service very high speed digitial subscriber line) Uses existing copper wire twisted-pair infrastructure combined with fibre to the neighborhood.

Gov (.gov) The top level domain designated for agencies and branches of the United States Federal Government. State and local governments in the United States should use the us top level country code domain. Prior to October 1, 1997, registration in gov was handled by InterNIC; the General Services Administration (GSA) began handling registration in the top level domain gov starting October 1, 1997.

FTP file transfer protocol In communications, a method of transferring one or more files from one computer to another;often over a modem and a telephone line. The protocol divides the file into smaller units, and each unit is processed in sequence. The transfer protocol also handles error detection and correction, by one of several methods.The protocol used to access a remote Internet host, and then transfer files between that host and your own computer. Ftp is also the name of the program used to manage this protocol. Ftp is bade on client/server architecture; you run an ftp client program on your system, and connect with an ftp server running on the Internet host computer. The ftp program originated as a Unix utility, but versions are now available for almost all popular operating systems. The traditional Unix ftp program starts a text-based command processor; modern versions use a graphical user interface with pull-down menus instead. The general consensus seems to be that the graphical versions are easier to use, but once you get the hang of things, the command processor versions, while not as pretty , are usually faster.

FTP site A computer which stores files that can be retrieved using FTP. FTP sites which allow anyone to retrieve files (without having an account on that computer) are known as Anonymous FTP sites.

FUD (fear, uncertainty, and doubt) The practice of spreading general unease about a situation where all the details are not known or not controllable. Don't let FUD ruin your day.

Fud factor The threshold of confusion in a market sufficient to allow an uncompetitive company to prepare products, while users delay purchasing.

FUD (fear, uncertainty, and doubt) The object of marketing campaigns launched by otherwise uncompetitive companies.

Full duplex Refers to the transmission of data in two directions simultaneously. For example, a telephone is a full-duplex device because both parties can talk at once. In contrast, a walkie-talkie is a half-duplex device because only one party can transmit at a time.

Most modems have a switch that lets you choose between full-duplex and half-duplex modes. The choice depends on which communications program you are running.

In full-duplex mode, data you transmit does not appear on your screen until it has been received and sent back by the other party. This enables you to validate that the data has been accurately transmitted. If your display screen shows two of each character, it probably means that your modem is set to half-duplex mode when it should be in full-duplex mode.

Full parity This is synonymous with full duplex, but most often used when describing dial-up modem communications standards.

Full screen anti-aliasing (FSAA) A method used by 3D graphics cards to provide anti-aliasing to all objects in a 3D environment. This acts to smooth out the jagged appearance of edges on some 3Dobjects. Different graphics cards have different implementations of FSAA, and image quality varies greatly.

Full-custom A technique used for the design of integrated circuits that involves the manipulation of circuit designs at the semiconductor device level.

Full-duplex A method of transmitting information over an asynchronous communications channel, in which signals may be sent in both directions simultaneously. This technique makes the best use of line time but substantially increases the amount of logic required in the primary and secondary stations.

Fullerenes Fullerenes, those soccer ball–shaped carbon molecules also known as "buckyballs," have generated outsized expectations ever since their discovery in 1985. Scientists think they could eventually be used in chemical sensors, fuel cells, drug delivery, cancer medicines, and smart materials. Yet while commercial demand for fullerenes is gradually emerging, so are fears that these molecules, which measure only a few billionths of a meter across, pose serious health and environmental hazards.

Full-motion video Video reproduction at 30 frames per second (NTSC-original signals) or 25 frames per second (PAL-original signals).

Full-text indexing A search engine feature in which every word in a document, significant or insignificant, is indexed and retrievable through a search.

Fully qualified domain name (FQDN) A host specification including the entire domain structure complete to the top-level domain(.com, .edu, .mil, and so on), in host.site.domain.name format.

Function An instruction to the application that performs operations or returns a value, or both.

Function key (F1, F2, etc.) One of the set of 12 keys at the top of a standard computer keyboard. These keys are labelled F1 through F12. The keys are basically general purpose extra keys so that programmers can assign the keys to special functions in their programs. One handy and common use of F3 in applications is to "Find again," or find the value again for which you most recently searched.

Function point A unit for estimating the functionality of a program.

Functional language A general purpose, high-level programming language based on the mathematical notion of functions. A functional program consists of a set of (possibly recursive) function definitions. Its execution consists of the evaluation of a function . Programs written in a functional language are generally compact and elegant, but tend to run slowly and consume a lot of memory.

Funding The raising of funds for hardware, software, and development. Grants are available from a variety of sources.

Fuse A device used to protect devices from excessive electrical current. It contains a conductor that melts and breaks the current flow when too much electricity flows through it. Once a fuse is blown it must be replaced with another one to close the circuit and allow electricity to flow again.

Fusion An object oriented object-oriented analysis and design method developed by Hewlett Packard.

Fuzzy logic Logic without an absolute true or false. Instead, you have gradients of true and false. This is necessary for solving some problems, especially those involving artificial intelligence. For example, the question, "Do I get some food now?" isn't always yes or no, and varies due to environmental factors and degrees of hunger.

G

G2 A real-time real-time expert system expert-system from Gensym Corporation.

GaAs Gallium Arsenide. A semiconducting material characterised by extremely fast switching times for transistors. The material also consumes relatively low power. In the early 80s, this material was thought to replace silicon. Research investment on this material has now lowered.

Gadget A dialog control that presents application output in some form and provides a way for an application to receive administrator input.

Gadget library Object-oriented abstractions for manipulating dialogs.

Gallium arsenide A chemical used in the production of semiconductor devices; chemical symbol GaAs.

Game console A consumer gaming system that is usually sold in retail stores and toy stores. It differs from a standard computer in that it is designed from the ground up to provide a certain amount of game playing power at a specific price point, and typically is very limited in upgradeability and expansion.

Game port A 15-pin analog port on a PC used specifically for game controllers like a joystick. It also doubles as a MIDI connector. Usually you find one on the back of your sound card.

Games Interactive entertainment programs that can be played back on computers or special playing machines connected to television sets. Some games are sold on compact discs that can either be played in CD-ROM drives connected to computers or CD players that are proprietary. For example, Sega games play on Sega players, Data Discman games play on Data Discman players, CD-I games play on CD-I players, etc. Games are generally authored by game vendors and cannot be modified or updated for education uses by users. Educators who think that their students are spending many hours in computer labs for academic purposes may discover that a large portion of computer lab time is taken up with game playing. More research needs to be conducted on the fascination of games so that educators can make better use of building these motivational factors into more serious learning materials.

Gamma correction The process of altering the gamma of computer graphics, pictures, or video in order to make the picture show up properly and enable the proper recognition of shades of color. Some graphics accelerators have gamma correction features, as early 3D games often had issues with colors appearing too dark.

Gamma In computer graphics and digital video, this refers to a numerical parameter that describes the nonlinearity of intensity reproduction.

Basically, as colors get lighter the human eye has more trouble discerning them, and a gamma setting is used to compensate for this so that shades of color on an object, such as those caused by shadows, can be discerned properly. Incorrect gamma settings can cause colors to look too dark or too light, losing detail to the viewer.

Gamut The limited range of colors provided by a specific input device, output device or pigment set.

Gang scanning Sequential scanning of multiple originals using the same previously defined exposure setting for each.

Garbage collection A process where dynamically allocated blocks of memory are reclaimed while a program executes. Garbage collection is normally performed by the garbage collector, which is part of the runtime system. However, it is possible to explicitly write code to do garbage collection as well. Automatic garbage collection is triggered when the amount of free memory blocks falls below a certain threshold.

Gas plasma display A type of monitor technology that was initially used to create small monochrome displays for early portable computers. Now it is typically used to create large monitors that are a only a few inches thick. Older models produced only orange images, but now gas plasma technology can be used to create full color displays. The technology works by creating a matrix of red, green, and blue pixels from plasma bubbles that are turned on or off by selectively powering them.

Gate A gate is a tiny electronic switch. These switches, when linked together, can perform logical functions. Basically, gate is the logical term for transistor.

Gated (gateway daemon) A program that must run on a computer using TCP/IP's RIP protocol.

Gateway In networking, a shared connection between a local area network and a larger system, such as a mainframe computer or a large packet-switching network. Usually slower than a bridge or router, a gateway typically has its own processor and memory, and can perform protocol conversions. Protocol conversions allows a gateway to connect two dissimilar networks; data is converted and reformatted before it is forwarded to the new network.

Gaussian classifiers Classifiers constructed on the assumption that the feature values of data will follow a Gaussian distribution.

GB gender changer A special intermediary connector for use with two cables that both have male or both have female connectors.

GB (Gigabyte) A unit of data storage size which represents 109 (one billion) characters of information.

Gbit (gigabit) This refers to approximately one billion bits. More exactly, it is 230, or 1,073,741,824 bits.

Gbps (gigabits per second) A rate of data transfer of one gigabit of data per second.

GCA Graphic Communications Association.

GCAC (generic connection admission control) This is a process to determine if a link has potentially enough resources to support a connection.

GCG (grey component replacement) A technique for replacing all the neutral tones of an image with an appropriate amount of black.

GCRA (generic cell rate algorithm) The GCRA is used to define conformance with respect to the traffic contract of the connection. For each cell arrival the GCRA determines whether the cell conforms to the traffic contract. The UPC function may implement the GCRA, or one or more equivalent algorithms to enforce conformance. The GCRA is defined with two parameters: the Increment (I) and the Limit (L).

GDI (graphics device interfaces) Link graphics hardware devices with the CPU. Much of the power of graphics processing depends upon whether the system has 8-bit, 16-bit, 32-bit, or

64-bit graphics power. Limitations of customer hardware often detract from the ability to develop operating systems to take full advantage of graphics power. For example, when developing Windows Chicago for 32-bit processors, Microsoft Corporation had to leave 16-bit GDI capacity on its 32-bit operating system.

Geek (1) A formerly derogatory term given to the outcast elite, usually lacking in social graces. The term has been used so liberally by the masses of people that computer gurus have taken it to heart as not being derogatory, but rather the name given to scientifically savvy folk.

(2) A carnival performer who performs grotesque acts, such as biting the heads off of live chickens.

General packet radio service (GPRS) A mobile phone 2.5G technology that allows short bursts of data between a phone and a network such as the Internet. The short transmissions allow for less costly connectivity than a constant connection, but work best with specialized services designed for such types of communication.

General protection fault GPF, short for General Protection Fault, is a computer condition that causes a Windows application to crash. The most common cause of a GPF is two applications trying to use the same block of memory, or more specifically, one application trying to use memory assigned to another application.

The following situations can also cause GPFs:

Running an application with insufficient resources.

Using improper hardware device drivers.

Corrupted or missing Windows files.

Applications exchanging data that cannot be read.

GPFs are often preceded by an invalid page fault.

General purpose interface bus (GPIB) A 24-pin parallel interface bus that conforms to the IEEE 488 interface definition standard, often used to connect scientific instruments together or to a computer. Originally developed by Hewlett-Packard, a GPIB is also known as the Hewlett-Packard Interface Bus(HPIB).

Generation backup A backup strategy in which several sets of backup disks or tapes are retained, sometimes called grandfather-father-son.

Generation gap What happens when you skip one of your backups.

Generic markup In computerised document preparation, a method of adding information to the text indicating the logical components of a document, such as paragraphs, headers or footnotes: SGML is an example of such a system. Specific instructions for layout of the text on the page do not appear in the markup.

Genericity The possibility for a language to provided parameterized modules or types. e.g. List(of:Integer) or List(of:People).

Genetic algorithm An algorithm that uses fuzzy logic and can refine itself based on its ability to select proper answers. Often, a human must tell the algorithm what it did right and what it did wrong so that it can select better results the next time it is run.

Genlocking A contraction of generator lock. The synchronization and superimposition of computer-generated text or graphics onto a video signal, so that the two images can be combined onto the same signal and displayed at the same time.

In the PC, a board containing the circuitry required for genlocing often plugs onto the display adapter. It converts the VGA signal into a standard NTSC video signal, which it then synchronizes with an external video signal.

Geographic information system (GIS) A system for capturing and manipulating data relating to the Earth. A common use of GIS is to overlay several types of maps (for example, train routes, elevation data, street maps) to determine useful data about a given geographic area.

Geometric Relating to the principles of geometry, a branch of mathematics related to the properties and relationships of points, lines, angles, surfaces, planes, and solids.

Germanium A chemical often used as a high performance semiconductor material; chemical symbol Ge.

Gershwin The name given to Apple's planned operating system 9.0 for Mac and PowerPC computers. New features were to include advanced speed recognition, interfacing that adapts to individual users, and new microkernal architecture. However, the System 9.0 has been abandoned in favor of an entirely new operating system called Rhapsody. Apple's hopes are riding heavily upon the evolution of a new operating system called Rhapsody that is a revolutinary operating system based upon NEXTStep technology.

GFC generic flow control GFC is a field in the ATM header which can be used to provide local functions (e.g., flow control). It has local significance only and the value encoded in the field is not carried end-to-end.

Gflop (gigaflop) The ability of a system to compute one billion floating point operations in one second. AMD's K6-2 processor and Motorola's G4 processor can achieve speeds of over 1 Gflop, for example, and newer chips can do multiple Gflops. The problem with trying to measure Gflops is determining a standard method of measuring floating point operation or instructions. Even if you do this, it's not clear that the measurement would reflect on real world usage.

Ghostview An X window interface to the ghostscript ghost script interpreter.

GIF This acronym stands for Graphic Interchange Format, a commonly used file compression format developed by CompuServe for transferring graphics files to and from online services. This is an extremely popular standard because it is so widely read in graphics software alternatives and is commonly used as the "GIF" file extensions of images carried on bulletin boards and transported across networks. A major drawback is the loss of color depth in GIF compression. Animated GIFs are popular at web sites.

Fig. GIF

GIF animation A technique using Graphic Interchange Format where many images are overlaid on one another and cycled through a sequence to produce an animation.

GIF (graphic interchange format) A file compression format developed by CompuServe for transferring graphic files to and from on-line services.

GIF image The acronym for Graphic Interchange Format where a static image is represented by binary bits in a data file.

Giga Prefix corresponding to a one billion quantity. One GB (Giga-Bytes) is equal to 1,000 MB or 1,000,000 KB or 1,000,000,000 Bytes. In 1995, disk storage have a capacity expressed in GB : generally between 0.2 and 4 GB.

Gigabyte 230, or 1,073,741,824 bytes. It would be 1 billion bytes,but bytes are generally counted in powers of 2 Gigabyte, roughly a billion bytes of disk storage. (1,024MB)

Gigaflop (Gflop) The ability of a system to compute one billion floating point operations in one second. AMD's K6-2 processor and Motorola's G4 processor can achieve speeds of over 1 Gflop, for example, and newer chips can do multiple Gflops. The problem with trying to measure Gflops is determining a standard method of measuring floating point operation or instructions. Even if you do this, it's not clear that the measurement would reflect on real world usage.

Gigahertz (GHz) A unit or measure of frequency, equivalent to a thousand million (billion, or 109) hertz, or cycles per second.

Gigapixel 1,073,741,824 pixels. This is a measure of how fast data can be moved through a graphics accelerator, as in gigapixels/second.

GIGO It's an acronym that stands for Garbage In, Garbage Out.

GILS (government information locator service) A plan for a decentralised collection of information locators and associated public services to find information throughout the US government.

GIMP (gnu image manipulation program) A free, Open Source program designed for creation or manipulation of images, much like Photoshop or Paint Shop Pro, but for use on Linux/UNIX platforms.

Gina A graphical interface (formerly known as GUIDE) for the Internet. This is a low-cost option for graphically interfacing with e-mail, bulletin boards, databases, library catalogs, news services, and conferencing.

GIS (geographic information system) A system for capturing and manipulating data relating to the Earth. A common use of GIS is to overlay several types of maps (for example, train routes, elevation data, street maps) to determine useful data about a given geographic area.

Glidepad A touch-sensitive pad about 2" x 2" that will track the touch of a finger. It is not a pressure sensor, so there is no need to press down, only to touch. This device acts like a mouse for pointing, and you can tap quickly on the pad to mimic a click.

Glitch This often refers to a bug in a program that is somewhat different than a freeze or a crash, usually causing erroneous or garbage results to be displayed. The term glitch sounds like a mess, and that's what programs with glitches create.

Global positioning system (GPS) A system of satellites around the Earth that broadcast the time via radio signals based on an internal atomic clock. GPS devices can receive the signals from multiple satellites, and by measuring the time it took the signal to arrive they can determine your current position on the Earth.

Global system for mobile communications (GSM) A 2G digital standard for cellular phone communications that is used in many countries. GSM communications bands range from 900-1800MHz. The GSM initials were initially derived from the French "Groupe de travail Sp,ciale pour les services Mobiles.".

Globally unique identifier (GUID) A unique 128-bit value generated by some Microsoft applications. An example of the GUID format is: 12345678-1234-1234-1234-123456789ABC. The GUID will use the MAC address of your network card as part of itself if you do have a network card installed, potentially marking documents created by Microsoft applications with a number that could be traced back to your PC.

Glue record A record in DNS to provide the IP addresses for a subdomain specified as self-responsible via a previous NS record.

Glyph A graphic symbol whose appearance conveys information; for example, the vertical and horizontal arrows on cursor keys that indicate the directions in which they control cursor movement.

GNU (gnu's not unix) A free software movement whose acronym stands recursively for "GNU's Not Unix." GNU was started in 1984 as a means to create an entire system of software, including operating systems, programming languages, and applications that are all free. In this context free means free of cost, free to distribute, free to modify, and free to distribute modified versions. The main thing you are not free to do is claim ownership of GNU software.

GNU public license (GPL) The short of it is quite simple: if you based anything on GPLed software, you MUST provide the source code to your software upon request. The legalities of this simple concept go on at great length, and periodically new revisions of the GPL appear as holes are found and fixed. The primary rival to this is the BSD license, which is "free beer" for the community, but developers of FreeBSD license software can choose to keep their source hidden.

Gnutella This is a distributed file swapping program developed by Nullsoft, which is owned by AOL. AOL attempted to shut down Gnutella, but once it was released onto the Web AOL could no longer control it. Gnutella connects you to a large network of users who make files available on their computers, allowing you to download those files and share your own files if you like. Unlike other file swapping mechanisms, Gnutella is fully distributed and does not depend on any one corporation or entity to keep it running. Gnutella clients function as clients and servers.

Gold master The final beta version of a program that is ready to be released to the public. The entire goal of the beta process is to arrive at the gold master candidate. Once it is tested successfully, it becomes the gold master and is shipped out to be duplicated (if it's a CD or floppy) and/or uploaded to the Web. The process of creating the gold master is often referred to as "going gold," or you could say that certain software "went gold" when the golden master was released.

Goldfinger One of the generic terms used to describe the group of gold connectors inside the AMD Athlon Slot A cartridge. The connector allows you to plug devices into it that can change the clock multiplier and voltage of the Athlon cartridge. However, you must break open the plastic cartridge to get to the connectors. There are many devices available that can be used to connect to the Goldfingers; these are also referred to as Golden Fingers or Goldfingers. Nowadays Slot A Athlons are outdated.

Good An object-oriented object-oriented framework framework for graphical applications from TU Ilmenau running under X Windows X-Window-System with special support to IRIS GL, OpenGL OpenGL, VOGL, etc.

Googol This stands for the number 10 raised to the power of 100 (10100), or a one followed by 100 zeros.

Googolplex The number 10 raised to the power of 1 google.

Gopher A menu-driven and user-friendly system of Internet sites that facilitate searching and browsing of documents and files around the world. Gopher has been largely overtaken by more modern web browsers. Gopher was the first system that communicated easily between different types of operating systems and computer installations. The term "Gopher" arises from the fact that the system originated with graduate students at the site of the "Golden Gophers" at the University of Minnesota. The Gopher is one of the most popular of various menu-driven systems such as WAIS and World Wide Web. NOTIS Systems developed a Windows' front end to Gopher. A graphical interface called WinGopher is available from NOTIS Systems Inc. Gopher became very popular on the Internet, but it is now being replaced by a similar and more graphics-oriented system called Mosaic that has Gopher services available.

Gopher mail The process of navigating Gopherspace via e-mail rather than via a Gopher client.

Gopher space The worldwide collection of Gopher servers and the information they publish on the Internet.

Gouraud shading This method analyzes the color at each corner of the triangle and takes an average of the colors where the corners meet. This causes the triangles to "bleed" together, making for a smoother, clearer, more colorful image.

GPF (general protection fault) An error that is caused in a Microsoft Windows operating system when a program tries to access a protected section of memory that it should not be accessing. These errors are typically caused by lack of hard drive space for virtual memory, poorly written software or drivers, or hardware conflicts.

GPL (gnu public license) The short of it is quite simple: if you based anything on GPLed software, you MUST provide the source code to your software upon request. The legalities of this simple concept go on at great length, and periodically new revisions of the GPL appear as holes are found and fixed. The primary rival to this is the BSD license, which is "free beer" for the community, but developers of FreeBSD license software can choose to keep their source hidden.

GPM General Purpose Macrogenerator written by C. Strachey around 1965. The author said "It contains in itself all the undesirable features of every possible machine code... It can also be almost impenetrably opaque".

GPRS (general packet radio services) It is an ETSI standard and is the first implementation of a packet switched wireless protocol, is that GPRS only uses the network when data is to be sent. GPRS enables uses to send data at speeds of up to 115 Kb per second. GPRS is often referred to as "always on" technology. Because it is particularly well suited to a "burst" type of data transmission, it effectively brings IP capabilities (e-mail, Internet access) to a GSM network.

GPS (global positioning system) A system of satellites around the Earth that broadcast the time via radio signals based on an internal atomic clock. GPS devices can receive the signals from multiple satellites, and by measuring the time it took the signal to arrive they can determine.

GPU (graphics processing unit) A microprocessor specifically designed for processing 3D graphics data. This term was first coined by NVIDIA to describe its GeForce 256 chip. NVIDIA justified the name by stating that its graphics chip had a similar amount of transistors as then-current CPU chips. Now GPU has become a more widely used term to describe the complex chips that power 3D graphics cards.

Graceful recovery Termination of a process that allows the operating system or parent process to regain normal control. Does not crash the machine or result in a GPF or blue screen. User is not required to close the application, and can continue to use the other functionality. Also called graceful exit.

Graft Add a branch to a multipoint router network when a site on that branch subscribes to or asks to join a multicast call.

Grammar A grammar is a mathematical system for defining a language, as well as a device for giving the sentences in the language a useful structure.

Grammar checker An application feature that is used precisely once in the lifetime of an application. Grammar Checkers explain to the user in Post-Graduate level English why the writing is at a Third Grade level.

Granularity A description of the level of precision that can be achieved in making measurements of a quantity; for example coarse granularity means inexpensive but imprecise measurements

Grapevine A distributed system project .

Graphical accelerator Specialised component in charge of processing graphical data display instead of the CPU. Mainly used for workstations large screens display.

Graphical interchange format (GIF) Invented by CompuServe for efficient transmission of graphics, this format can only support 256 colors, or 8 bits. The newer revision, 89a, allows for multiple images in one file to simulate animation. Unisys owns the patent to a form of compression used in GIF files and occasionally decides to demand licensing fees. Thus, you may want to use the newer and completely free PNG format instead of using GIF files.

Graphical user interface (GUI) A graphic-based user interface that allows users to select files, programs, or commands by pointing to pictorial representations on the screen rather than by typing long, complex commands from a command prompt. Application programs execute in windows, using a consistent set of pull-down menus, dialog boxes, and other graphical elements such as scroll bars and icons. This consistency among interface elements is a major benefit for the user,because as soon as you learn how to use the interface in one program, you can use it in all other programs running in the same environment.

Graphics Computer images that contain pictures, drawings, and other forms of imagery other than text. Popular file extensions for graphics files are bmp, pcx, tif, and cgm.

Graphics accelerator board A specialized expansion board containing a graphics coprocessor as well as all the other circuitry found on a video adapter. By offloading most of the graphics processing tasks from the main processor onto the graphics accelerator board, you can improve the performance of your system considerably, particularly if you are a Microsoft Windows user.

Graphics adapter The hardware inside a computer that enables the computer to display graphics on the screen. In contrast to Mac computers, PCs have a larger variety of graphics adapters that complicate compatibility between different PCs. In the early days, the PC standard was the Color Graphics Adapter (CGA) that, by today's standards, is low resolution and low in color combinations. This was replaced by EGA Enhanced Graphics Adapter and then VGA Video Graphics Array having a standard 480 lines vertical and 640 pixels horizontal resolution. Today Super VGA extensions (to at least 600 lines vertical and 800 pixels horizontal) are the choice among most PC users for whom graphics displays are important. Be aware, however, that there are different Super VGA resolutions and monitor options that can affect the compatibility of graphics images among different PCs. Also be aware that LCD panels are not able to handle the higher resolutions of cathode ray monitors; therefore, images may not look as good during class delivery as they did on a monitor during the authoring process. The top-rated graphics adapters at the end of 1994 are Impression Plus (Rank 1) with 4Mb of video RAM from Matrox, Imagine-128 (Rank 2) with 4Mb of video RAM from Number Nine, and Graphics Pro Turbo (Rank 3) with 4Mb of video RAM from ATI.

Graphics card The graphics card is an add-in board that plugs into the motherboard and sends signals out to the monitor to represent what should be shown on the screen. A graphics card can send simple text, or it can be designed to represent intense 3D graphics, as most cards do today.

Graphics coprocessor A fixed-function graphics chip, designed to speed up the processing and display of high-resolution images. Research:S386C9xx accelerator chips.

Graphics device interface (GDI) A standard set of programming functions provided by Microsoft for the production of graphic output in Windows. Microsoft provides these functions in its Software Development Kits. The functions are device-independent, so you can use them on any graphics card as long as Windows is installed.

Graphics interchange format (GIF) A graphics format pioneered by CompuServe that has a maximum of 256 colors, interlacing, and transparency (one color can be defined as transparent, allowing the background color to be visible); one of the most common graphics formats on the World Wide Web (WWW).

Graphics processing unit (GPU) A microprocessor specifically designed for processing 3D graphics data. This term was first coined by NVIDIA to describe its GeForce 256 chip. NVIDIA justified the name by stating that its graphics chip had a similar amount of transistors as then-current CPU chips. Now GPU has become a more widely used term to describe the complex chips that power 3D graphics cards.

Graspin An Esprit Esprit project to develop a personal software engineering environment to support the construction and verification of distributed and non-sequential software systems.

Grasshopper An experimental operating system for persistent systems.

Gray market The market where goods are sold in an unauthorized manner, or before their expected release date. Sometimes gray market goods have been stolen from the manufacturer, or have been dumped by the manufacturer to create a result such as flooding the market. Gray market products are more likely to be remarked as different products or unsupported by their manufacturers than products purchased through proper channels. However, gray market goods are sometimes cheaper or available before their time, making them attractive to potential purchasers. One of the largest sources of gray market products are computer shows, where many gray market goods are sold "as is."

Gray-scale monitor A monitor and video adapter that uses a set of gray shades from black to white instead of using colors. Gray-scale monitors are expensive and are used in medical and photographic imaging systems.

Greenie A slang term for a CD-Recordable disk. The media was originally green on the recording side, thus the term. Nowadays CD-R media may be green, blue, or gold on the recording side.

Grep A UNIX program, now also available on other OSes, that allows you to search through one or more text files for a specific text string. As well, Grep allows the replacement of the found string.

Ground Electrically speaking, this is a neutral point that can absorb excess electricity. Often it is the ground itself (as in the ground you stand on), but it is also commonly a large piece of metal, such as the chassis on a car. Electrical devices have to be connected to a ground so that the ground can disperse any excess electrical charges.

Grey balance The balance between CMY colorants required to produce neutral greys without a color cast.

Grey levels Discrete tonal steps in a continuous tone image, inherent to digital data. Most CT images will contain 256 grey levels per color.

Greyscale A continuous tone image comprising black, white, and grey data only.

Group alias A mail alias for a group of people; a mailing list. Consists of the group alias or mailing list, a request alias for submission and resignation requests, and an owner alias for problems.

Group ID (GID) A numeric value for the user account's group permissions.

Group In networking, an account that contains other accounts, called members. Permissions and rights granted to a group are also granted to its members.

Group policy Used to specify settings for groups of users and computers, including software policies, scripts, user documents and settings, application deployment, and security settings.

Group rights Rights given to a collection of users.

Groupware "Groupware" was originally coined to describe a new class of applications designed to provide electronic support for groups of individuals working together toward a common goal. In the last several years, the term has been applied to applications ranging from unstructured electronic mail to rigorously structured work-flow systems. Groupware is more useful as a concept when it is broken down into three major stages : communication, coordination and cooperation. In this light, groupware applications can be viewed in terms of the degree of structure in the group interaction and in complexity of that structure, and the rigor with which the activity itself is monitored.

GSM (global system for mobile communications) A 2G digital standard for cellular phone communications that is used in many countries. GSM communications bands range from 900-1800MHz. The GSM initials were initially derived from the French "Groupe de travail Sp,ciale pour les services Mobiles.".

GTL (gunning transceiver logic) A low-power standard for electrical signals used in CMOS circuits which allows for low electromagnetic interference at high speeds of transfer. GTL requires only 50% voltage swings to switch between on and off states, which is a small deviation compared to previous technologies. GTL is a parallel bus standard that typically operates at speeds of between 20 and 40MHz.

GTLP (gunning transceiver logic plus) This is an improvement to the GTL standard that allows for bus operation at speeds of between 60 and 125MHz typically. It remains a parallel signaling standard.

Guardian An authorization and authentication scheme developed by InterNIC that helps protect domain name records, contact records, and host records from unauthorized updates. Guardian is available free of charge and helps support secure registration transactions in an automated environment. It also provides flexible security mechanisms that can accommodate changes in organizations, personnel, and security needs.

GUI An acronym for Graphical User Interface, this term refers to a software front-end meant to provide an attractive and easy to use interface between a computer user and application, which historically gave rise to the icon-based operating system of Apple Corporation computers. The GUI concept actually had its origins in Xerox Corporation's Palo Alto Research Center (PARC) in the early 1970s. However, it was Apple Corporation who eventually exploited the technology that is now the fundamental basis of Mac, Windows, and other GUI operating systems that perform commands based upon bit-mapped graphics icons. This paved the way for object-oriented systems of the 1990s.

GUID (globally unique identifier) A unique 128-bit value generated by some Microsoft applications. An example of the GUID format is: 12345678-1234-1234-1234-123456789ABC. The GUID will use the MAC address of your network card as part of itself if you do have a network card installed, potentially marking documents created by Microsoft applications with a number that could be traced back to your PC.

Guide A hypertext hypertext system from the University of Kent (GB) and OWL for displaying online documentation.

Guidelines Recommended actions to follow in implementing the current policy. Guidelines should always be considered in the context of the best business practices. Guidelines change with the bank computer environment. Adherence to guidelines is advisable but discretionary.

Gunning transceiver logic (GTL) A low-power standard for electrical signals used in CMOS circuits which allows for low electromagnetic interference at high speeds of transfer. GTL requires only 50% voltage swings to switch between on and off states, which is a small deviation compared to previous technologies. GTL is a parallel bus standard that typically operates at speeds of between 20 and 40MHz.

Gustafson's law In response to Amdahl's Law on limitation of effectiveness of parallel computing due to a serial (non-parallelizable) component of code, Gustafson's Law was developed to show that you can achieve over a 1000-fold speed-up using 1024 processors. It states that if the size of most problems is increased sufficiently, you can achieve any given efficiency by increasing the amount of processors.

Gyros A contraction of gyroscopes; a mechanical device that uses one or more spinning discs which resist changes to their position in space.

H

H.323 Handheld Device Markup Language is a subset of HTML and is a text bade way of defining data, sent for display on handheld devices through the use of a microbrowser.

H_key (hive_key) A part of the Windows registry hive. The hive contains several different pieces, or keys.

H0 channel A 384 kbps channel that consists of six contiguous DS0s (64 kbps) of a T1 line.

Hacker Someone who seeks to understand computer, phone, or other systems strictly for the satisfaction of having that knowledge. Hackers wonder how things work, and have an incredible curiosity. Hackers will sometimes do questionable legal things, such as breaking into systems, but they generally will not cause harm once they break in. Contrast a hacker to the term cracker or malicious hacker.

HAL (hardware abstraction layer) The portion of the operating system that lets programs deal with hardware directly. This allows programs needing more speed from the computer to bypass the standard OS calls to hardware. So, instead of calling the Windows' API to draw a dialog box, you would go through the pain of actually drawing it out line by line—that's much faster, but much harder to write. This is of particular importance when coding games.

Half tones Black and white dots of certain sizes, which provide a perception of shades of gray

Half-duplex mode Also called half-duplex point-to-point link. This is a type of point-to-point connection in which devices take turns using a single wire. When one device is finished transmitting, it must "turn over" the communication channel so that the other device knows that is is permitted to transmit. When both devices can transmit at the same time, the operation is called full-duplex mode.

Half-duplex Refers to the transmission of data in just one direction at a time. For example, a walkie-talkie is a half-duplex device because only one party can talk at a time. In contrast, a telephone is a full-duplex device because both parties can talk simultaneously.

Most modems contain a switch that lets you select between half-duplex and full-duplex modes. The correct choice depends on which program you are using to transmit data through the modem.

In half-duplex mode, each character transmitted is immediately displayed on your screen. (For this reason, it is sometimes called local echo — characters are echoed by the local device). In full-duplex mode, transmitted data is not displayed on your monitor until it has been received and returned (remotely echoed) by the other device. If you are running a communications program and every character appears twice, it probably means that your modem is in half-duplex mode when it should be in full-duplex mode, and every character is being both locally and remotely echoed.

Half-height drive A space-saving drive bay that is half the height of the 3" drive bays used in the original IBM PC. Most of today's drives are half-height drives.

Halftone A simulation of continuous tones by the use of black or overlapping process color dots of varying size or position.

Halo A light line around object edges in an image, produced by the USM (sharpening) technique.

Ham radio A legal (or licensed) amateur radio.

Hand scanner An optical device used to digitize a relatively small image or artwork.

Hand-held computer A portable computer that is small enough to be held in one hand.

Handheld devices markup language (wireless markup language) Part of the Wireless Application Protocol (WAP) , allowing text portions of Web content to be separated from graphical content for display on wireless devices.

Handle Unique character string identifier assigned to each entry in the NIC WHOIS database.

Handshaking The process by which two devices initiate communications. Handshaking begins when one device sends a message to another device indicating that it wants to establish a communications channel. The two devices then send several messages back and forth that enable them to agree on a communications protocol.

Harassment Effectively an issue of corporate liability to employees and those with whom employees communicate using the corporate network. Recent court cases have involved the use of email to transfer information of a sexual, racial or generally offensive nature. Increasingly the organization and not the employee is seen as the owner of email sent using the corporate network. For this reason the employers need to demonstrate that they have a security policy and the technology to police corporate communication, including scanning for key words and tracking of email.

Hard boot A hard reboot (also known as a cold reboot) is when power to a computer is cycled (turned on and off) or a special reset signal to the processor is triggered (from a front panel switch of some sort). This restarts the computer without first performing the usual shut-down procedure. (With many operating systems, especially those with disc caches, after a hard reboot the system may well be in an "unclean" state, and require that checks and repairs to on-disc filesystem structures be performed before normal operation can begin.) It may be caused by power failure, be done by accident, or be done deliberately as a last resort because nothing else to retrieve the system from a "hung" state works.

Hard card A single expansion board that contains a small hard disk and associated controller circuitry. A hard card allows you to add another hard disk, even when all your drive bays are occupied, as long as there is still a single expansion slot available. Hard cards were brought to prominence by Plus Development Corporation.

Hard copy This refers to information printed out on paper, as contrasted to information stored in electronic formats.

Hard disk (HD) This is commonly the slang term for a hard drive. It refers to the type of re-writeable media that is inflexible, as opposed to a floppy disk. A hard drive typically contains multiple hard disk platters.

Hard disk controller An expansion board that contains the necessary circuitry to control and coordinate a hard disk drive. Many hard disk controllers are capable of managing more than one hard disk, as well as floppy disks and even tape drives.

Hard disk drive A storage device that uses a set of rotating, magnetically coated disks called platters to store data or programs. In everyday use, the terms "hard disk," "hard disk drive," and "hard drive" are all used interchangeably, because the disk and the drive mechanism are a single unit. A typical hard disk platter rotates at up to 3600 rpm, and the read/write heads float on a cushion of air from 10 to 25 millionths of an inch thick so that the heads never come into contact with the recording surface. The whole unit is hermetically sealed to prevent airborne contaminants from entering and interferring with these close tolerances. Hard disks range in capacity from a few tens of megabytes to several gigabytes of storage space; the bigger the disk, the more important a well-thought out backup strategy becomes. Hard disks are very reliable, but they do fail, and usually at the most inconvenient moment.

Hard disk interface A standard way of accessing the data stored on a hard disk. Several different hard-disk interface standards have evolved over time, including the ST-506 interface, enhanced small device interface, integrated drive electronics interface, and small computer-system interface.

Hard disk units Direct access storage unit containing unmovable disks. The hard disks are composed of metallic circular plates, covered with a magnetic layer allowing data recording. They are sealed in a box. Synonymous of "Fixed Disk".

Hard drive A "hard disc" file storage disc (usually a magnetic disc) on a computer that has higher storage capacity and faster access time (e.g., under 20 ms) than slower devices such as floppy disc drives and optical disc (e.g., CD-ROM) drives. This is not the same as memory or random access memory (RAM). Usually the term "hard drive" refers to rigid discs coated with magnetic material.

Fig. Hard drive

Hard reset (hardware reset) This refers to the forced, immediate shutdown and restart of a PDA or other device by means of hardware. This is typically done by pushing a sequence of buttons or a reset button, and usually only after it has become impossible to do a soft reset.

Hardlock Token-based software security system that ensures license compliance and provide innovative licensing, trial and upgrading solutions for software developers and publishers.

Hardware The physical components of your computer system, that is, the boxes. Your computer hardware may include the computer, terminal, keyboard, screen, modem, printer, mouse, trackball, diskdrive, and even a scanner.

Hardware abstraction layer (HAL) The portion of the operating system that lets programs deal with hardware directly. This allows programs needing more speed from the computer to bypass the standard OS calls to hardware. So, instead of calling the Windows' API to draw a dialog box, you would go through the pain of actually drawing it out line by line—that's much faster, but much harder to write. This is of particular importance when coding games.

Hardware address The physical address for the NIC (network interface card). Used by the low-level hardware layers of a network. TCP/IP's ARP protocol translates IP addresses into hardware addresses. The NIC vendor gets the address from the IEEE and assigns it permanently to the NIC. Also called the MAC (Media Access Control) address.

Hardware branch The hardware archive root key in the registry that is a superset of the memory-resident hardware tree. Although the hardware tree contains information only about those devices currently detected and running in the system, the registry contains a complete list of all hardware ever installed on the particular computer.

Hardware compatibility list (HCL) A list of computers and peripherals that have been tested by Microsoft to work with Windows NT or Windows 2000. If you run those operating systems on equipment that is not listed on the HCL, it is not guaranteed to work, but it might. Basically, if you install NT/2000 on hardware that's not on the HCL, you are on your own. However, it is done frequently with decent success.

Hardware compatibility tests A suite of tests from WHQL to verify hardware and device driver operations under a specific operating environment. These tests exercise the combination of a device, a software driver, and an operating system under controlled conditions to verify that all components operate properly.

Hardware description language A language used for the conceptual design of integrated circuits. Examples are VHDL VHDL and Verilog Verilog.

Hardware emulation layer (HEL) This provides software-based emulation of features that are not directly available in hardware.

Hardware ID A vendor-defined string used by the Plug and Play Manager to find an INF-file match for a device.

Hardware interrupt An interrupt or request for service generated by a hardware device such as a keystroke from the keyboard or a tick from the clock. because the processor may receive several such signals simultaneously, hardware interrupts are usually assigned a priority level, and processed according to that priority.

Hardware token A device that generates code to authenticate a user when logging on to a secure network or application.

Hardware tree A record in RAM of the current system configuration based on the information for all devices in the hardware branch of the registry. The hardware tree is created each time the system is started or whenever a dynamic change occurs to the system configuration.

Hardware-dependence The requirement that a specific hardware component be present for a program to work. Hardware-dependent software is often very difficult to move or port to another computer.

Hardware-independence The ability to produce similar results in a wide variety of environments, without requiring the presence of specific hardware. The Unix OS and the Post-Script page-description language are both examples fo hardware independence. Unix runs on a wide range of computers, from the PC to a Cray, and PostScript is used by many printer manufacturers.

Hardwired Describes a system designed in a way that does not allow for flexibility or future expansion. May also refer to a device or computer connected directly to a network.

Harmony A real-time real-time operating system developed by the SEL SEL in Canada.

Harvard cyclotron A specialized machine (cyclotron) developed in 1948 at Harvard University; it is used to carry out experiments in sub-atomic physics and medicine

Harvest An information discovery and access system for the Internet Internet from the University of Colorado.

Hash code Short ciphertext created by a one-way hash algorithm to uniquely identify the total keystrokes in a document.

Hash table A table that contains "hash values," generally used for speeding up searching algorithms on sorted data. For example, a hash table for a dictionary might contain all the letters of the alphabet and the page numbers where each letter starts. That way, instead of searching through from start to finish for each word, you just use the hash table and get a big head start.

Hashing A process that help generate aliases for long file names. For instance, Windows NT uses a hashing process to generate characters three through five of the file name, after it encounters four file names having the same first six characters and extension.

Haskell A functional language functional-language.

HASP Token-based software security system that ensures license compliance and provides innovative licensing, trial and upgrading solutions for software developers and publishers.

Hawthorne effects Refer to distortions and possibly non-sustaining effects of a treatment just because its newness captures more of an individual's attentiveness. In double blind studies of the impact of technologies upon learning, Hawthorne effects are particularly troublesome. Students are more apt to be more attentive to newer technologies simply because they are "new" curiosities. Positive results on learning impacts may not be sustaining, however, after the novelty and curiosity factors decline with repeated use of the technology over time.

Hayes compatible Hayes Microcomputer Products is one of the leading manufacturers of modems and has developed a language called the AT command set for controlling modems that has become the de facto standard. Any modem that recognizes Hayes modem commands is said to be Hayes-compatible. This is very useful because most communications programs use Hayes modem commands. Virtually all modems manufactured today are Hayes-compatible.

Hayes-compatible modem Any modem that recognizes the commands in the industry-standard AT-command set, defined by Hayes Microcomputer Products,Inc.

HBFG (host behavior functional group) The group of functions performed by an ATM-attached host that is participating in the MPOA service.

Hc The compiler for the h hyperbook language.

H-channel H-Channels are ISDN bearer services that have pre-defined speeds, starting and stopping locations on a PRI and are contiguously transported from one PRI site through networks to another PRI site.

HCL (hardware compatibility list) A list of computers and peripherals that have been tested by Microsoft to work with Windows NT or Windows 2000. If you run those operating systems on equipment that is not listed on the HCL, it is not guaranteed to work, but it might. Basically, if you install NT/2000 on hardware that's not on the HCL, you are on your own. However, it is done frequently with decent success.

HDLC (high level data link control) An ITU-TSS link layer protocol standard for point-to-point and multi-point communications.

HDML (handheld devices markup language) This stands for Handheld Devices Markup Language, now called Wireless Markup Language.

HDSL (high bit-rate digital subscriber line) Is generally used as a substitute for T1/E1. HDSL is becoming popular as a way to provide full-duplex symmetric data communication at rates up to 1.544 Mbps) over moderate distances via conventional telephone twisted-pair wires. Traditional T1 requires repeaters every 6000 ft. to boost the signal strength. HDSL has a longer range than T1/E1 without the use of repeaters to allow transmission over distances up to

12,000 feet. It uses pulse amplitude modulation (PAM) on a 4-wire loop.

HDTV (high definition television) A new standard of displaying and broadcasting television signals that uses at least twice the scan lines of normal television and a 16x9 aspect ratio, as opposed to the old 4x3 aspect ration of a standard TV set. Japan first used an analog form of HDTV. The United States began with a digital form of HDTV, or DTV.

Head The electromagnetic device used to read and write to and from magnetic media such as hard and floppy disks, tape drives, and compact discs. The head converts the information read into electrical pulses sent tot he computer for processing.

Head crash An unexpected collision between a hard disk head and the rapidly rotating magnetic recording surface of the disk resulting in damage to the disk surface,and in some severe cases resulting in damage to the head itself.A head crash in the file allocation table(FAT) area of a disk can be especially devastating because the FAT contains instructions for the OS on how to find all the other directories and files ont he disk, and if it is damaged, the other files and directories may become completely inaccessible.

An aluminum radiator that dissipates heat. Fast CPU's like the 586/Pentium have heatsinks, and often also cooling fans.

Head end Central distribution point for a CATV system. Video signals are received here from satellites and maybe other sources, frequency converted to the appropriate channels, combined with locally originated signals, and rebroadcast onto the HFC plant. The headend is where the CMTS is normally located.

Header The portion of a packet, preceding the actual data, containing source and destination addresses, error checking and other fields. A header is also the part of an electronic mail message that precedes the body of a message and contains, among other things, the message originator, date and time.

Header verify Anti-spam technology that analyzes the email headers, and compares the actual IP address of the originating SMTP server with the IP address listed in the message header.

Head-mounted displays (HMD) Helmets worn by a virtual reality (VR) participant that include speakers and screens for each eye, which display three- dimensional images.

Heap Most commonly, this is a segment of memory claimed by a program. Within the heap, pieces of memory can be used and freed as needed. Depending on usage, heaps can become fragmented as small pieces of memory are used and freed. In formal computer science terms, a heap is the same as a partially ordered tree.

Heatsink A device that makes contact with a microprocessor (or other object in need of cooling) and removes heat by exchanging it with air in a more efficient manner than the flat surface the heatsink is attached to. The heatsink does this by providing more surface area than a flat surface. This is usually accomplished by having a group of fins built into the shape of the heatsink. The longer the fins, and the more of them, the higher the surface area, and the better the efficiency. Most heatsinks are aluminum for cost and weight reasons. Copper heatsinks are more efficient, but are seldom used because they are much more expensive, heavier, and harder to build. It is common for a fan to be mounted onto a heatsink to increase the efficiency of heat exchange by blowing cooler air through the fins on the heatsink.

Heatsink fan (HSF) This is the common combination of a fan attached to a heatsink that is placed in contact with a microprocessor that needs to be cooled. The heatsink draws heat away from the processor, and the fan expedites the removal of the heat by moving air across the heatsink. Faster airflow generally equals better cooling.

Hebbian Refers to the most common way for a neural network to learn, namely supervised learning. Using a training sample which should produce known responses, the connection weights are adjusted so as to minimize the differences between the desired and actual outputs for the training sample.

HEL (hardware emulation layer) This provides software-based emulation of features that are not directly available in hardware.

Helical-scan recording A technique used by the 8mm and 4 mm data backup cartridges to increase data density on tapes. The tape moves at a relatively slow speed pasta drum that contains the recording head and revolves at high speed. The drum is tilted, and the recording head records data in diagonal stripes on the tape. Helical-scan recording increases data density by revolving the recording head more rapidly. Tape speeds are low and tape stress is minimized.

Hello packet A type of PNNI Routing packet that is exchanged between neighboring logical nodes.

Help desk If you've ever worked in an office environment, you may have called the help desk. This is the support organization designed to take care of your computer and phone problems. Help Desk staff work long hours, have a never ending workload, get harassed by everyone, and get crappy pay.

Help System function allowing the user to obtain information about the computer or the program being executed.

Helper application A program allowing you to view multimedia files (images, audio, video) that your web browser cannot handle internally. The file must be downloaded before it will be displayed. There are some plug-ins that allow you to view the file over the Internet without downloading it first.

HEP High Energy (Particle) Physics.

Herf guns - emp bombs HERF stands for High Energy Radio Frequency. HERF guns are able to shoot a high power radio signal at an electronic target and put it out of function. The damage can be moderate (e.g. that a system shuts down, but can be restarted) or severe (e.g. the system hardware has been physically damaged). Electronic circuits are more vulnerable to overload that most people would suspect. This mechanism uses HERF guns with big success. In essence, HERF guns are nothing but radio transmitters. They send a concentrated radio signal to the target. The target can be a mainframe inside a business building, an entire network in a building, or as today's planes and cars are stuffed with electronic equipment, the target can even be a moving vehicle with all the inherent dangers for the people who are inside. EMP stands for electromagnetic pulse. The source can be a nuclear or a non-nuclear detonation. It can be used by special forces teams who infiltrate the enemy's and detonate a device near their electronic devices. It destroys the electronics of all computer and communication systems in a quite large area. The EMP bomb can be smaller than a HERF gun to cause a similar amount of damage and is typically used to damage not a single target (not aiming in one direction) but to damage all equipment near the bomb.

Hermes An experimental object-oriented object-orienteddistributed systems language from IBM Watson Research Centre.

Hertz A rental company, formerly represented by O.J. Simpson. It is also a measure of speed. One Hertz means one cycle per second, so one megahertz (MHz) means one million cycles per second. This is the common measure of speed for processors and electronic activities inside a computer.

Heterogeneous data sources A data-warehousing term that describes the idea of drawing data from several different (heterogeneous) data sources on different platforms and computers.

Heuristic analysis Analysis of how a program behaves, rather than looking for a known virus signature in order to identify a virus.

Heuristic scanner Anti-virus scanner that can evaluate file structure and activity patterns to identify previously unknown viruses.

Heuristics This describes a set of rules developed to attempt to solve problems when a specific algorithm cannot be designed. For example, if the problem is "When do you eat food?", if you answer, "When I'm hungry" then you would have to eat immediately every single time you were hungry. Instead, we follow heuristics to determine when to eat by gauging our hunger level, the situation we are in, and our ability to get food. As you can imagine, heuristics are very important for solving artificial intelligence problems.

Hewlett-packard (HP) Hewlett-Packard Corporation, Palo Alto, California. Computer manufacturer, second largest income in 1994. Rather successful, mostly in the server and printer markets.

Hexadecimal (Hex) A base 16 number system where 16 digits are used instead of 10. In addition to the standard base 10 system numbers 0-9, letters A-F are used to represent the numbers 10-15. Thus, a one digit hexadecimal number is a value between 0 and 15 (where F is 15). A two digit hex number is the value between 0 and 255 (represented as 00 and FF in hex, where 00 is 016 + 01, and FF is 1516 + 151), and so forth. Hexadecimal numbers are often used to represent data because they are easily translatable to base 2 numbers, which are commonly used to apply to the 0 and 1 (off and on) conditions present in electronics, while base 10 numbers are not.

Hexidecimal (hex) The base-16 numbering system that uses the digits 0 to 9, followed by the letters A to F (equivalent tot he decimal numbers 10 through 15). Hex is a very convenient way to represent the binary numbers computers use internally, because it fits neatly into the 8-bit byte. All of the 16 hex digits 0 to f can be represented in four bits, and so two hex digits (one digit for each set of four bits) can be stored in a single byte. This means that one byte can contain any one of 256 different hex numbers, from 0 through FF. Hex numbers are often labled with a lower-case h (for example,1234h) to distinguish them from decimal numbers.

HFC (hybrid fiber-coaxial) Older CATV systems were provisioned using only coaxial cable. Modern systems use fiber transport from the headend to an optical node located in the neighborhood to reduce system noise. Coaxial cable runs from the node to the subscriber. The fiber plant is generally a star configuration with all optical node fibers terminating at a headend. The coaxial cable part of the system is generally a trunk-and-branch configuration.

HGC (hercules graphics card) A video adapter for DOS computers, introduced by Hercules Computer Technology. HGC provides monochrome graphics with 720 horizontal pixels and 348 vertical pixels.

Hi-8 A professional-quality format for high-end video cameras. Whereas the standard consumer resolution 8mm camera records 250 lines, the Hi-8 versions record 400 lines or more so as to produce more detail in video images.

Hibernate This allows computer users to save the contents of their computer's memory to disk before shutting down the PC. When restarted, the contents are read back into RAM and the computer is brought back to the exact state it was in before hibernation was initiated. This is different from sleep mode, where the computer is not fully shut down.

Hidden file A file with a filename that begins with a period. These files do not appear on regular ls directory listings. Use ls -a to include hidden files in your home directory, or in subdirectories of your home directory.

Hidden surface removal (Z-buffering) This tracks the depth of each triangle in a 3D graphics representation, from the perspective of the viewer, to ensure that objects behind other objects in a scene don't appear until the viewer has them in his or her line of sight. This is why you can't see through walls to what lies behind, but why you can play multiplayer Quake and have people at many different areas in a level.

Hierarchical file system (HFS) (General) A structured, hierarchical file system, such as the fast file system (FFS) or the Unix File System (UFS). (Specific) The hierarchical file system used on the Macintosh system in MacOS 6 through MacOS 9.

Hierarchical relationship This relationship is one where elements at lower levels are submissive to elements at higher levels. Just think of the military hierarchy, where the General is above a Captain who is above a Private.

Hierarchically complete source route A stack of DTLs representing a route across a PNNI routing domain such that a DTL is included for each hierarchical level between and including the current level and the lowest visible level in which the source and destination are reachable.

High availability Configuration of clusters or redundant servers to provide continuous access to a network resource application, such as a VPN, firewall, or Web server. The servers are continuously synchronized to provide automatic failover. High availability solutions enable redundant servers to detect when the primary server is unavailable and transparently switch to a secondary server.

High bit-rate dsl (HDSL) A form of DSL that provides T1 (1.5Mbits/second) or better transfer rates and is meant to displace business T1 connections. HDSL requires much less bandwidth than standard T1 encoding to transfer the same amount of data.

High color The name given to a graphics card setting that can display 16-bit color (65,536 colors).

High definition television (HDTV) A new standard of displaying and broadcasting television signals that uses at least twice the scan lines of normal television and a 16x9 aspect ratio, as opposed to the old 4x3 aspect ration of a standard TV set. Japan first used an analog form of HDTV. The United States began with a digital form of HDTV, or DTV.

High key A light image that is intentionally lacking in shadow detail.

High memory area (HMA) In an IBM-compatible compter, the first 64K of extended memory above the 1 MB limit of 8086 and 8088 addresses. Programs that conform to the extended memory specification can use this memory as an extension of conventional memory although only one program can use or control hma at a time; dos, Microsoft Windows, or an application. If you load DOS into the hma, you can recover approximately 50K of conventional memory for use by your applications.

High performance addressing (HPA) A form of passive matrix LCD display that improves the response time of the display. HPA screens still suffer from the same contrast problems that make passive matrix inferior to active matrix TFT LCD screens. HPA screens are no longer made, as the cost of active matrix LCD screens has dropped.

High performance file system (HPFS) A file system available in OS/2 and win nt that supports long, mixed-case file names up to 256 characters, up to 64K of extended attributes per file, faster disk access with an advanced disk cache for caching files and directory information, highly contiguous file allocation that eliminates file fragmentation, and support for hard disks up to 64GB in size. Dos does not recognize the hpfs file structure. Hpfs cannot be used on a floppy disk.

High performance peripheral interface (HiPPI) A high-speed (800Mb/sec or 1.6Gb/sec, depending on the width) network interface connection, typically to one or more mainframes or supercomputers.

High precision/low recall A phenomenon that occurs when a search yields a small set of hits; although each one may be highly relevant to the search topic, some relevant documents are missed

High resolution In monitors and printers, a description of high-quality output; resolution refers to the sharpness and detail of the image.

High speed serial interface (HSSI) A serial interface that runs on high speeds.

High voltage regulation Ability of the high voltage to respond to changes in beam current. Good high voltage regulation means a stable display even when changing between different intensity levels.

High-bandwidth A communication channel that permits many signals of differing frequencies to be transmitted simultaneously.

High-contrast support Part of Accessibility options set by users to indicate that they require a high degree of contrast to improve screen legibility.

High-density disk A floppy disk with more recording density and storage capacity than a double-density disk. In the Macintosh, high-density disks contain 1.44MB. In IBM-compatible computers, high-density 5.25" floppy disks contain 1.2MB, while high-density 3.5" floppy disks contain either 1.44MB or 2.88MB of storage space.

High-level format The process of preparing a floppy disk or a hard disk partition for use by the operating system. In the case of DOS, a high-level format ceates the boot sector, the file allocation table (FAT), and the root directory.

Highlight The lightest tones in an image. A spectral highlight is a bright, reflected light source.

High-persistence phosphor In a monitor, a phosphor that glows for a relatively long time after being energized by electrons. This can lead to ghost images on the screen.

High-speed data links Digital communications systems that permit digital data to be reliably transferred at high speed.

High-speed SDRAM (HSDRAM) A form of SDRAM memory made by Enhanced Memory Systems. It is designed to operate comfortably at speeds of up to 150MHz or higher at CAS 2 latency levels. It was mainly used by overclockers and was a niche product.

Himem.sys The dos and Microsoft Windows device that manages the use of extended memory and the high memory area on ibm-compatible computers. Himem.sys not only allows your application programs to access extended memory, it also oversees that area to prevent other programs from trying to use the same space at the same time. Himem.sys must be loaded by a device command in your CONFIG.SYS file.

Hipac An active DBMS active-DBMS from Xerox Advanced Information Technology.

HIPPI (high Performance Parallel Interface) A 100 Mbyte/sec data transfer system with associated interfaces and switches, developed at Los Alamos National Lab and now ANSI ANSI standard X3T9/88-127.

Histogram A chart displaying the tonal ranges present in an image as a series of vertical bars.

History file A file on your hard disk where your browser normally stores the URLs that you visit whenever you use the Internet.

History For on the history of computing.

Hit When a user requests an HTML document, image, or external object on the World Wide Web, the server records that request as a "hit." The problem with measuring popularity based on "hits" is that webservers, depending on the logging level, count each graphic on that page as a hit. For example, if you look at a page with 5 images on it, some servers count that as 6 hits: one for the HTML page and 5 for the graphics. For this reason "hits" are a questionable measurement of how popular a website actually is.

Hkey_classes_root One of the five subtrees found in a Windows registry. Hkey_classes_root contains object linking and embedding (OLE) and file-class association data. Information in this subtree is duplicated in hkey_local_machine.

Hkey_current_config One of the five subtress found in a Windows registry, hkey_current_config contains current hardware configuration, derived from the configuration used to boot the system. This is the area of the registry that is used and modified during the current session. When the system shuts down, the current configuration is copied back to hkey_local_machine under the appropriate area.

Hkey_current_user One of the five subtrees found in a Windows registry, hkey_current_user contains user-profile data for the currently logged-on user.

Hkey_local_machine This subtree contains computer hardware information. Part of this subtree is reconstructed each time the computer is started to reflect the current hardware configuration.

Hkey_users This subtree contains all actively loaded user profiles, including the default profile and a duplicate of information in hkey_current_user. Profiles fro remotely logged-on users are stored in the Registries of their local computers.

HL (hyper-learning) Using hypertext, hypermedia, and computer networks. Authors like Perelman tend to use the term in the context of learning from servers on an information highway such as the Internet after multimedia transmissions become more common.

H-node resolution names One of the four name resolution modes used on Windows networks. H-node is a hybrid mode wich favors WINS. First, an attempt is made to use p-node to resolve a name via WINS(Windows Internet Naming Service). Because it typically results in the best network utilization, h-node is the default mode of operation for MS TCP/IP clients configured to use WINS for name resolution.

Hoax Email message warning of a non-existent virus. The hoax can disrupt work in organizations that panic to deal with the hoax, while they wait for an update to their anti-virus software. The anti-virus software does not "catch" hoax email because there is no virus to catch.

HOL An interactive theorem proving system based on Higher Order Logic.

Hole Any means by which an intrusion may occur.

Holistic Looking at the entire system, rather than just its parts.

Holographic storage This form of storing data uses a three-dimensional array of storage media. Lasers are aligned vertically and horizontally to read or write a specific section of the media. Holographic storage densities should be superior to standard storage techniques because you are using three dimensions to store data instead of two. Think of holographic storage media looking like a stationary cube with lasers moving around it quickly to read data, while normal storage media is on a flat circular surface that spins.

Home directory The directory you start in when you log in, usually a subdirectory of /usr. You should keep your files in your home directory, or in subdirectories of your home directory.

Home page The starting point for a WWW session. Many system adminstrators set up "home pages" which are the default page shown when a user begins a session. These pages usually have a lot of options and menu items that apply to that particular institution and then have links to other places.

Honeypot A system left open and unprotected to entice hackers to break into it. Usually this is done so that system administrators can monitor the methods used to break in, the frequency of attack, or just to throw off attackers from the real goodies.

HOOD (hierarchical object oriented design) A method for Architectural Design primarily for software to be developed in Ada, leading to automated checking, documentation and source code generation.

Hoot & holler (H&H) A dedicated point-to-point voice facility between international offices of a trading facility.

Hop One piece of the TCP/IP networking protocol route that a computer needs to take in order to send or receive information. Think of all the main computers in the world that are physically connected as stones in a lake. To get from your stone to the stone on the other side you need to "hop" on a certain number of other stones. A similar method is used for communicating over the Internet.

Hop count A measure of distance between two nodes in an internet. A hop count of n means there are n-1 gateways between the source and the destination nodes.

Hop-by-hop route A route that is created by having each switch along the path use its own routing knowledge to determine the next hop of the route, with the expectation that all switches will choose consistent hops such that the call will reach the desired destination. PNNI does not use hop-by-hop routing.

Hope A functional language.

Hopfield John Hopfield in the early 1980's investigated a particular kind of neural network which is now commonly referred to as the Hopfield network or Hopfield model. In the Hopfield network, there are no special input or output neurons, but all are both input and output, and all are connected to all others in both directions (with equal weights in the two directions). Input is applied simultaneously to all neurons which then output to each other and the process continues until a stable state is reached, which represents the network output.

Horizontal frequency This indicates how long it takes to scan each of the Horizontal fines that make up the display. The unit of measurement is kilohertz (kHz). It is directly related to the number of lines and the Vertical Refresh (Frequency) so that the higher the Vertical Refresh or the number of lines, the higher the Horizontal frequency required.

Horizontal link A link between two logical nodes that belong to the same peer group.

Horizontal scanning frequency In a monitor, the frequency at which the monitor repaints the horizontal lines that make up an image. Horizontal scanning frequency is measured in kHz, and is standardized at 31.5 kHz for a VGA. For SuperVGA, this frequency ranges from 35 to 48 kHz, depending on the refresh rate of the video adapter.

Host The central or controlling computer in a networked or distributed processing environment, providing services that other computers or terminals can access via the network. Computers connected to the Internet are also described as hosts, and can be accessed using ftp, telnet, Gopher, or a World Wide Web browser.

Host adapter This term is synonymous with SCSI adapter. It refers to an add-in board, such as a PCI SCSI card, that allows PCs to communicate with SCSI devices.

Host alias A nickname for a host, such as "chimailhost" for the machine in Chicago that handles mail.

Host apparent address A set of internetwork layer addresses which a host will directly resolve to

Host form (host template) The electronic form used to register a new host (name server) or modify information for an existing host. Formerly referred to as the Host Template.

Host names Each host on IP Network is assigned a unique software address called an Internet or IP address. This address uniquely identifies each host within your internet work. By convention, this address is usually represented in dotted decimal notation such as the address 217.17.20.19.Each segment or network on your internet work is also assigned a network address that represents a portion of the IP address of each host on the network. From a user point of view, it is convenient to associate a name to each hosts or network.

Host part The host-specific portion of a CIDR address. The host part identifies the specific interface on a host.

Host tables Host Tables is an ASCII file containing the names and address of systems that you commonly access. For example, if you are trying to establish a telnet session with the host Pugmarks.com, the file is examined to find internet address. The file generally look like this 202.19.162.27 Pugmarks.com.

Hostmaster A role account established by InterNIC to handle email related to domain name registrations. Hostmaster also is a term commonly used by other organizations for role accounts that handle email related to network administration responsibilities.

Hosts file A text file that lists host names and their IP addresses on a network. For small networks, the hosts file is an alternative to DNS. Also called a host table by some TCP/IP vendors.

Host-to-host layer The DoD model layer that references to the Transport layer of the OSI model.

Hot fix Novell, Inc.'s term for the feature of their network file server operating system, Novell NetWare, which handles errors in disk write operations. The OS re-reads every block it writes to disk while it holds the data to be written in memory. In the case of an error, the data block is written to a spare area on the disk.

The feature lost much of its importance with the widespread use of hard disk drives with built-in error correction and bad block re-mapping.

Hot spare A drive in a RAID configuration that sits idle until one of the RAIDed drives fails. The hot spare then assumes the role of the dead drive. When the dead drive is replaced you can make it the hot spare. (The old hot spare doesn't revert back because it's got data on it now.) Hot spares are most often used in RAID 5 configurations, but can also be used in RAID 1 or RAID 10. When a drive fails the hot spare must be populated with information regenerated from the other drives. During this time performance is degraded.

Hot spots Buttons or other programmable objects that can activate objects or linked events.

Hotlist A file containing lists of Internet Web pages, enabling you to easily access your favorite Web pages.

Hot-pluggable Same as hot-swappable, but also connotes a simple plug-in mechanism for easy swapping.

Hot-swappable This type of mechanism implies that you can remove or add things while the system is powered on and running. For example, hard drives and power supplies are often candidates for this term, but more expensive servers may even have hot-swappable memory, PCI cards, and processors. Normally they come in special proprietary form factors in server machines and RAID boxes. If you've got mission-critical applications, you want your servers to have as many hot swappable components as possible.

HP VEE Visual Engineering Environment from Hewlett-Packard: a package similar in intention to LabVIEW running on UNIX workstations with OSF /Motif.

HPA (high performance addressing) A form of passive matrix LCD display that improves the response time of the display. HPA screens still suffer from the same contrast problems that make passive matrix inferior to active matrix TFT LCD screens. HPA screens are no longer made, as the cost of active matrix LCD screens has dropped.

HPM Hyper page mode, also known as EDO.

HPPI An earlier name for HIPPI.

HP-UX Hewlett-Packard's System V-based Unix implementation, with real-time extensions added.

HSCSD High Speed Circuit Switched Data is a circuit switched (as opposed to packet switched) Protocol that extends the capabilities of GSM to increase its transmission speeds by up to 4 times its GSM equivalent (57.6 Kb per second). It achieves this by using 4 GSM time slots rather than one.

HSDRAM (high-speed SDRAM) A form of SDRAM memory made by Enhanced Memory Systems. It is designed to operate comfortably at speeds of up to 150MHz or higher at CAS 2 latency levels. It was mainly used by overclockers and was a niche product.

HSF (heatsink Fan) This is the common combination of a fan attached to a heatsink that is placed in contact with a microprocessor that needs to be cooled. The heatsink draws heat away from the processor, and the fan expedites the removal of the heat by moving air across the heatsink. Faster airflow generally equals better cooling.

HSM (hierarchical storage manager) Software aiming at managing mass storage data in order to let very active data reside on hard disk, and to migrate less active data from/to less expensive storage such as tape units.

HSSI (high-speed serial interface) Is a short distance communications standard for data rates from 2Mbps to 52 Mbps.Common uses include connecting a LAN router to a high-speed line (like T3 or OC-3), host-to-host linking, image transmission, or connecting web servers or e-commerce servers to the Internet.

HST (high speed technology) Before the invention of the CCITT V.32 modem standards for 9600 BPS modems, US Robotics invented a proprietary protocol that runs even faster at 14,400 BPS. It became popular on US bulletin board system, but never caught on outside the USA. It is gradually being replaced by V.32.

HTML An acronym for a HyperText Markup Language DTD. HTML is the language used to tag various parts of a Web document so browsing software will know how to display that document's links, text, graphics and attached media. The popular HTML and the emerging HTML are subsets of the GML text scripting conceived in1969. IBM researchers depicting Generalized Markup Languages (and not-so-coincidentally the lead researchers were named Goldfarb, Mosher, and Lorie). Between 1978 and 1987, Dr. Charles F. Goldfarb led the team that developed the SGML Standard GML that is became International Standard ISO 8879. In 1990, Tim Berners-Lee led a team of particle physicists that invented the World Wide Web using a very small part of SGML that became the widely known and used scripting language known as Hypertext Markup Language (HTML). SGML is tremendously powerful but inefficient and complex. HTML is marvelously simple but not very powerful. In 1996, Jon Bosak of Sun Microsystems spearheaded the development of the XML standard to lend power, efficiency, cross-platform standards, and simplicity to the networking of databases on the Internet.

HTML document A document with a HyperText Markup Language DTD. It must be read using HTTP protocol.

HTTP (hypertext transfer protocol) The way the data in an HTML document is transferred. A document coming in over the HTTP protocol, usually TCP/IP port 80, is read as an HTML document.

HTTPS (secure hypertext transfer protocol) A secure means of transferring data using the HTTP protocol. Typically HTTP data is sent over TCP/IP port 80, but HTTPS data is sent over port 443. This standard was developed by Netscape for secure transactions, and uses 40-bit encryption ("weak" encryption) or 128-bit ("strong" encryption). If you are at a secure site, you will notice that there is a closed lock icon on the bottom area of your Navigator or IE browser. The HTTPS standard supports certificates. A webserver operator must get a digital certificate from a third-party certificate provider that ensures that the webserver in question is valid. This certificate gets installed on the webserver, and verifies for a period of a year that that server is a proper secure server.

Hub A common connection point for devices in a network. Hubs are commonly used to connect segments of a LAN. A hub contains multiple ports. When a packet arrives at one port, it is copied to the other ports so that all segments of the LAN can see all packets.

A passive hub serves simply as a conduit for the data, enabling it to go from one device (or segment) to another. So-called intelligent hubs include additional features that enables an administrator to monitor the traffic passing through the hub and to configure each port in the hub. Intelligent hubs are also called manageable hubs.

A third type of hub, called a switching hub, actually reads the destination address of each packet and then forwards the packet to the correct port.

Hue The color of an object perceived by the eye due to the fact that a single or pair of RGB primary colors predominates.

Huffman coding A terribly clever method of compressing information (like the stuff in your files) so that it takes up less space.

HX-pro An audio tape monitoring system marketed by Dolby that facilitates recording of analog audio tapes at higher decibel levels to reduce tape hiss. This is a feature available on high-end tape decks.

Hybrid A device or system combining two types of mechanisms, circuits, or design approaches, each of which could of itself accomplish the total function but in a different and usually less effective manner. A hybrid computer combines digital and analog computers into one functioning system.

Hydraulic Motion being powered by a pressurized liquid (such as water or oil), supplied through tubes or pipes.

Hyperbase An experimental active multiuser database for hypertext systems from the University of Aalborg, written in C++.It is built on the client-server model enabling distributed, concurrent, and shared access from workstations in a local area network.

Hypercard A software package for the Macintosh for storage and retrieval of information. It can handle images, and is designed for browsing. The powerful customisable interactive user interface allows new applications to be easily constructed by manipulating objects on the screen, often without conventional programming.

Hyperfacts Hypertext and/or hypermedia versions of fact books. The best known of these are encyclopedia CD-ROMs such as the Compton and Grolier options. But there are many other widely selling hyperfact books such as The Way Things Work by David Macauley, a CD-ROM book that has sold over 3 million copies to readers interested in guides and graphics of important inventions. This and several other innovative CD-ROM fact books ranging from sign language to art collections.

Hyperfiction Hypertext and/or hypermedia versions of fiction, usually on CD-ROM discs. The main feature of hyperfiction is that alternative navigations through the plot are possible. In some cases the reader creatively determines certain outcomes.

Hyperlink or link When you are browsing pages on the Web, you will find that some of the text you see may be underlined or highlighted. This is telling you that there is about this underlined or highlighted word or phrase. If you are using a computer equipped with a mouse, then all you need to do is point the mouse to the underlined or highlighted word and click. You will be taken to the place which has this additional information. This could be at the same location or anywhere in the world.

Hypermedia Hypertext with added features for audio and video features. Hypermedia may also entail touchscreen or remote control capabilities such that users can navigate by touching the computer screen or remote control devices. Eventually hypermedia will entail other senses such as smell. The key to hypermedia is random access that allows lightning-fast non linear navigation based upon reader choice or other reader actions such as responses to questions. The term "multimedia" is not totally synonymous with "hypermedia," because multimedia may not entail hypertext authoring.

Hypertext links A Hypertext Link is a method of embedding a URL into an object, such as a segment of text, or an image. When this object is clicked on the browser then addresses the embedded URL to retrieve its WWW document. Hypertext Links are responsible for the "world wide" aspect of the web, as they make any Web server a simple click away from any other Web server. As a general rule of thumb, any colored words and graphics are normally linked and can be clicked on.

Hypertext Pages of computer text that are authored in software allowing for non linear navigation based upon button controls, hotwords, or other controls that make sequencing of pages virtually irrelevant. Hypertext authoring packages typically differ from word processing packages that are intended primarily for preparing text for hard copy printing. Hypertext software may have options to print particular pages, but the intent is for computer use rather than printing. The key to hypertext is random access that allows lightning-fast non linear navigation based upon reader choice or other reader actions such as responses to questions. Popular software terminology for hypertext includes HyperCard "stacks," Authorware "network icons," and ToolBook "books."

Hypertext preprocessor (PHP) Created in 1994, this is a versatile embedded scripting language that can be placed into HTML documents. As long as the webserver supports it, PHP can be used to generate HTML pages by accessing a database. PHP code is executed on the server, and offers an alternative to CGI or SSI calls, or the use of languages such as ColdFusion.

Hyper-threading Hyper Threading Technology is Intel's trademark for their implementation of the simultaneous multithreading technology on the Pentium 4 microarchitecture. It is basically a more advanced form of Super-threading that first debuted on the Intel Xeon processors and later added to Pentium 4 processors.

Hypertransport An industry standard serial connection method pioneered by AMD for the internal connection of different buses inside of a PC or network device. It initially allows for connection speeds of up to 6.4GB/second. The first main consumer product using HyperTransport was the NVIDIA nForce2 chipset. AMD's Opteron has up to three HyperTransport links, while the Athlon 64 has one.

Hz Hertz. A measure of electromagnetic frequency. One Hz equals one cycle per second.

I

I/O (input/output) This abbreviation refers to any operation in a computer where data is transferred in or out of the computer. I/O may seem like a vague concept, but it refers to the basic power of a computer to communicate with the world outside of the box.

I/O devices Devices that can accept "input" data to a computer and to other devices that can produce "output".

I/O port address Every I/O device in a computer—including network interface cards(NICs)—must be assigned a unique address.

I/O port A location in a separate memory address map maintained for CPU/device communication. Each device's I/O ports must be uniquely assigned within the map. I/O ports come in sets of 2, 4, 8, 16 and 32, and are referred to only by their Base Address. Often used in PC's in conjunction with memory-mapped I/O, where I/O Ports form the control channel, and memory access forms the data channel. Except for PCs, totally obsoleted by memory-mapped I/O. Currently used in DEC's 250MHz Alpha PC.

I2O The I2O standard was designed to simplify and speed up I/O operations on servers. It was going to eliminate the need for different drivers for each OS, and for each SCSI card and network card. The speed-up was achieved by using an Intel 960 chip on the server's motherboard to handle a lot of the I/O processing that would normally be handled by the processor or I/O subsystem. The I20 SIG disbanded in late 2000, and it's no longer in existence, much like the technology.

IA-32 (intel architecture-32 bit) Intel's 32-bit instruction architecture that runs on the company's 386, 486, Pentium, Pentium Pro/II/III/4, and future consumer chips.

IA-64 (intel architecture-64 bit) Intel's 64-bit instruction architecture that features EPIC and runs on the Itanium processor. It's a fully 64-bit architecture built new from the ground up.

IAB (internet architecture board) The coordinating committee for the management of the Internet. They are a group of people responsible for research intot he direction of the Internet and the development of TCP/IP. They also create task forces to research Internet issues. Previously, the abbreviation IAB stood for Internet Activities Board.

IAD A dynamic analyser from IBM giving information on run time performance and code utilisation.

IANA (internet assigned numbers authority) The function that currently oversees registration for various Internet Protocol parameters, such as port numbers, protocol and enterprise numbers, options, codes, and types. The IANA function is currently located at the Information Sciences Institute at the University of Southern California in Marina del Rey, California.

IASG Internetwork Address Sub-Group: A range of internetwork layer addresses summarized in an internetwork layer routing protocol.

IBM 3270 A general name for a family of IBM system components-printers,terminals, and terminal cluster controllers—that can be used with a mainframe computer by an SNA link. Terminal emulation software that emulates a 3270 terminal is available for both DOS and Microsoft Windows, as well as for OS/2.

IBM cabling system IBM has specified a wide variety of cables for its Token-Ring network. The most common cable types follow:

Type1. Includes two data-grade, twisted pairs consisting of solid copper conductors. Both pairs are enclosed by a single shield.

Type2. Includes two solid-conductor, data-grade, twisted pairs enclosed by the same shield. In addition, the cable incorporates two voice-grade cables, enabling the same cable to be used for voice and data.

Type3. An unshielded twisted-pair cable similar to Category 3 UTP. IBM specifications originally limited use of Type3 cable to 4-Mbps token ring.

Type6. Includes two data-grade twisted pairs constructed with stranded wires. The stranded wires make Type6 cables more flexible and, therefore, better suited for cables that frequently are moved. Stranded cables, however, cannot carry signals as far as cables with solid conductors.

IBM data connector A fairly bulky connector that has several interesting features. When disconnected, it shorts pairs of conductors together, enabling you to disconnect devices from the network without introducing a break into the ring wiring of a token-ring network.

IBM international business machines corporation A giant present and historic leader in mainframe and PC computing. Having survived an enormous downturn of bad fortunes in the 1980s, IBM has struggled back with new products and joint ventures. In 1997, IBM announced that network software would all be sold under the banner eNetwork Software. IBM developed a superior operating system called OS/2, but poor marketing and timing resulted in a loss of momentum to Microsoft's Windows and Windows 2000 operating systems. IBM's joint venture with Apple Corporation resulted in the Power Mac and Power PC desktop computers. Most interesting is the IBM Global Campus initiative and the IBM Higher Education home page.

IBM MSAU (IBM multistation access unit) IBM's Token-Ring cabling uses MSAUs. MSAUs are a type of hub and the more modern ones often have 16 or more ports to which devices can be connected. Each MSAU has two special ports called Ring In(RI) and Ring Out(RO). A ring network is created by connecting the RO port of each MSAU to the RI port of the next MSAU in the ring. Each device on the network is connected to an MSAU by an individual cable. There are relays in the MSAUs that operate to configure the network as a logical ring. These relays normally are closed, permitting signals to flow around the ring. When a device connects to the network, the relay for that station opens, forcing signals to flow out tot he device. The device returns the signal to the MSAU, and the signal continues around the logical ring.

IBM PC A series of personal computers based on the Intel 8088 processor, introduced by IBM in mid-1981. The specifications for the IBM PC seem puny in comparison to current computer systems; the PC was released containing 16K of memory, expandable to 64K on the motherboard, and a monochrome video adapter incapable of displaying bit-mapped graphics. The floppy disk drive held 160K of data and programs. There was no hard disk on the original IBM PC; that came later with the release of the IBM PC/XT. In 1983, IBM released an improved version of the PC, the IBM PC-2, which came with 64K of memory, expandable to 256K on the motherboard, and a double-density floppy disk drive capable of storing 360K fo programs and data. The Color/Graphics Adapter (CGA) and an RGB color monitor were also introduced at the same time.

IBM PC/at A series of personal computers based on the Intel 80286 processor, introduced by IBM in 1984. The AT represented a significant performance increase over previous computers, up to 75 percent faster than the PC/XT, and the AT bus standard is used in many clones or IBM compatible computers.

IBM PC/xt A series of personal computers based on the Intel 8088 processor, introduced by IBM in 1983. The PC/XT was the first IBM personal computer to offer a built-in hard disk and the capability to expand memory up to a whopping 640K on the motherboard. The original PC/XT used an Intel8088 running at a clock speed of 4.77 MHz- very slow when compared with today's 66 and 100 MHz clock speeds.

IBM PC /2 A series of personal computers using several different Intel processors, introduced by IBM in 1987.

The main difference between the PS/2 line and earlier IBM personal computers was a major change to the internal bus. Previous computers used the AT bus, also known as industry-standard architecture, but IBM used the proprietary micro channel architecture in the PS/2 line instead. Micro channel architecture expanison boards will not work in a computer using ISA.

IBM RC /6000 A set of seven or nine separate 32-bit chips used in IBM's line of risc workstations. With up to 7.4 million transistors depending on configuration, the RS/6000 uses a superscalar design with 4 separate 16K data cache units and an 8K instruction cache. There is a single-chip version called the PowerPC.

IBM thinkpad A series of innovative and popular notebook computers from IBM.

IBM-compatible computer Originally, any personal computer compatible with the IBM line of personal computers. With the launch of IBM's proprietary microchannel architecture in the PS/2 line of computers, which replaced the aT bus, two incompatible standards emerged, and so the term became misleading. Now, it is becoming more common to use the term"industry-standard computer" when referring to a computer that uses the AT or ISA bus, and the term "DOS computer" to describe any PC that runs DOS and is based on one of the Intel family of chips.

IC (integrated circuit) A combination of multiple circuits into a single integrated device. Today the common microprocessor uses many millions of transistors, with each transistor counting as a single circuit. This combination is an integrated circuit.

ICADD International Committee for Accessible Document Design. Dedicated to making printed materials accessible to persons with print disabilities.

ICCP Institute for Certification of Computing Professionals.

ICD International Code Designator: This identifies an international organization. The registration authority for the International Code Designator is maintained by the British Standards Institute. The length of this field is two octets.

ICMP (internet control message protocol) A message control and error-reporting protocol between a host server and a gateway to the Internet. ICMP uses Internet Protocol (IP) datagrams, but the messages are processed by the IP software and are not directly apparent to the application user.

ICMP flood A type of Denial of Service attack that sends large amounts of (or just over-sized) ICMP packets to a machine in order to attempt to crash the TCP/IP stack on the machine and cause it to stop responding to TCP/IP requests.

Icon A cute, little picture used in conjunction with a GUI. A well-designed icon is supposed to be an obvious, unmistakable symbol of whatever it stands for, occupy much less space than do the equivalent words, and be cute. In practice, many icons are peculiar little pictures with no obvious meaning.

ICQ (i seek you) One of the first and most popular instant messaging clients. It was developed by Mirabilis, which was later purchased by AOL.

ICR (intelligent character recognition) A technology that employs either software only or software and hardware to automatically recognise and translate raster images into structured data.

IDE (integrated development environment) A programming environment integrated into an application. For example, Microsoft Office applications support various versions of the BASIC programming language. You can develop a WordBasic application while running Microsoft Word.

IDE (integrated drive electronics) In 1986, Compaq started work to integrate Western Digital controller technology with Control Data Corporation hard drives, IDE is the result of this work. IDE had several advantages. Besides a power cable, only a single cable was required. More important, however, close integration of controller and hard drive has resulted in dramatic performance improvements, even while drive costs have been plummeting. IDE drives now offer outstanding performance at costs of less than 40 percent per megabyte. IDE drives do not require an elaborate controller on the motherboard, just a simple, inexpensive interface is all that is required. Virtually all motherboards now have built-in IDE controllers, but inexpensive IDE expansion boards also are available. A PC can support two IDE controllers, each of which can support two drives. A PC, therefore, can support four IDE drives.IDE drives are excellent for workstations, but poor choices for servers and disk mirroring.

Note:As of 1997, Standard IDE drives allow for only 512 MB of disk space to be accessed without special drivers. This is dure to a 1,024 cylinder limit in the original IDE specification. EIDE allows newer systems to access sizes aboe 512MB on one drive, up to 2 GB.

IDL (interface definition language) That facilitates interfacing between servers and IDL compliant client computers. For example, a Java IDL enables Java to communicate with non-Java objects on networks.

IDSL ISDN based DSL developed originally by Ascend Communications. IDSL uses 2B1Q line coding and typically supports data transfer rates of 128 Kbps.

IDSS Intelligent Decision Support Systems.

IDTV (improved definitional tv) That uses a computerized line doubling technique to simulate HDTV at higher resolutions.

IDU (interface data unit) The unit of information transferred to/from the upper layer in a single interaction across the SAP. Each IDU contains interface control information and may also contain the whole or part of the SDU.

IEEE (institute of electrical and electronics engineers) A professional ANSI- accredited body of scientists and engineers based in the United States. IEEE promoters standardization, and consults to the American National Standards Institute on matters relating to electrical to electrical and electronic development. The IEEE 802 Standards Committee is the leading official standard organization for LANs.

Ieee 1394 A serial protocol that runs at speeds ranging from 100 to 400 megabits per second, depending upon the implementation. Devices that are prime candidates for IEEE 1394 include digital camcorders and VCRs, digital audio amplifiers, and video teleconferencing.

IETF (internet engineering task force) An international group open to the public, generally made up of network designers, operators, vendors, and researchers concerned with the evolution of Internet architecture. The IETF meets three times per year, and does most of its work in smaller groups via mailing lists. The IETF is perhaps most famous for having control of which documents become RFC documents and define interoperability standards or suggested methods of practice for the Internet.

IETM Interactive Electronic Technical Manual.

IIIS International Institute of Informatics and Systemics.

IIOP (internet inter-orb protocol) An evolving wire-level protocol that defines how distributed objects communicate with each other. IIOP—which is similar to Microsoft's Distributed Common Object Model (DCOM) specification—is based around the Common Object Request Broker Architecture (CORBA). In theory, any IIOP-compliant client software on any platform will be able to access the same object, a programming function that performs a specific task (such as authenticating a user against a server).

IIS (internet information server) A web server that comes with BackOffice, which runs on WinNT Server; or in a more limited way on NT Workstation as a Peer Web service. IIS can support 3 different Internet data transfer protocols: FTP,Gopher, and HTTP. It can communicate with data sources to display web pages that are created "on demand." It functions as either as an Internet or intranet service provider, can be configured as a virtual server etc.

I-link Sony's name for the IEEE 1394, or FireWire, interface. For some reason Sony decided to pick its own name for the IEEE 1394 interface when it is used on Sony's devices. There are no differences between "i-Link" and IEEE 1394.

Illegal Within the context of a computer program, this refers to any operation that attempts to access an area of memory or perform an instruction that is not within the rules of the computer architecture or computer programming language.

Illiquid Lacking in liquid assets; or something that is not easily transferable into currency.

ILMI(integrated local managment interface) An ATM Forum defined interim specification for network management functions between an end user and a public or private network and between a public network and a private network. This is based on a limited subset of SNMP capabilities.

Image map A graphic image at WWW sites that is a navigational tool. It contains two elements: (1) the graphic that is visible on the screen and (2) a text file that contains the HTML or other hyperlink coding.

Imagesetter A device used to record digital data (images and text) onto monochrome film or offset litho printing plates by means of a single or multiple intermittent light beams. Color separated data is recorded as a series of slightly overlapping spots to produce either solid areas of line-art or halftone dots for printing continuous tones.

IMAP (Internet Message Access Protocol) IMAP is gradually replacing POP as the main protocol used by email clients in communicating with email servers. Using IMAP, an email client program can not only retrieve email but can also manipulate messages stored on the server without having to actually retrieve the messages. So messages can be deleted, have their status changed, multiple mail boxes can be managed, etc.

IMAP4 (internet message access protocol, version 4) A still-evolving protocol that allows a client to access and manipulate e-mail messages on a server. IMAP4—designed for disconnected e-mail use—lets you perform such tasks as managing folders remotely, viewing just message subject lines, and selectively downloading messages and attachments based on various criteria (size or author, for example). IMAP4 also allows for shared mail folders.

IMHO (in my humble opinion) A shorthand term appended to a comment in an online forum or email. IMHO indicates that the writer is aware that they are expressing a debatable or dissenting view.

ImmersaDesks Large 4 x 5 foot screens that allow for stereoscopic visualization; the 3-D computer graphics create the illusion of a virtual environment.

ImmersaWalls Large-scale, flat screen visualization environments that include passive and active multi-projector displays of 3-D images.

Immersive Involved in something totally.

IMODE (i-mode) A packet-based means of wireless data transfer used widely in Japan and offered by Japanese mobile phone company NTT DoCoMo. iMode uses CWML (Compact Wireless Markup Language) instead of WAP's WML for data display. i-Mode was introduced in 1999 and was the first method available to browse the Web from a cellular phone.

Impact printers Printers that work by hitting a ribbon against the paper. They're old-fashioned, but they still work.

Impedance An electrical property of a cable that combines capcitance, inductance, and resistance. Impedance can be described as the apparent resistance to the flow of alternating current at a given frequency; mismatches in impedance along a cable cause distortions and reflections.

Import The process of pulling data into a program. Normally it refers to taking a plain text file and pulling it into a database format so that you can work with it using a database program. For example, you call a company you need some data from and ask it to send you some data to add to your database. The company sends the data as a text file, and you import it into your database. Now you can run queries on the data in your database program. However, you could import any data format your database program supports. There are hundreds out there.

Impression When a user looks at a single page on the World Wide Web, that visit is counted as one impression regardless of how many images are on that page. Most access log analysis tools remove server requests that reference ".gif" or ".jpg" (image tags) from their analysis. This is the most accurate measurement yet developed. An impression could almost be called a "page look.".

IMT-2000 International Mobile Telecommunications 2000 is an ITU concept that defines that group of technological solutions that enable 3rd Generation mobile systems.

In In terms of data flow, indicates consumption of data. An in pin is compatible with an out pin.

In the wild Collection of viruses known to be in circulation throughout many organizational networks. This is in contrast a general collection of viruses, known as a "zoo.".

Inactive window A window that is open but is not the top window.

Inappropriate content Transmission or access to unauthorized information. Some employees misuse their Internet privileges for illegal or unproductive activities such as running side businesses. Employees often use company Internet connections to download software for personal use, to download pornography, and to conduct businesses on the side. Apart from tying up valuable bandwidth, these activities often expose organizations to legal liabilities.

In-band Pertaining to elements or objects that are within the limits of a certain local area network (LAN).

Incident A collection of data representing one or more related attacks. Attacks may be related by attacker, type of attack, objectives, sites, or timing.

INCOSE (international council on systems engineering) An international organization formed to develop nurture and enhance the system engineering approach to multi-disciplinary system product development.

Index (Multiple meanings) (a) A term used to describe a web page which contains links to other webpages of a specific category. (b) Another term used to describe the means by which a search engine catalogs a web site. (c) Most commonly, the main or starting page of a website.

Infiniband A standard created by Intel and other server manufacturers to link servers and network devices externally at high speeds. It should scale as high at 30GB/second, but initially will run at 2.5Gbits/second (0.3 GB/second).

Information highway A world wide combination of fiber optic cable and satellite receivers in a future time when homes and offices around the world will be linked by highways of electronic information that can be traversed interactively both to and from a connected user. Technologies are coming to a head and plans are being laid to bring the digital information highways to Main Street USA and elsewhere in the world. In homes and offices, a single piece of interactive TV digital television equipment (let's call it the PCTV computer/television superhighways terminal) will combine what are now television sets, telephones, stereos, videotape players, videodisc players, compact disc players, and computers. The PCTV will be networked to hundreds of millions of "servers" ranging from the computer files of individuals to the systems of computer files that contain *virtually* all the movies ever made, all the contents of daily newspapers, all the "television" shows ever recorded, all the cataloged products and services available from vendors, all public documents of governments, all the contents of libraries, all instructional and training courses on most anything known in the world, and so on to limits beyond our present imaginations. Even before the information superhighways come to town via digital satellites, telephone fiber optics, and cable digital TV, technology is presently in place to make vast amounts of digitized financial information publicly available in hypermedia structures. The hardware for a fiber optic superhighway across the United States made great progress when AT&T Corporation announced that "Sonet" service is operational initially between 200 cities. In 1994, Macromedia teamed up with Microware Systems Corporation in Des Moines, Iowa, to extend the Director software into PC and Mac utilities for authoring interactive network television titles.

Information technology (IT) The field of work dealing with computers and technology, or more specifically, the organization within a company that takes care of all of the computers, telephones, webservers, and Internet connectivity that keeps a company able to communicate with the outside world by electronic means.

InfraRed data association (IRDA) These people developed the IRDA port standard that transfers data through the use of infrared light. Of course, you must have two IRDA devices to get any real use out of this technology. Most notebooks today come standard with this port, as do PDAs and some printers as well. It's handy if you road warriors want to print a document and you've got all the right equipment.

INI file (initialization file) Commonly used under Windows 3.x and earlier, INI files have been used by both the operating system and individual applications to store persistent settings related to an application, driver, or piece of hardware. In Windows 32-bit operating systems, INI files are supported for backward compatibility, but the registry is the preferred location for storing such settings.

Init method A special function in an object oriented program that is automatically called to initialize the elements of an object when it is created.

Inkjet printer The next generation of dot matrix printers. It uses a head that sprays tiny droplets of ink onto print material. There are three major benefits to this method: 1) it is quieter than standard dot matrix printers,

2) it is able to make smaller dots to make print look better, and

3) since the ink is in liquid form it mixes better when printing in color. On the downside, early models printed slower than standard dot matrix printers, and since they do not print by impact they cannot print carbon copies. Nowadays inkjet printers can easily outpace dot matrix printers.

Installation The process of configuring new hardware, software or both to work on a computer.

Installer A utility that copies system software or an application from floppy disks or a CD-ROM to your hard disk. An Installer may also decompress the new files, remove obsolete files, place extensions and control panels in their proper folders, and/or create new folders.

Instance A particular object of an object type.

Instance ID A string that distinguishes a device from other devices of the same type on a computer. An instance ID is a string without any path-separator characters that contains serial-number information if supported by the underlying bus or some kind of location information. The format of the string is bus-specific.

Instance manager (IM) Provides the fundamental operations that support the management of multiple instances of an object type.

Instant messaging (IMING) Messaging between to or more individuals who are simultaneously online. It is more like a telephone conversation than email. America OnlineAOL introduced instant messaging and has had an ongoing dispute with Microsoft over its use in Internet Explorer. Instant Messenger can be used by AOL members but there is no requirement to be connected to the Internet through AOL. An Open Source alternative to AOL's instant messaging is called Jabber.

Instantiate In object-oriented programming, to create an instance of a class.

Instantiation A more precisely defined version of some object which was already partially defined. In object-oriented object-oriented programming, a particular example of an object produced from its class template.

Instruction The simplest direction that you can give to a processor. Programs are made up of these, but usually don't go down to such nitty-gritty levels unless you are programming in assembly language. An example of what a single instruction would do is increment a piece of data by one, or clear a piece of data out of a register.

Instruction decode unit The part of a microprocessor pipeline that decodes instructions that are sent to the microprocessor. It can decode and optimize the order of instructions before it sends them to the execution unit to be run.

Instrumentation A mechanism for reporting information about the state of PC hardware and software to enable management applications to ascertain and change the state of a PC and to be notified of state changes.

Integrated circuit (IC) A combination of multiple circuits into a single integrated device. Today the common microprocessor uses many millions of transistors, with each transistor counting as a single circuit. This combination is an integrated circuit.

Integrated modem A modem device that is built into a computer, rather than being attached as a separate peripheral.

Integrated services digital network (ISDN) A new network standard that allows high-speed communication over ordinary category 3 or 5 copper cabling. It may someday replace conventional phone systems with high-speed, digital lines.

Integrity (system) The ability of a system to perform its intended function in an unimpaired manner, free from unauthorized manipulation.

Integrity file A file created and updated in the directory of any file scanned when the smart scan heuristic method is used.

Intel architecture personal computer A general descriptive term for computers built with processors conforming to the architecture defined by the Intel processor family based on the 486 instruction set and having an industry-standard PC architecture.

Intel overdrive The original Intel OverDrive microprocessor was designed as a user-installable upgrade toa n 80486SX or 80486DX-based computer; while the Pentium OverDrive chip is designed as a replacement for 486-based systems. OverDrive chips boost system performance by using the same clock multiplying technology found in the Intel 80486DX-2 and DX4 chips. Once installed, an OverDrive processor can increase application performance by an estimated 40 to 70 percent.

Interchange A commercial network service introduced by a computer book publishing firm called Ziff-Davis. Although designed to compete with CompuServe and other commercial network services, Interchange tries to provide more services for technology monitoring of computer users.

Interconnectivity The ability of more than one physical computer to operate with one or more other physical computers; interconnectivity is usually accomplished by means of network wiring, cable, or telephone lines.

Interface That point whee a connection is made between two different parts of a system, such as between two hardware devices, between a user and a program or operating system, or between two application programs.

In hardware, an interface describes the logical and physical connections used, as in RS 232-C and is often considered to be synonymous with the term "port".

A user interface consists of all the means by which a program communicates with the user, including a command line, menus, dialog boxes, online help systems, and so on. User interfaces can be classified as character-based; menu-driven, or graphical.

Software interfaces are application program interfaces; the codes and messages used by programs to communicate behind the scenes.

Interframe coding Compression techniques that track the differences between frames of video. This results in more compression over a range of frames than intraframe coding. interlaced (1) A scanning method that divides the screen into two fields, alternately drawing odd-numbered and even-numbered scan lines.

(2) A scheme to display a video image by displaying alternate scan lines in two discrete fields. Interlaced signals are used in broadcast video and are required for video to be compliant with NTSC.

Interior Denotes that an item (e.g., link, node, or reachable address) is inside of a PNNI routing domain.

Interleave factor The order in which the sectors were arranged on your hard disk by the initial low-level format.

Introduced as a compensation for slow computers, interleaving eliminates the delay that results when a drive is not ready to read or write the next sector as soon as it has read or written the previous one. With a 3:1 interleave factor, sequentially numbered sectors are located three sectors apart on the disk. An interleave that is either too high or too low can lead toa sevre degradation in performance, because the computer spends its time waiting for the next sector to arrive at the read/write heads. Thanks to increases in PC speed, interleaving is obsolete, and most modern disks use a 1:1 interleave factor (which actually indicates a non-interleaving drive).

Interleave This typically refers to the numbering scheme of sectors of data on hard drives. With an interleave of one, sectors are numbered sequentially. With an interleave of two, sequential data is stored on every second sector, and so forth. The reason for interleaves higher than one is that hard drives cannot always keep up with the spin speed of the disk and sometimes need a break before getting to the next region of data. For example, if the data were listed as 11111 xxxxx 22222 yyyyy (interleave of two) then while the hard drive spins over xxxxx it can take some time and get ready to start reading 22222. If a hard drive read head is quick enough to have an interleave of one, data is simply put sequentially onto the media.

Interleaved memory A method of speedin up data access by dividing dynamic RAM (DRAM) memory into two separate banks so that the processor can read one bank while the other is being refreshed. DRA requires that its contents be updated at least every thousandth of a second, and while it is being refreshed it cannot be read by the processor; interleaving memory speeds up access times. The introduction of static RAM (SRAM) has removed the need for interleaved memory, because SRAM memory can retain its contents without the need for refreshment.

Internal hard disk A hard disk drive housed inside the computer's system unit and integrated with it, rather than an external drive packaged with its own case, cables, and independent power supply.

Internal modem A telecommunications device that renders your mouse inoperative and cannot be used at the same time as your LAN card.

Internet A global network made up of a large number of individual networks interconnected through the use TCP/IP protocols. The individual networks comprising the Internet are from colleges, universities, businesses research organizations, government agencies, individuals and other bodies. The government body of this global network is the Internet Activities Board (IAB). When the term Internet is used with an upper-case I, it refers to global network, but with a lower-case i, it simply means a group of interconnected networks.

Internet address A thirty-two-bit number that uniquely identifies an Internet Internet host. It is usually represented as four 8-bit numbers separated by dots e.g. 128.121.4.5. It consists of a network number and a host number, and can be subdivided in several ways.

Internet assigned numbers authority (IANA) The organization responsible for matching unique numerical addresses (IP addresses) to computer names for the Internet.

Internet audio and video The transport of audio and video such that users can hear sounds and watch video while reading text and graphics on the Internet. It is no longer necessary to download these media files and install them on a local computer or a local server. These files can be played live on the Internet.

Internet control message protocol (ICMP) A TCP/IP messaging protocol that runs specifically over IP (as opposed to UDP). This protocol is used to announce network errors, timeouts, and congestion. PING is based on ICMP.

Internet engineering task force (IETF) An international group open to the public, generally made up of network designers, operators, vendors, and researchers concerned with the evolution of Internet architecture. The IETF meets three times per year, and does most of its work in smaller groups via mailing lists. The IETF is perhaps most famous for having control of which documents become RFC documents and define interoperability standards or suggested methods of practice for the Internet.

Internet explorer A web browser developed by Microsoft Corporation to compete with Netscape.

Internet gateway protocol (IGP) A protocol used to communicate routing information between Internet routers.

Internet group management protocol (IGMP) A protocol used to form and dissolve groups on the MBONE.

Internet message access protocol (IMAP) The industry standard protocol for accessing electronic information on a mail server. Originally developed at Stanford University in 1986, IMAP includes standards for:

Creating, deleting, and renaming mailboxes.

Checking for new messages.

Permanently removing messages.

Setting and clearing flags.

Server-based RFC-822 and MIME parsing.

Searching and selective fetching of message attributes and text.

Internet messaging technologies for sending messages across the Internet. Leading technologies are shown below.

Internet phones and videoconferencing Emerging telephony on the Internet coupled with the extension to video telephony. Technology in this area is reviewed in *PC Magazine*, March 26, 1996, pp. 143-145.

Internet protocol (IP) A connectionless communications protocol that forms part of the basis for the TCP/IP protocol suite. It is a fast protocol, but it has no mechanism for sequencing or error conditions—error packets are simply lost. IP will basically just move datagrams. TCP and UDP run on top of the Internet Protocol, where TCP is the more robust protocol and UDP is intended for applications that don't require exact quality of service—like voice transmission.

Internet protocol security (IPSEC) A simple version of the emerging Internet IP security protocol. IPSEC includes ESP (Encapsulated Security Payload) protocol for encryption and AH (Automatic Header) protocol for authenticating TCP/IP packets. It is typically used to create VPNs across untrusted Internet links and is appropriate for data with a short lifespan.

Internet protocol version 6 (IPv6) Also known as IP Next Generation (IPNG), the next generation of the Internet Protocol. Reserves a larger address space and several new configuration and security options to fix shortcomings that the current version of IP (v4), created in the 1960s, doesn't address.

Internet relay chat (IRC) A client/server protocol where IRC clients can connect to an IRC server and "chat." There are several networks of these computers, and there are thousands of channels (or rooms) and hundreds of thousands of people. There is a channel for any interest you could have—it is simply a matter of finding the name. You need to use an IRC client to get to the channels, but as long as you have an Internet connection you can get hooked in. There are also methods of directly transferring files between IRC clients.

Internet server API An API proposed by Microsoft to replace CGI. Programs written to ISAPI are compiled as DLLs and stored in memory so they can be run faster than CGI scripts—or at leastCGI scripts not using FastCGI or Mod-Perl, which both have similar caching features.

Internet service provider (ISP) A company that provides Internet access to people or corporations. Early ISPs generally had pools of modems awaiting dial-up connections, but many ISPs nowadays only deal in high-end business communications. Smaller ISPs buy bandwidth from larger ISPs.

Interprocess communication A term that describes all the methods used to pass information between two programs running on the same computer running a multitasking operating system, or between two programs running on a network, including pipes, shared memory queues, the Clipboard,DDE(Dynamic Data Exchange) and OLE (Object Linking and Embedding).

Interrupt handler Special software invoked when an interrupt occurs. Each type of interrupt, such as a clock tick or a keystroke, is processed by its own specific interrupt handler. A table, called the interrupt vector table, maintains a list of addresses for these specific interrupt handlers.

Intranet The use of the Internet and Internet-type software for subsytems of computing for private organizations and individuals. Companies are storing key forms and documents on web sites inside their operations, making it easy for employees to find information using standard web browsers, not special-purpose database programs. Most intranets use the "free" connections of the Internet, and turn the Internet into an intranet with passwords or other access barriers to documents and databases. Combinations of free Internet lines connected with leased (usually from telephone companies) private nodes are termed "virtual private networks" or VPN. A VPN functionality of a dedicated line, but which is really like a private network within a public one, because it is still controlled by a telephone company. VPN's use encryption and other security mechanisms to ensure that only authorized users can access the network and that the data cannot be intercepted. Some security mechanisms exist that are not available on intranets.

Intruder An adversary who is conducting or has conducted an intrusion or attack against a victim host, site, network, or organization. Since the label of intruder is assigned by the victim of the intrusion and is therefore contingent on the victim's definition of encroachment, there can be no ubiquitous categorization of actions as being intrusive or not. From the victim's viewpoint, an intruder is usually an entity (person or organization) that has successfully attacked the victim. It is unclear whether one who conducts an unsuccessful attack is an intruder. If an intrusion is required to be an intruder, then it seems that all intruders are attackers, but all attackers are not necessarily intruders.

Intrusion detection technologies A broader term (than intrusion detection system) meaning a combination of intrusion detection systems, intrusion analysts, and other supporting tools (such as those that process raw network packets or log files). Used together, intrusion detection technologies can provide accurate indicators of whether or not an attack or intrusion has occurred.

IP address A unique 32-bit number that identifies computers and other devices on a TCP/IP network. Two computers directly connected to the Internet cannot have the same IP address at the same time. IP addresses can either be static (permanently assigned to a specific computer) dynamic (temporarily assigned to a computer when that computer logs on to a network).

The format of an IP address is a 32-bit numeric address written as four numbers separated by periods. Within an isolated network, you can assign IP addresses at random as long as each one is unique. However, connecting a private network to the Internet requires using registered (legal) IP addresses.

IP family The Internet Protocol (IP) family consists of many different protocols, including:

Address Resolution Protocol (ARP).

Internet Control Message Protocol (ICMP)—Internet Control Message Protocol (ICMP).

Internet Protocol (IP)—Internet Protocol (IP).

Transmission Control Protocol (TCP)—Transmission Control Protocol (TCP).

User Datagram Protocol (UDP)—User Datagram Protocol (UDP).

IRDA (infrared data association) These people developed the IRDA port standard that transfers data through the use of infrared light. Of course, you must have two IRDA devices to get any real use out of this technology. Most notebooks today come standard with this port, as do PDAs and some printers as well. It's handy if you road warriors want to print a document and you've got all the right equipment.

IRDS (information resource dictionary system) A set of ISO standards for CASE repositories. It governs the definition of data dictionaries to be implemented on top of relational databases.

Iridiumò A communication system that uses a 66 strong satellit network orbiting the earth. The system was first developed by Motorola and established itself as a separate company in 1991. It provides a mobile wireless communication network across the world and is connected to terrestrial telephone systems. It allows a mobile user to place and receive calls from anywhere in the world.

Iris explorer A visualisation system.

ISDN Integrated Services Digital Network. The technical standards and design philosophy according to which digital networks will be designed. ISDN provides high-speed, high-bandwidth channels to every subscriber on the network, achieving end-to-end digital functions with standard equipment interface devices. The network will enable a variety of mixed digital transmission services to be accommodated at a single interface. Access channels under definition include basic (144 Kbps, or 2B+D) and primary (1.544 Mbps or 23B+D in North America, and 30B+D, or 2.048 Mbps in Europe) interface rates. Signalling System 7 (SS7), an out-of-band signalling scheme, is key to current ISDN implementation; the International Telegraph and Telephone Consultative Committee (CCITT) general assembly finalised a variant.

ISR (interrupt service routine) A routine whose function is to service a device when it generates an interrupt.

ISV (independent software vendor) A software company that creates software to run on a platform or platforms that it doesn't create. For example, Microsoft is not an ISV because it owns its own OS. Often the term refers to companies that write "valuable" software applications. OS makers will often give them sweet deals and help them distribute their software if they feel it benefits their OS.

Isync Basically, the iSync platform adds mobile phones to Apple's digital hub strategy. It works with the Mac OS X Jaguar Address Book and iCal (Apple's calendar program) to synchronize contacts and calendars among Bluetooth-enabled mobile phones, PalmOS devices, Apple's iPod portable digital music player and other Macs using Apple's .Mac service. With iSync 1.0, users can sync their Jaguar Address Book with the new .Mac Address Book, making it possible to access contacts while using .Mac Web Mail from virtually any computer, the company said in a statement. iSync 1.0 also includes a feature that allows for regularly scheduled Mac-to-Mac synchronization.

IT (information technology) The field of work dealing with computers and technology, or more specifically, the organization within a company that takes care of all of the computers, telephones, webservers, and Internet connectivity that keeps a company able to communicate with the outside world by electronic means.

It8 Industry standard color reference target used to calibrate input and output devices.

ITAD (integrated telephone answering device) That avoids tape recording by using direct digital recorders for telephones.

Italics A type style with slightly slanted characters, used for emphasis. Best used to set off quotes, special phrases, and foreign words, italic letters have a redesigned structure that allows them to slant to the right. The first italic type was designed by Aldus Manutius in AD 1501 and was based on the handwriting style of that time. Furthermore, lowercase letters were in italics while capital letters were Roman (or vertical stance).

Iteration (iterative) This is a programming term. It refers to a process that can be described by a fixed number of variables and a set of rules that describes what happens to those variables to achieve the next step of the process. If the process is interrupted, it can be continued if the state of all the variables is known. Contrast this to a recursive process. An iteration is a single step.

IWS (intelligent workstation) A term synonymous with programmable workstation. A personal computer.

J

Jackson method A proprietary structured method for software analysis, design and programming.

Jacquard's loom A weaving loom, developed by Joseph-Marie Jacquard (1752-1834), controlled by punched cards; identified as one of the earliest examples of programming automation.

Jargon A general term used to talk about the many abbreviations used on the net. Here are some of those terms and their meaningsLOL - Laughing Out Loud.

ROFL - Rolling on the Floor Laughing.

FYI - For your Information.

IMO - In My Opinion.

IMHO - In My Humble Opinion.

TTYL - Talk To You Later.

BBL - Be Back Later.

Java A programming (a slow running derivative of C++) language also known as "Hot Java" from Sun Microsystems that is designed for browser plug-in running of applications called "applets." In 1997, IBM became the world leader in Java development with its subsidiary Taligent developer leading the way. Java has spread like wildfire among software developers. and can now be run from leading browsers such as the Netsacape Navigator and Microsoft's Internet Explorer. An especially important advantage of Java is the ability to run applets on virtually any operating system (Windows, Macintosh, OS/2, etc.) or even without a GUI operating system. Plug-in utilities are now available on most WWW browsers. An important advantage on network computers is the Remote Method Invocation (RMI) standard. RMI is that part of the Java programming language library which enables a Java program running on one computer to access the objects and methods of another Java program running on a different computer. Java is extremely controversial since it allows for "centralized" housing of software to run on inexpensive networked computers (as opposed to decentralized installation of software on higher-capacity desktop machines). Many users hope to rent software (e.g., word processors) as opposed to purchasing and installing software on individual machines. Although it has been possible for some time to purchase LAN versions of software for multiple machines, Java makes it possible to run software world wide from a single server. Traffic jams on the Internet, however, are serious obstacles to the future of Java. Java has put Sun Microsystems in head-to-head combat with Microsoft's newer OLE options for running applications on the Internet. Microsoft is also attempting to thwart Java success by extending Windows OLE capabilities.

Java applets Applets written in the Java programming language and executed with the support of a Java Virtual Machine (JVM) or a Java enabled browser.

Java directory access protocol (JDAP) The Java answer to LDAP. It really means "Java implementation of the Lightweight Directory Access Protocol."

Java server page (JSP) A specification that uses Java Servlets run on the webserver to generate Web pages that feature dynamic content. JSP is freely available, and a competitor to Microsoft's ASP.

Java servlets (servlets) A Java application that is designed to execute on a webserver instead of on the client's computer. Servlets can be used in the same way that CGI programs can to move data between a client and the webserver.

Java virtual machine (JVM) A program that runs under an operating system and interprets Java programs. The Java Virtual Machine ideally will not allow any harm to come to the computer because it has no control of the operating system and acts as if it is a separate computer. Thus, if a malicious Java program were to crash the Java Virtual Machine the operating system would remain stable. Another advantage of this mechanism is that different OSes can have their own Java Virtual Machines that should act identically. Thus Java should be able to be run across different platforms easily with no code changes. In the real world, however, this is not always the case.

Javabeans An object-oriented API created by Sun Microsystems for developers to create re-useable Java applications or components.

Javascript This differs from Java and currently can only run in a browser that supports it. However, under a browser, JavaScript is basically auto-executable. JavaScript is relatively easy to write and does not require a compiler, making it an ideal tool for many hackers to create vandals. An Active Server Page (ASP) containing JavaScript or a Windows Scripting Host (WSH) script containing JavaScript is potentially dangerous because these environments allow scripts unrestricted access to machine resources (file system, registry, etc.) and application objects (via COM). Web administrators should take the same precautions for ASP pages as for CGI scripts.

Javastation A low cost hardware unit that provides users an internet browser specifically designed to employ Java. JavaStation is based on the Pico-Java technology that Sun licenses to developers for WWW-based microcomputing.

JBOD (just a bunch of disks) One or more disk drives that form a single volume. However, the information on these disks is not striped in any way or protected a JBOD is not a RAID. It's usually comprised of leftover drives, and the term JBOD can be used to refer to a volume on a single drive, where anything that's not a RAID is a JBOD.

JCL (job control language) The batch file and script language of the IBM 360, 370, 390 and ES/9000 family mainframes, though the acronym was used by other manufacturers as well.

JDAP (java directory access protocol) The Java answer to LDAP. It really means "Java implementation of the Lightweight Directory Access Protocol."

JDBC (java database connectivity) Standard that allows Java to interface with databases.

JDK (java development kit) A software development package from Sun Microsystems containing the basic tools needed to write, test, and debug Java applications and applets.

JEDEC (joint electron device engineering council) The standardization body of the Electronic Industries Alliance trade association. It was created in 1958 to form discrete semiconductor device standards, and was expanded to include integrated circuits in 1970. Examples of JEDEC's work include the SDRAM and DDR memory standards.

JEPI (joint electronic payment initiative) A joint project between W3C W3C and CommerceNet in the field of electronic payment using WWW.

Jini An initiative developed by Sun Microsystems that allows for spontaneous communication and information sharing over a network.

Jiro An open software development frame initially provided by Sun Microsystems that enables the management of network storage systems from different manufacturers and designs.

JITT (just-in-time training) In many technical and complex areas it is not practical for employees or other persons to be knowledgeable about all details at all times. For example, it has become impractical for auditors to have a working knowledge of every accounting and auditing standard in the United States and other nations. Physicians and other medical practitioners cannot have instant recall of details of every disease and combination of medical symptoms and treatments. JITT refers to a process (that is usually aided by computers, compact discs, computer networks, and/or teleconferencing) in which the person receives training just-in-time. when it is needed for a particular purpose. The JITT process may change the entire process of education and training, because the focus may become how to effectively access and utilize JITT rather than how to teach students and or employees technical details that have to be memorized long before they are needed in practice.

Job A program you started from the shell that can start, stop, and move between the foreground and background.

Joining The phase in which the LE Client establishes its control connections to the LE Server.

Joint electron device engineering council (JEDEC) The standardization body of the Electronic Industries Alliance trade association. It was created in 1958 to form discrete semiconductor device standards, and was expanded to include integrated circuits in 1970. Examples of JEDEC's work include the SDRAM and DDR memory standards.

JOOP Journal of Object-Oriented Object-Oriented Programming.

Joystick An input device first found on arcade game machines, then home game systems, and finally on computers. It consists of any stick-like object attached to a base that can be pushed in four or more directions. Usually there's a button in the vicinity of the joystick. Joysticks come in many shapes and sizes, with the typical arcade joystick having a large ball at the top that can be easily gripped; but lately, joysticks have been replaced by cheap button pads in many home gaming systems. However, smaller joysticks that can be pushed around with a single finger have been added to some of the pads as well.

JPEG (joint photographic expert group) Standards for image compression that is an increasingly popular compressed graphics image file, the extension for which is usually jpg. Because large and high resolution graphics images with considerable color depth require massive amounts of storage (e.g., over 30 Mb) for each image, compression routines that create images almost as good with substantially fewer storage requirements are highly desirable. Doyle calls several options "awesome," including the $940 Fast Electronic's Movie Machine Pro (415-802-0772) with M-JPEG and Avi file capturing options. Similarly, he calls the $570 Intel Smart Video Recorder (800-538-3373) and the $890 Micro Computer microVIDEO DC1 tv (800-249-6476) awesome. JPEG images are generally of sufficient quality that it is not necessary to utilize more storage space for uncompressed files. JPEG compression of graphics images requires no special playback boards. When using any compression utility such as JPEG, it pays to study the limitations. For example, JPEG compression does not work especially well with hard edges and lines in graphics images. Black and white images should never be compressed into JPEG images. Also conversions from GIF to JPEG may be disappointing since GIF images are usually color reduced before becoming GIF images. Also math coprocessors will not speed up JPEG graphics since JPEG algorithms use only integer arithmetic. JPEG can be used with motion video cards such as the RasterOps MoviePak2 video compression daughter card for Mac computers.

JSA Japanese Standards Association

JSP A specification that uses Java Servlets run on the webserver to generate Web pages that feature dynamic content. JSP is freely available, and a competitor to Microsoft's ASP.

Jughead An Internet search mechanism used to construct an index of high-level Gopher menus.

Jukeboxes Hardware devices for stacking discs, especially compact discs such as CD-ROM discs for a computer. Two hardware options for moving from one active CD to another are called jukeboxes and arrays. Jukeboxes typically take up only one SCSI device spot but they can be slow to access while the robot finds, extracts, moves, and inserts each disc. Arrays are linked CD devices that are both faster and cheaper than jukeboxes.

Jumper A jumper fits on two metal connectors. It provides an electrical connection between the two wires to enable a semi-permanent hardware configuration. The Plug-and-Play initiative was designed to help eliminate jumpers, and this is slowly happening. Most hard drives and motherboards still have some jumpers that users can utilize to make the devices act in different ways.

Junk email Also known as spam, unwanted marketing and promotional email has become both disruptive and a source of viruses and vandals. In addition to random junk mail, other unsolicited email can be undesirable, such as email that attempts to lure employees with job offers.

Just a bunch of disks (JBOD) One or more disk drives that form a single volume. However, the information on these disks is not striped in any way or protected—a JBOD is not a RAID. It's usually comprised of leftover drives, and the term JBOD can be used to refer to a volume on a single drive, where anything that's not a RAID is a JBOD.

JVM A program that runs under an operating system and interprets Java programs. The Java Virtual Machine ideally will not allow any harm to come to the computer because it has no control of the operating system and acts as if it is a separate computer. Thus, if a malicious Java program were to crash the Java Virtual Machine the operating system would remain stable. Another advantage of this mechanism is that different OSes can have their own Java Virtual Machines that should act identically. Thus Java should be able to be run across different platforms easily with no code changes. In the real world, however, this is not always the case.

K

K (KB or kilobyte) A measure of memory or disk size which is 1,024 bytes of information. This number happens to be 2 multiplied by itself 10 times, which is a nice round number for computers.

K desktop environment (KDE) The KDE project was started in 1996 by Matthias Ettrich as a way to bring a more user-friendly GUI experience to UNIX users. KDE is an Integrated Desktop Environment for UNIX and Linux that adds functionality to X-Windows.

K56 flex A technology developed by Lucent Technologies and Rockwell International for delivering data rates up to 56 Kbps over plain old telephone service (POTS). It was long believed that the maximum data transmission rate over copper telephone wires was 33.6 Kbps, but K56flex achieves higher rates by taking advantage of the fact that most phone switching stations are connected by high-speed digital lines. K56flex bypasses the normal digital-to-analog conversion and sends the digital data over the telephone wires directly to your modem where it is decoded.

Lucent and Rockwell have announced that future K56flex modems will conform to the new V.90 standard approved by the ITU. And users with older K56flex modems may upgrade their modems to support V.90.

While K56flex offers faster Internet access than normal modems, there are several caveats to using an K56flex modem:

The high speeds are available only with downstream traffic (e.g., data sent to your computer). Upstream traffic is delivered using normal techniques, with a maximum speed of 33.6 Kbps.

To connect to the Internet at K56flex speeds, your Internet Service Provider (ISP) must have a modem at the other end that supports V.90.

Even if your ISP supports V.90, you might not achieve maximum transmission rates due to noisy lines.

Karnaugh mapping A means of showing the relationship between logic inputs and desired output. Generally a truth table is mapped to a smaller, more workable grid of output values (1s and 0s). Karnaugh Mappings are often used when working with electronic circuits and trying to predict their output.

Kbps (kilobits per second) A measure of data transfer. A 56Kbps dial-up modem transfers data at about 7.2 kilobytes (KB) per second, or about 432 KB per minute.

KBS Knowledge-based system.

KDD (knowledge discovery in databases) A branch of Artificial-Intelligence.

KDE (k desktop environment) The KDE project was started in 1996 by Matthias Ettrich as a way to bring a more user-friendly GUI experience to UNIX users. KDE is an Integrated Desktop Environment for UNIX and Linux that adds functionality to X-Windows.

KE shell (knowledge executive shell) Software from Arthur Andersen Worldwide Organization, Center for Professional Education, St Charles, IL. The software called.

Kerberos Kerberos is a network authentication protocol. It is designed to provide strong authentication for client/server applications by using secret-key cryptography. A free implementation of this protocol is available from the Massachusetts Institute of Technology. Kerberos is available in many commercial products as well.

Kernel The central module of an operating system. It is the part of the operating system that loads first, and it remains in main memory. Because it stays in memory, it is important for the kernel to be as small as possible while still providing all the essential services required by other parts of the operating system and applications. Typically, the kernel is responsible for memory management, process and task management, and disk management.

Kernel mode The processor mode that allows full, unprotected access to the system. A driver or thread running in kernel mode has access to system memory and hardware.

Kernel size The number of pixels sampled as a unit during image manipulation and sharpening processes.

Kernel-mode driver Driver for a logical, virtual, or physical devices.

Key The secret that is used to encrypt and decrypt ciphertext. successful encryption requires that this key remain secret.

Key board The thing you type on to tell your computer what to do. There are many different keyboards, with a wide variety of keys on them.

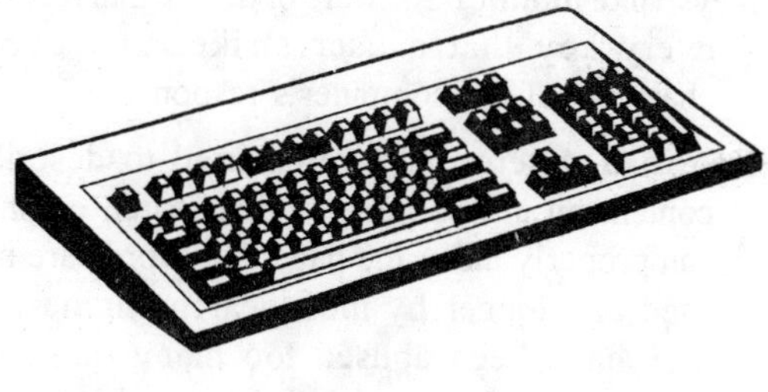

Fig. Key board

Key escrow The system of giving different parts of a key to a number of trustees in such a way that all the trustees must collaborate to recover the key.

Key exchange algorithm A public method for agreeing on a symmetric key without comprising the key.This is used by the U.S. government to implement the Diffie-Hellman key agreement when sending classified military messages.

Keyboard buffer A small amount of system memory used to store the most recently typed keys, also known as the type-ahead buffer. Some utility programs let you collect a number of keystrokes or commands and edit or reissue them.

Keyboard layout Most computers use a keyboard based on the traditional QWERTY typewriter-like keyboard.In the IBM PC and DOS computers, the most common keyboard currently used has 101 keys, with 12 function keys arranged over the top of all the other keys.

Keyboard template A plastic card that fits over certain keys (usually the function keys) on the keyboard to remind you how to use them. These templates are specific to an application, and can be very useful if you are an occasional user, or you are learning to use the program.

Key-ring Key-rings are used in public-key encryption systems such as Pretty Good Privacy (PGP). A pair of keys that consists of both a public key and its corresponding private key. Data encrypted with someone's public key can only be decrypted with the corresponding private key, and vice versa. Key-rings are associated with an encryption system known as Pretty Good Privacy (PGP).

Keystroke monitor Software or device that records every key that a user strikes and every character of the computer's response.

Keyword A term most often used to describe content on a Web page so that search engines can properly index the page. Keywords are not used any longer by most search engines, as they have been abused too many times by people listing keywords that have nothing to do with their pages in an attempt to get extra traffic.

Kilo A prefix indicating 1000 in the metric system. Because computing is based on powers of 2, in this context kilo usually means 2(to the tenth), or 1024. To differentiate between these two uses, a lowercase k is used to indicate 1000 (as in kHz), and an uppercase K to indicate 1024(as in KB).

Kinematics A branch of physics and mechanical engineering that involves the study of moving bodies and particles.

Kinetics A branch of physics or chemistry concerned with the rate of change in chemical or physical systems.

Kiosk A multimedia display system such as those used in marketing displays at conferences and in stores. Kiosks are typically used for demonstrations and may be self-contained hardware units having computer, video, and audio capabilities. For example, Computer and Control Solutions offers one such self-contained Kiosk machine. Also, a center of standalone interactive information or content. Large department store chains such as Sears and Kmart are installing web kiosks for accessing online catalogs and the entire inventories of items available for ordering.

K-nearest neighbors A classifier that assigns a class label for an unknown data item by looking at the class labels of the nearest items in the training data.

KNI (katmai new instructions) This is the original code-name for Intel's SSE instruction set, named after the first Pentium III processor core, code-named "Katmai."

Knowledge engineering The acquisition of knowledge from a human expert or similar source and its coding in an expert system expert-system.

Knowledge executive shell (KE Shell) Provides facilities for integrating multimedia components of text, video, audio, and graphics.

Knowledge management A term that can have multiple meanings. In business information technology knowledge management refers to an entire integrated system for accumulation, integration, manipulation, and access of data across multiple organizations, including such data as credit data, consumer profiles, market data, product development data, etc.

Kohonen T. Kohonen of the University of Helsinki has been studying neural networks for many years with the idea of modelling as closely as possible the behaviour of biological systems, and his name is commonly associated with a particular kind of neural network in which there are only two kinds of neurons, input and others. All the input neurons are connected to all others, and the others are connected only to their other nearest neighbors. The training algorithm is a relatively simple one based on the geometric layout of the neurons, and makes use of annealing annealing.

Korn shell An enhanced version of the Bourne shell, written by a guy named Korn. For your purposes, it's mostly like the Bourne shell,and prompts you with a $. Its program name is ksh.

KVM switch (keyboard video mouse switch) A switch that connects two or more computers to the same keyboard, mouse, and monitor. The KVM switch fools each computer into thinking that it is actively connected to a separate keyboard, mouse, and monitor. There is always some mechanism (a button and or keyboard command) on a KVM switch to decide which computer (at a given time) accepts the input of the keyboard and mouse and displays output to the monitor. Thus, when you move the mouse connected to the switch your mouse movement is only echoed to the active computer. Some

KVM switches also accept audio input so that more then one computer can use the same set of speakers, although not simultaneously. Most KVM switches use PS/2 ports for keyboard and mouse operations, but more and more are coming Lwith USB support.

L

Lag A condition caused by network congestion. When more traffic is flowing than a network or connection can handle, it causes programs waiting to send or receive data over the network to slow down, or lag. This term is often used to describe a slowdown while playing games online, especially over dial-up modems or any connection with high latency.

LAN A computer network that spans a relatively small area. Most LANs are confined to a single building or group of buildings. However, one LAN can be connected to other LANs over any distance via telephone lines and radio waves. A system of LANs connected in this way is called a wide area network (WAN).

Most LANs connect workstations and personal computers. Each node (individual computer) in a LAN has its own CPU with which it executes programs, but it is also able to access data and devices anywhere on the LAN. This means that many users can share expensive devices, such as laser printers, as well as data. Users can also use the LAN to communicate with each other, by sending e-mail or engaging in chat sessions.

There are many different types of LANs Ethernets being the most common for PCs. Most Apple Macintosh networks are based on Apple's AppleTalk network system, which is built into Macintosh computers.

Lapping The practice of sanding down the surface of a microprocessor package to make it flatter than it was initially in order to make better contact with a heatsink. You do not sand down the microprocessor itself, but the metal surface on the top of the microprocessor that comes into contact with a heatsink. Typically you start with a rougher (but still fine) grit of sandpaper and lightly sand the surface flat, moving to finer and finer sandpaper until the metal has a mirror shine. Uneven chip package surfaces make the microprocessor contact the heatsink poorly. Lapping can be dangerous, especially with newer processors that are smaller than their older counterparts and have less metal on top of them. If you sand through the metal you will ruin the processor.

Laptop computer A small portable computer light enough to carry comfortably, with a flat screen and keyboard that fold together. Laptops are battery-operated, often have a thin,backlit or sidelit LCD display screen, and some models can even mate with a docking station to perform as a full-sized desktop system back at the office. Advances in battery technology allow laptop computers to run for many hours between charges, and some models have a set of business applications built into ROM.

Fig. Laptop Compuer

Laser pointer This is typically a pen-shaped device that emits a bright red laser light that appears as a red dot on any surface at which it is aimed. In a smoke-filled room, fog, or other similar environmental conditions, you can see the entire beam and not just the endpoint of the laser. Laser pointers started out as a means for presenters to easily point to specific areas of their presentations on large displays, and as their price came down they evolved into a means to harass people at sporting and other events. Laser pointing devices are also used to target long-range rifles, as the distance a laser light beam can travel without dispersing is quite impressive, and light travels in a relatively straight line unless it is reflected or refracted. Newer pointers also come in green.

Laser printer A high-resolution non-impact printer that uses a variation of the electrophotographic process used in photocopying machines to print text and graphics onto paper.

Laser printer uses a rotating disc to reflect laser beams onto a photosensitive drum, where the image of the page is converted into an electrostatic charge that attracts and holds the toner. A piece of charged paper is then rolled against the drum to transfer the image, and heat is applied to fuse the toner and paper together to create the final image.

LaTeX A document preparation system based on TeX, popular in the HEP community. It adds a collection of commands to simplify typesetting, and lets the user concentrate on the structure of the text rather than on formatting commands.

LB (leaky bucket) Leaky Bucket is the term used as an analogous description of the algorithm used for conformance checking of cell flows from a user or network. The "leaking hole in the bucket" applies to the sustained rate at which cells can be accommodated, while the "bucket depth" applies to the tolerance to cell bursting over a given time period.

LCD (liquid crystal display) A type of display used in digital watches and many portable computers. LCD displays utilize two sheets of polarizing material with a liquid crystal solution between them. An electric current passed through the liquid causes the crystals to align so that light cannot pass through them. Each crystal, therefore, is like a shutter, either allowing light to pass through or blocking the light.

Monochrome LCD images usually appear as blue or dark gray images on top of a grayish-white background. Color LCD displays use two basic techniques for producing color: Passive matrix is the less expensive of the two technologies. The other technology, called thin film transistor (TFT) or active-matrix, produces color images that are as sharp as traditional CRT displays, but the technology is expensive. Recent passive-matrix displays using new CSTN and DSTN technologies produce sharp colors rivaling active-matrix displays.

LCD monitor A monitor that uses liquid-crystal display technology. Many laptop and notebook computers use LCD displays because of their low power requirements.

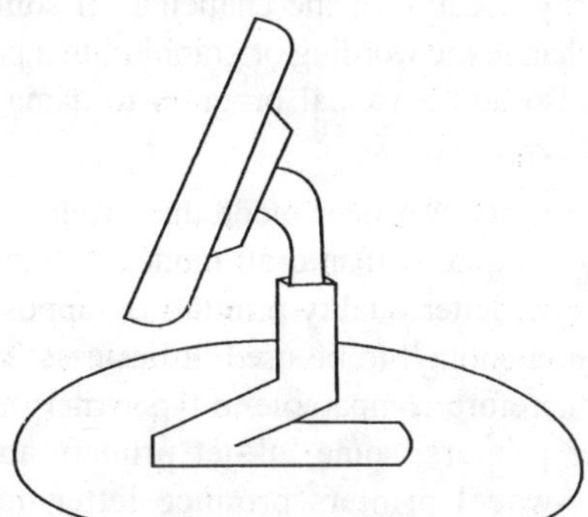

Fig. LCD monitor

LDT (lightning data transfer bus) An interconnection standard introduced by AMD that allows for fast data transfers among the Northbridge part of a chipset, the PCI bus(es), and the Southbridge part. In a multiprocessing machine the LDT bus can transfer data between sets of two processors. AMD now calls this technology HyperTransport.

LED (light emitting diode) This piece of electronics emits light when a current is passed through it. It does not work the same way as a light bulb, so it does not have the problem of burning out. It also only emits a few frequencies of light, so it can be a specific pure color.

Legacy system Any old computer system that was set up before your time and now continues to work and need support. Often legacy systems are problematic to upgrade because the people that put them together aren't around any more. One great example was the Year 2000 problem. Legacy systems were driving everyone nuts because no one programmed in COBOL anymore, and lots of legacy code was written in COBOL.

Legitimate sites Just because a user is viewing a "trusted" Web site does not mean that the content could not have been altered to include vandal programs. For example, in August 1996, the CIA Web site was altered. Since then and until now, thousands of Web sites have been hacked, or as hackers call it, "defaced." In fact, hackers often target traditional bastions of security because of the challenge. If someone can change the wording or graphics, that person can also add a vandal program to damage or steal data.

Letter quality A printer mode that produces text higher in quality than draft mode. As the name suggests, letter quality printing is supposed to be good enough to be used in business letters, and therefore comparable to typewriter output. Laser printers, some ink-jet printers and all daisy-wheel printers produce letter-quality output; certain high-end dot-matrix printers can produce letter-quality output, but most do not.

LFN A standard introduced by Microsoft with Windows 95 that allowed users to break from the file naming conventions of DOS. DOS only allowed filenames of eight letters then a period then three more letters. Almost all other file systems allow for longer names. They can be 255 characters long, containing spaces or even periods. Besides the 255 character limit the only real restriction is that none of the following characters may be used in filenames: \/:?"<>.

License (software license) Most corporations need multiple copies of software, but do not need the media in which they come, either because they already have it or because they allow users to install software from a server on the network. Companies still need to purchase a copy for each user, however, so they need a way to prove they have actually purchased a copy of each. These companies purchase software licenses with no associated media. Such licenses are typically just sheets of paper that cost a lot of money, but allow you to legally use additional copies of the software.

Life-cycle The software life-cycle consists of phases: requirements analysis, design, construction, testing and maintenance. The development process tends to run iteratively through these phases rather than linearly; several models (spiral, waterfall etc) have been proposed to describe this process.

Lightning data transfer bus (LDT) An interconnection standard introduced by AMD that allows for fast data transfers among the Northbridge part of a chipset, the PCI bus(es), and the Southbridge part. In a multiprocessing machine the LDT bus can transfer data between sets of two processors. AMD now calls this technology HyperTransport.

Line printer Any printer that prints a complete line at a time, rather than printing one character at a time (as a dot-matrix or daisy wheel printer does), or one page at a time(as a laser printer does). Line printers are very high-speed printers,and are common in the coroporate environment where they are used with mainframe computers,minicomputers, and networked systems.

Line sharing device A small electronic device that allows a fax machine and a telephone answering machine to share the same phone line. The device answers the call and listens for the characteristic high-pitched fax carrier signal. If this signal is detected, the call is routed to the fax machine; if it is not detected, the call is sent to a telephone or answering machine instead.

Linear tape-open (LTO) An open tape storage standard developed by HP, IBM, and Seagate. The standard consists of two formats: Accelis and Ultrium. Accelis is designed for faster access speed and uses a two-reel 8 mm tape to store up to 25 GB of data natively. Ultrium uses 1/2" tape on a single reel to offer 100 GB of native storage capacity for the initial format, with roadmaps scaling up to 1.6 TB per tape. DDS and DLT are competing standards.

Link (hyperlink) Part of an HTML document that points to another resource. When you view an HTML document using a browser, it is common practice to display hyperlinks in blue with an underlined font. When you click on a hyperlink you will jump, or link, to another area in that document or a different document. The linked document or item may be on the same page, the same server, or a server hundreds of miles away. The work all goes on behind the scenes as long as you are connected to the Internet.

Linux A version of UNIX that runs on a variety of hardware platforms including x86 PCs, Alpha, PowerPC and IBM's product line. Linux is open source software, which is freely available; however, the full distribution of Linux along with technical support and training are available for a fee from vendors such as Red Hat Software and Caldera. Due to its stability, Linux has gained popularity with Internet Service Providers as the Operating System of choice for hosting Web servers.

Liquid cooling This form of cooling refers to water cooling, or any other method of cooling where a liquid is used to keep something cool.

Liquid crystal display CD) A display technology common in portable computers that uses electric current to align crystals in a special liquid. The rod-shaped crystals are contained between two parallel transparent electrodes, and when current is applied, they change their orientation, creating a darker area. Many LCD screens are also back-lit or side-lit to increase visibility and reduce the possibility of eyestrain.

LMP Link Manager Protocol is the layer of the Bluetooth protocol stack responsible for the set up of the link between Bluetooth devices. This includes security aspects (authentication, encryption), the control and negotiation of packet sizes, power mode control and connection states of a Bluetooth unit in a piconet.

Local bus A PC bus specification that allows peripherals to exchange data at a rate faster than the 8 megabytes per second allowed by the ISA, and the 32 megabytes per second allowed by the EISA definitions. Local bus can acheive a maximum data rate of133 megabytes per second with a 33MHz bus speed, 148 megabytes per second with a 40MHz bus, or 267 megabytes per second with a 50 MHz bus. VESAs video cards have been the main peripheral to benefit from local bus use. Also defined as, a fast expansion bus found on 486 and Pentium computers that operates at a higher speed than the old ISA bus and allows 32-bit data transfers. Two types are commonly found:VESA and PCI. Many 486 comps include several VESA local bus slots, but newer Pentium comps use PCI slots. For best network performance,all servers should have VESA or PCI disk I/O and network interface cards(NICs).

Localtalk Apple's scheme for cabling Macintosh networks by using the Mac's printer ports. PhoneNET is a cabling scheme that's compatible with Local Talk but less expensive.

Logic This is broken down into two categories:

Software logic: The sequence of instructions performed by a program.

Hardware logic: A set of circuit elements that perform a function.

Logical block addressing (LBA) A form of addressing used by Enhanced IDE to recognize hard drives over 528 MB, as specified in the original IDE standard. LBA literally translates the hard drive's parameters into logical parameters that are able to be recognized by the computer BIOS.

Logical drive The internal division of a large hard disk into smaller units. One single physical drive may be organized into several logical drives for convenience; DOS supports up to 23 logical drives on a system. On a single-floppy system, the disk drive can function as both logical drive A and logical drive B, depending on the exact circumstances.

Long file name (LFN) A standard introduced by Microsoft with Windows 95 that allowed users to break from the file naming conventions of DOS. DOS only allowed filenames of eight letters then a period then three more letters. Almost all other file systems allow for longer names. They can be 255 characters long, containing spaces or even periods. Besides the 255 character limit the only real restriction is that none of the following characters may be used in filenames: \/:?"<>.

Loopback A diagnostic test that returns the transmitted signal back to the sending device after it has passed through a network or across a particular link. The returned signal can then be compared to the transmitted one. The discrepancy between the two help to trace the fault. When trying to locate a faulty piece of equipment, loopbacks will be repeated, eliminating satisfactory machines until the problem is found.

Lotus notes A networking set of application programs from Lotus Development Corporation, now owned by IBM Corporation, which allows organizations to share documents, databases, and exchange electronic mail messages. Purportedly, Lotus Notes was the major reason why Lotus was purchased by IBM Corporation. An interactive web server called Domino was introduced in 1996 so that Lotus Notes users could build intranets on the internet. For example, the accounting firm of Coopers & Lybrand makes extensive use of Domino for worldwide groupware applications. Java applets will give web browsers the look and feel of Notes.

Low key A dark image that is intentionally lacking in highlight detail.

Low precision/high recall A phenomenon that occurs during a search when a large set of results are retrieved, including many relevant and irrelevant documents.

Low-level format The process that creates the tracks and sectors on a blank hard disk or floppy disk; sometimes called the physical format. Most hard disks are already low-level formatted; however, floppy disks receive both a low and a high-level format (or logical format) when you use the DOS or OS/2 command format.

LUN (logical unit number) A term used in the context of devices connected to a SCSI controller. Each device on a SCSI controller has a SCSI ID, but each SCSI ID may have several LUNs that translate to several hard disks or removable media.

Lurking To read through mailing lists or newsgroups and get a feel of the topic before posting your own messages. It is considered good netiquette to "lurk" a while before joining an online discussion.

LYNX A UNIX program which allows character based terminals to access websites. Lynx users do not ordinarily see the graphics on a web page.

M

M/mb/megabyte A measure of memory and disk size that is 1,048,576 bytes, or 1K times 1K, or 2 multiplied by itself 20 times.

Mac An abbreviation of the popular Macintosh computers manufactured and sold by Apple Corporation. These computers contain what is called the Macintosh Operating System that will only run software written for that processor. Although software can be added so that Mac computers will run (in emulation form) many DOS and Windows programs (slowly), the PC computers cannot as a rule run Mac programs. Differences between Mac and PC operating systems have led to constant frustrations for authors since there is no single standard for authoring materials that can be used across the computer market. This is especially frustrating for authors of CD-ROM learning and entertainment materials. Mac computers took an early lead in graphics computing and menu-driven operating systems emulated later in Windows and OS/2 operating systems. A drawback for hypermedia developers, however, has been market share. Apple Corporation has less than 5% of the worldwide desktop computer market and has lost much of its competitive lead in graphics and hypermedia computing. In 1994, Apple's disturbing declines in market share, even after PowerMacs were introduced, led Apple Corporation to the first-time licensing of its operating system to other hardware manufacturers, notably IBM which undertake a new joint venture to produce a new computer running forthcoming versions of the Mac operating system. Analysts, however, are skeptical that Apple's licensing agreements may be too little too late to stop the market share momentum of Windows 95 and Windows 2000. Apple also has videotape rendering workstations known as AV or Mac Video Computers.

Macintosh A range of personal computers manufactured by Apple Computer Inc.

Macro A means of executing a group of instructions within a program. Many programs offer the capability to put together macros so that you don't have to do the same group of repetitive instructions one by one. You can program the macro to do any number of instructions. Many programs allow you to extend the simple macro languages that they provide with other, more complex programming languages.

Macro virus A virus written into an MS Office document using the VBA scripting language. Macro viruses are the number one cause of all virus infections. The nearly universal prevalence of Microsoft Office and the simplicity with which macro viruses can be created, continue to make macro viruses one of the fastest growing threats.

Macrovision A method of copy protection that rapidly modulates colorburst signals and pulses the vertical blanking signal in order to make videotaped copies of protected materials unwatchable. Some older VCRs even have trouble viewing Macrovision-protected movies. DVD players typically have Macrovision circuits built-in to make copying of DVD movies impossible; however, some DVD players allow Macrovision to be disabled.

Magnetic field effects As described in the paragraph "Rotation Control", the Monitor is affected by magnetic fields. If your screen develops wrong colors in areas or the picture becomes distorted you must check what is near to your Monitor. If your Monitor is positioned near a steel cabinet, on a steel desk or bench, or a steel girder imbedded in a wall or ceiling, then all of these things could be magnetized and therefore interfering with the picture tube's Electron Beams. Try moving the Monitor two to three feet away from the suspected source of magnetic field and see if the picture improves. If the picture only looks colored or distorted during certain times check if you have any speakers near the Monitor because these could radiate magnetic fields strong enough to distort the picture when they are powered-up.

Magnetic RAM (MRAM) A form of memory that stores information magnetically instead of electrically like DRAM. IBM has been working on developing MRAM since 1974, and has recently touted it—along with German memory-maker Infineon—as a viable main memory competitor that will be faster than DRAM and able to hold as much information, without requiring the electrical refresh of DRAM—it will hold onto data like Flash memory.

Mail A message to one or more users or groups sent over the computer. Mail can include other documents as attachments. Mail can traverse multiple machines and networks.

Mailbox The file in which the electronic mail system puts your incoming mail.

Mail-from One of the authentication schemes used by InterNIC. In the mail-from scheme, the email address that is used to send a modification request is compared to the email addresses that are on file for the individuals or organizations who are listed as authorized points of contact/agent for the domain name, the contact, or the host. The mail-from option under the Guardian] plan allows the contact to specify two email addresses, rather than just one, which can help avoid problems with authentication later if one of the email addresses should change.

Mailing list An email-based discussion group. Sending one email message to the mailing list sends email to all other members of the group. Mailing lists are usually joined by subscribing, and can be left by unsubscribing.

Mailslots A connectionless messaging IPC mechanism that Windows NT USES for browse requests and logon authentication.

Mainframe/ Mainframe computer 1. A large computer featuring downloadable microcode, rich I/O paths, substantial integrity enforcement, degradated mode capability, multiple virtual machines, and terabyte address spaces.

2. The central patch panel for a facility's cabling system.

3. *Slang* Any computer bigger then a PC or Macintosh.

Maintenance An important part of the software life-cycle. Maintenance is expensive in manpower and resources, and software engineering techniques aim to reduce its cost.

Male connector Any cable connector with pins designed to engage the sockets on the female part of the connector.

Malicious code Program instructions that are intended to carry out malicious or hostile actions; e.g., deleting a user's files.

Malware All types of software that prevent users from using their computers as they were intended. This includes hostile java applets,

ActiveX vandals, Trojan horses, script vandals, and viruses that are designed to corrupt or steal digital information.

Managed hosting A dedicated server that is accompanied by a full suite of technical support, maintenance and monitoring services. This differs from dedicated Web hosting, where customers are provided with their own servers but are still responsible for virtually all administrative and maintenance duties.

Managed service provider (MSP) A company that provides Internet services beyond basic connectivity to other companies. An MSP may also implement and manage the services it provides. For example, an MSP may use Gateway to filter content for companies that use it to connect to the Internet.

Manufacturer 1. A commercial entity that imports, labels, and markets goods, expecting VAR's to support them.

2. A factory for hire in a developing country, with accomodating labor and environmental laws.

MAPLE Mathematics computing software also known as Waterloo Maple, because it was developed at the University of Waterloo in Canada. This is a very popular software for both research and teaching of mathematics. New enhancements include a spreadsheet interface and interfacing with mathematics text processors. There are also interactive graphics and symbolic computing utilities. MAPLE runs on DOS, Windows, UNIX, and Macintosh platforms at present.

Masking To conceal a web site's URL in some manner, normally by using a domain name. For example, if a URL shows up as "http://www.example.com/" but the web site is actually located at "http://www.somewhere-else.com/example/", that URL is said to be "masked".

Master boot record (MBR) The first sector on a hard disk or other disk media. When a computer boots up it searches for a master boot record wherever the BIOS tells it to (usually the master hard drive on the first IDE channel, but this can also be checked for in CD/DVD drives and floppy drives) and, based on what the master boot record says, loads up an operating system. Thus, if the master boot record becomes corrupt or is tampered with by a virus, it can cause your computer to be unable to boot.

Master browser The computer on a network that maintains a list of computers and services available on the network and distributes the list to other browser. The Master Browser may also promote potential browses to be browsers.

Master clock Controls the rate of reference time within a graph and is used by filters within the graph to synchronize presentation times. Provides a standard mechanism to query the reference time, to query the physical clock time and rate (compared to the system clock) of the owner of the master clock, and to establish event notifications based on position changes in the master clock's reference time.

Mathematica Mathematics computing software from Wolfram Research Inc. in Champaign, Illinois. This is a widely popular software package used by many major universities. It is capable of two- and three-dimensional animated graphics. There are both Mac and Windows versions that allow users to choose between direct interaction with the kernel and interaction through a front end that supports a GUI. The front end allows users to create Mathematica Notebooks that incorporate text, graphics, animation, and audio. Many universities supplement or replace traditional curriculum materials with Mathematica curricula.

Maximum transmission unit (MTU) The largest size of a data packet that can be sent over a TCP/IP or other packet- or frame-based network. Ethernet uses an MTU of 1,500 bytes, while the standard Internet MTU is 576 bytes. Using a higher MTU is recommended for fast networks, while slower or more congested networks need a smaller MTU, as there is a greater chance that not all of the packet will make it through in one shot. Of course, using a small MTU on a fast network causes a lot of extra traffic to be generated, as the packet has to be split into smaller pieces with more conversations for data to be transmitted.

Mbps (megabits per second) This is a measure of throughput roughly in millions of bits per second. More exactly, that is 220 (1,048,576) bits per second.

MCA (micro channel architecture) A 32-bit proprietary expansion bus first introduced by IBM in 1987 for the IBM PS/2 range of computers, and also used in the RS/6000 series. MCA is incompatible with expansion boards that follow the earlier 16-bit AT bus standard, physically because the boards are about 50 percent smaller, and electronically as the bus depends on more proprietary integrated circuits. MCA was designed for multiprocessing, and it also allows expansion boards to identify themselves, thus eliminating many of the conflicts that arose through the use of manual settings in the original bus.

MCI (media control interface) Established by Microsoft Corporation that has become a popular standard for Windows authors and users. MCI menus drop down to let users select input sources such as CD-Audio inputs, videodisc inputs, MIDI sequencers, and auxiliary sources such as inputs from a stereo set or a videotape player. These standards also mean that certain types of files should play on MCI systems (e.g., WAV files should play audio and AVI files should play video on MCI systems). It is recommended that any hardware/software purchased for the PC go beyond MCI standards and be Sound Blaster compatible. This does not mean that you must buy multimedia upgrades from Creative Labs. It only means that your system is compatible with the popular standard established by Sound Blaster. Also, a standard control interface for multimedia devices and media files, including a command-message interface and a command-string interface.

MCSE (microsoft certified system engineer) A certification program offered by Microsoft. To become an MCSE you must pass a series of standardized tests at Microsoft-approved testing facilities. On the positive side, the MCSE certification is designed to give employers an easier way of screening candidates. On the negative side, a candidate with an MCSE and little practical knowledge may unfairly receive consideration over a more qualified non-MCSE. Some Geeks think it's worthy to aspire to be an MCSE, but others think it's just a waste of time and money to learn the "Microsoft way."

Mechanical control A dial or knob whose physical setting directly affects some measurement. For example, the power button in early PCs was a mechanical control, as were the huge, hand-controlled electrical switches in old horror movies and light switches on your wall. By pushing the power button you used to physically make an electrical contact so that power could flow to your PC. Nowadays most power buttons only send signals to the motherboard and are no longer mechanical controls.

Media 1. Objects on which data can be stored. These include hard disks, floppy disks, CD-ROMs, and tapes.

2. In computer networks, media refers to the cables linking workstations together. There are many different types of transmission media, the most popular being twisted-pair wire (normal electrical wire), coaxial cable (the type of cable used for cable television), and fiber optic cable (cables made out of glass).

3. The form and technology used to communicate information. Multimedia presentations, for example, combine sound, pictures, and videos, all of which are different types of media.

Media access control address (MAC address) A unique 128-bit address of a network card or device. The first part of the address is unique to the company that produced the device, and beyond that it is a sequence of digits unique to a single device manufactured by a company.

Mega Abbreviated M. A prefix meaning one million in the metric system. Because computing is based on powers of 2, in this context mega usually means 220or 1,048,576; the power of 2 closest to 1 million bits.

Megabits per second A measurement of the amount of information moving across a network or communications link in one second, measured in multiples of 1,048,576 bits.

Megapixel One million pixels. This term is most often used when talking about how fast 3D graphics cards can pump data to the display device, or how much data a digital camera can capture. As a general rule higher megapixel ratings typically equate to higher maximum performance for graphics, or better quality pictures for digital cameras.

Membrane keyboard A pressure-sensitive keyboard covered by a protective plastic sheet used in a hostile environment where operators may not always have clean hands. While it is very difficult to type quickly and accurately on a membrane keyboard, they are most often used for occasional data entry in factories or in fast food restaurants.

Memory Internal storage areas in the computer. The term memory identifies data storage that comes in the form of chips, and the word storage is used for memory that exists on tapes or disks. Moreover, the term memory is usually used as a shorthand for physical memory, which refers to the actual chips capable of holding data. Some computers also use virtual memory, which expands physical memory onto a hard disk.

Every computer comes with a certain amount of physical memory, usually referred to as main memory or RAM. You can think of main memory as an array of boxes, each of which can hold a single byte of information. A computer that has 1 megabyte of memory, therefore, can hold about 1 million bytes (or characters) of information.

Memory chip A chip that holds data or program instructions. A memory chip may hold its contents temporarily , as in the case of RAM, or permanently as in the case of ROM.

Memory configuration The amount of memory in an IC and how it is accessed.

Memory management The way in which the computer handles memory. In the PC you may find the following kinds of memory:

Conventional memory: This is the area of memory below 640KB.

Upper memory: Also known as reserved memory. The 384KB of memory between 640KB and 1MB. This space is used by system hardware such as the video adapter. Unused portions of upper memory are known as upper memory blocks (UMBs), and on some PCs UMBs can be used for loading device drivers or terminate-and-stay-resident programs.

Extended memory: That memory above 1MB on 386's (or later) processors. Extended memory requires an extended-memory manager, such as HIMEM.SYS.

High memory area: The first 64K of extended memory.

Expanded memory: Memory above conventional memory that can be used by certain DOS applications.

Memory types cache Static random access memory containing recently used information

DRAM: Dynamic random access memory.

SDRAM: Single data rate synchronous dynamic random access memory.

DDR SDRAM: Double data rate synchronous dynamic random access memory. Usually referred to as DDR.

SLDRAM: Synchronous link dynamic random access memory.

RDRAM: Rambus dynamic random access memory.

RAM: Random access memory.

ROM: Read only memory (permanent memory that cannot be changed).

SRAM: Static random access memory.

Menu A list of choices, usually commands, from which you can choose.

Menu bar The horizontal bar that contains the names of available menus. The menu bar is located below the title bar.

Menu label The text or icon on a menu item in a program with a graphical user interface.

Message In object-oriented object-oriented programming sending a message to an object (to invoke a method) is equivalent to calling a procedure in traditional programming languages, except that the actual code executed may only be selected at run-time depending on the class of the object. Thus, in response to the message "drawSelf", the method code invoked would be different if the target object were a circle or a square.

Message channel A form of interprocess communication found in multitasking OSes. Interprocess communications allow two programs running the same computer to share information.

Method set Used in Windows NT, Windows 2000, and WDM drivers to perform an action, such as allocating memory, and to provide a way to access related actions. Each method set has a unique identifier used to retrieve that method set and can be fulfilled either synchronously or asynchronously. A resource method set contains resource-specific methods for manipulating a type of resource by a kernel-mode client, and is used in resource allocation by enumerated devices on a bus.

Methodology A term for a codified set of procedures for some phase of software engineering, such as analysis and design.

MIB (management information base) When SNMP devices send SNMP messages to the management console, it stores information in this file or database. The MIB collects and contains information on managed objects.

Micro channel architecture (MCA) A 32-bit standard developed by IBM for expansion cards. The standard offered improvements over 16-bit ISA, but never caught on outside of IBM computers. The industry chose to go with EISA, which was only found in servers and workstations for the most part and was eventually replaced by PCI.

Microchip Synonymous with microprocessor. This term is commonly used to describe the CPU. More specifically, it refers to the part of the CPU that actually does the work, since many CPUs now contain L1 and L2 caches on-chip.

Microcode The microinstructions, especially of a microprocessor, that govern the details of operations. For example, the hardware of 3081 fetches and executes 108-bit microinstructions wholly different from the instruction set of System/370. Yet IBM supplies a microprogram that causes the 3081 to act like a System/370. The instructions in such a program are referred to as microcode. The execution of each System/370 instructions puts the hardware into a subroutine of microinstructions that execute the function defined for that instruction. Microcoded functions can improve performance but add a layer of complexity. For example, microcode errors appear to software as being hardware failures.

Microcomputer . 1. A computer designed for use by a single user, employing a single chip Processing Unit with fixed microcode and a single-user operating system.

2. An embedded system employing a single chip CPU.

Microphone (mic) A device that changes audio into an electric signal. You can plug a microphone into most sound cards, and they are required for certain operations, such as Internet telephony.

Microprocessor A silicon chip that contains a CPU. In the world of personal computers, the terms microprocessor and CPU are used interchangeably. At the heart of all personal computers and most workstations sits a microprocessor. Microprocessors also control the logic of almost all digital devices, from clock radios to fuel-injection systems for automobiles.

Three basic characteristics differentiate microprocessors:

Instruction set: The set of instructions that the microprocessor can execute.

Bandwidth: The number of bits processed in a single instruction.

Clock speed: Given in megahertz (MHz), the clock speed determines how many instructions per second the processor can execute.

In both cases, the higher the value, the more powerful the CPU. For example, a 32-bit microprocessor that runs at 50MHz is more powerful than a 16-bit microprocessor that runs at 25MHz.

In addition to bandwidth and clock speed, microprocessors are classified as being either RISC (reduced instruction set computer) or CISC (complex instruction set computer).

Microsoft A vendor of systems and application software for personal computers and similar platforms. Software world leader. The main products are Windows and MS-Office which is composed of WORD, EXCEL, PowerPoint and MAIL.

Microsoft certified system engineer (MCSE) A certification program offered by Microsoft. To become an MCSE you must pass a series of standardized tests at Microsoft-approved testing facilities. On the positive side, the MCSE certification is designed to give employers an easier way of screening candidates. On the negative side, a candidate with an MCSE and little practical knowledge may unfairly receive consideration over a more qualified non-MCSE. Some Geeks think it's worthy to aspire to be an MCSE, but others think it's just a waste of time and money to learn the "Microsoft way."

Millions of Instructions per second (MIPS) A rating of how quickly a processor can process instructions. A processor rated at 100 MIPS can process 100,000,000 instructions per second. Although it seems straightforward enough, for an accurate comparison you must define which instruction(s) you are going to run, and a rating such as this could lead processor makers to build chips that have high MIPS ratings but aren't useful in the real world.

Minicomputer This term refers to "mini" mainframe computers that are a step smaller than a large corporate mainframe. They were once popular in small businesses that couldn't afford real mainframes, but now you only find reference to them in free subscription surveys for computer industry print magazines ("Do you work with mini-computers, microcomputers, etc.?") or in some college campuses or large business networks.

Minidisc Is used in a variety of contexts to depict miniature "MD" optical discs and/or magnetic discs smaller than the standard 4.72 inch CD. Some MD alternatives such as the Sony MD Data 2.5 inch disk are smaller than floppy discs but hold nearly as much as a CD-ROM. The Sony version holds up to 74 minutes of CD quality audio or 140 Mb of data storage. The most typical MD size is the 2.5 inch audio disc. The term MD-Data refers to a minidisc used to record computer files and hypermedia presentations.

Mirror Generally speaking, "to mirror" is to maintain an exact copy of something. Probably the most common use of this term on the Internet refers to "mirror sites" which are web sites or FTP sites that maintain exact copies of material originated at another location. This is usually in order to provide more widespread access to the resource. Another common use of the term "mirror" refers to an arrangement where information is written to more than one hard disk simultaneously, so that if one disk fails, the computer keeps on working without losing anything.

Mission critical application Any application that is critical to the proper running of a business. If this application fails for any length of time you may be out of business. For example, an order-entry system may be considered mission critical if your business relies on taking lots of orders.

MMC (multimedia card) A postage stamp-sized Flash memory card that allows data to be saved onto it. MMC cards are a means of exchanging data between PDAs, phones, digital cameras, and other devices, but they can also serve the function of acting similar to a hard drive on a PC for the storage of data and programs. The MMCA (MMC Association) was founded in 1998 to push the MMC standard.

MNP (microcom networking protocol) These protocols were developed for error recovery and data compression (in order to speed up the transmission). They are now in the public domain.

Modem Process of converting digitized data into analog form for a carrier wave. Demodulation transforms data transmitted in analog form back into digital form for computer storage and/or processing. Modems modulate and demodulate computer data for transmission on telephone lines. Fax modems have the added capability of importing facsimiles received over phone lines directly into computer files. Cable TV modems offer transmitting speeds of over five times those of ISDN modems. The term "ricochet modem" is sometimes used to depict a wireless connection of a computer to the Internet. The product Ricochet Modem is brick-sized connector from Metricom Inc. that is a special kind of radio connector to the Internet in metropolitan areas having Ricochet's receivers for Internet connections.

Modification The process of updating an existing domain name record, contact record, or host (name server) record per the request of a domain name's contact/agent. There is no additional charge to modify an existing domain, contact, or host record. Keeping these records up to date is critical to the smooth operation of the Domain Name System (DNS), and it is the responsibility of the registrant to ensure that domain name record(s) are kept up to date.

Modified frequency modulation encoding (MFM) The most widely used method of storing data on a hard disk. Based on an earlier technique known as frequency modulation (FM) encoding, MFM achieves a two-fold increase in data storage density over standard FM recording, but it is not as efficient a space saver as run-length limited encoding.

Monitor A video output device capable of displaying text and graphics, often in color.

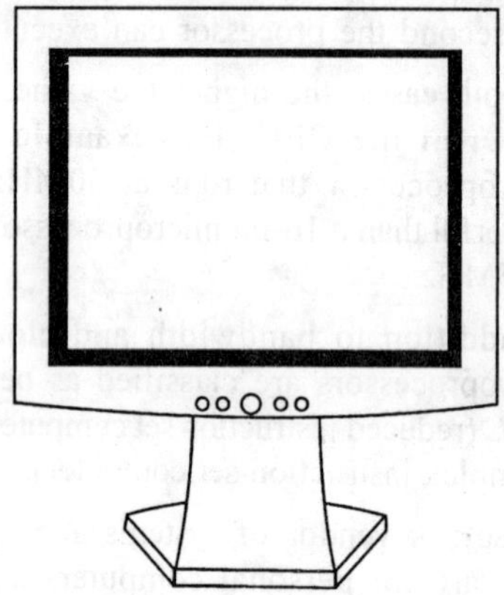

Fig. Monitor

Monochrome Single-colored. An image or medium displaying only black-and-white or greyscale information. Greyscale information displayed in one color is also monochrome.

Moore's law Former Intel chairman Gordon Moore is credited with predicting the trend that transistor counts in processors double every 18 months. This law has held true since the 1970s. The law can also be applied to other technologies, and works frighteningly well with hard drive and memory chip density, processor speeds, processor power, and processor size (micron process). More than ever the end of Moore's Law is being discussed, as smaller, more compact designs and electrical leakage threaten to throw Moore's Law off track.

Mosaic A menu-driven and user-friendly hypertext system (also called NCSA Mosaic) of Internet sites that facilitate searching and browsing of documents and files around the world. Mosaic has largely been overtaken by more modern web browsers. For users not connected to the Internet, Mosaic can also be used with SLIP. Mosaic combines various former Internet servers such as Gopher Servers, World Wide Web, InterNIC InfoSource, ftp Sites, Finger Gateway, Whois Gateway, and Home Pages. Key features include world wide free networking by graphical interfacing to text, pictures, digitized video, and audio. Clicking on a highlighted Mosaic hotword or phrase (indicating a hyperlinked term) will complete a connection to the appropriate server to display documents, graphics, audio, or other multimedia files. Mosaic is becoming even more popular than Gopher largely due to the graphics-orientation of Mosaic and commercial developers of Mosaic interfaces.

Motherboard The main circuit board of a microcomputer. The motherboard contains the connectors for attaching additional boards. Typically, the motherboard contains the CPU, BIOS, memory, mass storage interfaces, serial and parallel ports, expansion slots, and all the controllers required to control standard peripheral devices, such as the display screen, keyboard, and disk drive. Collectively, all these chips that reside on the motherboard are known as the motherboard's chipset.

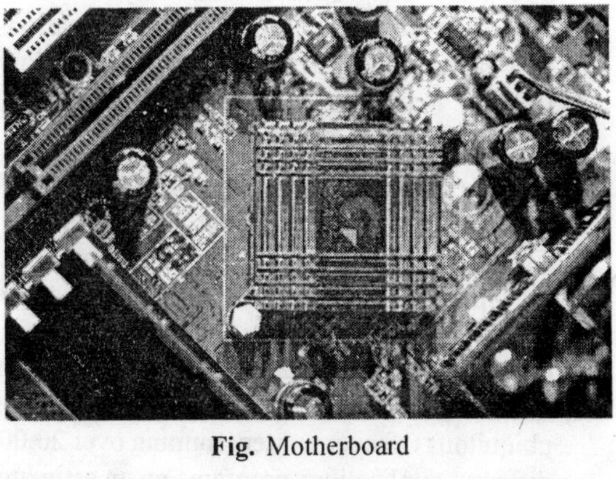

Fig. Motherboard

On most PCs, it is possible to add memory chips directly to the motherboard. You may also be able to upgrade to a faster CP by replacing the CPU chip. To add additional core features, you may need to replace the motherboard entirely.

Mount This term comes from the days when tape media had to be physically mounted at the instruction of an operating system. The terminology is still used in UNIX/Linux environments. When the system is powered on all hard drives are normally set to mount automatically, but removable media such as CD-ROMs and floppy disks have to be manually set to be recognized by the operating system (mounted) after they are inserted into the computer. Some newer GUI UNIX/Linux interfaces will mount media for you automatically and save you the trouble of typing in a potentially complex mount command.

Mouse A pointing device that is pushed around a desk area with the palm of your hand. Traditionally mice have used roller balls to detect motion, but newer models feature no moving parts and use integrated circuits that detect movement over the desktop and translate that into motion.

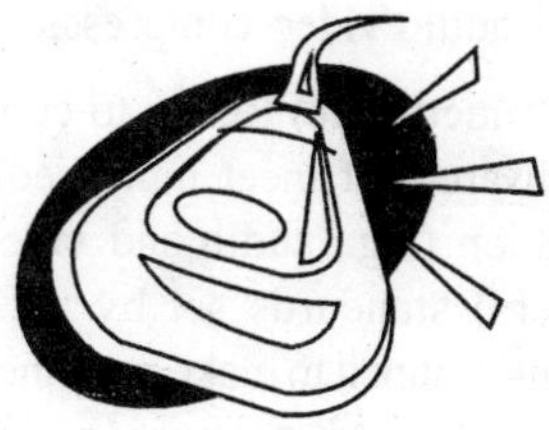

Fig. Mouse

Mousepad A pad that has a surface made for providing traction for a mouse that uses a roller ball.

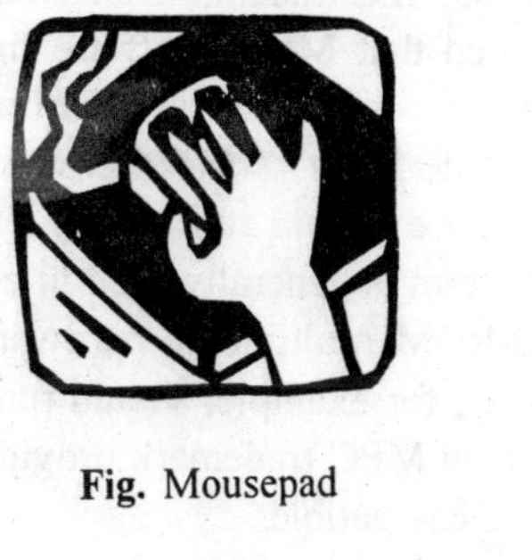

Fig. Mousepad

Moving pictures expert group (MPEG) An ISO group that works to develop standard formats for compressing video. The standards associated with the group include MPEG-1, MPEG-2 (used in DVD movies), and MPEG-4 (used sometimes to further compress DVD movies onto CD-ROM media). There are other MPEG standards as well. MPEG standard are typically not open standards, and require licensing fees. MPEG files in Windows often have the ".mpg" file extension.

Mozilla An Open Source project put together to create the next generation of Netscape Web browsers starting after Netscape Navigator 4.x. The project is run by developers who work for Netscape, but development is done by both Netscape employees and independent developers.

MP3 (mpeg-1 audio layer-3) A compression standard for audio. It enables compression of CD-audio by about 10 times, depending on the bit and sampling rate. It does not stand for MPEG-3, but rather it is the audio part of the MPEG-1 audio/video compression standard.

MPC (multimedia pc) Refers to combinations of PC hardware that meet multimedia hardware-combination (e.g., audio and video boards for computers) standards set by the Multimedia Marketing Council to make multimedia hardware products of vendors more compatible. The MPC1 Level 1 standard requires a 386 PC with a minimum of 2 Mb of RAM. The MPC2 Level 2 standard requires a 486SX or greater PC with 4 Mb of RAM. A variety of PC manufacturers use the MPC trademark. Consumers can then be assured that MPC hardware from one vendor will be compatible with hardware of another vendor. Also, software written for MPC hardware should run on any MPC equipment. The term is generally used in conjunction with CD-ROM multimedia hardware. A CD-ROM player, for example, should run on a computer with an MPC trademark provided the player is MPC compatible.

MPEG (moving pictures experts group) Systems boards and compression standards (e.g., MPEG-2 and MPEG-1) for the most popular emerging form of compressed full-motion video standard for computer file storage. MPEG compression requires MPEG playback boards and/or MPEG authoring boards such as the Optibase MPG-1000 digital video codec (compression/decompression) board (800-451-5101). Although MPEG-2 is superior to MPEG-1, MPEG-2 requires at least quad speed CD-ROMs that, thereby, limits the use of MPEG-2 in the commercial market. MPEG-2 works much better with CD-DVD. However, even MPEG-1 is considered a better video compression alternative than its competitors. Full-motion video at over 30 frames per second takes up so much digitized storage that video must be compressed to make it more useful in hypermedia.

MRAM (magnetic ram) A form of memory that stores information magnetically instead of electrically like DRAM. IBM has been working on developing MRAM since 1974, and has recently touted it—along with German memory-maker Infineon—as a viable main memory competitor that will be faster than DRAM and able to hold as much information, without requiring the electrical refresh of DRAM—it will hold onto data like Flash memory.

Ms windows Any of five versions of a graphical operating environment that enables Task Switching between Productivity Applications. Also, an extended memory manager that allows DOS to load four Megabyte EXE's plus 10 Megabytes of DLL's for one.

MS-DOS (microsoft disk operating system) MS-DOS allocates system resources such as hard and floppy disks, the monitor and the printer to the applications programs that need them. MS-DOS is a single-user, single-tasking operating system, with either a command-line interface, or a shell interface. Its is the most ubiquitous OS ever written, running over 20,000 different applications programs on an estimated 60 million computers.

MTU The largest size of a data packet that can be sent over a TCP/IP or other packet- or frame-based network. Ethernet uses an MTU of 1,500 bytes, while the standard Internet MTU is 576 bytes. Using a higher MTU is recommended for fast networks, while slower or more congested networks need a smaller MTU, as there is a greater chance that not all of the packet will make it through in one shot. Of course, using a small MTU on a fast network causes a lot of extra traffic to be generated, as the packet has to be split into smaller pieces with more conversations for data to be transmitted.

Multicast IP - A form of TCP/IP being proposed that will allow for high-bandwidth transmissions (like television channels) to be broadcast over the Internet to all the routers in the world (possibly) that are connected to someone watching that channel. To see the benefit, think of 1,000 people making separate connections to the USA network. Each packet of data sent out would have to be sent to 1,000 people. Thus, you have 1,000 conversations active among the USA network server and people's machines, each one saying the same thing. That's poor scalability. Now imagine that in this fantasy network we only have 10 routers with these 1,000 people connected to them. In simplistic terms, you only have to send each packet to 10 places, and each machine downloads packets directly from the router it is connected to. Thus the USA network server doesn't have to do much work to keep Gary Busey movies going to 1,000 people at once, and the rest of the network isn't clogged with all 1,000 conversations. However, there are lots of minute details that must be considered, such as how many channels are offered and how much router memory that takes.

Multicolor graphics array (MCGA) A graphics standard prior to VGA which allows 320x200 resolutions with 256 colors, or 640x400 resolutions with two colors. It is a bit better than CGA.

Multihomed A machine with more than one NIC attached to more than one network. If a machine has multiple NICs but is only attached to one network, it is not multihomed. A machine must have more than one network attached to be multihomed. The standard home version of a multi-homed machine is one that connects to the Internet and separately to a local network.

Multimedia extensions (MMX) A technology created by Intel Corporation that enhances audio and video capabilities. MMX is found in Pentium III and later CPU's and is also found in AMD K6 series CPU's. Microprocessors that have MMX can handle tasks that usually are handled by a separate component, such as; Digital Signal Processing (DSP) is a common multimedia operation that is normally handled by a separate audio or video card. The direct benefit of this technology includes speeding up such things as; image processing, motion video, speech synthesis, telephony, and 3D graphics.

Multimedia The ability to combine audio, visual, and possibly other types of hardware into a presentation. For example, a "multimedia" classroom will typically have projection hardware and switching controls that make it easy for teachers to switch back and forth between computer projections, videotape projections, audio CDs, 35mm slides, videodiscs, CD-I players, etc. Although hypermedia presentations may require multimedia facilities, the two terms are not synonymous.

Multiple DOS configurations DOS6 includes features that allow you to define different system configurations and choose the one you want to use at startup time. To do this you define a startup menu in your CONFIG.SYS file, and then create configuration blocks for each selection in the startup menu. When your system starts, the menu is presented on the screen, you choose the selection you want to use, and your system is configured accordingly.

Multiplexing In communications, a technique that transmits several signals over a single communications channel.

Frequency-division multiplexing separates the signals by modulating the data into different carrier frequencies.

Time-division multiplexing divides up the available time between the various signals.

Statistical multiplexing uses statistical techniques to dynamically allocate transmission space depending on the traffic pattern.

Multipoint-to-multipoint connection A Multipoint-to-Multipoint Connection is a collection of associated ATM VC or VP links, and their associated nodes, with the following properties:

1. All Nodes in the connection, called endpoints, serve as a Root Node in a Point-to-Multipoint connection to all of the (N-1) remaining endpoints.

2. Each of the endpoints on the connection can send information directly to any other endpoint, but the receiving endpoint cannot distinguish which of the endpoints is sending information without additional (e.g., higher layer) information.

Multipoint-to-point connection A Point-to-Multipoint Connection may have zero bandwidth from the Root node to the Leaf Nodes, and non-zero return bandwidth from the Leaf Nodes to the Root Node. Such a connection is also known as a Multipoint-to-Point Connection. Note that UNI 4.0 does not support this connection type.

Multiprocessing The ability of an OS to use more than one CPU in a single computer.

Symmetrical multiprocessing refers to the OS's ability to assign tasks dynamically to the next available processor; this ensures that each processor is being used fully.

Asymmetrical multiprocessing requires that the original program designer choose the processor to use for a given task at the time of writing the program. This approach is relatively easy to implement, but can result in some processors being busier than others.

Multipurpose internet mail extensions (MIME) Functions used for the attachment of binary files to an e-mail message. MIME is the most common group of functions used to make this translation, and allows us to tack on graphics, sound, and executable files to our e-mail messages.

Multi-tiered architecture This is the most scalable application architecture (over two-tier and three-tier). This architecture refers to 4-, 5-, or even higher-tiered architectures. It is the most complex type of architecture, splitting the application and database management tasks into many discrete components. For example, take the three-tier architecture and change it so that the application logic is separate from the database management system—this gets you to four-tier architecture. With this structure you can more easily change one of the tiers without compromising your entire application. To get to 5 tiers you could move some of the application logic to the client to optimize performance.

Multi-user . 1. A pejorative used against UNIX type systems, as in, "you really don't want the overhead of a multi-user OS."

2. The ability to remotely log-in, diagnose and repair software problems.

MVS (multiple virtual storage) An IBM mainframe operating system. The term MVS is used to describe an entire family of mainframe operating systems. The term "multiple virtual storage" refers to the use of multiple virtual memory areas in the operating system.

MX record (mail exchange record) A record that exists on a DNS server and tells e-mail servers where to send mail for any particular DNS entry. The address is prefaced by a precedence number; for example, "10 mailserver.geek.com" could be an MX record that tells an external e-mail server to try sending mail to the address "mailserver.geek.com." You can have several MX records per domain with different precedence. For example, assuming you have the

MX record we just mentioned listed for your domain, you may point to your backup mail server at "5000 backupmail.geek.com" in case your main mail server is down. Of course you could use any number over 10, but a higher number ensures that no mail will go to the backup server unless your main mail server is inaccessible. You can also set a group of e-mail servers with the same number so that traffic will be equally dispersed among them. This is useful if you get a lot of e-mail and need to balance the load.

Mylar A synthetic film, invented by the DuPont corporation, used in photographic printing and production processes, as well as disks and tapes.

N

N+1 disk shadowing/mirroring A system- or storage subsystem-level facility to provide significantly improved apparent disk reliability without the cost of two-times disk shadowing (e.g., N+1 redundant array of inexpensive disk).

NAK (no acknowledgement) A none acknowledgement (disapproval) from an authorized point of contact/agent for a domain name record, contact record, or host record that a requested modification should not be completed. When a modification request is received from a source that is not an authorized contact, the request will be rejected and a message will be sent to the listed contacts asking them to ACK (Acknowledge) or NAK (disapprove) the modification.

Name service (domain name service) Providing individuals or organizations with domain name-to-Internet Protocol (IP) number resolution by maintaining and making available the hardware, software, and data needed to perform this function. Many Internet Service Providers (ISPs) operate name server and provide their customers with name service when they register a domain name. Most individuals are not in a position to operate a name server on their own and will need to make arrangements for name service with an ISP or some other person or organization.

Nano machines and microbes Nano machines and Microbes provide the possibility to cause serious harm to a system. Unlike viruses, we can use these to attack not the software but the hardware of a computer system. Nano machines are tiny robots (smaller than ants) that could be spread at an information center of the enemy. They crawl through the halls and offices until they find a computer. They are so small that they enter the computer through slots and shut down electronic circuits. Another way to damage the hardware is a special breed of microbes. We know that they can eat oil, what about if they were bred for eating silizium? They would destroy all integrated circuits in a computer lab, a site, a building, a town.

Napster The most infamous file swapping utility/company. The Napster client allows you to connect to Napster servers and download MP3 files, or allows your own MP3 files to be downloaded by others. The popularity of Napster erupted into lawsuits brought by the RIAA and various recording artists. The actual Napster company had its assets sold off to the highest bidder, but the client lives on through Open Source projects like OpenNap.

Narrowband A general term in communication systems pertaining to a signal that has a small collection of differing frequency components (as opposed to broadband which has many frequency components) .

NAS (network attached storage) The use of specialized devices that function simply as hard drives connected to a network. NAS devices typically consist of one or more hard drives in a housing that contains a simple operating system and a network connection. The use of NAS devices allows for cheaper and more easily expandable storage without requiring more complex and expensive multi-purpose servers to do the work of delivering files to network users.

NAT (network address translation) A method that many ISPs use to extend their IP addressing to support more addresses than they own. The interior network uses one addressing scheme, and the exterior network uses the standard IPv4 Internet addressing. NAT devices can be routers, firewalls, or proxy-servers. To program a NAT device you must supply translation rules for how interior IP addresses are displayed to the outside world. You could, for example, set your firewall to act as if all traffic coming from inside your corporate network was coming from the firewall's IP address.

Native The availability of a software package written directly for an operating system as opposed to running in emulation under some type of translation process. Emulation usually runs slower and possibly less effectively than native versions. For example, Word Perfect and Microsoft Word have native versions for both Power Mac and Windows Chicago operating systems. Most Windows and DOS programs must be run in emulation on PowerPCs such that the speed advantages of the PowerPC are virtually lost due to not being able to run in native form. Market share determines the number of native software applications being developed for operating systems. Mac, UNIX, and other operating systems are losing the native software development war to Windows Chicago and Windows 2000. Windows Chicago is almost certain to become the PC operating system standard of choice until its upgrade called Windows Cairo rolls off the line and/or Windows 2000 with upgraded object-oriented programming features become the operating systems of choice among users having newer hardware speed and memory components.

Natural language This refers to a human language as opposed to a computer language. While computer languages such as C++ or Perl are very structured and are (arguably) designed to be clear in meaning to a parser, natural languages evolved over thousands of years and took on characteristics like accents, slang, inflection, local terminology, and meaning of words and phrases in context. The understanding and use of natural languages is a much harder problem for computers than understanding computer languages.

Navigation The navigation of a reader or user through learning and entertainment materials such as electronic books, courseware, and networks.

Navigation tools Allows users to find their way around a website or multimedia presentation. They can be hypertext links, clickable buttons, icons, or image maps.

Navigator A browser developed by Netscape, and the first to support Java Script.

Net (.net) The top level domain designated for entities and computers that represent part of the Internet's infrastructure. Originally intended for use by Network Information Centers (NICs), Network Operations Centers (NOCs), administrative computers (such as a name server) and network node computers. One of the worldwide top level domains.

Netscape A web browser created by Netscape Communications Corporation. The Netscape browser was originally based on the Mosaic program developed at the National Center for Supercomputing Applications (NCSA). It provided major improvements in speed and interface over other browsers, but also engendered debate by being the first to create browser-specific elements for HTML.

Network A group of computers and associated peripherals connected by a communications channel capable of sharing files and other resources between several users. A network can range from a peer-to-peer network connecting a small number of users in an office or department, to a local area network connecting many users over permanently installed cables and dial-up lines, or to a wide area network connecting users on several different networks spread over a wide geographic area.

Network access point (NAP) Telecommunications term for the location where a call (data or voice) enters the telecommunications network.

Network adapter This is a hardware unit that connects a device to a communication line. For wide area networks (WAN), these adapters connect routers to the specific type of connection (T1, BRI) that is installed. For local area networks (LAN), these adapters connect workstations to the LAN (Ethernet or TokenRing) cabling.

Network Computer (NC) A concept that came from the old days of dumb terminals and was a rehash of this idea promoted largely by Sun Microsystems. Network Computers were supposed to reduce the cost of standardized computers in the office environment but never really took off, as increasing application complexity demanded high-powered PCs.

Network driver interface specification (NDIS) This spec was designed by Microsoft to allow multiple protocols to easily communicate with Network Interface Cards (NICs) without knowing anything about those cards. In theory you just have to install the NDIS driver for the particular NIC and you can bind multiple protocols to it. Previously you had to unload one protocol stack to load another. NDIS allows multiple stacks on the same card.

Network operating system (NOS) An operating system designed to run across a network. It refers to the operating system that runs on a server, not the client. Network OSes are typically designed to provide access to server resources to clients, making the server function as a file server, print server, or other type of server.

Network security Protection of networks and their services from unauthorized modification, destruction, or disclosure, while still allowing them to perform their critical functions without harmful side-effects.

Network-to-network interface (NNI) The connection on telecommunications equipment between two disparate telecommunications networks.

Neural network A computing device which converts one or more input signals to one or more output signals by means of an interconnected set of elementary non-linear signal processors called neurons. Animal brains are examples of biological neural networks. Artificial Neural Networks are man-made computing devices modelled after their biological counterparts. The features which distinguish artificial neural networks from traditional Von Neumann (sequential) computers are: (a) the elementary processors are highly non-linear (in the limit, they are simple threshold discriminators), (b) the neurons are highly interconnencted which allows a high degree of parallelism and (c) there is no idle memory containing data and programs, but rather each neuron is pre-programmed and continuously active.

Newsgroups (usenet newsgroups) Also referred to simply as "newsgroups," Usenet newsgroups are a huge bunch of Internet discussion groups that replicate across the Internet every so often. If you get a bunch of people together and request a group for yourself, you'll probably be able to create it. Topics range from technical discussions and debate to flame wars. However, the most infamous use of the newsgroups is the distribution of binary pictures and files as text.

Nextstep An operating system developed by Steve Jobs, co-founder of Apple Computer. NEXTStep is a leader in GUI interfaces and has some native applications software such as Word Perfect and Mathematica up and running. The future of

NEXTStep was uncertain until Apple Corporation purchased the OS for $400 million in 1997 with the intention of making it the core of the future Mac and PowerMac operating systems. a revolutionary operating system from Apple Corporation that is based upon NEXTStep technology. Apple plans to deliver two operating systems for the next several years. First will be the Mac OS, which we will continue to upgrade and improve to support the current Macintosh customers worldwide, approximately 60 million users. Second will be a new OS based on NeXT Software's operating system technologies, NEXTStep and OPENStep. The powerful and advanced NeXT technologies are years ahead of competitive offerings, and will provide the foundation for a new OS, code-named Rhapsody. In addition to leveraging the NeXT technologies, Rhapsody is designed to run Mac applications through a Mac OS compatibility environment. Rhapsody's user interface will combine elements from both the Mac OS and NEXTStep, but will be closer in look and feel to the Mac OS Finder. We realize that customers need a consistent interface in the two operating systems to deploy them throughout a single organization. It's important for training and ease of use. One of the advantages of NeXT's technology is the easy support of multiple user interface paradigms.

NIS+ An extension to the Network Information Service (NIS) including hierarchical domains, incremental updates to other servers, multiple indices to database tables, and built-in security. Requires the Solaris operating system.

Nitroinspection Content Inspection technology built around a concept similar to the "stateful" inspection technologies that allows clients and the CI to receive the file at the same time. This method of scanning files is far superior to the older proxy method.

As soon as the last packet is received, it is held until the CI completes inspection. Once the CI scans and approves the file, the final packet is forwarded to the requesting client. In the event that the file contains a content threat, the final packet is prevented from completing its journey to the requesting client.

If the end user still attempts to open a file whose last packet has been blocked, the operating system informs the user that the file is corrupted and cannot be executed. This prevents a malicious file from endangering the end-user.

NLX (new low profile extended) The NLX form factor features a number of improvements over the previous design LPX form factor and began heavy usage in late 1997. The popularity of the design was confirmed by massive design use in 1998. The popularity has made it Intel's flagship line and one of the profit leaders in chipsets. Its features include:

1. Support for larger memory modules and DIMMs.

2. Support for the newest microprocessors, including the Pentium II using SEC packaging.

3. Support for AGP video cards.

4. Better access to motherboard components.

5. Support for dockable designs in which the motherboard can be removed without tools.

Node One computer/machine or address on a network. If you managed a network with 10 printers, 50 servers, and 150 client machines, you could say you managed a network with 210 nodes.

Noise In communications, extraneous signals on a transmission channel that degrade the quality or performance of the channel. Noise is often caused by interference from nearby power lines, from electrical equipment, or from spikes in the AC line voltage.

Non-breaking space (NBSP) An HTML command that is used to display a single text space without a visible character in that space. The format in HTML for this is   and it can be used to position text or to fool a browser into behaving like text is in a space when there is no text visible.

Non-productive content Any distractive content, which is not work related according to corporate policy. It includes spam, and Web sites in subjects such as gambling, travel, sports, nudity, racism, etc. Some surveys estimate that 75 percent of Web surfing occurs at work.

Employees often use valuable time and bandwidth accessing unproductive sites contrary to company policy. Additionally, there are hundreds of Web sites that hold collections of hacker tools or other malicious software. Employees with malicious intent often use these tool collections. Abuse of Internet privileges often leads to lost productivity, wasted bandwidth, or collections of illegal software and images.

Non-volatile ram (NVRAM) A typically small amount of RAM that stores information even after you turn off your computer. It is used in modems for storing your settings and in hardware keys for protecting software. Flash memory is a type of non-volatile RAM.

Normalize A verb used to describe what can be done to data to remove useless or extraneous entries. For example, if you set up a survey with choices A, B, and No Response, and then wanted to report the % of respondents that picked A or B, you could cut out the "No Responses" and thus normalize the data. Another example would be changing the loudness of an MP3 file by analyzing the file for the loudest part and then setting the loudness of the entire file to a percentage of that. That way, if you are putting together a mix file from many separate sources, you get a more uniform loudness.

Notebook computer A portable computer about the size of a standard ring binder notebook. Original laptop computers were about the size of a briefcase. Notebook computers later emerged that could be carried inside a briefcase. Next, sub-notebook computers were introduced that could be carried inside a suit pocket, although the most popular models presently are notebook size portables. Multimedia versions are slightly larger and heavier. Although notebook computers do not have expansion slots for hardware modifications, SCSI, Ethernet, ISBN, video caputure, and other hardware options are available on PCMCI cards.

Novell Network operating system vendor based in Provo, Utah. It designs, manufactures markets and service high-performance local-area network software and systems.

NP complete (nondeterministic polynomial time complete) Generally this is a class of problems that are so difficult that even the best solutions cannot consistently determine their solutions in an efficient way. Specifically, NP Complete problems can only possibly be solved in polynomial time using a nondeterministic Turing machine (a computer capable of making guesses and checking them in polynomial time). Problems such as weather prediction, how to fill a box with odd-sized objects, and the Traveling Salesman problem fall into the realm of NP Complete problems. Because of the problem with finding the "best" solution, programs are often developed to find a usually reasonable solution. Take this into account the next time your weatherperson can't predict the weather—there are just too many variables.

Null A character that has all the binary digits set to zero(ASCII 0), and therefore has no value.In programming, a null character is used for severa special purposes, including padding fields, or serving as delimiter characters. In the C language, for example, a null character indicates the end of a character string.

N-way A method of multiprocessing where each processor runs separate tasks with no special programming required. This is different from SMP, where one task can run across several processors and all processors must act together, requiring special programming to speed up specific tasks. The "N" stands for a number greater than one, where a system with two microprocessors would be a Two-Way system, and so on.

Nysernet An Internet network that links rural libraries with a high speed communications network. This network is a nonprofit, equal-access network that has strong backing from major computer vendors and publishing firms.

O

OAM(operations administration and maintenance) A group of network management functions that provide network fault indication, performance information, and data and diagnosis functions.

OBEX (Obeject exchange protocol) Is a sesson protocol developed by the IrDA that allows the exchange of data in a simple and spontaneous mannr. Previously known as IrOBEX, it provides the same basic functionality aHTTP.

Object management system In an IPSE IPSE, the system which maintains information about the system under development.

Object-oriented Applied to analysis, design and programming. The basic concept in this approach is that of objects, which consist of data structures encapsulated with a set of routines, often called "methods" which operate on the data. Operations on the data must be performed via these methods, which are common to all instances of objects of a particular class. Thus, the interface to objects is well defined, and allows the code implementing the methods to be changed so long as the interface remains the same.

OC(Optical Carrier) Representing the speed of fiber-optic networks. OC speeds can range anywhere between 1 and 48. Most hosting companies have OC3 connections, which allows for the transfer of data at a rate of up to 155.52 Mbps.

OCR (optical character recognition) Software and hardware used to interpret scanned symbols into characters of text or numbers recognized as something other than mere graphics images. The term is commonly used in such software as OmniPage Pro to indicate options of translating scanned words and numbers into computer text files that can be read by word processing and spreadsheet software. Leveraging ScanSoft's world-leading optical character recognition (OCR) and PDF conversion technology, the OmniPage Search Indexer creates index data from your document images, without changing the original. The ScanSoft OmniPage Search Indexer includes an OCR engine that is very fast and accurate, as well as a lightning fast PDF indexing engine - both tuned for search applications.

ODBC (open database connectivity) Support Open Database Connectivity (ODBC) refers to a standard for accessing different database systems in Visual Basic and Visual C++. Applications in most any software (e.g., Asymetrix ToolBook) can submit statements to ODBC using the ODBC type of SQL. ODBC then translates the code for use in common database systems such as Access, Paradox, dBase, Text, Excel and Btrieve databases. ODBC is based on Call-Level Interface and was defined by the SQL Access Group. Microsoft was one member of the group and was the first company to release a commercial product based on its work (under Microsoft Windows) but ODBC is not a Microsoft generated standard. ODBC drivers and development tools are available now for Microsoft Windows, Unix, OS/2, and Macintosh.

Office suite The set of software products that are required by an office, most often comprised of a spreadsheet program, a word processor, a scheduler, and a presentation manager. Sometimes the suites will include a financial package and a database program as well. These are put together by a single company, so they are made to work with one another.

Offline Being away from your computer or the Internet, or your computer being off and disconnected from the Internet. If you were a character in the movie Tron, you died when you went offline.

OLE (object linking and embedding) Standards established by Microsoft Corporation for Mac and Windows operating systems. In 1997, Microsoft declared that OLE no longer stands for object linking and embedding . Before 1997, however, OLE standards allowed the creation of links between documents and the embedding of documents in multiple applications. The OLE standards are designed to be "dynamic" in that as changes are made in an object in one document, the changes are simultaneously made automatically in all linked documents. For example, in pasting from the clipboard, authors choose the Paste Link or Paste Special command rather than the Paste command in the Edit menu. Pasting in this way creates a dynamic link between the source document and the destination document. OLE also supports embedding which embeds the source document (or a portion of the document) into the destination file such that the two documents become a "compound" file. Embedding is often used where a server file (creating embedded items) and client files (receiving embedded files) are in the system. In contrast to OLE linkages, OLE embedding edits in client files will not alter server files. This is not the case with OLE linkages, where any changes in a linked file will change all other linked files. Most word processor and spreadsheet software options have OLE capabilities.

Omtool A graphical tool from General Electric Advanced Concepts Center for design and analysis of systems with the OMT methodology with some C++/SQL code generation.

On-line service A computer you can call, log in to, and use, usually for a fee per hour. Some services provide a pecific set of information:Lexis, for example, provides legal information, and Nexis provides news. Others provide general information: CompuServe, Delphi, and Prodigy, for example provide a wide range of information, including weather, airline flights, and support for many software programs. Others, like MCI Mail, provide electronic mail.

OnLine transaction processing (OLTP) A group of programs that allow real-time inputting, recording, and retrieval of data to/from a networked system. The speed of recording the data is critical, as is the reaction time of the system, so that people entering data are not bogged down.

On-the-fly recording Sending data from your hard disk directly to the CD-R burner, without creating a *physical image file* first.

Ontology web language (OWL) The OWL Web Ontology Language is designed for use by applications that need to process the content of information instead of just presenting information to humans. OWL facilitates greater machine interpretability of Web content than that supported by XML, RDF, and RDF Schema (RDF-S) by providing additional vocabulary along with a formal semantics. OWL has three increasingly-expressive sublanguages: OWL Lite, OWL DL, and OWL Full.

Open A public standard in computer contexts that is the opposite of "proprietary." Open refers to software and hardware made from published specifications that anyone can copy — so customers have choice among multiple suppliers that compete on price and innovation.

Open architecture A vendor-independent cmputer design that is publicly available and well understood within the industry. An open architecture allows the user to configure the computer easily by adding expansion cards.

Open database connectivity (ODBC) A standard API for communicating with database servers. There are different ODBC drivers supporting most of the major database servers, such as Oracle and Microsoft SQL Server. If you program to ODBC you get the advantage of (theoretically) being able to easily use your application on different databases without reprogramming. However, ODBC drivers are not always perfect.

Open systems A concept based on offering hardware and software and capabilities defined by standards - produced by standards committees as well as those supported or demanded by users (i.e., de facto standards, such as those developed by Unix International or the Open Software Foundation). Typically, an open system provides Unix as a basic operating system, although that is not a requirement; what is required is that the system provide standard interfaces. An open system is a compliant implementation of an evolving set of vendor-neutral specifications for interfaces, services, protocols and formats. It is designed to let users configure, operate and substitute an entire system, its applications and components with other equally compliant implementations, preferably available from different vendors.

Openwindows A server program for the Sun which handles SunView SunView, NeWS NeWS and X Window System X-Window-Systemprotocols.

Operands When a computer is executing instructions in a program, the elements on which it performs the instructions are known as the operands.

Operating system The master control software system that serves as a foundation for applications software. Examples of past, present, and forthcoming operating systems include MS-DOS, Amiga DOS, Windows, Windows XP, Windows 2000, Windows Chicago, Windows Cairo, OS/2, Workplace OS, Apple/Mac Systems 7 and 8, Taligent (Pink), PowerOpen, NEXTStep, Rhapsody, Unix, SCO, AIX, HP/UX, HP/MPE, SCO Open Desktop, Solaris, and UnixWARE (Novell). A second class of operating systems is known as real time processing. These are used more for on-the-fly control systems such as aviation control systems and military applications. Examples include the Intel Multibus and iRMX operating systems. For 10 years, Apple Corporation would not license its proprietary Mac operating system to other manufacturers. However, in 1994 Apple announced that it would license its System 7 operating system to other vendors on PowerPC computers. In 1997, plans for Copeland and Gershwin upgrades were abandoned in favor or Rhapsody. However, Microsoft Windows still remains the market share choice. Then along came Linux to challenge the Microsoft's operating systems. Linux (pronounced Leenicks) is a freely-distributable implementation of UNIX that runs on a number of hardware platforms, including Intel and Motorola microprocessors. It is very popular among computer scientists who have freely given their time to develpment of Linux.

Optical disk (disque optique) Disk whose reading and writing mechanisms use laser optics instead of magnetism. Their lifetime is probably long : more than 30 years for the support, but can we ensure to find decades later compatible reading mechanisms. They can record relatively large quantities of data (500 MB in 1995), but their access time is slow.

Optical drive Any medium or device using a laser beam for accessing data stored on an optical disc. Typical optical drives are CD drives and videodisc drives. However, there are many types of optical drives including those that can be written on and re-written on much like floppy discs or computer tape. To date, most optical drives have slower access time than magnetic drives.

Oracle A vendor of database management systems.

Oracle card A hypercard hypercard-like product from Oracle Oracle for constructing DB applications, running on PC and Macintosh.

OS/2 (operating system 2) Introduced by IBM Corporation in 1992 and upgraded to OS/2 Warp in 1994. This is the first 32-bit processing system designed for PCs. It beat its rival Microsoft Windows 2000 to the market by almost two years. In early 1994, neither Windows 2000 nor OS/2 have made a huge dent in the DOS and Windows market. For example, there were only four million OS/2 adopters and 250,000 Windows 2000 adopters at the end of 1993 in comparison with over 40 million Microsoft Windows adopters. As older PCs are replaced by higher speed PCs with more memory, 32-bit processors will become more popular. OS/2 gets some high praises when compared with current 32-bit alternatives in PC/Computing Special Report. At issue is whether OS/2 or Windows 2000 or Pink or some other operating system will saturate the market (after DOS, Windows, Apple/Mac, and Windows Chicago stubbornly fade from the scene). OS/2 is a very reliable operating system that requires less PC capacity than Windows 2000. However, Windows 2000 has more networking utilities that may give it the competitive edge in the future. Until software vendors offer a wider array of options for either OS/2 or Windows 2000, the operating systems most widely used worldwide will continue to be DOS, Windows, and Windows Chicago. An alternate IBM operating system called Workplace OS combines the object-oriented Workplace with the OS/2 operating environment. Since OS/2 Warp has such a small market share, developers are not generating significant native software applications that run more efficiently in OS/2 vis-a-vis Windows. Although OS/2 Warp runs DOS applications better than MS-DOS itself, it is very slow when trying to run Windows applications. Neither Apple Corporation nor IBM Corporation have been able to significantly gain market share against Microsoft Windows.

Outsourcing A contractual relationship with an external provider characterised by the transfer of assets (both physical and human), to include facilities management, network management, network management, PC services, and/or application development/maintenance.

Overburning The process of recording more than 74 minutes of audio or more than 650 MB of data onto a CD-R disk. There are software programs that allow you to do this, and now there is media that supports larger storage than the standard CD-R normally holds.

Overclock To run a microprocessor faster than the speed for which it has been tested and approved. Overclocking is a popular technique for eking out a little more performance from a system. In many cases, you can force your CPU to run faster than it was intended simply by setting a jumper on the motherboard. Overclocking does come with some risks, however, such as over-heating, so you should become familiar with all the pros and cons before you attempt it.

Overclocking is sometimes called speed margining.

Overdrive A processor upgrade sold by Intel that is used to upgrade an older processor to a newer, faster processor.

Overflow This is when there is more information than can be properly handled. It is often used to describe the production of a number larger than a variable can handle. For instance, if you are expecting 10 digits but receive 11, that's overflow.

Owner alias An alias that points to the owner of a group alias triplet.

P

P2P (peer to peer) A method of distributing files over a network. Using P2P client software a client can advertise, send, or receive files with another client. Some P2P file distribution systems require a centralized database of available files (such as Napster), while other distribution systems (like Gnutella) are more decentralized.

PABX Private Branch Exchange. A telephone switch located on a customer's premises that primarily establishes voice-grade circuits (over tie lines to a telephone company central office) between individual users and the public-switched telephone network. The PABX also provides switching within the customer premises local area, and usually offers numerous enhanced features, including least-cost routing and call-details recording.

Page A web page is not comparable to a real page of printed material, such as a brochure or a page from this document. Web pages can be nearly any length, although for practical reasons most people limit them to less than 400 lines of 80 column text or less. A Web Page is a computer file written in the Hyper Text Markup Language (HTML).

Page-mode RAM A memory-management technique used to speed up the performance of dynamic RAM. In a page-mode memory system, the memory is divided into pages by specialized dynamic RAM chips. Consecutive accesses to memory addresses in the same page results in a page-mode cycle that takes about half the time of a regular dynamic RAM cycle.

Pages per minute (PPM) This term usually refers to the amount of printed pages a printer can output over a minute's time. The time is based on some average amount of ink or toner coverage on a page. If you are printing complex graphics on inkjet color printers, expect your printer to function more slowly than its PPM rating, as it has to make up to four passes over each area of a page instead of a single pass for black ink only.

Paintbrush software Software used to create new or modify imported graphics images and photographs. Options and prices vary widely. Important features to look for are the variety of filters that enable importing a wide variety of types of graphics images, the ability to resize and change aspect ratios of pictures, and the layering of objects in an image such that images behind layers can be recovered (this is a feature of Adobe Photoshop that is not available in most other software options). Alternative software features and options are reviewed in the annual NewMedia Tool Guide from NewMedia magazine in the 1995 edition. 2-D graphics software options are listed on pp. 40-43.

Palmtop computer A very small battery-powered portable computer that you can hold in one hand, often weighing about a pound.

Parallel This means in unison, or many things at the same time. It most commonly refers to a computer with multiple processors that can all function independently at the same time. It also refers to cabling or connection standards that use several wires to transmit data.

Parallel communications The transmission of information from computer to computer, or from computer to a peripheral, where all the bits that make up the character are transmitted at the same time over a multiline cable.

Parallel debugging Specialized approaches to locating and correcting errors in computer programs that are to be executed on parallel computing machine architectures.

Parallel port A parallel interface for connecting an external device such as a printer. Most personal computers have both a parallel port and at least one serial port. On PCs, the parallel port uses a 25-pin connector (type DB-25) and is used to connect printers, computers and other devices that need relatively high bandwidth. It is often called a Centronics interface after the company that designed the original standard for parallel communication between a computer and printer. (The modern parallel interface is based on a design by Epson.).

A newer type of parallel port, which supports the same connectors as the Centronics interface, is the EPP (Enhanced Parallel Port) or ECP (Extended Capabilities Port). Both of these parallel ports support bi-directional communication and transfer rates ten times as fast as the Centronics port.

Macintoshes have a SCSI port, which is parallel, but more flexible.

Parameter RAM A small part of the Macintosh random-access memory that holds information including the hardware configuration, the date and time, which disk is the startup disk, and information about the state of the Desktop. The contents of PRAM are maintained by a battery, and so the contents are not lost when the Mac is turned off or unplugged at the end of session.

Parent directory The directory that contains the current working directory. That is the current working directory is a subdirectory of the parent directory.

Parent node The logical group node that represents the containing peer group of a specific node at the next higher level of the hierarchy.

Parent peer group The parent peer group of a peer group is the one containing the logical group node representing that peer group. The parent peer group of a node is the one containing the parent node of that node.

Parity In communications, a simple form of error checking that uses an extra, or redundant bit, after the data bits but before the stop bit(s).

Parity may be set to odd, even, mark, space, or none. Odd parity indicates that the sum of all the 1 bits in the byte plus the parity bit must be odd. If the total is already odd, the parity bit is set to zero; if it is even, the parity bit is set to 1.

In even parity, the sum of all the 1 bits is even, the parity bit must be set to 1; if it is odd, the parity bit must be set to 1.

In mark parity, the parity bit is always set to 1, and is used as the eighth bit.

In space parity, the parity bit is set to 0, and used as the eighth bit.

If parity is set to none, there is no parity bit, and no parity checking is performed.

The parity setting on your computer must match the setting on the remote computer for successful communications. Most online services use no parity and an eight-bit data word.

Parity bit An extra or redundant bit used to detect transmission errors.

Parity checking A check mechanism applied to a character or series of characters that uses the addition of extra or redundant bits known as parity bits. Parity checking is used in situations as diverse as asynchronous communications and computer memory coordination.

Park To move the hardisk read/write heads to a safe area of the disk (called a landing zone) before you turn your system off, to guard against damage when the computer is moved. Most modern hard disks park their heads automatically, and so you do not need to run a special program to park the heads.

Parking All domain names have to be stored on a server in order to be purchased. Most domain registration services will therefore temporarily place a newly purchased name on their servers until a hosting plan is purchased or the owner points the DNS to a different site. This is known as parking.

Parlog++ An object-oriented extension to MacParlog. It combines object-oriented object-oriented and parallel logic programming logic-programming, giving the benefits of both paradigms within a single coherent development environment.

Parser Aprogram that receives input from sequential source program instructions, interactive online commands, markup tags, or some other defined interface and breaks them up into parts (for example, the nouns (objects), verbs (methods), and their attributes or options) that can then be managed by other programming (for example, other components in a compiler). A parser may also check to see that all input has been provided that is necessary.

Partition A section of a hard drive. You must create at least one partition to begin using a new hard drive, and you can create multiple partitions and keep chunks of your data separate. It is also possible to install multiple OSes on these multiple partitions. Usually it's just one OS per partition, but some OSes, like Windows 95/98/Me and Windows NT/2000/XP, for example, are designed to run together in the same partition as long as you use a compatible file system to format the partition.

Partition table In DOS,an area of the hard disk containing information on how the disk is organized.

It also contains information that tells the computer which OS to load.

Pascal A programming language that was designed to teach computer science students the concepts of programming. It's almost like C for dummies. In fact, the two languages are very similar, but the stoic brackets of C are changed to happy and fluffy "Begin" and "End" statements. Also, many of the more complex functions of C are missing, but Pascal is still a fully functional language. Borland used Pascal as the basis for its Delphi programming language.

Password A code used to gain access to a locked system. Effective passwords should contain both letters and non-letters and not be common or easily guessed words.

Password authentication protocol (PAP) The most basic access control protocol for logging onto a network. A table of usernames and passwords is stored on a server. When users log on, their usernames and passwords are sent to the server for verification. Contrast with CHAP, which encrypts the username and password before transmitting it.

Password encryption The encryption of passwords to prevent sniffers from obtaining a password.

Paste To insert information from the Clipboard. Information can be pasted multiple times.

Patch A set of tone-generating parameters that determine the instrument imitation (flute, violin, etc.) of a synthesizer.

Patch cable The common name for any network cable that is used to connect, or "patch," any two network ports.

Patch panel A group of network ports stuck

together for easy accessibility. Usually this panel resides in a wiring closet or server room. Connections are made between this panel and ports on a hub to enable a network connection at a remote port. Each port on the patch panel is connected by a longer cable (often run through the ceiling) to a remote port anywhere in an office that needs a computer hooked up to the network.

Path A path can be described as a file's address on your file system, describing where the file lives: An absolute path gives the complete path, starting at the root directory, or the very top of the file system; A relative path looks for a file from the directory you are currently in down.

Path constraint A bound on the combined value of a topology metric along a path for a specific connection.

Pathname Instructions for how to get to a file. An absolute pathname tells you how to find a file beginning at the root directory and working down the tree. A relative pathname tells you how to find the file starting where you are now.

Pathologically eclectic rubbish lister (PERL) A programming scripting language used heavily in systems administration and web programming with the Common Gateway Interface (CGI).

Pathway Emulation software produced by the Wollongong company.

Pattern recognition A process used by some artificial-intelligence systems to identify a variety of patterns, including visual patterns, information patterns buried in a noisy signal, and word patterns imbedded in text.

PAW (physics analysis workbench) General purpose portable tool for analysis and presentation of physics data.

Payload The eventual action taken by a virus once it has installed itself on a system. This action may be immediate, or it could wait for some trigger in the future, such as a specific date or a certain amount of time, to take action. The possible actions of a virus are limited to your imagination, although some payloads include deletion of files, formatting hard drives, or simply displaying a message to the user.

PB (petabyte) This is 250 bytes. One thousand terabytes/one million gigabytes/one billion megabytes/one trillion kilobytes/one quadrillion bytes (approximately).

PC (personal computer) That is compatible with the IBM desktop computers. PCs that are not manufactured by IBM Corporation are typically referred to as "clones." Generally, programs written on any PC will play on another PC. Most PC users now run under Microsoft DOS or Microsoft Windows operating systems. Newer and more advanced processors include OS/2 from IBM and Windows 2000 from Microsoft Corporation. Programs written on a Mac operating system will not usually run on a PC. Differences between Mac and PC computers have led to constant frustrations for authors since there is no single standard for authoring materials that can be used across the computer market. This is especially frustrating for authors of CD-ROM learning and entertainment materials. PC computers using the early Intel 8088 processor were called XT models. The XT's gave way to the AT models containing the 80286 or higher level Intel processors. Now the model names usually contain the processor specifications such as Intel 386, 486, and Pentium designations. The top-rated PCs at the end of 1994 are Dell Dimension (Rank 1), Micron PCI (Rank 2), Gateway P% (Rank 3), and IBM ValuPoint (Rank 4) according to PC Computing, December 1994, p. 126. Two pages later, that same magazine ranks the best-buys in portables as TravelMate 4000M from Texas Instruments (Rank 1), Latitude XP from Dell (Rank 2), and ThinkPad755C from IBM (Rank 3).

Pc card A Hardware and Software specification for small add-in cards for portable PC's. It builds on the old PCMCIA technology that failed to work correctly.

Pc card slot An opening in the case of a portable computer intended to receive a PC Card; also known as a PCMCIA slot.

PC protocol control Protocol Control is a mechanism which a given application protocol may employ to determine or control the performance and health of the application. Example, protocol liveness may require that protocol control information be sent at some minimum rate; some applications may become intolerable to users if they are unable to send at least at some minimum rate. For such applications, the concept of MCR is defined. Refer to MCR.

PC/SC A standard developed by for ensuring compatibility between smart cards, card reader/writers, and computers produced by different manufacturers. It supports business-specific application standards such as EMV (Europay, MasterCard, Visa) and GSM (Global Standard for Mobile Communication).

PC100 (pc100 SDRAM) The standard that SDRAM makers adhere to to be sure that SDRAM running at 100MHz works properly. PC100 SDRAM normally works fine in 66MHz SDRAM motherboards.

Pc1066 SDRAM Rambus RDRAM that runs at a speed of 533MHz double-pumped to an effective speed of 1.06GHz. Memory throughput in systems featuring this type of DRAM is 2.1GB/second per 16-bit channel, or 4.2GB/second per 32-bit channel.

PC133 (pc133 SDRAM) A type of SDRAM that is designed to be run at 133MHz operation. It is pin-compatible with PC100 SDRAM and 66MHz SDRAM, and comes in a DIMM form factor.

PC1600 (pc1600 DDR SDRAM) DDR SDRAM running at 100MHz double-pumped to an effective speed of 200MHz. It has a maximum data transfer rate of 1.6GB/second for one PC1600 channel.

PC200 DDR SDRAM The DDR memory chips used to assemble PC1600 DDR memory modules.

PC2100 DDR SDRAM A type of DDR SDRAM running at 133MHz double-pumped to an effective speed of 266MHz. It is referred to as PC2100 because systems featuring DDR SDRAM at 266MHz have a maximum data transfer rate of 2.1GB/second.

PC266 DDR SDRAM The DDR memory chips used to assemble PC2100 DDR memory modules.

PC2700 (pc2700 DDR SDRAM) A type of DDR SDRAM running at 166MHz double-pumped to an effective speed of 333MHz. It is referred to as PC2600 because of its maximum data transfer rate of 2.7GB/second.

PC3200 (pc3200 DDR SDRAM) A type of DDR SDRAM running at 200MHz double-pumped to an effective speed of 400MHz. It is referred to as PC3200 because of its maximum data transfer rate of 3.2GB/second in a single 64-bit channel.

PC333 DDR SDRAM The DDR memory chips used to assemble PC2700 DDR memory modules.

PC400 DDR SDRAM The DDR memory chips used to assemble PC3200 DDR memory modules.

PC600 RDRAM Rambus RDRAM that runs at a speed of 266MHz double-pumped to an effective speed of 532MHz. Memory throughput in systems featuring this type of DRAM is about 1.06GB/second.

PC700 RDRAM Rambus RDRAM that runs at a speed of 356MHz double-pumped to an effective speed of 712MHz. Memory throughput in systems featuring this type of DRAM is about 1.42GB/second.

PC800 RDRAM Rambus RDRAM that runs at a speed of 400MHz double-pumped to an effective speed of 800MHz. Memory throughput in systems featuring this type of DRAM is 1.6GB/second.

PCA A dynamic analyser from DEC giving information on run time performance and code utilisation.

P-CAD A CAE CAE system marketed by CADAM, an IBM company.

PCB (printed circuit board) The normally green plastic board that is imprinted with one or more layers of circuitry. Examples of common PCBs include motherboards, PCI cards, and AGP cards. The boards can hold microchips and other components, and are a way to link such components together.

Pc-dos The version of the DOS operating system supplied with PCs sold by IBM.

PCI(peripheral component interconnect) A specification introduced by Intel that defines a local bus that allows up to ten PCI-compliant expansion cards to be plugged into the computer. One of these ten cards must be the PCI controller card, but the others can include a video card, network interface card,SCSI interface, or any other basic I/O function.The PCI controller exchanges information with the computer's processor as 32- or 64- bits, and allows intelligent PCI adapters to perform certain tasks concurrently with the main processor by using bus mastering techniques.

PCI-X (peripheral component interconnect extended) An extension to the PCI interface developed by IBM, HP, and Compaq. The extension allows data to be transferred at 1 GB per second using a 64-bit bus running at 133MHz. PCI-X peripherals are fully compatible with PCI and vice-versa, but will not run faster than the chipset or peripheral allows.

PCL (printer control language) A set of commands used to communicate with Hewlett Packard printers. Each printer company has its own language, but PCL has become a generic term to describe these languages.

PCM (pulse code modulation) Of audio waveform sampling that records actual values rather than the ADPVM difference between samples. This decreases fidelity with higher resolution than ADPCM.

PCMCIA (personal computer memory card international association) Defined standards for memory card external slots (ports) to peripheral devices such as fax modems. PCMCIA slots are common in printers, and notebook/laptop computers, but these "slots" have been troubled technologies from the start. The Type I slots are 3.3 mm thick and serve mainly as memory cards. The Type II slots are more input/output compatible with fax modems and LAN adapters. The Type III slots are 10.5 mm thick and can be used for porting to some auxiliary storage devices such as external hard drives. One problem is that some vendors who claim to have Type III slots are really manufacturing with only Type II slots stacked on top of each other giving rise to a .5 mm incompatibility difference. There is also some doubt whether PCMCIA technology can be expanded to 32 bit and 64 bit processors of the future.

PCO(point of control and observation) A place (point) within a testing environment where the occurrence of test events is to be controlled and observed as defined by the particular abstract test method used.

PCR (program clock reference) A timestamp that is inserted by the MPEG-2 encoder into the Transport Stream to aid the decoder in the recovering and tracking the encoder clock.

PCTE(portable common tool environment) An ECMA ECMA standard framework for software tools developed in the Esprit Esprit programme. It is based on an entity-relationship Object Management System Object-Management-System and defines the way in which tools access.

PCX A bit-mapped file format for graphics designed by Z-Soft. The programs Paintbrush and Paint Shop Pro let you create and edit PCX images.

PDA (personal digital assistant) PDAs are basically beefed-up organizers or toned-down laptops. They have small LCD screens, some form of pen or keyboard input, and software for organization, OCR, and contact management. Some have even more features, such as Web browsing or Internet e-mail. Most PDAs are designed to fit in one hand while you use the other hand for input.

PDA and PDF Portable Document Aassistant PostScript formatting technology that attempts to provide a viable way of exchanging documents across operating systems and different types of software. The of the best known PDA option is the Acrobat tools from Adobe Corporation that gives rise to PDF documents in Protable Document Format file extensions. Acrobat also provides other utilities such as the Distiller tool that translates PostScript files into a PDF format, the Exchange tool that facilitates insertion of hypertext linkages, the PDF Writer containing printer drivers, and other utilities.

PDF (portable document format) A format developed by Adobe. Adobe makes a freeware Adobe Acrobat Reader program that is available for a variety of platforms. Thus, using a variety of operating systems, you can download and read a PDF document with very little hassle. In addition, the PDF format strives for easy printing, viewing, and compact storage. On PCs .pdf is the file extension for this type of file.

Peer-to peer communication A network computer that both shares resources with other computers and accesses the shared resources of other computers.

Pen drive A small keyring-sized device that can be used to easily transfer files between USB-compatible systems. Available in a range of capacities (and in some cases, with an MP3 player built-in). Plug it in to any USB port and it will be automatically detected by the Operating System.

Pentium A CISC high speed processor that followed the 486 processors of Intel. The Pentium runs much faster than the 486 in most instances and, thereby, is a better alternative for graphics, audio, and video processing. It is also better suited to newer operating systems such as Windows Chicago and Windows 2000. Early versions tended to overheat and had an unknown life and reliability. Later versions of Pentium processors such as the P54C overcame all doubts about Intel's ability to produce a cool running CISC processor at speeds up to 100 MHz and plans to produce even faster Pentiums. These newer versions dispel all doubts about "Intel's aim to crunch the PowerPC" according to Information Week, February 21, 1994, p. 60. The comparative advantages, and they are serious advantages in the market, are the ability to run DOS and Windows applications in direct rather than emulation form in Pentium processors. This is not the case with PowerPC alternatives. Also, some users prefer CISC to RISC.

Peripheral Any device that is not part of the motherboard, aside from memory and the CPU. For example, video cards, sound cards, modems, and hard drives are peripherals. When speaking about the exterior of a PC peripheral refers to anything that can be connected to the exterior of a PC, like an LCD monitor or FireWire hard drive.

Permanent IP address An IP address that is defined for the PC and is not used by any device on the network.

Personal digital assistant (PDA) PDAs are basically beefed-up organizers or toned-down laptops. They have small LCD screens, some form of pen or keyboard input, and software for organization, OCR, and contact management. Some have even more features, such as Web browsing or Internet e-mail. Most PDAs are designed to fit in one hand while you use the other hand for input.

Phishing Short for Password Harvesting Fishing. It is the luring of sensitive information, such as passwords and other personal information, from a victim by masquerading as someone trustworthy with a real need for such information. Popular targets are users of online banking services, and auction sites such as eBay. Phishers usually work by sending out spam e-mail to large numbers of potential victims. Typically the email will appear to come from a trustworthy company and contain a subject and message intended to alarm the recipient into taking action.

A common approach is to tell the recipient that their account has been de-activated due to a problem and inform them that they must take action to re-activate their account. The user is provided with a convenient link in the same email that takes the email recipient to a fake web page appearing to be that of a trustworthy company. Once at that page, the user enters her personal information which is then captured by the fraudster.

Photo CD A CD that contains up to 100 high quality photographs developed by Kodak from 35 mm film directly onto a CD-ROM or a CD-I disc. PhotoCD files generally have a pcd extension and can be played back on Kodak software. New Photo CD Portfolio and Create-It software from Kodak (800-CD-KODAK) facilitate presentations such as classroom lectures and outside presentations to be pressed to Photo CDs. However, the Photo CD disc only stores graphics images (including text stored as a graphic) and will not store files that can be executed in computer software such as playing back a ToolBook book or HyperCard stack or storing a Lotus or Excel spreadsheet file. (In contrast, a CD-ROM disc will store computer files that can be read into execution files.) Reading of such discs requires special software. Also, CD-ROM drives have to be sufficiently fast (e.g., double or triple speed) to playback Photo CD discs. CD-I and related machines that play on television sets rather than computers will also play Photo CD discs.

PHP (hypertext preprocessor) Is a server-side, HTML-embedded scripting language used to create dynamic Web pages. In an HTML document, PHP script (similar syntax to that of Perl or C) is enclosed within special PHP tags. Because PHP is embedded within tags, the author can jump between HTML and PHP (similar to ASP and Cold Fusion) instead of having to rely on heavy amounts of code to output HTML. Because PHP is executed on the server, the client cannot view the PHP code. PHP can perform any task any CGI program can, but its strength lies in its compatibility with many types of databases. Also, PHP can talk across networks using IMAP, SNMP, NNTP, POP3 or HTTP.

Phreaker The skilled saboteur who relies on guile and the fallibility of employees in an information system. Employees do not necessarily have to be co-conspirators. The phreaker takes advantage of their innocence and trusting nature. The term is used in contrast to a hacker and a cracker. A hacker is a person who relies only upon technology to hack into the system (e.g., by breaking the encryption code.) Whereas a hacker usually breaks in without intention to harm the system or for personal gain, a "hacker" turns into a "cracker" when the intention becomes more sinister. A "phreaker" may do some hacking or cracking, but the to be a phreaker the saboteur must also rely upon human fallibility.

Physical drive A real device in the computer that you can see or touch, rather than a logical drive, which is a part of the hard disk that functions as if it were a separate disk drive but is not. One physical drive may be divided into several logical drives.

PICS (protocol implementation conformance statement) A statement made by the supplier of an implementation or system stating which capabilities have been implemented for a given protocol.

Piezoelectric crystal An electronic component that when subjected to a current will produce a waveform signal at a precise rate, which can then be used as a clock signal in a computer.

PIN (personal identification number) A password, usually numeric, used in conjunction with a cryptographic token, smart card, or bank card, to ensure that only an authorized user can activate an account governed by the token or card.

Pin An exposed and rigid metal wire. A group of pins make up a "male" connector, and you can plug it into a compatible female connector. On motherboards and add-on cards you can often connect pins electrically with a jumper to change features on the boards. Pins are also found on cables with male connectors.

Ping of death A DoS exploit that uses the Ping utility. The exploit requires the transmission of a packet greater than 65536 bytes. This leads to a buffer overflow on the receiving system, with sometimes disastrous and often unpredictable results. This exploit was widely used because many different platforms were susceptible, and the attacker only needed to know the system's IP address. Most platforms now have effective patches and fixes, and the exploit is no longer as dangerous as it once was.

PIO (programmed input/output) Input/Output standards on IDE hard disk drives. If you have a hard drive that supports one PIO mode, you need your interface to support it as well for maximum performance. The data transfer rates for the various PIO modes are: PIO mode 0 - 3.3Mbps; PIO mode 1 - 5.2Mbps; PIO mode 2 - 8.3Mbps; PIO mode 3 - 11.1Mbps; PIO mode 4 - 16.6Mbps. Ultra IDE doubles the data transfer rate of PIO mode 4.

Pipeline The technique of processing multiple parts of an instruction at the same time. Many processors have two or more instruction pipelines—think of them as automobile assembly lines. As one instruction is executed, the next instruction is being decoded, and the one after that is being fetched from memory (i.e., Ellen welds the frame of one car, while Frank paints another one, and Jimmy puts the tires onto the finished frame of another car). The pipeline is only as fast as its slowest member (i.e., if it takes Jimmy an hour to put on some tires then it doesn't matter that Ellen can weld the frame in 20 minutes; either the line will slow down, or you need three Jimmys for optimal performance). The speed-up you get from having a pipeline is about equal to the amount of pieces of pipe, though it's slightly slower due to the fact that the first instruction executed begins to fill the empty pipeline (i.e., Jimmy can't put on any tires if Ellen is still welding the frame of the first car through the line!). If something happens that empties the pipeline then performance suffers—the penalty is greater with larger pipelines. For some practical examples, the original PowerPC G4 has a 7-stage pipeline, while the Pentium 4 has a 20-stage pipeline. Processors with smaller pipelines are typically seen as more efficient, but at higher speeds the short pipeline can be limiting.

Pixel (picture element) The smallest dot that a monitor can display at a particular resolution. Screen size is often referred to in pixels: 800 x 600, for example. This means that the screen is 800 pixels across by 600 pixels vertically.

A pixel is a single point in a graphic image. Graphics monitors display pictures by dividing the display screen into thousands (or millions) of pixels, arranged in rows and columns. The pixels are so close together that they appear connected.

The number of bits used to represent each pixel determines how many colors or shades of gray can be displayed. For example, in 8-bit color mode, the color monitor uses 8 bits for each pixel, making it possible to display 2 to the 8th power (256) different colors or shades of gray.

On color monitors, each pixel is actually composed of three dots — a red, a blue, and a green one. Ideally, the three dots should all converge at the same point, but all monitors have some convergence error that can make color pixels appear fuzzy.

The quality of a display system largely depends on its resolution, how many pixels it can display, and how many bits are used to represent each pixel. VGA systems display 640 by 480, or about 300,000 pixels. In contrast, SVGA systems display 1,024 by 768, or nearly 800,000 pixels. True Color systems use 24 bits per pixel, allowing them to display more than 16 million different colors.

Plastic fiber optics An optical fiber where the core transmission media is plastic in contrast to glass or silica cores. Proposed plastic fibers generally have larger attenuation and dispersion than glass fiber but may have applications where the distance is limited. Plastic systems may also offer lower cost connectors that may be installed with simple tools and a limited amount of training.

Plug in Has a meaning that can vary with context. The most common meaning in WWW browsers is reader (runtime, playback, view) software that will "plug" into the browser such that when a file extension (e.g., PDF, TBK, WAV, AVI, MOV, etc.) is encountered the browser will view or download the file automatically and run that file. Most plug-in readers are free. Examples include the PDF Acrobat reader from <http://www.adobe.com/>, the shockwave reader from <http://www.macromedia.com/>, the neuron reader from <http://www.asymetrix.com/>, and movie readers from <http://www.texas.net>. VRML readers are usually browser plug-ins.

Podcasts Those amateur or professional audio or video programs delivered automatically to a subscriber's computer or MP3 player—let consumers listen to their favorite shows whenever and wherever they want. But though the technology for podcast subscriptions has been around for several years, the mainstream has only recently caught on.

POH (path overhead) A maintenance channel transmitted in the SONET overhead following the path from the beginning multiplexer to the ending demultiplexer. This is not implemented in SONET Lite.

Point of presence (POP) A local telephone number through which you can access your ISP. The largest national ISPs have POPs all over the country.

Point to point A type of network communication where information is sent from a single source to a single destination, eliminating any extraneous data transmission.

Pointer (1) In programming, think of a pointer as an address. The address can point to just about anything, including another pointer. Ultimately, if you follow the trail of pointers you'll probably find some data—pointers are most often used to point to data. The purpose of pointers is so that when you are programming you can pass around a small address that points to some data, instead of passing the actual data around.

(2) Pointers can also refer to the icon on the screen that you move around with a mouse or other pointing device. In a GUI environment you need a pointer to point to things so that you can select them.

Point-to-multipoint connection A Point-to-Multipoint Connection is a collection of associated ATM VC or VP links, with associated endpoint nodes, with the following properties: One ATM link, called the Root Link, serves as the root in a simple tre e topology. When the Root Node sends information, all of the remaining nodes on the connection, called Leaf Nodes, receive copies of the information.

2. Each of the Leaf Nodes on the connection can send information directly to the Root Node. The Root Node cannot distinguish which Leaf is sending information without additional (higher layer) information.

Polling The process by which a computer periodically ask each terminal or device on a LAN if it has message to send, and then allows each to send data in turn. On a multipoint connection or a point-to-point connection, polling is the process whereby data stations are invited one at a time to transmit.

Polymorphic virus A virus that attempts to evade all but the most advanced scanners by changing itself each time it creates a new copy. It does this by using different machine code commands which accomplish the same thing, or by re-arranging the order of the commands.

Polymorphism In object-oriented object-orientedprogramming, the term is used to describe variables which may refer at run-time to objects of different classes. For example, the variable "myVehicle" could refer to an object of class "motorCar" or "Truck".

Polyvinyl chloride (PVC) The common vinyl shielding used to cover the pairs in the copper four-pair wire used for numerous Ethernet standards. When burned it gives off deadly fumes, so plenum wire must be used in certain office buildings instead of PVC.

POP (point of presence, also post office protocol) Two commonly used meanings: A Point of Presence usually means a city or location where a network can be connected to, often with dial up phone lines. So if an Internet company says they will soon have a POP in Belgrade, it means that they will soon have a local phone number in Belgrade and/or a place where leased lines can connect to their network.

A second meaning, Post Office Protocol refers to a way that e-mail client software, such as Outlook, gets mail from a mail server. When you obtain an account from an Internet Service Provider (ISP) you almost always get a POP account with it, and it is this POP account that you tell your e-mail software to use to get your mail. Another protocol called IMAP is replacing POP for email.

Port First and most frequently, a port is where information goes into and/or out of a computer, such as the serial port on a PC. Secondly, a "port" often refers to the number appearing after the colon (:) in a domain name, such as http://www.example.com:7000/. Thirdly, to "port" something refers to translating a piece of software from one computer platform to another (for example, from Windows to Macintosh).

Port replicator A device that is used to provide laptops—with limited ports and expansion options built-in—with a larger amount of ports and expandability. Most port replicators are proprietary devices that work with one particular model of laptop and add extra ports such as additional USB and PS/2 ports and sound line-in and line-out ports.

Portable computer Technically, any computer that features a self-contained screen to allow it to easily be moved around. The first "luggable" portables were as big as a suitcase and had small CRT monitors, then came the with orange gas-plasma screens, and then laptops with LCD screens. Portable computers also usually have their own power source.

Portal (web portal) A term coined to describe the large search engine sites, such as Yahoo! and Lycos, that have branched off to offer a wide variety of services. The idea is that a Web user would peer at the Web by using only one website: the portal. For example, you go to a portal to do searches, get stock quotes, buy things, etc. It would be your everything site. Each portal site wants to offer one of each type of service so that a user never has to leave the site.

POSIX The IEEE portable operating system interface. POSIX defines a family of definitions of how parts of computer systems work with each other and incidentally, with users. POSIX is intended to look just like Unix but to be independent of any specific vendor. There are about a dozen members of the POSIX family; the one you care about is 1003.2 (known as "dot two") and the related user portability extension (UPE). Together, they define the way the commands and shells work. A system that compiles with 1003.2 and UPE looks enough like Unix that everything in this book applies to it.

POST (power-on self test) A series of diagnostic tests that run automatically when you turn your computer on. The actual tests can differ depending on how the BIOS is configured, but usually the POST tests the RAM, the keyboard, and the disk drives. If the tests are successful, the computer boots itself. If the tests are unsuccessful, the computer reports the error by emitting a series of beeps and possibly displaying an error message and code on the display screen. The number of beeps indicates the error, but differs from one BIOS to another.

Postscript A page description language page-description-language from Adobe Systems Inc. Its primary application is to describe the appearance of text, graphical shapes and sampled images on printed or displayed pages. A program in PostScript can communicate a document description from a composition system to a printing system in a device-independent way. Many printers now interpret PostScript directly.

Power supply A part of the computer that converts the power from a wall outlet into the lower voltages, typically 5 to 12 volts DC, required internally in the computer. PC power supplies are usually rated in watts, ranging from 90 watts at the low end to 300 watts at the high end. If the power supply in your computer fails, nothing works, not even the fan.

PowerPC A revolutionary new desktop RISC computer emerging from a joint venture between Apple Corporation, Motorola, and IBM. What is revolutionary is the ability of the PowerPC to run under Apple, OS/2, DOS, Windows, and Unix operating systems. This is a remarkably fast and cheap CPU using RISC chip technology. IBM was the first company to introduce the PowerPC notebook computer. For a time it looked like the PowerPC would indeed capture enormous chunks of market share from Intel, but then in hurried desperation Intel introduced its 90-MHz and 100-MHz O54C CISC processors. With the new CISC Pentiums and RISC NexGen alternatives selling at a much faster clip than Mac and IBM PowerPC processors, it appears that PowerPC will have a tough time selling to users other than Mac users who want faster processors for the Apple operating systems. Later versions of Pentium processors such as the P54C overcame all doubts about Intel's ability to produce a cool running CISC processor at speeds up to 100 MHz and plans to produce even faster Pentiums. These newer versions dispel all doubts about "Intel's aim to crunch the PowerPC" according to Information Week, February 21, 1994, p. 60. The comparative advantages of the Intel processors, and they are serious short-term advantages in the market, are the abilities of Intel processors to run DOS and Windows applications in direct rather than the emulation form used in PowerPCs and Macs. The main drawback of the PowerPC is that PowerPC users can only run DOS and Windows applications in emulation form such that all speed advantages of the PowerPC are lost. For this reason, the "PC" part of the tradename "PowerPC" is somewhat misleading since most PC users run under DOS and/or Windows operating systems. Certainly users who prefer to stay in a DOS and/or Windows operating system are advised to stick with the 486, Pentium, or some other CPU alternative that does not require emulation. When applications vendors bring applications to market in PowerOpen, Pink, and planned PowerPC native software, Intel and NexGen may lose market share to PowerPC, but this probably will not happen to a major extent in this century, largely due to the fact that PowerPC requires replacement of existing computers with new PowerPC computers. Worldwide, this will not happen for years due to tight budgets in business and government. It will be years before software developers offer PowerPC native software anywhere close to the present Windows product lines. IBM is also working with Apple to develop the PowerOpen operating system for the PowerPC. Taligent is developing the Pink operating system for the PowerPC. It will only be a short time before portable (e.g., Tadpoles and PowerBooks) and multimedia PowerPC lines are produced, although demand for these portable versions leads to long delivery delays. Another drawback of the PowerPC is that the alliance between IBM and Apple was weakened somewhat by delays in developing a PowerPC that will switch back and forth between Mac and IBM operating systems (e.g., between Mac and OS/2 or Mac and Windows). Users still have to make that big choice between one operating system or another. Good news includes the current availability of some popular software packages designed specifically for the PowerPC such as WordPerfect native Power Macintosh. Bad news includes the decision of Lotus Corporation not to produce native PowerPC versions at the present time. Even more discouraging for PowerPC hopefuls are analyst forecasts of the pent up demand for Windows 95 and Windows 2000 that will probably lead consumers toward Intel and NexGen processors. At the moment, it's still a horse race between Intel and PowerPC with PowerPC far behind and waning hopes for a burst of speed. A huge area of concern has been the tapering off of demand for the new Power Mac versions of the PowerPC. Apple's share of the PC market reached 14% in 1993, but has since slipped back down to less than 5%. Apple admits to losing the operating system war to Microsoft. Mac, UNIX, and other operating systems are losing the native software development war to Windows 95, 97, and Windows 2000. Windows 2000 is almost certain to become the PC operating system standard of choice until its upgrade called Windows Cairo rolls off the line and/or Windows 2000 with upgraded object-oriented programming features become the operating systems of choice among users having newer hardware speed and memory components.

PPP (point to point protocol) PPP is a superset of the TCP/IP protocols. Built upon that foundation, but instead of allowing one computer to be able to talk to many, it relies on the fact that the other computer it's linked with has that ability and therefore does not need it.

Language spoken by printers and the programs that communicate with these printers. PostScript enables printers to print a wonderful array of characters in all kinds of sizes and shapes, as well as pictures. When a program wants to print something on a PostScript printer, rather than just send the characters to print, it has to send a PostScript program that tells the printer how to print the stuff.

Practical extraction and report language (PERL) Created by system admin Larry Wall in the mid 1980s, this programming language was originally intended to fill a gap and help out with administration tasks. From those meager beginnings PERL has become a programming language often associated with the Web and UNIX. PERL is the most common programming language used to program CGI scripts. It is a very powerful language that can be used to easily modify large amounts of text files with hardly any programming required. PERL aficionados use it for doing everything.

PRAM Am small portion of the Mac's RAM set aside to hold basic information such as the date and time, speaker volume, desktop pattern, and key-board and mouse settings. PRAM is powered by a battery, so it doesn't lose the settings when you shut down. Sometimes, however, the PRAM data gets corrupted, causing crashes or other problems.

Precision vs. accuracy (accuracy vs. Precision) If the actual value is 4.321 and you say that it is 4.30, then you are precise to the first decimal place but inaccurate by .021. If a value is represented as a bulls-eye on a target, a group of guesses or measurements represented by closely grouped points have a high degree of precision. If that group is near the center, it is highly accurate as well. On a bullseye, think of accuracy as how close to the center your arrow hits, and your measurement of precision as how closely you can group your shots.

Preemptive multitasking A form of multitasking where the OS executes an application for a specific period of time, according to its assigned priority. At that time, it is preempted, and another task is given access to the CPU for its allocated time. Although an application can give up control before its time is up, such as during input/output waits, no task is ever allowed to execute for longer than its allotted time period.

PRI primary rate interface An ISDN standard for provisioning of 1.544 Mbit/s (DS1 - North

America, Japan, et al) or 2.048 Mbit/s (E1 - Europe) ISDN services. DS1 is 23 "B" channels of 64 kbit/s each and one signalling "D" channel of 64 kbit/s/ E1 is 30 "B" channels of 64 kbit/s each and one signalling "D" channel of 64 kbit/s.

Primary cache Primary cache is the cache located closest to the CPU. Usually, primary cache is internal to the CPU, and secondary cache is external. Some early-model personal computers have CPU chips that don't contain internal cache. In these cases the external cache, if present, would actually be the primary (L1) cache.

Primary server The name server that will contain authoritative information for the domain name and will be used to resolve that domain name to its corresponding IP number(s). The designation of "primary" means that this name server will be used first and will be relied upon before any of the other name servers that may be listed on the Domain Name Registration Agreement. This information is required for domain name registration.

Primary-DOS partition In DOS, a division of the hard disk that contains important OS files. A DOS hard disk can be divided into two partitions, or areas; the primary DOS partition, and the extended DOS partition. If you want to start your computer from the hard disk, the disk must contain an active primary DOS partition that includes the three DOS system files:MSDOS.SYS,IO.SYS,and COMMAND.COM. The primary DOS partition on the first hard disk in the system is referred to as drive C.

Print screen This button is intended to print whatever is on your screen. If you are using DOS, or you are in your BIOS and have a printer set up, the Print Screen button should do just that. In Windows OSes,hitting the Print Screen button will copy your current desktop so that you can paste it into a graphics program, or a program that will support graphics, such as many word processors today. Additionally, hitting Alt-Print Screen will copy just the window that is active at the time.

Printed circuit board (PCB) The normally green plastic board that is imprinted with one or more layers of circuitry. Examples of common PCBs include motherboards, PCI cards, and AGP cards. The boards can hold microchips and other components, and are a way to link such components together.

Printer Any device that makes an impression on media, usually paper, and is connected to a computer. The invention of the computer with printer has almost made the typewriter obsolete. The simplest printers are located in cash registers printing out receipts, while more advanced printers are capable of magazine-quality photo images. Printers come in several types, including daisy-wheel, dot matrix, inkjet, laser, and dye sublimation.

Fig. Printer

Private key encryption An encryption method in which both the sender and recipient of a message share a single, common key that is used to both encrypt and decrypt the message.

Private key The part of an asymmetric encryption scheme that is known only to the owner and never transmitted over the network. A sender can use a private key to "sign" a message (or message digest), thereby allowing the recipient to authenticate the sender by using the sender's public key. A private key can also be used by a recipient to decrypt a message that was encrypted using the recipient's public key.

Privileged mode An operating mode supported in protected mode that allows the OS and certain classes of device driver to manipulate parts of the system including memory and I/O ports.

Proactive Active approach that prevents problems before they occur, as opposed to a reactive approach that responds to problems after they occur. Proactive security measures prevent hackers from exploiting the type of content that is difficult to protect against using traditional anti-virus technologies. The most recent developments in vandal and virus activity have involved active content that traditional anti-virus protection can neither detect nor protect against.

Processor A processor is a device that processes programmed instructions and performs tasks. Your processor sends and receives information from the different parts of the system (from hardware and software). The speed at which the CPU processes information internally is measured in MegaHertz (MHz) and GigaHertz (GHz). 1 GHz is equal to 1,000 MHz.

Processor clock The processor is regulated by a crystal that vibrates at a regular frequency when an electrical current is applied to it. Each vibration counts as one tick of the clock.

Processor serial number (PSN) An embedded serial number in Intel Pentium III microprocessors. It allows software manufacturers and websites to identify individuals more precisely. Intel caught a lot of flack for this "feature," and there is no benefit to home users, as websites are not using this technology. Network management could use the software to identify systems, but AMD and other brand microprocessors do not support the PSN—neither do earlier Intel processors. Intel left the PSN out of its Pentium 4 processors.

Production A description of a product's development status during the release phase, marking the end of Research & Development. The same as Beta Test, except that there exists no mechanism for users to report bugs.

Productivity application Spreadsheets, functional WYSIWYG Word Processors, and other software that contributes directly to the success of a commercial enterprise. Does not include Word Perfect for Windows.

Profanity The use of bad language in email. Profanity is considered a Content Security threat because use of company email to send sexual or racial content can open a company up to legal liability and loss of reputation.

Profile Configuration information that describes a certain capability or setup; a prototype for configuration information or properties that are common to a group of machines or that apply to an application.

Programmable Capable of being programmed. The fact that a computer is programmable is what sets it apart from all other instruments that use microprocessors; it is truly a general-purpose machine.

Programmable logic device (PLD) An integrated circuit that consists of an array of AND and OR gates whose operation can be modified. The programming of the devices is done by blowing fuses on the PLD.

Programmable read only memory (PROM) This is a memory device. Once data is written to a PROM it is there forever, unlike with an EPROM. A PROM is also a curious high school ritual involving strangely colored dresses, tuxedos, and sometimes limousines, unconsciously mirroring the wedding rituals most of its participants will undergo at some point in the following 10-15 years. PROMs leave some traumatized and others gleeful, but everyone agrees the post-PROM activities are always better than the PROM itself.

Programmed input/output (PIO) Input/Output standards on IDE hard disk drives. If you have a hard drive that supports one PIO mode, you need your interface to support it as well for maximum performance. The data transfer rates for the various PIO modes are: PIO mode 0 - 3.3Mbps; PIO mode 1 - 5.2Mbps; PIO mode 2 -

8.3Mbps; PIO mode 3 - 11.1Mbps; PIO mode 4 - 16.6Mbps. Ultra IDE doubles the data transfer rate of PIO mode 4.

Project assurance The process of specifying the support system: techniques, internal standards, measurements, tools, and training for a project; counseling the project team in the application of these elements and monitoring the adherence to the standards.

Properties Information about an object, including settings or options for that object. For example, you look at properties of a file for information such as the file size, file type, and file attributes.

Proprietary software Software created by an individual or company that is sold under a license that dictates use and distribution.

Protected mode An operating state that supports advanced features, such as hardware support for multitasking,virtual memory management, and the prevention of programs from accessing blocks of memory that belong to other executing programs.

Protocol An agreed-upon format for transmitting data between two devices. The protocol determines the following:

The type of error checking to be used.

Data compression method, if any.

How the sending device will indicate that it has finished sending a message.

How the receiving device will indicate that it has received a message.

There are a variety of standard protocols from which programmers can choose. Each has particular advantages and disadvantages; for example, some are simpler than others, some are more reliable, and some are faster. From a user's point of view, the only interesting aspect about protocols is that your computer or device must support the right ones if you want to communicate with other computers. The protocol can be implemented either in hardware or in software.

Proxy The use of one computer or device to make requests in place of another over a network. Proxies are often used for Internet security, or to control connections. You can use a proxy or proxy server to pass data between your internal network and the Internet. A machine on your network sends a request to the proxy; the proxy sends the request to a server on the Internet. Thus, it stands in for the computer on your network—the server on the Internet never knows that the request is coming from anywhere but the proxy. Thus 100 machines on your network could all access an Internet server and it would look like the proxy were making all of the requests. Some proxies have caching and site filtering built-in.

Proxy ARP A technique in which one machine, usually a gateway, answers ARP requests for another machine. By pretending to be the physical network location of another machine, the gateway takes over the responsibility of routing packets destined for the other machine. For instance, a gateway can proxy ARP for addresses that the gateway identifies as being off the local network and that the gateway has a route for. The originating computer receives the gateway's proxy ARP reply and sends the datagram on to the gateway, which routes the datagram to its actual destination network.

Proxy inspection Proxy inspection methods require that the Content Security device receive the entire file and scan or approve it before allowing any traffic to reach the requesting client. This causes time-outs, user complaints, and bandwidth usage problems.

Proxy server A server that acts as an intermediary between a workstation user and the internet so that the enterprise can ensure security, administrative control, and caching service. A proxy server is associated with, or part of, a gateway server that separates the enterprise network from the outside network and a firewall server that protects the enterprise network from the outside intrusion.

PS/2 port:A type of port developed by IBM for connecting a mouse or keyboard to a PC. The PS/2 port supports a mini DIN plug containing just 6 pins. Most PCs have a PS/2 port so that the serial port can be used by another device, such as a modem. The PS/2 port is often called the mouse port.

Pseudocode A notation resembling a programming language but not intended for actual compilation. It usually combines some of the structure of a programming language with an informal natural-language description of the computations to be carried out. It is often produced by CASE systems as a basis for later hand coding.

PSN (processor serial number) An embedded serial number in Intel Pentium III microprocessors. It allows software manufacturers and websites to identify individuals more precisely. Intel caught a lot of flack for this "feature," and there is no benefit to home users, as websites are not using this technology. Network management could use the software to identify systems, but AMD and other brand microprocessors do not support the PSN—neither do earlier Intel processors. Intel left the PSN out of its Pentium 4 processors.

PTT (postal telegraph and telephone) An agency in a European country, usually a government-run monopoly, that is responsible for all postal, telegraph and telephone services. It also has certain regulatory functions for telecommunications, such as providing specifications for modems and certifying that equipment may connect to the telephone network. In some countries, the PTT also provides its own line of equipment, such as modems. Now also called Telecommunications Administrations (TAs), these entities are undergoing varying amounts of structural change.

Public key encryption An encryption method that uses the concept of a key-ring. The key-ring has two keys - a public key that is made available to everyone and a private, or secret, key that is known only by the private key holder. The public and private keys are designed to work together. Anyone can use the public key to encrypt data, but only the person with the corresponding private key can decrypt the data; this helps to protect the content of messages. Alternatively, anyone can use the public key to decrypt data, but only if it was encrypted with the corresponding private key; this helps to ensure the identity of the person sending the data. Pretty Good Privacy (PGP) is a type of Public Key Encryption.

Public switched telephone network (PSTN) A global network of interconnected digital and analog communication links originally designed to support voice communication between any two points in the world. It was quickly adapted to handle digital data traffic when the in the world. It was quickly adapted to handle digital data traffic when the computer revolution occurred. In addition to its voice support role, the PSTN now functions as the Physical layer of the Internet by providing dial-up and leased lines for private and public use.

Purge A synonym for deleting something, usually in such a way that it cannot be easily recovered. It is used in several contexts, including the deletion of print jobs from a print queue and the final deletion of files from the NetWare operating system. You can purge print jobs to clean out a print queue that is not behaving, or purge files in NetWare to free up space and fully delete files that were specified for deletion.

Purity The ability of the electron beam to lit precisely the correct phosphor color dot. If a full page of red color is shown on the display, impurity would result in a purple or greenish color region. This impurity can occur if the shadow mask has been damaged or if the screen has become magnetized. Degaussing the screen may fix the problem.

Push technology This technology was first popularized by Pointcast, a company offering a client that would allow data to be "pushed" into it from an external server. The client would then display parts of that data based on what the user was interested in looking at, such as news, weather reports, stock info, and so on. Push technology has lost popularity due to bandwidth requirements and the general undesirability of having data pushed into corporate networks. Now the same services are offered through standard Web pages.

PVPC (permanent virtual path connection) A Virtual Path Connection (VPC) is an ATM connection where switching is performed on the VPI field only of each cell. A Permanent VPC is one which is provisioned through some network management function and left up indefinitely.

Q

QA (quality assurance) The practice of checking hardware, software, or systems for defects, identifying such defects, and then checking to make sure that such defects are corrected when future revisions of software or hardware are ready for testing. QA workers typically work closely with the people who develop hardware and software, and often program exhaustive scripts to automate checking and identify problems.

QD (queuing delay) Queuing Delay refers to the delay imposed on a cell by its having to be buffered because of unavailability of resources to pass the cell onto the next network function or element. This buffering could be a result of oversubscription of a physical link, or due to a connection of higher priority or tighter service constraints getting the resource of the physical link.

Qemm 386 A memory-management program from QuarterDeck Office Systems for IBM-compatible computers. QEMM 386 moves terminate-and-stay resident programs and device drivers, including network drivers, into high memory, leaving more conventional memory available for running application programs. QEMM 50/60 is a special version of the program designed for use on IBM PS/2 Model 50 and 60 computers.

Quake This was a revolutionary 3D, first-person perspective game full of blood and gore. Designed by id Software, it is now perhaps the most well-known and most user-modified line of 3D shooter games. Other competitors include the Unreal series and Doom (also from id Software).

Quality factor A multiplication factor (between 1 and 2) applied to output screen ruling to calculate scanning resolution for optimum output quality. This is also known as the halftoning factor.

Quality of service (QoS) An effort to provide different prioritization levels for different types of traffic over a network. Various methods are used to achieve quality of service, including the RSVP protocol. For example, streaming video may have a higher priority than ICMP traffic, as the consequences of interrupting streaming video are more obvious than slowing down ICMP traffic.

Quantum mechanical Something influenced by the set of rules that govern the energy and wave behavior of subatomic particles on the scale of sizes that are comparable to the particles themselves.

Quantum-dot cellular automata (QCA) The theory of automata as applied to quantum dot architectures, which are a proposed approach for the development of computers at nanotechnology scales.

Quartz A powerful graphics system that delivers a rich imaging model, on-the-fly rendering, anti-aliasing, and compositing of PostScript graphics. Quartz also implements the windowing system for Mac OS X and provides low-level services such as event handling and cursor management. It also offers facilities for rendering and printing that use PDF as an internal model for graphics representation.

Query Criteria for sorting out irrelevant information in a report. For example: by selecting only sandbox violations and a specific date, you can generate a report of sandbox violations that occurred on that date.

Queue A data construct that is first-in, first-out (FIFO). Think of a check-out line at a supermarket, or any type of line formed by people in society. Queues are used throughout the architecture of computers and are necessary in programming languages to accomplish certain tasks.

Quicktime Animation and video files that originally were designed for by Apple Corporation for Mac computers. Next came the software for playing quicktime video on PC computers. In late 1996, Apple announced that it was letting go of its proprietary rights so that Quicktime could become an open-platform recording standard. Now PC users can record and well as play back Quicktime video.

QWERTY keyboard The standard typewriter and computer keyboard layout, named for the first six keys at the top left of the alphabetic keyboard.

R

Rack units (U) This refers to the distance of 1.75" between screw holes in a rack used to hold server equipment. Most computer equipment racks are between 24 and 42 rack units in height. If you are shopping for rack equipment, keep in mind the height of the rack you have to work with and the "U" rating of the equipment. Heights of 1U indicate equipment that can fit into a 1.75" tall rack space, and 2U would indicate twice that at 3.5", and so forth with 3U, 4U, and up.

RAD (rapid application development) In the context of development applications software. The term is used in the context of object oriented, component-based and visually-aided software that allows for faster development of applications software. For example, Netscape Corporation in 1997 introduced a component-based Visual Java-Script intended to be for the web what Microsoft's Visual Basic software was for earlier applications development. Visual Java Scrip also licensed TV-Objects from TV-Objects Corporation in Princeton, N.J. for translating Visual Basic applications into JavaScript.

RAID (redundant array of inexpensive drives) A method of linking storage devices together so that they function as a single logical unit. RAID requires all drives to be of the same size, as compared to JBOD setups. RAID can be used for increased performance, but is also used to increase redundancy.

RAM (random access memory) Portion of a computer. The term "memory" typically refers to RAM as opposed to hard disc and optical disc storage of files that cannot be randomly accessed without searching by sectors. RAM stores instructions and other files potentially needed for immediate processing of a task at hand. Memory usually can be accessed "randomly" at relatively high speeds. Files stored on computer tape, floppy discs, hard drive, optical drives, etc. are not available in RAM until they are "loaded" into RAM. Four important types of RAM in PCs running DOS are conventional memory, high (upper) memory, expanded memory, and extended memory. When DOS first was designed, 640 Kb of memory seemed like a lot, so out of the then standard 1 Mb of base memory, 640 Kb was designated as conventional memory reserved for DOS and the remaining 360 Mb was high (upper) memory available for other internal system computing functions. Later, memory managers and the Windows HIMEM.SYS file made some of the high memory available for software usage. Another gimmick entailed use of peepholes of size 64 Kb swapping of chunks of memory. However, today the 1 Mb base memory utilized in the most efficient way is not sufficient to run most newer types of software. Memory SIMM chips can be added to raise the RAM to higher levels such as 64 Mb currently popular in multimedia authoring. Upper limits for extended memory options vary with types of PCs. Extended memory is much more important than expanded memory. Often the term extended memory applies to all RAM above the 640 Kb of conventional RAM, although from a technical standpoint it applies to RAM above the 1 Mb base. The term "RAM cache" refers to a section of RAM set aside to serve as a buffer between the central processing unit and auxiliary disc drives.

RAM chip A semiconductor storage device, either dynamic RAM or static RAM.

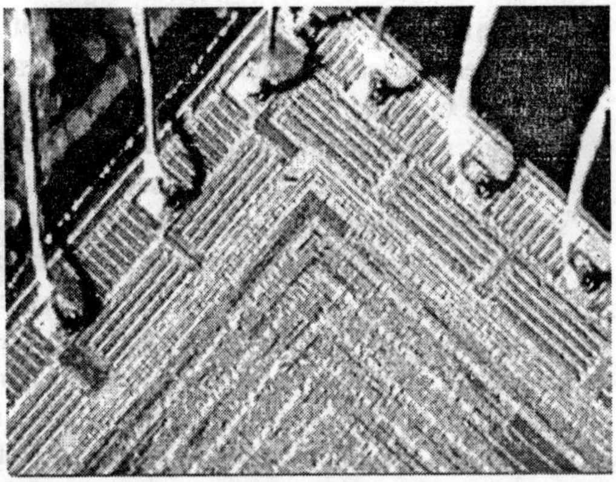

Fig. Ram chip

RAM disk An area of memory managed by a special device driver and used as a simulated disk.

Because the RAM disk operates in memory, it works very quickly, much faster than a regular hard disk. Remember that anything you store on your RAM disk will be erased when you turn off your computer, so you must save its contents onto a real disk first. RAM disks may also be called virtual drives.

RAM bus DRAM (direct RAM bus DRAM) One possible future successor to SDRAM, and competitor to DDR SDRAM. DRDRAM (also now simply called RDRAM) was originally developed by Rambus, Inc. This RAM architecture is capable of speeds starting at 266, 356, and 400MHz, and transfers data on the up and down ticks of a clock cycle, where standard SDRAM tops out at about 200MHz. You may see RDRAM referred to at 532, 712, and 800MHz, but that is actually 2662, 3562, and 400MHz2, where the 2 denotes transfer on the up and down tick of the clock. Intel picked RDRAM to be the future of RAM for PCs, but RDRAM ran into many stumbling blocks due to the complexity of manufacturing it. RDRAM was used in the popular Nintendo 64 game machine for its high-speed capabilities and low pin count, necessary for the intense 3D rendering being done on a low complexity system. RDRAM started out using a 16- bit bus, while SDRAM and DDR have 64-bit buses. Thus, 100MHz SDRAM has half the throughput of RDRAM at 400MHz (10064 = 6,400Mbits/second; 400216 = 12,800Mbits/second). However, newer RDRAM uses a 32-bit bus and is clocked up to 533MHz2. Still, it never achieved dominance in the PC market.

RAM drive The DOS device driver used to create a RAM disk.

Random access Describes the ability of a storage device to go directly to the required memory address without having to read from the beginning every time data is requested. There is nothing random or haphazard about random access; a more precise term is direct access. In a random-access device, the information can be read directly by accessing the appropriate memory address. Some storage devices, such as tapes, must start at the beginning to find a specific storage location, and if the information is towards the end of the tape, access can take a long time. This access method is known as "sequential access."

Raw Any data that has not been translated. It also refers to sending print data directly to a printer instead of translating it first to an EMF file. Printing to raw format uses less CPU power for translation, but skips the print spooler and makes printing more dependent on the application and less on the OS.

RDRAM (direct RAM bus DRAM) One possible future successor to SDRAM, and competitor to DDR SDRAM. DRDRAM (also now simply called RDRAM) was originally developed by Rambus, Inc. This RAM architecture is capable of speeds starting at 266, 356, and 400MHz, and transfers data on the up and down ticks of a clock cycle, where standard SDRAM tops out at about 200MHz. You may see RDRAM referred to at 532, 712, and 800MHz, but that is actually 2662, 3562, and 400MHz2, where the 2 denotes transfer on the up and down tick of the clock. Intel picked RDRAM to be the future of RAM for PCs, but RDRAM ran into many stumbling blocks due to the complexity of manufacturing it. RDRAM was used in the popular Nintendc 64 game machine for its high-speed capabilities and low pin count, necessary for the intense 3D rendering being done on a low complexity system. RDRAM started out using a 16- bit bus, while SDRAM and DDR have 64-bit buses. Thus, 100MHz SDRAM has half the throughput of RDRAM at 400MHz (10064 = 6,400Mbits/second; 400216 = 12,800Mbits/second). However, newer RDRAM uses a 32-bit bus and is clocked up to 533MHz2. Still, it never achieved dominance in the PC market.

Read only memory (ROM) Memory containing a program, data, or information about the device that has been programmed onto the chip at the factory and cannot be changed. There is no easy mechanism to write to ROM, but it is usually possible to do it. It's just not made easy, as writing to ROM is not intended to done.

Real-time Tasks that are time-critical and must happen in our time (as opposed to the much faster computer time). Real-time is the highest priority you can give to a thread or process in the Windows environment. Even though this is accounted for in the operating systems, Windows has historically been a poor real-time OS. The user interface should always be real-time. If you move the mouse, your pointer should move on screen immediately. Unfortunately, Windows can bog down enough so that this doesn't happen. Other real-time applications can include medical applications and control of real world systems. For example, you want to make sure that the train switches tracks on time and not too late because your server is bogged down.

Reboot To restart a computer. It comes from "boot," which is a term that means starting the operating system on the computer. When you are using your computer and have weird problems, the tech guy comes over and says, "Time to reboot." If you are the tech guy you'll find yourself saying this far too often.

Redirection To hijack the output of a command, which is usually on-screen, and put it somewhere else (this process is called output redirection). Alternatively, you can use information from somewhere else as the input for a command (called input redirection) rather than take the input from the keyboard. To redirect the output of a command to a file, use the character. To redirect the output of one command to become the input to another command, use the pipe(|) character.

Refresh Generally, to update something with new data. For example, some Web browsers include a refresh button that updates the currently display Web pages. This feature is also called reload.

To recharge a device with power or information. For example, dynamic RAM needs to be refreshed thousands of times per second or it will lose the data stored in it.

Similarly, display monitors must be refreshed many times per second. The refresh rate for a monitor is measured in hertz (Hz) and is also called the vertical frequency, vertical scan rate, frame rate or vertical refresh rate. The old standard for monitor refresh rates was 60Hz, but a new standard developed by VESA sets the refresh rate at 75Hz for monitors displaying resolutions of 640x480 or greater. This means that the monitor redraws the display 75 times per second. The faster the refresh rate, the less the monitor flickers.

Registry A registry is responsible for delegating Internet addresses such as Internet Protocol (IP) numbers and domain names, and keeping a record of those addresses and the information associated with their delegation. Examples of regional IP registries include Asian-Pacific Network Information Center (APNIC), American Registry for Internet Numbers (ARIN), and Reseaux IP Europeens (RIPE). Examples of domain name registries include InterNIC' InterNIC operation (.com, .net, and .org) and the ISO 3166 country code registries (e.g., .fr, .de, .uk, and .us).

REL (recorder element)The minimum distance between two recorded points (spots) in an imagesetter.

Relay Use of a private mail-relay server by someone from outside of the organization. Hackers use this technique for mail-spoofing or for initiating DoS attacks against third-party mail servers, and can put unnecessary load on your mail servers.

Release engineer The individual whose job it is to oversee the mechanics of the development process of software. The release engineer controls when new code is entered into the current working release, and makes sure the proper pieces of code are compiled and ready when the program has to be sent to a media duplication plant, or simply made live on a network.

Remote control A means of taking control of a remote computer, usually on a remote network. Programs like Symantec's pcAnywhere and a host of others offer this ability. Usually you connect to the remote computer via the Internet or a phone line, and control the computer by interacting with your computer while seeing on your screen a representation of what is actually happening on the remote computer. The downside to remote control is that each remote connection requires a separate computer. You can't easily have multiple people controlling one computer remotely and seeing a useful representation of what is on the remote display.

Removable canister A removable hard drive casing. There are two parts to the canister: the bay itself, and the casing that goes around the hard drive. These canisters can be used with SCSI or IDE/ATA hard drives, and have the advantage of easy portability of hard drives, especially if you have multiple computers with the same type of bay in them. Integrating a bare hard drive into a removable canister can be an annoying chore, as space is limited and you have lots of extra wires to deal with. This term can also be used to refer to the hard drives that are used in server machines and integrated into cases that can be plugged into servers and removed easily. Removable canisters can be hot pluggable, but usually only in servers with RAID systems.

Removable hard disk Hard disk that can be removed from a laptop computer. This type of unit generates a special risk in terms of security.

Render This synonym for hacking up animals for human consumption determines how colors are used on each triangle displayed in a 3D image. Very complex images take a long time to render; less complex 3D images, such as those in a 3D game, can be rendered in real time. When they make computer animated movies or effects of very high quality, effects companies use many computers to render images.

Report program generator (RPG) A programming language for minicomputer mainframes such as the IBM AS/400. RPG began as a program to generate reports—as you could have guessed from the name—but is now a full programming language that is widely used.

Request for comments (RFC) A document that was created to define accepted or proposed Internet standards or standards of practice. The acceptance of a document as an RFC is governed by the IETF (Internet Engineering Task Force). RFCs begin life as Internet-Drafts, which may be written by anyone. The IETF decides which Internet-Drafts become RFCs. RFCs are most often created by groups of interested individuals hoping to create a standard for interoperability over the Internet; however, they also describe such suggested practices, such as how to set up a mailserver to avoid being used to transmit SPAM mail.

Request ID The ID number of a print job as it waits in the print queue for the printer daemon to get around to printing it. You need to know the request ID if you want to cancel printing when, for example, the output is horribly fouled up and wasting lots of paper.

Reserved memory In DOS, a term used to describe that area of memory between 640K and 1MB, also known as upper memory. Reserved memory is used by DOS to store system and video information.

Reserved word Any word that has a special meaning and therefore cannot be used for any other purpose in the same context.

Resistor A two-terminal electronic component that resists an electrical current and turns the extra current into heat. Resistors are rated in ohms, and can be used to regulate the voltage and current in a circuit. Basically, a resistor resists the flow of electricity. Resistors are used to lower voltages and currents so that components that require smaller voltage/current can function properly. If a power supply puts out 12 volts and you have a chip that runs on three, you need a resistor to cut down the voltage.

Resolution Refers to the sharpness and clarity of an image. The term is most often used to describe monitors, printers, and bit-mapped graphic images. In the case of dot-matrix and laser printers, the resolution indicates the number of dots per inch. For example, a 300-dpi (dots per inch) printer is one that is capable of printing 300 distinct dots in a line 1 inch long. This means it can print 90,000 dots per square inch.

For graphics monitors, the screen resolution signifies the number of dots (pixels) on the entire screen. For example, a 640-by-480 pixel screen is capable of displaying 640 distinct dots on each of 480 lines, or about 300,000 pixels. This translates into different dpi measurements depending on the size of the screen. For example, a 15-inch VGA monitor (640x480) displays about 50 dots per inch.

Printers, monitors, scanners, and other I/O devices are often classified as high resolution, medium resolution, or low resolution. The actual resolution ranges for each of these grades is constantly shifting as the technology improves.

Resource description framework (RDF), rdf site summary (RSS), and podcasting A framework for metadata and provides for interoperability for applications in "machine-understandable" information on the Web. RDF draws upon several technologies such as XML (Extensible Markup Language). RDF a recommendation of the World Wide Web Consortium currently headed by Tim Bermers-Lee, the creater of the HTML markup language and the http protocol that is the basis of the World Wide Web. Over the long run, Berners-Lee envisions a time when Web sites can be devoid of most broken links and difficult-to-find information.

Return key When you use a Unix shell, pressing Return means that you have just typed a command and you want Unix to do it. When you use a text editor, pressing Return means that you want to begin a newline. The Enter key and the Return key usually do the same thing (your keyboard may have one, the other, or both).

Reusability The possibility of using code developed for one application in another application: traditionally achieved using program libraries. Object-oriented Object-oriented programming offers the potential for greater reusability of code via its techniques of inheritance inheritance, genericity genericity etc.

Class libraries with intelligent browsers and application generators are under development to help in this process.

Reverse address resolution protocol (RARP) Is a protocol by which a physical machine in a local area network can request to learn its IP address from a gateway server's Address Resolution Protocol (Address Resolution Protocol) table or cache. A network administrator creates a table in a local area network's gateway router that maps the physical machine (or Media Access Control - MAC address) addresses to corresponding Internet Protocol addresses. When a new machine is set up, its RARP client program requests from the RARP server on the router to be sent its IP address. Assuming that an entry has been set up in the router table, the RARP server will return the IP address to the machine which can store it for future use. RARP is available for Ethernet, Fiber Distributed-Data Interface, and token ring LANs.

Reverse engineering The process of analyzing an existing system to identify its components and their interrelationships, and create representations of the system in another form or at a higher level of abstraction. Usually undertaken in order to redesign the system for better maintainability.

Revolutions per minute (RPM) A measurement that applies commonly to hard drives, and removable drives like CD-ROMs and DVD-ROMs. It also applies to anything that moves in a circular motion. If you are using a drive with higher RPMs, you usually have better performance. Since the disk is spinning faster the drive can usually read data at a faster rate. For example, 5,400 RPM hard drives are generally slower than 7,200 RPM hard drives. The downside to higher RPM rates is that it is harder to stabilize and read data from a disk that is spinning faster, so the mechanism may be more complex and more expensive. Also, faster spinning drives are usually louder and run hotter.

RFID (radio frequency identification) Refers to the technology that uses devices attached to objects that transmit data to an RFID receiver. An alternative to bar coding. Advantages include data capacity, read/write capability, and no line-of-sight requirements.

Rhapsody A one time revolutionary operating system from Apple Corporation that was based upon NEXTStep technology. Apple plans to deliver two operating systems for the next several years. First will be the Mac OS, which we will continue to upgrade and improve to support the current Macintosh customers worldwide, approximately 60 million users. Second will be a new OS based on NeXT Software's operating system technologies, NEXTStep and OPENStep. The powerful and advanced NeXT technologies are years ahead of competitive offerings, and will provide the foundation for a new OS, code-named Rhapsody. In addition to leveraging the NeXT technologies, Rhapsody is designed to run Mac applications through a Mac OS compatibility environment. Rhapsody's user interface will combine elements from both the Mac OS and NEXTStep, but will be closer in look and feel to the Mac OS Finder. We realize that customers need a consistent interface in the two operating systems to deploy them throughout a single organization. It's important for training and ease of use. One of the advantages of NeXT's technology is the easy support of multiple user interface paradigms.

Rich-text format A text formatting standard established by Microsoft Corporation to enable text to be transferred between a word processor and other software without losing all of its formatting properties. Many modern word processors have the option of saving documents in rich-text format (RTF). Increasingly, authoring software vendors of hypertext, hypermedia, and CMS software are adding RTF importing utilities to overcome the frustrations of importing in ASCII or ANSI forms that lose all or most formatting properties.

RISC (reduced instruction set computing) Chipsets such as the MIPS R4000 and R4400 intended to outperform CISC complex instruction chipsets such as the Intel family of popular 386, 486, and Pentium competitors and the Motorola 680x0 family in Mac computers. The concept of RISC evolved from IBM laboratories where it was noted that most routine processing of consumers does not require full use of the processor. RISC processors consume less power and generate less heat than CISC processors powerful enough to compete at the same speed and capacity as RISC processors. They do this by reducing the number of operations and executing multiple instructions in what is known as "superscaler" processing. However, INTEL intends to keep its CISC lines competitive with RISC processors. At this juncture, it is impossible to know who will win the RISC versus CISC processor competitions of the future. The RISC-architecture is the foundation of the new PowerPCs and the PA-RISC systems of Hewlett-Packard Corporation. The HP 32-bit PA-7100 chip, for example, runs about 25% faster than the PowerPC RISC chips and the Pentium CISC chips. A new RISC processor from Texas Instruments called the Multimedia Video Processor is claimed to be 20 to 50 times more powerful than Intel's Pentium. RISC chipsets may become more of a threat to CISC in the form of NexGen alternatives to Pentium that are being manufactured by Alaris for Compaq, IBM, and other major PC manufacturers.

Riser card A card that plugs into a motherboard and enables other cards to be plugged into it horizontally. Architectures that support riser cards are typically designed to allow tall cards to be plugged into shorter enclosures. Servers often use riser cards, since if they didn't the motherboard would be too large to fit into a standard sized enclosure.

RM (resource management) Resource Management is the management of critical resources in an ATM network. Two critical resources are buffer space and trunk bandwidth. Provisioning may be used to allocate network resources in order to separate traffic flows according to service characteristics. VPCs play a key role in resource management. By reserving capacity on VPCs, the processing required to establish individual VCCs is reduced.

RMS (root mean square) Mathematically, this refers to the square root of the average of a group of numbers. You will most often see RMS referring to the power rating of an audio amplifier. RMS power is different than peak power, and is a more accurate rating of power than peak. If an amplifier lists a power rating in watts and doesn't say whether it is RMS or peak, you can assume it is peak, as peak ratings are typically much higher than RMS power. Manufacturers of high quality audio components will always list the RMS power of their amplifiers.

Root directory In a hierarchical directory structure, the directory from which all other directories must branch. The root directory is created by the FORMAT command, and can contain files as well as other directories. It is wise to store as few files as possible in the root directory,because in DOS there is a limit to number of entries that the root directory can hold. Also, you cannot delete the root directory. The backslash(\) character represents the root directory, and you can use this character to make the root directory the current directory in a single step, if you type CD\ from the system prompt.

Root mean square (RMS) Mathematically, this refers to the square root of the average of a group of numbers. You will most often see RMS referring to the power rating of an audio amplifier. RMS power is different than peak power, and is a more accurate rating of power than peak. If an amplifier lists a power rating in watts and doesn't say whether it is RMS or peak, you can assume it is peak, as peak ratings are typically much higher than RMS power. Manufacturers of high quality audio components will always list the RMS power of their amplifiers.

Root server A machine that has the software and data needed to locate name servers that contain authoritative data for the top level domains (e.g., root, servers know which name servers contain authoritative data for .com, .net, .fr, .uk. etc.). The root servers are, in fact, name server, and contain authoritative data for the very top of the Domain Name System (DNS) hierarchy. Currently, technical specifications limit the number of root servers to 13. These machines are located around the globe, in the U.S., the U.K., Sweden, and Japan.

Rot-13 A simple encryption scheme often used to scramble posts to USENET newsgroups, it makes the article unreadable until the text is decoded, and is often used when the subject matter might be considered offensive.

Round tripping A term used mainly to refer to the transformation of a computer file into a different type with the option to return to the original type. Microsoft uses this term in conjunction with Office 2000 products. For example, an Excel worksheet or an Excel chart can be saved as an HTML file with many of the interactive features of Excel (such as replacement of data and recomputation of functions) in the browser rather than Excel. However, the HTML files have round-trip recovery features for saving the file back to an Excel worksheet or Excel chart.

Router A special purpose computer that attaches to two or more networks and routes packets from one network to the other. A router uses network layer addresses *(such as IP Addresses)* to determine if packets should be sent from one network to another. Routers send packets to other routers until they arrive at their final destination.

Routing computation The process of applying a mathematical algorithm to a topology database to compute routes. There are many types of routing computations that may be used. The Djikstra algorithm is one particular example of a possible routing computation.

RPC (remote procedure call) Protocol that allows a program on one computer to execute a program on a server computer. Using RPC, a system developer need not develop specific procedures for the server. With RPC you call a specific function whereas with an ORB you call a method within a distributed object. In ORB each object manages its own private instance of the data whereas in RPC you can only call a specific function and all functions get implemented in the same way. ORB allows for differential processing.

RPG (report program generator) A programming language for minicomputer mainframes such as the IBM AS/400. RPG began as a program to generate reports—as you could have guessed from the name—but is now a full programming language that is widely used.

Runtime Permissive use of a portion of a software system that allows for the "running" or "viewing" or "delivery" or "playback" of an application in contrast to its "authoring." An author may write an electronic book in Asymetrix ToolBook authoring software, for example, which can then be played by readers using ToolBook runtime software. Many types of software (e.g., word processor, spreadsheet, and database software) have no runtime versions. Most hypertext and hypermedia authoring packages have runtime versions. Vendors vary as to whether fees are charged for runtime versions. Apple Media Kit from Apple Corporation and ScriptX from Kaleida Labs are examples of options that can have costly runtime fees, especially for items sold in large-scale markets. Some options have free runtime within an organization but charge a royalty on all sales of applications outside the organization. A professor who writes a CD-ROM textbook in some types of software (Apple Media Kit, Icon Author, Tencore, etc.) can use the free runtime versions for discs distributed free to students and faculty within his or her university but would have to pay a royalty on each CD-ROM sold for a profit. There is a strong incentive for authors to seek out hypertext and hypermedia authoring packages that are accompanied by free runtime (reader, player, playback, delivery) files for all customers.

RW (read-write) Attributes which are read-write can not be written by the PNNI protocol entity. Only the Network Management Entity may change the value of a read-write attribute. The PNNI Protocol Entity is restricted to only reading such read-write attributes. Read-write attributes are typically used to provide the ability for Network Management to configure, control, and manage a PNNI Protocol Entity's behavior.

RXD (receive data) A hardware signal defined by the RS-232-C standard to carry data from one device to another.

S

S.M.A.R.T.. (self-monitoring analysis and reporting tool) This technology reports on a variety of hard drive attributes. You need a compliant BIOS and SCSI and/or IDE controller, a hard drive that supports SMART, and some sort of software package that reports on these conditions. Once you have that you should be able to receive system warnings about your hard drive. Many hard drive manufacturers have added onto the SMART technology or changed it around so that it has proprietary features for their drives. The good news about SMART is that having SMART is much better than not having it, and you can be warned of hard drive failure before it happens and backup your drive while it still works. Thus, your data is safer with SMART around.

Safe mode An operating mode used in Microsoft operating systems. It was first introduced in Windows 95 and was loaded automatically if Windows 95 crashed during boot up. You can access Safe Mode if you press the "F8" key when new Windows operating systems are booting—this will bring you to a menu that allows you to boot into safe mode. Safe Mode boots the operating system with minimal driver support. The purpose of it is to help resolve boot problems. For example, if you install the wrong graphics driver, Windows could crash when it's loading. When you Windows it will boot into Safe Mode and use the standard VGA driver with 60Hz refresh rate. This will allow you to go to the Display Properties function and switch the video driver back to something that works. There is no reason to go into Safe Mode unless you are crashing during boot-up or you are trying to diagnose a driver problem.

Sample A small portion representative of something. It usually means a small amount of sound from an instrument, enough to reproduce the sounds of that instrument.

Sampling rate The frequency with which samples are taken and converted in digitizing operations. This is measured in kilohertz (KHz). The MPC standard requires a sound card with a recording sampling rate of at least 11 KHz and an output rate of 11 and 22 KHz.

SAP (service access point) A SAP is used for the following purposes:

1. When the application initiates an outgoing call to a remote ATM device, a destination_SAP specifies the ATM address of the remote device, plus further addressing that identifies the target software entity within the remote device.

2. When the application prepares to respond to incoming calls from remote ATM devices, a local_SAP specifies the ATM address of the device housing the application, plus further addressing that identifies the application within the local device.

There are several groups of SAPs that are specified as valid for Native ATM Services.

Save This term describes the movement of data from a computer's volatile DRAM to the non-volatile hard disk or other media. Basically, when you save something you are making sure that if your computer loses power you will be able to get back to the information that you have saved. This information may be saved to a floppy disk, a hard drive, or a CD-R. The information also can be saved to these devices connected to your local machine, or to a server on a network.

Scandisk A Microsoft program that first shipped with DOS version 6, replacing the venerable chkdsk.exe program. Technically the program is scandisk.exe. It is available in MS-DOS version 6.x, and non-NT versions of Windows. It added the ability to do a surface scan for physical defects on drive media, and a nicer UI than chkdsk, which had no graphical UI. Windows NT/2000/XP still uses chkdsk.

Scanner Both hand-held and flatbed hardware and software for copying graphics images and text into computer files. Both color and black and white options are available. We have never had much luck with hand-held versions, but flatbed scanners do a terrific job. Text scanned as graphics must be converted into computer text via specialized software.

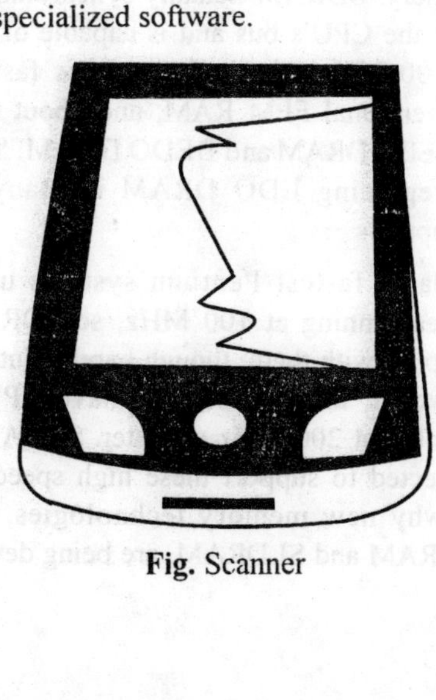

Fig. Scanner

Screen The TV-type thing that shows you what's going on in your computer. Also called a monitor, CRT, and VDU. Some screens can display many colors; others can do only one, usually green. Some screens can display many colors; others can do only one, usually green. Some screens can display pictures (graphics); others can do only characters.

Screen capturing The "capturing" of images on a computer screen onto a clipboard or into a graphics file so that they can be imported into other software. Screen captures are analogous to photographs of screen images. Captured text is normally in graphics mode such that it must be run through a text converter (e.g., OmniPage text conversion software) that translates graphics text back into word processor text.

Screen editor A text editor that deals with text an entire screen at a time. The vi and emacs programs are screen editors.

Screen flicker The phenomenon whereby a display screen appears to flicker. Screen flicker results from a variety of factors, the most important of which is the monitor's refresh rate, the speed with which the screen is redrawn. If the refresh rate is too slow, the screen will appear to glimmer. Another factor that affects screen flicker is the persistence of the screen phosphors. Low-persistence phosphors fade more quickly than high-persistence monitors, making screen flicker more likely. Screen flicker can also be affected by lighting. Finally, screen flicker is a subjective perception that affects people differently. Some people perceive screen flicker where others do not. Most people perceive no screen flicker if the refresh rate is 72 MHz or higher.

Screensaver A program that displays an image, animation, or just a blank screen on a computer after no input has been received for a certain length of time. Screensavers were originally designed so that images would not be burned into the phosphors of older CRT screens, but soon turned into a source of entertainment. Complex screensavers can use a good deal of

CPU power to run, and should be kept off of servers. Screensavers are largely unnecessary today as CRT screens are much more resistant to burn-in.

Script Program built into the HTML code of a Web page that work on almost all Internet applications. Scripts can also be used with a variety of applications that support their scripting syntax. One such application is Windows Scripting Host, an automation tool that was exploited by many vandals. Scripts can do almost anything - infect a system with Trojans, modify files, cause DoS attacks, or spread malicious code using Microsoft Networks or Microsoft Outlook. Scripts are written in VBScript , JavaScript , or other scripting languages.

Scroll lock The scroll lock key is, for most, a way to turn the "scroll lock" light on and off on your keyboard and nothing more. The scroll lock key was intended to function as a third "state" key, such as the Caps Lock and Num Lock keys. Some software makes use of it, but most does not. Some people mock the scroll lock key.

SCSI (small computer system interface) SCSI is a parallel interface standard used by Apple Macintosh computers, PCs, and many UNIX systems for attaching peripheral devices to computers. Nearly all Apple Macintosh computers, excluding only the earliest Macs and the recent iMac, come with a SCSI port for attaching devices such as disk drives and printers.

SCSI interfaces provide for faster data transmission rates (up to 80 megabytes per second) than standard serial and parallel ports. In addition, you can attach many devices to a single SCSI port, so that SCSI is really an I/O bus rather than simply an interface.

The following varieties of SCSI are currently implemented:

SCSI-1 Uses an 8-bit bus, and supports data rates of 4 MBps.

SCSI-2 Same as·SCSI-1, but uses a 50-pin connector instead of a 25-pin connector, and supports multiple devices. This is what most people mean when they refer to plain SCSI.

Wide scsi Uses a wider cable (168 cable lines to 68 pins) to support 16-bit transfers.

Fast scsi Uses an 8-bit bus, but doubles the clock rate to support data rates of 10 MBps.

Fast Wide SCSI Uses a 16-bit bus and supports data rates of 20 MBps.

Ultra SCSI Uses an 8-bit bus, and supports data rates of 20 MBps.

SCSI-3 Uses a 16-bit bus and supports data rates of 40 MBps. Also called Ultra Wide SCSI.

Ultra2 SCSI Uses an 8-bit bus and supports data rates of 40 MBps.

Wide Ultra2 SCSI Uses a 16-bit bus and supports data rates of 80 MBps.

SDH (synchronous digital hierarchy) A method used for multiplexing many circuits with a low bit rate onto fewer circuits with a higher bit rate, and vice-versa (de-multiplexing). Used primarily in the telecomms industry to carry telephony traffic. This network can also be used to carry IP traffic.

SDRAM (synchronous dynamic random access memory) A new type of DRAM that can run at much higher clock speeds than conventional memory. SDRAM actually synchronizes itself with the CPU's bus and is capable of running at 100 MHz, about three times faster than conventional FPM RAM, and about twice as fast EDO DRAM and BEDO DRAM. SDRAM is replacing EDO DRAM in many newer computers .

Today's fastest Pentium systems use CPU buses running at 100 MHz, so SDRAM can keep up with them, though barely. Future PCs, however, are expected to have CPU buses running at 200 MHz or faster. SDRAM is not expected to support these high speeds which is why new memory technologies, such as RDRAM and SLDRAM, are being developed.

Search engine Literally, this is the software used to search for information within a given database, and now often used to mean a website with a database of other websites and the information they contain. Since the Web is such a large place, it is handy to go to search engines when you can't find the information for which you are looking. (Google and Teoma are search engines).

Second level domain In the Domain Name System (DNS), the next highest level of the hierarchy underneath the top level domains. In a domain name, that portion of the domain name that appears immediately to the left of the top level domain. For example, the DomainMart in DomainMart.com.

Secondary server A server is a computer station on a network that handles special tasks, such as disk storage, printing, or communications. A dedicated server handles only its special tasks. An Internet server is a program that interacts with user programs. For example, a "web server" provides World Wide Web pages to your browser program. InterNIC's use of the designation of "secondary" indicates that the name server will be used in addition to and as a backup for the primary name server that is listed on the Domain Name Registration Agreement.

Sector The smallest unit of physical space on a disk. Typically the smallest unit of data that is read from or written to the disk.

Secure electronic transaction (SET) A method to protect credit card transactions that was developed by Visa and MasterCard.

Secure hypertext transfer protocol (HTTPS) A secure means of transferring data using the HTTP protocol. Typically HTTP data is sent over TCP/IP port 80, but HTTPS data is sent over port 443. This standard was developed by Netscape for secure transactions, and uses 40-bit encryption ("weak" encryption) or 128-bit ("strong" encryption). The HTTPS standard supports certificates. A webserver operator must get a digital certificate from a third-party certificate provider that ensures that the webserver in question is valid. This certificate gets installed on the webserver, and verifies for a period of a year that that server is a proper secure server.

Secure online payment system A system that allows InterNIC customers to pay for their domain name registration and renewal (re-registration) fee 24 hours a day, seven days a week, by entering their credit card information directly via the Web. The system provides a fast and secure method of payment and requires that the customer have a browser that will support Secure Sockets Layer (SSL).

Secure server A Web server that supports any of the major security protocols, which encrypt and decrypt messages. Making purchases from a secure Web server ensures that a user's payment or personal information can be encrypted into a secret code that is difficult to crack. Major security protocols include SSL, SHTTP, PCT, and IPSec.

Security certificate Information that is used by the SSL protocol to establish a secure connection. Security Certificates contain information about its ownership, issuer, valid dates, and an encrypted "fingerprint" that can be used to verify the contents of the certificate. In order for an SSL connection to be created, both sides must have a valid Security Certificate.

Segmented addressing An addressing scheme used in Intel processors that divides the address space into logical pieces called segments.

To access any given address, a program must specify the segment and also an offset within that segment. This addressing method is sometimes abbreviated to segment:offset, and is used in Intel processors in real mode; most other processors use a single flat address space.

Self-monitoring analysis and reporting tool (SMART) This technology reports on a variety of hard drive attributes. You need a compliant BIOS and SCSI and/or IDE controller, a hard drive that supports SMART, and some sort of software package that reports on these conditions. Once you have that you should be able to receive system warnings about your hard drive. Many hard drive manufacturers have added onto the SMART technology or changed it around so that it has proprietary features for their drives. The good news about SMART is that having SMART is much better than not having it, and you can be warned of hard drive failure before it happens and backup your drive while it still works. Thus, your data is safer with SMART around.

Semantics The study of how words acquire meaning and how those meanings change over time.

Semaphore In programming, an interprocess communication signal that indicates the status of a shared system resource, such as shared memory.

A material that is half-way between a conductor (which conducts electricity) and an insulator (which resists electricity), whose electrical behavior can be precisely controlled by the addition of impurities called dopants.

Semiconductor A material that is neither a good conductor of electricity (like copper) nor a good insulator (like rubber). The most common semiconductor materials are silicon and germanium. These materials are then doped to create an excess or lack of electrons.

Computer chips, both for CPU and memory, are composed of semiconductor materials. Semiconductors make it possible to miniaturize electronic components, such as transistors. Not only does miniaturization mean that the components take up less space, it also means that they are faster and require less energy.

Semiconductor diode laser A diode that emits electromagnetic radiation at wavelengths above about 630 nanometers, creating a laser beam for industrial applications.

Semipermanent connection A connection established via a service order or via network management.

Sensors Devices that can record and transmit data regarding the altitude, flight path, attitude, etc., so that they can enter into the system's calculations.

Sentry A process that monitors a variety of system activities, such as the amount of disk space available, and that can generate events or alarms based on thresholds.

Serial ATA A specification for consumer hard drive connections that boosts the data transfer rate up to 150MB/second. In addition, it changes IDE/ATA from a parallel interface requiring 40 separate wires to connect components to a serial interface requiring only 6 wires. 2x and 4x versions of Serial ATA double and quadruple the speed of Serial ATA.

Serial cable/serial port A cable used to connect peripheral devices through a computer's serial port. Normally a 25-pin connector on each end, yet can be a 9-pin on one. A Serial Port can either be plugged into an expansion slot on the motherboard of your computer or built into the motherboard itself. Serial ports are used for such devices as printers, mice, and modems.

Serial mouse A mouse that attaches directly to one of the computer's serial ports.

Serial port A port, or interface, that can be used for serial communication, in which only 1 bit is transmitted at a time. Most serial ports on personal computers conform to the RS-232C or RS-422 standards. A serial port is a general-purpose interface that can be used for almost any type of device, including modems, mice, and printers (although most printers are connected to a parallel port).

Server A system or a program that receives requests from one or more client systems or programs to perform activities that allow the client to accomplish certain tasks. A processor that provides a specific service to systems on a network. Routing servers connect subnetworks of like architecture, gateway servers connect networks of different architecture by performing protocol conversions and terminal, printer and file servers provide interfaces between peripheral devices and systems on the network.

Server farm A group of servers usually located in a secure area, and sometimes collocated at an ISP. These servers all serve a single purpose (such as serving Web pages, for example) and have some sort of load balanced across them. If one server in the farm dies, business carries on as usual. If performance is slow, you add more servers. This term is popular when dealing with Web-based applications, where a group of webservers all serve up the same content or pull data from a database server or group of database servers.

Server message block (SMB) A client method of communication that allows a client to make requests for resources over a network. A server responds to these requests.

Server side includes (SSI) A method of calling, or "including," code into a Web page. To utilize SSI your webserver must be set to check for and respond to these codes called in HTML pages. The SSI calls are embedded in HTML comments, so if they are called from a server that doesn't support SSI or is not actively looking for them, they are ignored. This can be used to create a single look and feel across multiple HTML pages.

Server skeleton Unmarshals the data associated with a request for presentation to a method, and marshals the data returned.

Service A process that performs a specific function in Windows NT and can be called by various other programs. Windows NT provides tools to monitor and administer services.

Session encryption Encryption used during a communication session, for example while using Secure Sockets Layer (SSL) protocol to communicate with a secure Web server.

SGRAM A type of DRAM used increasingly on video adapters and graphics accelerators. Like SDRAM, SGRAM can synchronize itself with the CPU bus clock up to speeds of 100 MHz. In addition, SGRAM uses several other techniques, such as masked writes and block writes, to increase bandwidth for graphics-intensive functions.

Unlike VRAM and WRAM, SGRAM is single-ported. However, it can open two memory pages at once, which simulates the dual-port nature of other video RAM technologies.

Shading (rendering) This synonym for hacking up animals for human consumption determines how colors are used on each triangle displayed in a 3D image. Very complex images take a long time to render; less complex 3D images, such as those in a 3D game, can be rendered in real time. When they make computer animated movies or effects of very high quality, effects companies use many computers to render images.

Shadow memory In PCs based on the 80386 (or later) processor, the technique of copying the contents of the BIOS ROM into faster RAM when the computer first boots up; also known as shadow RAM or shadow ROM.

Shadowing A technique used to increase a computer's speed by using high-speed RAM memory in place of slower ROM memory (RAM is about three times as fast as ROM). On PCs, for example, all code to control hardware devices, such as keyboards, is normally executed in a special ROM chip called the BIOS ROM. However, this chip is slower than the general-purpose RAM that comprises main memory. Many PC manufacturers, therefore, configure their PCs to copy the BIOS code into RAM when the computer boots. The RAM used to hold the BIOS code is called shadow RAM.

Shared memory An interprocess communications technique in which the same memory is accessed by more than one program running in a multitasking OS. Semaphores or other management elements prevent the applications from "colliding," or trying to update the same information at the same time.

Shareware Software distributed on the basis of an honor system. Most shareware is delivered free of charge, but the author usually requests that you pay a small fee if you like the program and use it regularly. By sending the small fee, you become registered with the producer so that you can receive service assistance and updates. You can copy shareware and pass it along to friends and colleagues, but they too are expected to pay a fee if they use the product.

Shareware is inexpensive because it is usually produced by a single programmer and is offered directly to customers. Thus, there are practically no packaging or advertising expenses.

Shell The outermost layer of a program. Shell is another term for user interface. Operating systems and applications sometimes provide an alternative shell to make interaction with the program easier. For example, if the application is usually command driven, the shell might be a menu-driven system that translates the user's selections into the appropriate commands.

Sometimes called command shell, a shell is the command processor interface. The command processor is the program that executes operating system commands. The shell, therefore, is the part of the command processor that accepts commands. After verifying that the commands are valid, the shell sends them to another part of the command processor to be executed.

Shortcut A pointer to an actual program or file, as opposed to a full copy of that file. Shortcuts can also point to other shortcuts, and are used mainly because they take up less space. For example, in Windows you can place a shortcut to a 200 KB file on the desktop which will only take up 1 KB, as opposed to copying the entire file to the desktop, which would take up the full 200 KB. Another benefit is that if you need to update a file that has several shortcuts, you don't have to update several copies of it, just one.

Silicon chip A common term for a semiconductor integrated circuit device.

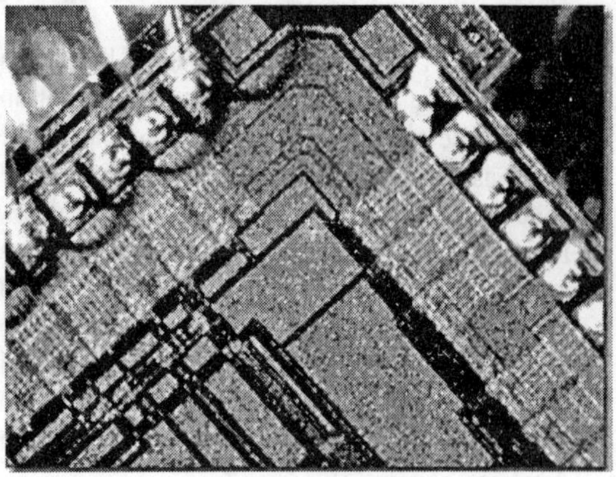

Fig. Silicon chip

Silicon on insulator (SOI) The practice of placing a thin layer of silicon on top of an insulating material in order to speed up the performance of a microprocessor by reducing the capacitance of the transistors and making them operate faster.

Silicon valley An area in California near San Francisco, which has been the home location of many of the most significant information technology orientated companies and universities.

SIMD (single instruction multiple data) A processor instruction that can perform operations across multiple data instructions. So, instead of saying "Add A,B" several times to add two groups of numbers, you may say "Add Row A, Row B" or something to that effect. Instructions of this nature are often associated with 3D graphics and multimedia.

SIMM (single in-line memory module) A small circuit board that can hold a group of memory chips. Typically, SIMMs hold up 8 (on Macintoshes) or 9 (on PCs) RAM chips. On PCs, the ninth chip is often used for parity error checking. Unlike memory chips, SIMMs are measured in bytes rather than bits. SIMMs are easier to install than individual memory chips.

The bus from a SIMM to the actual memory chips is 32 bits wide. A newer technology, called dual in-line memory module (DIMM), provides a 64-bit bus. For modern Pentium microprocessors that have a 64-bit bus, you must use either DIMMs or pairs of SIMMs.

Simulation Computer generated or enhanced emulation of real world happenings. In the early days of computing simulation was largely a numerical modeling of factory operations, weather systems, planetary movements, etc. The advent of flight simulation ushered in physical reproductions of reality that gave the look and feel of being in a real world happening such as landing an aircraft at night in simulated airports around the world or simulated combat situations. Modern day multimedia computing has ushered in countless applications of visual as well as numerical modeling simulations. The high end technology for simulation today is virtual reality.

Single large expensive drive (SLED) Back in the early days of hard disks you had two choices: SLED or RAID. SLED systems used a single high capacity hard drive to store lots of data. The drive may have contained a platter that was three feet (one meter) across, and it was very expensive. RAID allowed users to link a bunch of smaller, cheaper hard drives together for redundancy and to save the cost of a SLED. As costs and physical sizes of high capacity hard drives decreased and physical drive sizes were standardized, the term SLED has lost its meaning.

Site A logical group of interconnected physical machines all under the control of a single administrative unit. The administrative unit itself. The DNS domain name of the administrative unit. A site almost always contains multiple systems. Any one of these systems is not necessarily wholly contained within the site. Generally, the machines that make up a site are collocated geographically, hence the name. A site is frequently equated with its DNS domain name. James attacked site blue. James attacked blue.com.

Site license Usually software manufacturers will sell their software based on the amount of users using the software. As the amount of users increases and prices get higher, software manufacturers will sometimes sell a site license that entitles an entire site to use as many licenses as it needs to at a particular location for a single price. This makes management of a large amount of licenses unnecessary and simplifies things for the customer and the software vendor. For example, one company may have a 1-user, 5-user, 10-user, 25-user, and finally a site-license version of its software. The site license will be the most expensive, but may be more economical if you have a large amount of users.

Skeleton The ORB /o component which assists an object adapter in passing requests to particular methods. It is specific to an object and an interface.

Skin A graphic or graphic scheme that is placed over a 2D or 3D object. For 3D games such as Quake, you can wrap a 2D graphic skin around your 3D character to change its appearance. Another skin example would be a Web browser that customizes the way it looks. Most programs that allow the use of skins have publicly available standards for creating new skins.

Sleep mode The placement of a computing device into an inoperable mode, where less power is consumed by shutting down unnecessary devices, but leaving all data in RAM. Typically you return from sleep mode by using the keyboard or mouse, and devices are switched back on. Sleep mode in its early incarnations was very problematic in some PCs, and would often crash programs and operating systems that were not completely compatible with the sleep mode in the PC's BIOS.

Slot mask This form of mask is similar to a shadow mask, but instead of a sheet of metal with holes poked into it it is a series of fine, vertically-aligned metal wires.

Small computer systems interface (SCSI) Pronounced "skuzzy," this is a standard data pathway used mostly for hard drives and CD-ROM drives; but it was also a common interface for scanners and even printers at one point. It is the fastest (and the most flexible) method of interfacing with hard drives. It comes in numerous varieties, and is mainly used in servers and high-end workstations. SCSI drives are much more expensive than IDE drives, but SCSI drives can have features, like 15,000 RPM spin speeds and 5-year warranties, that IDE drives currently do not.

Small outline dimm (SO-DIMM) A small form factor DIMM that is designed for use in laptops, graphics cards, and other devices that require a smaller than normal DIMM. The SO-DIMM allowed for an easily interchangeable SDRAM module for small form factor devices, replacing numerous proprietary laptop memory standards.

SMART (self-monitoring analysis and reporting tool) This technology reports on a variety of hard drive attributes. You need a compliant BIOS and SCSI and/or IDE controller, a hard drive that supports SMART, and some sort of software package that reports on these conditions. Once you have that you should be able to receive system warnings about your hard drive. Many hard drive manufacturers have added onto the SMART technology or changed it around so that it has proprietary features for their drives. The good news about SMART is that having SMART is much better than not having it, and you can be warned of hard drive failure before it happens and backup your drive while it still works. Thus, your data is safer with SMART around.

Smartscan Heuristic scan, which first checks to see whether a file has changed before determining whether to scan it. An integrity file is created and updated in the directory of any file scanned.

SMS (short message service) A method of sending text messages that are 160 characters in length or shorter over a mobile phone. More and more mobile phones are supporting the sending and receiving of SMS messages.

Snail-mail A mail system in which you print the message you want to send to another person, address a paper envelope of the correct size to fit the paper, insert the paper in the envelope, close the envelope, find a postage stamp, and place the entire thing in a U.S mail box. Many Unix users find electronic mail simpler, faster, and more convenient.

Socket In UNIX and some other operating systems, a software object that connects an application to a network protocol. In UNIX, for example, a program can send and receive TCP/IP messages by opening a socket and reading and writing data to and from the socket. This simplifies program development because the programmer need only worry about manipulating the socket and can rely on the operating system to actually transport messages across the network correctly. Note that a socket in this sense is completely soft - it's a software object, not a physical component.

A receptacle into which a plug can be inserted.

A receptacle for a microprocessor or other hardware component.

Socket services Part of the software support needed for PCMCIA hardware devices in a portable computer, controlling the interface to the hardware. Socket services is the lowest layer in the software that manages PCMCIA cards. It provides a BIOS-level software interface to the hardware, effectively hiding the specific details from higher levels of software. Socket services also detect when you insert or remove a PCMCIA card and identify the type of card it is.

Software A set of instructions (also called programs) that tell a computer to do something. In contrast to hardware, which includes the physical components of your computer, software is composed of information on a disk (or tape, or whatever).

Software developer's kit (SDK) A programming tool that is tailored towards a particular purpose. The kit includes a compiler, linker, and an editor. Most hardware manufacturers have SDKs available that work specifically with their hardware.

Software engineering A systematic approach to the analysis, design, implementation and maintenance of software. It usually involves the use of CASE tools CASE-tools. There are various models of the software life-cycle, and many methodologies for the different phases.

Software license Most corporations need multiple copies of software, but do not need the media in which they come, either because they already have it or because they allow users to install software from a server on the network. Companies still need to purchase a copy for each user, however, so they need a way to prove they have actually purchased a copy of each. These companies purchase software licenses with no associated media. Such licenses are typically just sheets of paper that cost a lot of money, but allow you to legally use additional copies of the software.

Software metrics Measures of software quality which indicate the complexity, understandability, testability, description and intricacy of code.

Software modem A modem implemented entirely in software. Software modems rely on the computer's processor to modulate and demodulate signals.

Software-defined networks (SDNs) The same as virtual private networks (VPNs), where the subscriber can set up and maintain a communications system using management software, on a public network.

Sound board A hardware insert for computers that allows mono or stereo audio (e.g., from cassette players, microphones, and television audio tracks) to be sent to computer speakers "on the fly" and/or to be captured as computer files such aswav and voc files for PC computers. The wav file extensions run on Microsoft MCI standards and the voc files run on Soundblaster sound boards from Creative Labs. Hardware options are reviewed in the NewMedia 1996 Tool Guide. Software (audio editing) options are reviewed in the NewMedia 1996 Tool Guide. When available, it is often better to have audio hardware on the motherboard rather than as a board added to a computer's expansion slot.

Sound card A peripheral device in the form of a card used for producing sound and music. Although PCs come with a built-in speaker, it was originally tied to the CPU and did not do a good job of reproducing complex sounds. As for reproducing sound, the speaker takes most of the processor's power to produce only marginal sound, whereas a sound card does it effortlessly and creates a much better reproduction. Most motherboards today come with some kind of external sound chip built-in, just in case you want decent sound without attaching a separate sound card.

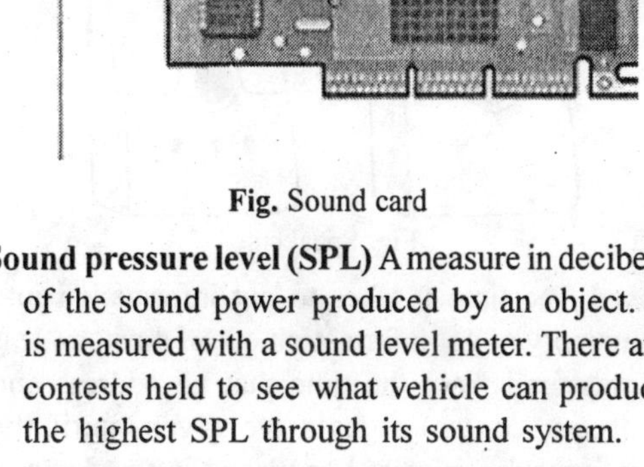

Fig. Sound card

Sound pressure level (SPL) A measure in decibels of the sound power produced by an object. It is measured with a sound level meter. There are contests held to see what vehicle can produce the highest SPL through its sound system.

Source code The uncompiled code of a computer program. Before compiling you can look at the instructions and tell what the program does—if you are familiar with the programming language. After compiling, the source code is transformed into machine code that is much more low level and hard to follow, making optimizations and fixes almost impossible. Thus, some developers package the source code with their software so that if people want to improve it or fix it—or just see how it works-they can do that.

Source code control system (SCCS) A suite of utilities to administrate source code such that only one person can change any given file at any given instant. Provides audit trails.

Spam Spam, also referred to as unsolicited bulk email, or "junk" email, is unrequested email that is sent to multiple recipients, with a purpose to promote, a business, idea or service. Spam is also used by hackers to spread vandals and viruses in email, or to trick users into visiting hostile or hacked sites, which will attack innocent surfers. Spam usually promotes "get rich quick" schemes, porn sites, travel/vacation services, and a variety of other topics.

Speaker shielding The ferro-magnetic shielding around the magnets of speakers that prevents interference with a CRT monitor and prevents damage to magnetic media such as floppies and hard drives.

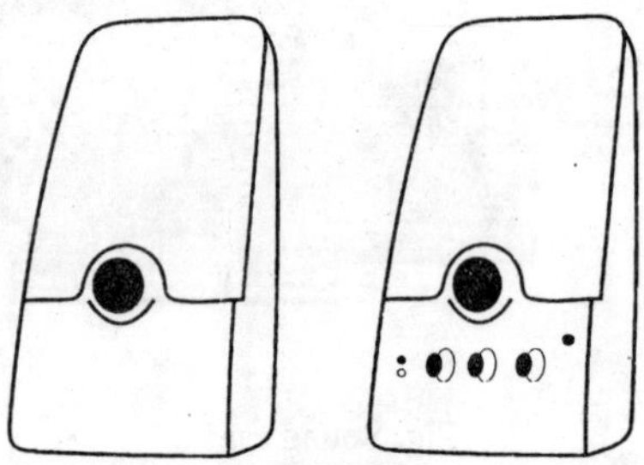

Fig. Speakers

Speed The time it takes to put information into memory or get information out of memory. It is measured from the time that an address and proper control signals are given, until the information is stored or placed in the device's output(s). RAM speed is typically expressed in nanoseconds (lower is faster) for EDO and FPM, and in MHz (higher is faster) for SDR SDRAM, DDR, SDRAM, and RDRAM.

Speedstep An Intel standard that allows its mobile processors to run at a lower MHz speed when used in a notebook that is not plugged into a power source.

Spell checker An application feature that users rely on to correct their grammar. The *de facto* industry standard requires the Spell Checker's dictionary to contain all the words in the English language *except* computer terminology and competing vendor's product names.

Spider This is also known as a Web crawler, a robot, Web spider, or sometimes a worm. It is a program that runs on the Internet, goes out to an URL (Web page), and requests all links that are referred to on that page. Spiders learn as they go, building a database of links. They index based on meta tags in the HTML, the title, or just about anything else you can imagine. Usually they come from search engines, and are designed to keep the search engines current.

Spindle The centerpiece of a hard drive which holds one or more hard drive platters. Often the term spindle is used to differentiate hard drives from hard disk platters in discussion when referring to large RAID subsystems holding many hard drives, such as "We'll be using 50 spindles instead of 10 spindles in the new RAID box." Basically a spindle is seen as a limiting factor in performance; generally, more spindles in a system mean higher possible performance.

Spoofing (email) Mail-spoofing is forging email senders addresses. This could be dangerous as someone might impersonate someone else. Spammers and hackers use it extensively. One example of a spoof is to send messages to users that appear to come from the administrator, and to request that the users change their password to the new value provided in the message.

Spoofing (file types) When a file extension is changed to create a backup or disabled working copy of a file, no harm is done. However, hackers can use this technique to hide the true nature of a file.

Spool The intermediary device between a computer and a printer. In the old days, if you had no spooler your computer would wait as the printer slowly printed a document. You would send your print data to a spooler to accept the data and save it temporarily to hard disk or memory while it dealt with the slow printer for you. Nowadays print-server is a more current term for describing this type of device. Most modern operating systems contain spooler processes that take care of printing in the background, and you don't notice any delays anyway Spool.

Spooler The intermediary device between a computer and a printer. In the old days, if you had no spooler your computer would wait as the printer slowly printed a document. You would send your print data to a spooler to accept the data and save it temporarily to hard disk or memory while it dealt with the slow printer for you. Nowadays print-server is a more current term for describing this type of device. Most modern operating systems contain spooler processes that take care of printing in the background, and you don't notice any delays anyway.

Spreadsheet A type of computer program that displays a group of cells (a 2D graph pattern) and allows for easy mathematical operations and relationships among the cells. The first major spreadsheet was Lotus 1-2-3. Today's most popular spreadsheet is Microsoft Excel.

SQL Structured Query Language. SQL is a relational data language that provides a consistent, English keyword-oriented set of facilities for query, data definition, data manipulation and data control. It is a programming interface to a relational database management system (RDBMS). SQL was introduced by IBM Research as the main external interface to System R, an experimental RDBMS developed in the 1970s. SQL statements include: Data manipulation language (DML) statements - SELECT, INSERT, UPDATE and DELETE; Data definition language (DDL) statements including the CREATE and DROP statements for tables and indexes and statements that control data consistency, and grant and revoke authority. SQL statements that are not completely specified until the program is executed are called dynamic. SQL statements that are completely specified when the program is compiled are said to be static.

SSA (serial storage architecture) Along with its FC-AL Fibre Channel alterative, that offer huge bandwidth networking schemes that operate within an Eithernet network. Shared discs in SSA or FC-AL systems can be operated over networks as fast as hard drives on a local computer. Furthermore, the connecting cables are "thin" relative to traditional SCSI connection cables. Whjile Ultra-Wide SCSI has a 40Mbps maximum bandwidth, SSA offers 80 MBps and FC-AL goes up to 100 MBps. SSA is fully duplex with two cables to devices. One advantage of SSA is that if a connected device fails, the entire loop does not fail since SSA does not require a hub. Over time, SSA systems and FC-AL will probably replace SCSI systems.

SSD (solid state drive) This type of storage is basically a huge block of RAM chips that functions like a hard drive. Solid state drives are extremely expensive, but offer very high data speeds that are necessary in some applications. They can also be used as large caches on huge RAID subsystems, but due to the volatile nature of the DRAM used as storage solid state drives should be used carefully.

SSE (streaming SIMD extensions) The name for Intel's additions to the x86 instructions set, introduced in its Pentium III processor. The SSE extensions are similar to AMD's 3DNow set of instructions. These extensions are a set of 70 instructions that perform SIMD operations. In addition, to support these instructions Pentium IIIs come with 8 128-bit registers dedicated to them.

Stack A reserved area of memory used to keep track of a program's internal operations, including functions, return addresses, passed parameters,etc. A stack is usually maintained as a "last in, first out" (LIFO) data structure, so that the last item added to the structure is the first item used.

Standardized general markup language (SGML) A generalized format for marking up documents, originally created by the United States government. One of the more common subsets of SGML is HyperText Markup Language (HTML).

Star network A network topology in the form of a star. At the center of the star is a wiring hub or concentrator, and the nodes or workstations are arranged around the central point representing the points of the star.

Start/stop bits A start bit signals the start of a unit of data in asynchronous communications. A stop bit signals the stop of a unit of data. The unit can vary in length depending on the protocol.

State database A database containing the state of each metadevice, stored in a dedicated (and non-metadevice) disk partition.

State transition diagram A diagram consisting of circles to represent states and directed line segments to represent transitions between the states. One or more actions may be associated with each transition. The diagrom represents a Finite State Machine.

Stateful Inspection The ability of a firewall to retain "state" information about ongoing network sessions. When a packet goes out through a stateful firewall (TCP/UDP/ICMP) it will only permit expected return traffic that would normally be returned in response to that packet from the remote site. This prevents spoofed packet attacks and other nasty things.

Statement A single line of a script or program.

Static IP address An IP address that does not change. Most IP addresses for client machines are handed out by a method such as a DHCP server that manages a range of IP addresses. Static IP addresses are typically reserved for servers or routers, but some companies still use them for all their PCs. Most IP addresses handed out by an ISP are not static, but you can find ISPs that offer static IP addresses.

Static RAM A type of computer memory that retains its contents as long as power is supplied; it does not need constant refreshment like dynamic RAM chips. A static RAM chip can only store about 1/4th of the information that a dynamic RAM chip can. However, SRAM is faster than DRAM , it has an access time of 15-30 nanoseconds. It is often used in caches.

Stock keeping unit (SKU) A number associated with a particular product, often represented by a barcode. The SKU is used to track inventory and may or may not be shown to customers when shopping on the Web.

Storage data acceleration (SDX) This technology was introduced by Western Digital. The idea behind it is that slower drives such as CD and DVD drives would attach directly to larger, faster hard drives. There would be a 10-pin connector between the hard drive and the other peripheral, as opposed to the 40-pin IDE connector. A portion of the hard drive would be used as cache for the CD drive or other device. This was touted to speed up CD-ROM drives by 50%-300% depending on what operations are being performed. You would have had to buy specialized hard drives and CD drives to take advantage of this technology, but it flopped, so don't worry about it.

Store-and-forward A delivery method for data within a network in which information moves from one node to another toward its target. If any node in the paths is unavailable, the last active node in the chain holds the information until thatm node becomes available, at which time the transfer continues. The originator need not maintain the information as each node receiving the object accepts responsibility for its delivery. Although store-and-forward is most often associated with electronic mail, it can be used for file transfer, software updates and other functions that do not require a "quick" or synchronised response.

Streaming SIMD extensions (SSE) The name for Intel's additions to the x86 instructions set, introduced in its Pentium III processor. The SSE extensions are similar to AMD's 3DNow set of instructions. These extensions are a set of 70 instructions that perform SIMD operations. In addition, to support these instructions Pentium IIIs come with 8 128-bit registers dedicated to them.

Streaming tape A high-speed tape backup system, often used to make a complete backup of an entire hard disk.A streaming tape is designed to optimize throughput so that time is never wasted by stopping the tape during a backup; this also means that the computer and backup software also have to be fast enough to keep up with the tape drive.

Structured query language (SQL) This is a means of managing data in a relational database. There is a SQL standard, and there are also many vendor-specific SQL packages which combine relational databases with tools SQL tools to manage them. Statements in SQL can be used to read or request data from a database, such as, "select from geek," which would return an entire table of data from the table named "geek." Queries can also be much more complex such as, "select from geek where name=sam" which would return records from the database where the field "name" was set to "sam." SQL statements can also be used to delete and update data.

Structured This adjective describes how data are stored and used at companies. Travel agents, for example, type information into designated spaces on electronic forms on their computer screens that are connected to database programs. That structures, or categorizes, the information so it can be searched and sorted using such criteria as a customer's name or destination. The Web, in contrast, stores data in an unstructured way that limits the kinds of searches that can be performed.

Stub A discontinuity in a SCSI bus. There are required lengths between stubs for the various SCSI standards. Each SCSI device counts as a stub. You can think of anything that's not a continuous SCSI cable as a stub.

Student response pads Hand-held wireless audience response pads which allow individual answers or group frequency responses to be immediately displayed in front of the class. The pads themselves must be separately purchased. HyperGraphics is the only CMS vendor that sells response pads with built in CMS software utilities. Barry Rice at Loyola College in Maryland performs Multimedia ToolBook authoring with student response pads for accounting applications in a Windows environment.

Studio classroom An application of computer technology pioneered by Jack M. Wilson at Rensselaer Polytechnical Institute for replacing large lecture courses with students working in pairs in front of computer screens where they interactively tackle problems and issues rather than listen to or passively watch lectures in front of a mass lecture section. The only lecture comes at the beginning and end of class where the instructor commences or wraps up the learning session. The "studio" is a combination lab and electronic classroom.

Stylus A pen-like pointing device used in pen-based systems and personal digital assistants.

Subdomain Typically known as a "domain within a domain", subdomains are individual Web addresses built upon a pre-existing domain name (such as clientname.yourhostingcompany.com). As a reseller, you will have the option of assigning subdomains to clients if they do not choose to have a domain name.

Subnet address An extension of the Internet addressing system that allows a site to subdivide a single Internet address to cover multiple physical networks. This is done by dividing up the host address part of an IP Address into a local network number and host address number.

Subnet mask A TCP/IP number used to determine to which TCP/IP subnet a device belongs. Devices in the same subnet can be communicated with locally without going through a router. When a TCP/IP device tries to communicate with another device the bits of the TCP/IP destination address are "ANDed" with the subnet mask to determine whether the address is a local address (broadcastable) or must be reached through a router. A subnet mask of 255.255.255.0 used by a computer with a TCP/IP address of 10.10.10.1 would include the addresses 10.10.10.0 through 10.10.10.255 in the local network, basically telling the computer to try a router if it's transmitting to any other IP address.

Super bypass A means of reducing memory latency in the AMD 750 chipset, the first chipset designed to work with the AMD Athlon. It was implemented in all versions of the AMD 750, but did not function properly in early versions. AMD corrected this problem with a new revision of the AMD 750 chipset. It is possible to identify the Super Bypass-capable chipsets electronically or through software, but the enabling or disabling of Super Bypass is done automatically by the motherboard BIOS.

Supercomputer A computer that is able to operate at a speed that places it at or near the top speed of currently produced computers. Most supercomputers cost millions of dollars, and the traditional model of using one large computer with proprietary hardware is being challenged by using a cluster of cheaper computers with more standard hardware.

Superscalar A processor that is capable of executing more than one instruction during a processor cycle. Processors can do this by fetching multiple instructions in one cycle, deciding which instructions are independent of other instructions, and executing them. To do this the processor must have an instruction fetching unit that can fetch more than one instruction at a time, built-in logic to determine if instructions are independent, and multiple execution units to execute all the independent instructions. Instructions that depend on the results of the previous instruction obviously can't be executed simultaneously with the instructions on which they depend. This type of instruction slows down superscalar processors. If all instructions are of this type you get no benefit from the superscalar architecture.

Support 1. The business activity that turns profitable products into unprofitable ones, and vice-versa.

2. The process of reducing user questions into three categories, a.) known problems with answers, b.) unsupported configurations, and c.) further profitable opportunities.

Surf This term is synonymous with browsing, as in browsing the Web with a Web browser.

Survivability The capability of a system to fulfill its mission, in a timely manner, in the presence of attacks, failures, or accidents. Timeliness is a critical factor that is typically included in (or implied by) the very high-level requirements that define a mission. However, timeliness is such an important factor that we include it explicitly in the definition of survivability. It is important to recognize that it is the mission fulfillment that must survive, not any particular subsystem or system component. Central to the notion of survivability is the capability of a system to fulfill its mission, even if significant portions of the system are damaged or destroyed. We will sometimes use the term survivable system as a less than perfectly precise shorthand for a system with the capability to fulfill a specified mission in the face of attacks, failures, or accidents.

Swap file On a hard disk, a file used to store parts of running programs that have been swapped out of memory temporarily to make room for other running programs. It may be permanent, always occupying the same amount of hard disk space even though the application that created it may not be running, or is temporary, and only created as and when needed.

Swap space Disk space used by the kernel as "virtual" RAM. It is slower than RAM, but because disk space is cheaper, swap is usually more plentiful. Swap space is useful to the kernel for holding lesser-used data and as a fallback when physical RAM is exhausted.

Switch A hub that directs network packets to the port for which they are intended, without broadcasting them to all connections. At one time switched hubs were a luxury used only on the backbone of a network; nowadays even consumer equipment is switched to allow for faster networking. For an example of the benefits of switches over simple hubs, a 24-port 100BaseT hub can only transfer 100Mbits of data at any given time. A 24-port 100BaseT switch could theoretically be used to transfer 2.4Gbits/second, assuming that the switch is built to handle that much throughput.

Switched connection A connection that requires a manual or an automated sequence to establish a connection before it can be used by any software or hardware component. Often referred to as a "dialled" connection because of the need to complete a phone call to establish the connection, its characteristics are different from a dedicated line (always available for use) and it requires different support. Applications using switched lines cannot assume the connection is made or that communication has been initialised.

Switching hub Short for port-switching hub, a special type of hub that forwards packets to the appropriate port based on the packet's address. Conventional hubs simply rebroadcast every packet to every port. Since switching hubs forward each packet only to the required port, they provide much better performance. Most switching hubs also support load balancing, so that ports are dynamically reassigned to different LAN segments based on traffic patterns.

Some newer switching hubs support both traditional Ethernet (10 Mbps) and Fast Ethernet (100 Mbps) ports. This enables the administrator to establish a dedicated, Fast Ethernet channel for high-traffic devices such as servers.

Switching system A set of one or more systems that act together and appear as a single switch for the purposes of PNNI routing.

Synchronization The timing of separate elements or events to occur simultaneously. In a multimedia presentation, synchronization ensures that the audio and video components are timed correctly. In a computer-to-computer communications, the hardware and software must be synchronized so that the file transfers can take place. The process of updating files on both a portable comp and a desktop system so that they both have the latest versions.

Synchronous (synchrome) Having a constant time interval between successive bits, characters or events. Synchronous transmission uses no redundant information to identify the beginning and the end of the characters, and thus is faster and more efficient than asynchronous transmission, which uses start and stop bits. The timing is achieved by transmitting sync characters prior to data ; usually synchronisation can be achieved in two or three character times.

Synchronous network architecture distribution services (SNADS) The distribution protocol, handling delivery and verification, for Synchronous Network Architecture (SNA).

Synchronous Optical network (SONET) A fiber optic network in a ring topology, often used to carry voice signals or Internet traffic. One ring is described as hot, or carrying data. The other ring is the protect—or standby—ring that transmits data in the opposite direction in case of service degradation or a fiber cut. Typically, within 50 milliseconds of a failure SONET equipment on the edge of the failing segment attempts to construct a new ring using a combination of standby fiber and hot fiber—if any of it is working.

Synchronous transmission In communications, a transmission method that uses a clock signal to regulate data flow. Synchronous transmissions do not use start and stop bits.

System A combination of the hardware, software, and firmware. A system typically consists of components (or elements) which are connected together in order to accomplish a specific function or set of functions.

System administrator The godlike being who keeps your system running. Responsible for everything involving your system and the network it's on, including but not limited to managing your account (creation, modification, closure, deletion), your workstation, your subnet, your routers, the system-wide hosts table, the mail subsystem, all mail aliases and groups, keeping time synchronized across the network, the news subsystem, the printer subsystem, any applications you use—basically, the person who keeps everything working smoothly and seamlessly.

System disk A disk that contains all the files necessary to boot and start the OS. In most computers, the hard disk is the system disk.

System file In DOS and OS/2, a file whose system attribute is set. In IBM's PC-DOS, the two system files are called IBMBIOS.COM and IBMDOS.COM; in MS-DOS, they are called IO.SYS and MSDOS.SYS. These files contain the essential routines needed to manage devices, memory, and I/O operations.

System management bus (SMB or SMBus) A standard created by Intel in 1995. It is a two-wire specification that uses a connector the size of an RJ-45 plug and allows for communications between an external UPS or power device and a computer. SMB connections are found on many motherboards designed for servers and workstations.

System monitor An application that monitors important system resources and allows you to undo changes made by Trojan horses and other malicious content. Important system resources should include: critical Registry Keys, system configurations, and the bootup sequence.

System software The programs that make up the operating system(OS), along with the associated utility programs, as distinct from an application program.

System time The time and date maintained by the internal clock inside the computer. This internal clock circuitry is usually backed up by a small battery so that the clock continues to keep time even though the computer may be switched off. The system time is used to date-stamp files with time of their creation or revision.

System tray (systray) The system tray is the location on the far right of the Windows 95/NT 4.0 (or newer version of Windows) taskbar. Within it always resides the clock, and often other user-installed programs that monitor the system or run constantly. If you double-click on items in the systray, you usually get some sort of window to open up and tell you about why the item is there and what you can do with it.

System unit The case that houses the processor, motherboard, internal hard- and floppy disks, power supply, and the expansion bus.

System.ini In Windows OSes, an initialization file that contains information on your hardware and the internal Windows operating environment.

Systems application architecture A set of IBM standards, first introduced in 1987, that define a consistent set of interfaces for future IBM software. Three standards are defined:

1.*Common User Access (CUA)* A GUI definition for products designed for use in an object-oriented operating environment.

2.*Common Programming Interface(CPI)* A set of APIs designed to encourage independence from the underlying OS. The standard database query language is SQL.

3.*Common Communications Support (CCS)* A common set of communications protocols that interconnect SAA systems and devices.

Systems network architecture (SNA) An IBM architecture for enterprise computing systems. IBM has created a complete suite of programs to work on its proprietary hardware for enterprise computing.

Systray (system tray) The system tray is the location on the far right of the Windows 95/NT 4.0 (or newer version of Windows) taskbar. Within it always resides the clock, and often other user-installed programs that monitor the system or run constantly. If you double-click on items in the systray, you usually get some sort of window to open up and tell you about why the item is there and what you can do with it.

T

T1 digital circuitry A type of digital network technology that can handle separate voice and/or digital communications lines.

Tab delimited A text file where data elements in the text file are separated by the tab character.

Tag image file format (TIFF) A bitmap graphics file format. It was developed by Aldus in 1986 to provide a common format for scanners, and is mainly used for that purpose, desktop publishing, and as the data format for scanned faxes.

Tag RAM A bank of SRAM that only holds addresses. Tag RAM is used to store addresses so that when the processor makes a call for memory it first checks to see if the data is in the cache by looking for the memory address in the tag RAM. If it's there, it gets the data from cache. If not, it gets the data from main memory. Tag RAM controls the amount of memory that can be cached. For example, the Tag RAM used with most Intel 430TX chipsets only allowed the first 64 MB of RAM to be cached. You could use more RAM in your machine but it won't be cached, and thus performance will be affected when memory over 64 MB is accessed.

TAG TAG memory acts as an index for the information stored in L2 cache. It is usually composed of SRAM.

Taligent A former software development venture initially commenced by Apple and IBM corporations. In 1994, Hewlett-Packard announced it would take 15% in Taligent and provide technical support. Taligent's primary mission is to develop cross-platform object-oriented operating systems and applications software, the first release of which will be in 1995 for IBM's Unix-based system called AIX. Versions for OS/2, PowerOpen, and Hewett-Packards HP-UX systems will follow. The future of Taligent along with a similar joint venture at Kaleida Labs is somewhat uncertain due to changing times and top management strategies in IBM and Apple.

Tangible Of a nature that is real, as opposed to something that is imaginary or abstract.

TAO (track at once) A method of writing data to a CD-R or CD-RW disc on a track by track basis. Recording can be paused between writing tracks, unlike Disc at Once, which requires an uninterrupted full-disc recording. You can create unclosed CDs with TAO recording that you can write to again at a later time.

Tap 1. A connector that attaches to a cable without blocking the passage of information along that cable.

2. In communications, a connection onto the main transmission medium of the network.

Tape A storage medium that consists of a long band of magnetic material wound around a couple of reels. Tapes can hold a lot of information, but are typically slow to access different parts of the tape, and can be unreliable for long-term storage due to their magnetic nature.

Tape archive (tar) A UNIX/Linux command that was designed to allow the storage of data spread across files and directories to exist in a single tape volume. Another handy use is to squeeze a directory or group of files into a single file on a hard drive, and then compact it with a compression program such as gzip to save some space. Simple usage includes "tar cvf" (cvf = create verbose-mode file), or "tar xvf" (x = extract) to extract a .tar file back to its original contents.

Tape drive A device that can store data on a tape. The advantage of storing data on a tape is that a tape can hold large amounts of data in a small and inexpensive package. On the downside, a tape cannot store the data indefinitely, and it is expensive and slower compared to a hard drive. But tapes themselves are cheaper, and are more easy to move around than hard drives.

Taskbar The space that normally sits at the bottom of the Windows 95/98/NT4/2000/XP interface. It displays the list of running programs so that you can easily switch among programs even when you have a maximized window taking up the entire screen otherwise. It can be moved to either side or the top of the screen.

TCP (transmission control protocol) Originally developed by the Department of Defense to support interworking of dissimilar computers across a network. A protocol which provides end-to-end, connection-oriented, reliable transport layer (layer 4) functions over IP controlled networks. TCP performs the following functions: flow control between two systems, acknowledgements of packets received and end-to-end sequencing of packets.

TCS (transmission convergence sublayer) This is part of the ATM physical layer that defines how cells will be transmitted by the actual physical layer.

Technographer This person types into a computer exactly what a person speaking at a meeting requests of them. The output is displayed on a screen for all to see. The important thing is that anyone can speak and ask the technographer to type in what he or she wants. The technographer doesn't type everything that is said, just what the speaker wants the technographer to type. What is typed cannot be changed by anyone but the speaker, even if it makes everyone else angry and has nothing to do with the meeting.

Teleconference A telephone communication in which more than two people are simultaneously connected so they can exchange verbal comments as if they were in the same room having a face-to-face conference. A teleconference need not have visual communications in addition to audio communications, but modern technology now makes it possible to see conference members on monitor screens or television screens.

Telematics The combination of computers in concert with telecommunications systems. This includes dial-up service to the Internet as well as all types of networks that rely on a telecommunications system to transport data.

Telemedicine The technology that permits remote diagnosis and treatment of patients by a medical practitioner; usually interactive bi-directional audio and video signals.

Telnet The Internet standard protocol for remote login service that allows users on the Internet to access programs and applications on computers in remote locations. Telnet allows a user at one site to interact with a remote timesharing system at another site as if the user's terminal were connected directly to the remote computer. When using the Internet, type "Telnet" followed by a space and the address of the computer for remote login. Note that the Telnet protocol should not be confused with the Telnet public data network.

Temporary swap file A sway file that is created every time it is needed. A temporary swap file will not consist of a single large area of contiguous hard disk space, but may consist of several discontinuous pieces of space.

Terabyte Abbreviated TB. In computing, usually 240, or 1,099,511,627,776 bytes. A terabyte is equivalent to 1,000 gigabytes, and usually refers to extremely large hard-disk capacities.

Terminal ready (TR) This light is illuminated when your computer has turned on the RS-232 (serial) interface. Sometimes this light will not come on until you have loaded your communications software into memory.

Terminal server A special-purpose computer with places to plug in several modems on one side, and a connection to a LAN or host machine on the other side. The terminal server does the work of passing connections on to the appropriate node. Most terminal servers can provide PPP or SLIP services if connected to the Internet.

Terminate and stay resident (TSR) A program that runs, loads into memory, and stays out of view until you call on it. TSRs were commonly used in DOS, and are not necessary in modern operating systems.

Terminate-and-stay-resident program A DOS program that stays loaded in memory, even when it is not actually running, so that you can invoke it very quickly to perform a specific task. Calendars, appointment schedulers, calculators are all popular TSR programs. TSRs occupy conventinal memory space that becomes unavailable for use by your applications programs

Termination (SCSI bus termination) Because of the amount of signals that SCSI format sends through small wiring, termination is required. The termination is accomplished by using resistors across certain signal wires. If the chain were not terminated, the signals would bounce off the end of the chain and cause interference with real signals.

Terminator A device attached to the end-points of a bus network or daisy-chain. The purpose of the terminator is to absorb signals so that they do not reflect back down the line. Ethernet networks require a terminator at both ends of the bus, and SCSI chains require a single terminator at the end of the chain.

A character that indicates the end of a string. In the C programming language, the null character serves as a terminator.

Text editor A class of computer programs that allows the opening, changing, and saving of text files. Text editors can be used to edit HTML files, and any file that is not binary in nature. Text editors are not good for working with graphics files or proprietary formats such as Word documents that contain formatting information that is not translated properly to plain text. Text editors differ from word processors because no formatting data (such as font type, font size, etc.) is added when a file is saved in a text editor.

Text file A file that consists of text characters without any formatting information. Also known as an ASCII file, a text file can be read by any word processor.

Tflop (teraflop) The ability of a system to compute one trillion floating point operations in one second.

TFT (thin layer transistor) Transistor type used in active matrix screens in laptop computers. Layers of TFT and condensers are put on a glass containing RGB filters.

TFTP (trivial file transfer protocol) A network transfer protocol that allows you to connect to a device and download code onto it. For example, it can be used to shove boot code onto a diskless workstation, or connect and download firmware updates to networking devices.

Thermal compound A paste that is applied between a microprocessor and heatsink. This paste fills in any tiny gaps that may be present on the visibly flat surfaces of the microprocessor package and heatsink. Without thermal compound cooling may be less efficient, as the heatsink and microprocessor package may have air gaps between them. Thermal compound has much more efficient heat exchange properties than air.

Thermal printer A nonimpact printer that uses a thermal printhead and specially treated paper to create an image. The main advangtage of a thermal printer is that it is virtually silent. Thermal printers are used in calculators and in terminals to provide a local printing capability.

Thicknet The type of cabling on which 10Base5 Ethernet runs. It can transfer data at up to 10Mbps using the 10Base5 Ethernet standard. It is thicker than 10Base2 cabling, and thus the name.

Thin client A thin client is similar to a dumb terminal in that it gets all of its information from the network. Some thin clients have their own memory, but lack a hard drive. They're basically stripped down computers that are supposed to lower the total cost of owning a computer. These computers are generally used in business or commercial applications.

Thin Ethernet Connecting coaxial cable used on an Ethernet network. The cable is 5 mm thick, and can be used to connect network nodes up to a distance of approx. 1000 feet. Primarily used for office installations.

Thin film transistor (TFT) A synonym for the Active Matrix display. You'll often see screens referred to as "TFT-Active Matrix," or just "TFT" if the manufacturer is low on space.

Third level domain In the Domain Name System (DNS, the next highest level of the hierarchy underneath the second level domains. It is that portion of the domain name that appears two segments to the left of the top level domain. Third level domains are not the portion of an email address that appears in front of the @ symbol - for example, the webmaster in support@DomainMart.com is not a third level domain.

Third party 1. Any company that is not Microsoft or IBM.

2. Any small company that pioneers an innovative technology, which will be immediately countered with a White Paper and later be superseded by an inferior version bundled in the Operating System.

Thrashing An excessive amount of disk activity in a virtual memory system, to the point where the system is spending all its time swapping pages in and out of memory, and no time executing the application. Thrashing can be caused when poor system configuration creates a swap file that is too small, or when insufficient memory is installed in the computer. Increasing the size of the swap file and adding memory are the best ways to reduce thrashing.

Thread Part of a program that runs independently or along with other threads to accomplish a task. To run multiple threads you must be running on an operating system such as UNIX or Windows NT/2000/XP that supports multiple threads. The performance benefit of allowing multiple threads to run at the same time is realized mainly on multi-processing systems. Different threads run on different processors, so they can run simultaneously.

Three-beam projector A computer/video projector having three color beams (guns) to project computer and/or video images on the wall or large screens. These are generally the top of the line in terms of projection quality and lowest in line in terms of portability. Most of these have scan converters to convert computer RGB into NTSC images. Early models could only scan CGA images from PC computers. Modern versions can scan almost any type of computer display, although they may require skilled technicians to adjust the display whenever a computer is first connected to the projector. These projectors are very popular as ceiling mounts in electronic classrooms.

Thumbnail (thumb) A small representation of a larger graphic. Detail is lost in the representation, but you get an idea of the content of the graphic. Thumbnails are often used on the Internet to display several graphics at once, or in imaging software so that you can sort through images more easily.

Title bar The top horizontal border of a rectangular region owned by a program running in a graphical user interface (GUI); it usually contains the program name and can be used to move the region around.

Titles The vast array of CD-ROM, CD-I, CD-3DO, videodisc, videotape,. and other "titles" of electronic books, electronic games, etc. available on the market.

TLV type / length / value A coding methodology which provides a flexible and extensible means of coding parameters within a frame. Type indicates parameter type. Length indicates parameter's value length. Value indicates the actual parameter value.

TM (traffic management) Traffic Management is the aspect of the traffic control and congestion control procedures for ATM. ATM layer traffic control refers to the set of actions taken by the network to avoid congestion conditions. ATM layer congestion control refers to the set of actions taken by the network to minimize the intensity, spread and duration of congestion. The following functions form a framework for managing and controlling traffic and congestion in ATM networks and may be used in appropriate combinations.

Connection Admission Control.

Feedback Control.

Usage Parameter Control.

Priority Control

Traffic Shaping.

Network Resource Management.

Toggle A function that allows a user to switch back and fourth between an OFF and ON position.

Token ring A computer network arbitration scheme in which conflicts in the transmission of messages are avoided by the granting of "tokens" which give permission to send. A station keeps the token while transmitting a message, if it has a message to transmit, and then passes it on to the next station.

Token-ring network A LAN with a ring structure that uses token-passing to regulate traffic on the network and avoid collisions. On a token-ring network, the controlling computer generates a "token" that controls the right to transmit. This token is continuously passed from one node to the next around the network. When a node has information to transmit, it captures the token, sets its status to busy, and adds the message and the destination address. All other nodes continuously read the token to determine if they are the recipient of a message; if they are, they collect the token, extract the message, and return the token to the sender. The sender then removes the message and sets the token status to free, indicating that it can be used by the next node in sequence.

Toner Basically this is ink in dust form. It is specially formulated to be sticky and to melt at a couple hundred degrees so that it bonds with paper when used in a laser printer or copier.

Toner cartridge When referring to laser printers (or copiers or fax machines) this is a cartridge that contains toner and the electrostatic drum used to transfer that toner.

Toolbar A common user interface term that refers to any rectangular bar of buttons or icons with a set of related functions. For example, most browsers use a toolbar for navigating forward or backwards through pages. You can often customize toolbars and add more functionality to them.

Torx A type of indent in a screw head that looks like a 6-pointed star. Compaq used torx screws for all of its computer equipment at one point. Torx sciews are also used in some automotive applications for body trim that should not be easily removed, such as to hold in the headlights on a '79 Chevy Malibu. Because a

Torx driver is rarer than a Phillips-head or flat-head screwdriver, Torx screws are used as a simple security method.

Total cost of ownership (TCO) This phrase was coined by the creators of the Network Computer (NC) to describe the benefits of using a system that is more mainframe and less client/server. Their logic states that NCs, although they may cost the same up front as cheap PCs, have a lower TCO than a network built on PCs.

Touchpad A pad that is electrically sensitive to touch, often used as the pointing device in laptops. You can also tap on it for clicks, but some people find that annoying if they bump the pad while typing.

Touchscreen An overlay for a computer monitor screen that allows users to control navigation and other actions by touching the screen. Although widely used for children, touchscreens are also useful when customers enter reception areas and library users want to search holdings listings.

Tower case A system unit case designed to stand on the floor rather than be placed on a desktop. Tower cases often have mor drive bays and expansion slots than the desktop units, and are commonly used for file servers and workstations.

Tracert (traceroute) A command that displays PING results for each router encountered between a source and a destination TCP/IP address. Traceroute is useful for getting some information along the entire path between two TCP/IP addresses. Firewalls or other security measures that block PING traffic also block traceroutes. The command itself is typed "tracert" on the command line of most operating systems.

Track A concentric collection of sectors on a hard- or floppy disk.

The outermost track on the top of the disk (or platter) is numbered track 0 side 0, and the outermost track on the other side is numbered track 0 side1. Numbering increases inwards towards the center of the disk. Tracks are created during the disk formatting process.

On tapes, tracks are parallel lines down the axis of the tape.

Track at once (TAO) A method of writing data to a CD-R or CD-RW disc on a track by track basis. Recording can be paused between writing tracks, unlike Disc at Once, which requires an uninterrupted full-disc recording. You can create unclosed CDs with TAO recording that you can write to again at a later time.

Track-at-once recording A mode that lets you record contents to a disk in multiple sessions, a track at a time.

Trackball An input device used for pointing, designed as an alternative to the mouse. It is almost an upside-down mouse; it is stationary and contains a movable ball that you rotate using your fingers to move the mouse cursor on the screen.

Tracking number The reference number assigned to an email message when the email message is received by InterNIC at the hostmaster@internic.net address. The tracking number has the following format: NIC-YYMMDD.#, where YYMMDD represent the year, month, and date that the acknowledgment is sent, and # is the unique number assigned to that particular request. The tracking number can be used to check on the status of a registration request as well as payment status for a domain name.

Trademark A word, phrase, graphic image, or other symbol used to represent a business, commercial, or other organization. Trademarks are used to identify the organization to the public and to consumers and are intended to identify the organization's products and services as well. To be recognized as a trademark, the word, phrase, graphic image, or symbol must be registered with the U.S. Patent and Trademark Office (in the United States) or, in the case of other countries, with the appropriate authority for that country.

Trademark rights A trademark is a name, symbol, or phrase that identifies a trading organization and is owned by that organization.

Transceiver Short for transmitter-receiver, a device that both transmits and receives analog or digital signals. The term is used most frequently to describe the component in local-area networks (LANs) that actually applies signals onto the network wire and detects signals passing through the wire. For many LANs, the transceiver is built into the network interface card (NIC). Some types of networks, however, require an external transceiver. In Ethernet networks, a transceiver is also called a Medium Access Unit (MAU).

Transfer The process of changing the party whom is listed as the domain name registrant. The party taking over the domain name is responsible for paying a new registration fee. Domain name transfers are processed using the Registrant Name Change Agreement (RNCA).

Transfer rate The speed at which a disk drive can transfer information between its platters and your CPU. The transfer rate is typically measured in megabytes per second, megabits per second, or megahertz.

Transport layer (couche transport) In the Open Systems Interconnection (OSI) model, the network processing entity responsible, in conjunction with the underlying network, data link and physical layers, for the end-to-end control of transmitted data and the optimized use of network resources.

Transport layer The OSI model layer responsible for the guaranteed serial delivery of packets between two computers over an internetwork. TCP is the Transport Layer Protocol for the TCP/IP transport protocol.

Transport protocol A service that delivers discrete packets of information between any two computers in a network. Higher level connection-oriented services are built upon transport protocols.

Trilinear filtering Like Bilinear Filtering, this is used to smooth flat surfaces by averaging the colors of adjacent pixels, which blurs them and removes blockiness when examined closely.

Trinitron A technology developed by Sony to enhance the clarity of graphics on its monitors. These screens were vertically flat and made the pixels appear more square and uniform.

Triodes Nearly obsolete electronic devices constructed of sealed glass tubes containing metal elements in a vacuum; triodes were used to control electrical signals.

Trojan horse (trojan) A computer program that appears to be something useful, but then does something malicious to your computer. This could range from destroying data to laying dormant and someday hijacking your computer to be used as part of a Denial of Service attack. Anti-virus programs will protect you from known Trojan horses, but strictly speaking Trojan horses are unlike viruses because they do not replicate. However, combination virus/Trojans can replicate.

Trolling The act of deliberately posting false or inflammatory information in order to start a flame war or cause aggravation to others.

True color Refers to any graphics device or software that uses at least 24 bits to represent each dot or pixel. Using 24 bits means that more than 16 million unique colors can be represented. Since humans can only distinguish a few million colors, this is more than enough to accurately represent any color image.

True parity This term has come about with the advent of logical parity memory. It simply means that the parity memory actually does something useful instead of just issuing positives over and over.

Tunes A project to design a new computing environment at all levels of software.

Tunneling A way of handling different communication protocols, by taking packets of a foreign protocol and changing them so that they appear to be a locally known type.

Tuple (n-tuple) This is a mathematical term for a finite sequence of n terms. For example, the set {1, 2, 3, 4} is a four-tuple. The set {Frank, Jane, Ed} is a three-tuple. Any time there is a list of n things in a certain order, you can think of it as an n-tuple.

Turbo-pascal Borland's version of the Pascal programming language.

Turing machine A proposed type of computing machine that takes inputs off paper tape and then moves through a sequence of states under the control of an algorithm; identified by Alan Turing (1912-1954).

Turnkey This usually refers to a server or a complex system that can basically be shipped from the manufacturer, turned on, and work right away. Many VARs pride themselves on providing turnkey servers on which their customers don't need to do any configuration. If you think of it in terms of an engine, a turnkey engine comes with all the parts and can be tossed into a car and work immediately. An engine that isn't turnkey will need additional parts and integration before it will run.

Turnkey system A system that already contains all the components and programs required for operation. The vendor takes care of installation and configurations so all the user has to do is "turn the key" to begin using the system.

Twisted pair An inexpensive, medium bandwidth communication channel commonly used in local area networks.

Twisted-pair cable Cable that comprises two insulated wires twisted together at six twists per inch. In twisted-pair cable, one wire carries the signal and the other is grounded. Telephone wire installed in modern buildings is often twisted-pair wiring.

Two-factor authentication Any method of authentication is based on two factors, such as something the user knows (a PIN, etc.) and something the user has (a hardware token or other physical device).

Two-phase commit Method for co-ordinating a single transaction across two or more database management systems or other resource managers. Two-phase commit guarantees the logical integrity of data by ensuring that transaction updates are finalised ("committed") in all of the separate databases or are fully backed out of all participating databases, i.e., all or nothing based on transaction boundaries. Two-phase commit is a necessary component of distributed database and is implemented in "transaction management" software, which may be part of a database management system, on-line transaction processing monitor, or front-end application tool.

TX (transmission) The act of uploading or sending data. Often the term "TX" is used on indicator lights on modems or network cards to indicate that data is flowing out of the device.

Txd Abbreviation for transmit data. A hardware signal defined by the RS-232-C standard that carries information from one device to another.

U

UART (universal asynchronous receiver/transmitter) An electronic module that combines the transmitting and receiving circuitry needed for asynchronous transmission over a serial line.

UBR (unspecified bit rate) UBR is an ATM service category which does not specify traffic related service guarantees. Specifically, UBR does not include the notion of a per-connection negotiated bandwidth. No numerical commitments are made with respect to the cell loss ratio experienced by a UBR connection, or as to the cell transfer delay experienced by cells on the connection.

UCD User Centered Design.

UDMA A protocol developed by Quantum Corporation and Intel that supports burst mode data transfer rates of 33.3 MBps. This is twice as fast as the previous disk drive standard for PCs, and is necessary to take advantage of new, faster Ultra ATA disk drives.

UDP (user datagram protocol) Part of the TCP/IP suite of protocols. UDP is the part of the TCP/IP suite used by applications to transfer datagrams. It is also the part of TCP/IP responsible for port addresses.

UI (unix international) A consortium including Sun and AT&T, promoting an open environment base on UNIX UNIX System V System-V including the Open Look Open-Look windowing system.

UIMX An interface builder for Motif Motif from Visual Edge.

ULSI (ultra large scale integration) A microchip with over one million transistors. Most popular chips today fit this description. Maybe in 10 years we will have the SDULSI, for Super-Duper Ultra Large Scale Integration. For now this is at the top of the heap.

Ultimedia video Is IBM Corporation's OS/2 equivalent of Video for Windows. Ultimedia Video IN/2 is priced at under $200 and supports video capture and editing in IBM Ultimation and Indeo compression formats. It can deliver up to 30 fps at 320 by 240 window size if the user's hardware can handle the upper-end capabilities.

Ultra 160M (160M) A form of SCSI that supercedes Ultra2 SCSI. It runs at up to 160 megabytes per second and uses 80-pin connections over copper wires.

Ultra 320M (320m) A form of SCSI that doubles the potential performance of Ultra 160M SCSI and offers throughput of up to 320 megabytes per second per channel.

Ultra ATA/100 Another extension to the ATA interface that adds a 50% increase in top speed over ATA/66, getting to 100MB/second, up from 66MB/second. This standard also adds some additional error-checking not found in earlier ATA standards. Like Ultra ATA/66, ATA/100 requires an 80-conductor cable to work at full speed.

Ultra ATA/133 This refers to what is most probably the final extension to the parallel ATA connection standard. The proposal was created by Maxtor, and allows a top data transfer rate of 133 megabytes per second. Intel didn't support this standard in its chipsets, instead opting to wait for Serial ATA.

Ultra ATA/33 An extension to the ATA interface (IDE) that effectively doubles the top data transfer speed of IDE from 16.6MBytes/second up to 33 MBytes/second. Also known as Ultra-IDE.

Ultra ATA/66 An extension to the ATA interface (IDE) proposed by Quantum that effectively doubles the data transfer speed of the Ultra ATA/33 interface to 66MBps. To achieve the increase in speed you must use a special 80-conductor cable with 40 data lines and 40 ground lines to keep the signal stable.

Ultra large scale integration (ULSI) A microchip with over one million transistors. Most popular chips today fit this description. Maybe in 10 years we will have the SDULSI, for Super-Duper Ultra Large Scale Integration. For now this is at the top of the heap.

Ultra sATA (serial ATA) A specification for consumer hard drive connections that boosts the data transfer rate up to 150MB/second. In addition, it changes IDE/ATA from a parallel interface requiring 40 separate wires to connect components to a serial interface requiring only 6 wires. 2x and 4x versions of Serial ATA double and quadruple the speed of Serial ATA.

Ultra SCSI This is SCSI that communicates twice as fast as standard SCSI-2. Normal Ultra-SCSI transfers data at 20MBps, and Wide Ultra-SCSI transfers data at 40MBps. Similar to Ultra-IDE, Ultra-SCSI works its magic by transferring data on the up AND the down stroke of a clock cycle, doubling throughput.

Ultra XGA (UXGA) A display with 1600x1200 pixel resolution.

Ultraviolet A spectrum of light with wavelengths from about four nanometers to 380 nanometers. Light below 4 nm is in the x-ray spectrum, and just above 380 nm is visible violet light, moving through the color spectrum of visible light as wavelengths get larger.

Ultrix A version of UNIX based on the Berkeley version, designed and implemented by DEC to run on their VAX and DECstation series of processors.

UME uni management entity The software residing in the ATM devices at each end of the UNI circuit that implements the management interface to the ATM network.

UML (unified modeling language) Initially created at Rational Software (now part of IBM), this is an industry-standard method of specifying, visualizing, constructing, and documenting the artifacts of object-oriented software systems using a graphical diagram that looks similar to a flowchart. You can use UML to effectively make a blueprint of the software you are developing, thus making additional development easier, as you can refer back to your UML model.

UMS (unfied messaging systems) A technology that allow users to access messages sent in different formats through one single interface.

Unassigned cells A cell identified by a standardized virtual path identifier (VPI) and virtual channel identifier (VCI) value, which has been generated and does not carry information from an application using the ATM Layer service.

Unbuffered memory This is where the chip set controller deals directly with the memory. There is nothing between the chip set and the memory chips on the module as they communicate.

UNC (universal naming convention) The name given for the naming used when one specifies:

\\the server\the volume\the path\then the file name of a file. So, a UNC filename would look like this: \\Myserver\Docdrive\Magazine\glossary.doc.

Undelete program A utility program that recovers deleted or damaged files from a disk. A file can be deleted accidentally, or can become inaccessible when part of the file's control information is lost.

Undelete To recover an accidentally deleted file. DOS 5 and later provides the undelete command, but many of the popular utility programs, which often have a much better user interface and are therefore easier to use.

Unformat The process of recovering an accidentally formatted disk.

Unformat program A utility program that recovers files and directories after a disk has been formatted by accident.

UNI (user-network interface) An interface point between ATM end users and a private ATM switch, or between a private ATM switch and the public carrier ATM network; defined by physical and protocol specifications per ATM Forum UNI documents. The standard adopted by the ATM Forum to define connections between users or end stations and a local switch.

Unicasting The transmit operation of a single PDU by a source interface where the PDU reaches a single destination.

Unicode A universal encoding scheme for characters and text. The goal of unicode is to enable the use of all characters for all languages of the world. Unicode supports a 16-bit character code for a possible 65,000 characters, as well as an extension of the 16-bit code called UTF-16 that allows for over one million characters and is sufficient for all known encoding requirements, including all known past and present written language characters in the world. Contrast that to the 8-bit 256 character limit of ASCII. Unicode is the default encoding of HTML and XML.

Unicos A version of the UNIX operating system adapted for CRAY computers.

Unified cache Multiple memory caches, most often L1 and L2 cache, that are treated as a single unit in that they don't ever hold the same information. In non-unified caching, both L1 and L2 could potentially hold parts of the same data.

Unified modeling language (UML) Initially created at Rational Software (now part of IBM), this is an industry-standard method of specifying, visualizing, constructing, and documenting the artifacts of object-oriented software systems using a graphical diagram that looks similar to a flowchart. You can use UML to effectively make a blueprint of the software you are developing, thus making additional development easier, as you can refer back to your UML model.

Uniform resource locator (URL) Also called a Universal Resource Locator. The pointer that defines the access method, host, path name, and file name to some reference or resource on an internet, accessible via a WWW browser.

Uniformity Comparison of one area's brightness to an adjacent area. In general, the brightest part of the image will be in the center area. When moving out to the edges, the intensity of image will vary in a non-linear function. This means that one comer of the screen will not be the same brightness as another comer of the screen. A typical CRT manufacturer's specification may call for up to a 30% difference between the center area and the corners.

Uninterruptible power supply (UPS) A device that contains a battery and some circuitry to supply your computer with power for a limited time (depending on the battery) if there is any sort of interruption in the outlet power. It must switch to battery power fast enough to keep the computer running during an outage. Large UPSes typically use lead-acid batteries like the one in car.

Union This consists of all of the items from two or more sets, similar to "AND" in a function. For example, the union of {1,2,3} and {3,4,5} is {1,2,3,4,5}.

Universal asynchronous receiver transmitter (UART) A chip that standardized serial communications. Its function is to change a byte into a standard sequence of electrical impulses.

Universal data format (UDF) A superset of data formats used with GIS, imaging, mapping, and CAD products. You can access data in UDF format instead of converting it from one format to another, with full geographic information preserved.

Universal resource locator (URL) This is what is used to give Web addresses for HTML, VRML, WAV, and other files. It simply contains the Internet name of the machine containing the data and the path to the file. URLs are much like the UNC, except specifically for the Internet. The address also includes what protocol should be used, such as HTTP, HTTPS, or FTP.

Universal serial bus port (USB) The new plug & play port standard for computer and peripheral connectivity that is standard on all new PCs, laptops, and a host of peripheral devices. The USB port allows users to insert or remove hardware while the computer is running without affecting the hardware. All USB devices use the same style port connection and automatically receive their identification numbers from the host controller inside the PC, thus allowing them to create a "daisy chain" of up to 127 devices.

Unix An operating system developed by Bell Laboratories for use on large workstations. Unix became one of the main operating systems for networked computers. It is especially suited for networks and is commonly used for Internet networks. The Unix System V Release 4 based operating system is called Sun's Solaris that runs off Sun Workstations and the PowerPC. IBM's Unix-based operating system is called the AIX, and the Hewlett-Packard version is called HP/UX.

Unix file system (UFS) The generic name for the modern implementations of the Berkeley fast file system (FFS). A hierarchical file system in common use on Unix systems.

Unix international (UI) A consortium of computer vendors that supports system V and gives guidance to USL.

Unix system laboratories (USL) The organisation that develops and maintains Unix system V. Originally owned primarily by AT&T, it is now part of Novell.

Unmoderated newsgroup A usenet newsgroup or mailing list in which posts are not subject to review before distribution.

Unshielded twisted pair (UTP) Cables that consist of pairs of unshielded wire twisted together. These cables are used for data and telephone networks. They are cheap to produce because they are unshielded, and they get their shielding by being twisted together in pairs.

Unsolicited commercial email (UCE) Electronic junk mail advertising a product, service, or web site, where the recipient did not request to receive the message.

UP (unwired planet) A set of technologies that enhances the number of services available for handheld devices, for example the UP-Browser.

UPC (usage parameter control) Usage Parameter Control is defined as the set of actions taken by the network to monitor and control traffic, in terms of traffic offered and validity of the ATM connection, at the end-system access. Its main purpose is to protect network resources from malicious as well as unintentional misbehavior, which can affect the QoS of other already established connections, by detecting violations of negotiated parameters and taking appropriate actions.

Upgradable computer A computer system specifically designed to be upgraded as technology advances.

Upgrade This normally refers to a newer version of software, or a version with an enhanced feature set. If you already own a previous version of the software, you can often purchase an upgrade version for a lower price than a new version. In terms of hardware, you can upgrade your system by adding more memory, or any component that makes your system better or faster. Some graphics cards let you upgrade them by plugging more memory onto the board.

Uplink port A special networking port on a hub or switch that is used to connect it to a larger network. Often you need a special crossover cable to make this connection function properly.

Uplinks Connections from a client machine to a large network; frequently used when information is being sent to a communications satellite.

Upload In communications, sending a file or files from one computer to another over a network using a modem.

Upnode The node that represents a border node's outside neighbor in the common peer group. The upnode must be a neighboring peer of one of the border node's ancestors.

Upper memory block The memory between 640KB and 1MB in an IBM-compatible computer running DOS was originally reserved for system and video use;however, not all the space is used, and the unused portions are known as upper memory blocks.

UPS (Uninterruptible Power Supply) A backup power unit that provides continuous power when the normal power supply is interrupted. UPS systems can be stand-by, only supplying power when the regular supply is interrupted, or fulltime, relying on regular power and/or batteries to supply it while it supplies power to the protected device. A UPS is not necessary on most computer systems, but can be important on systems that need to be up 24 hours a day, such as servers.

Upstream This refers to sending of data from a client machine across the Internet. With cable modems and ADSL, upstream speeds are slower than downstream speeds.

Upstream frequency The frequency used to transmit data from the CM to the CMTS. Normally in the 5-42 MHz range for US systems and 5-65 MHz for European systems.

Upward compatibility The design of software so as to function with other, more powerful, products likely to become available in the short term. The use of standards makes upward compatibility much easier to achieve.

Urban legend Urban legends are lies about what somebody said or wrote and are circulated wildly across the Web or some other network, including mouth-to-mouth dissemination.

URI (uniform resource identifier) A string of characters that represents the location or address of a resource on the Internet and how that resource should be accessed. A URI is a superset of the Uniform Resource Locator.

URL (universal resource locator) This is what is used to give Web addresses for HTML, VRML, WAV, and other files. It simply contains the Internet name of the machine containing the data and the path to the file. URLs are much like the UNC, except specifically for the Internet. The address also includes what protocol should be used, such as HTTP, HTTPS, or FTP.

URL blocking Preventing communication with specific URLs. Use of an extensive URL database provides companies the ability to restrict access to inappropriate sites.

USB (universal serial bus) A new external bus standard that supports data transfer rates of 12 MBps (12 million bytes per second). A single USB port can be used to connect up to 128 peripheral devices, such as mice, modems, and keyboards. USB also supports Plug-and-Play installation and hot plugging.

Starting in 1996, a few computer manufacturers started including USB support in their new machines. Since the release of Intel's 440LX chipset in 1997, USB has become more widespread. It is expected to eventually completely replace serial and parallel ports.

Usenet A distributed bulletin board system that runs on news servers, UNIX hosts, online services and bulletin board systems. Collectively, USENET is made up of all the users who post to and read newsgroup articles. The USENET is the largest decentralized information utility available today.

Usenet newsgroups Also referred to simply as "newsgroups," Usenet newsgroups are a huge bunch of Internet discussion groups that replicate across the Internet every so often. If you get a bunch of people together and request a group for yourself, you'll probably be able to create it. Topics range from technical discussions and debate to flame wars. However, the most infamous use of the newsgroups is the distribution of binary pictures and files as text.

User 1. A person trying to derive usefulness out of an application.

2. Someone not functioning primarily as a programmer, marketer, installer or maintainer of software.

3. Theoretically, the originator of requirements.

4. The financial foundation of the computer business.

User authentication The process of verifying the identity of a user. In an IPSEC compliant VPN, digital certificates are normally used to accomplish this.

User datagram protocol (UDP) Part of the TCP/IP suite of protocols. UDP is the part of the TCP/IP suite used by applications to transfer datagrams. It is also the part of TCP/IP responsible for port addresses.

User friendly 1. Specification for software to include Context Sensitive Help, three manuals and twenty hypertext documents on how to use the mouse, menus and buttons. Does not address documentation about installation errors, crashes, or actual functionality.

2. Software designed to be easy to learn and comprehend, with absolutely no thought to speed of use, ease of repetitive actions, or workflow.

User group A voluntary group of users of a specific computer or software package, who meet to share tips and listen to industry experts.

User Id The string of characters that identifies you. The name by which you are known to the network. Also known as username.

User interface (UI) The interface between the user and the program.

USL (unix system laboratories) USL, which develops and markets the Unix System V operating system, the Tuxedo Enterprise Transaction Processing System and other standards-based system software products, started in 1991 as a subsidiary spun off from AT&T. Novell acquired USL in December 1992, partially as a counter to Microsoft and its Windows products. The announcement virtually set the stage for the next-generation operating system war. Novell, which is likely to better integrate NetWare servers with Unix, seeks to achieve three goals: expand its market share, reduce its losses to Windows NT, and accelerate the expansion of Unix, the low-end commercial market.

USSD Unstructured Supplementary Services Data allows for the transmission of information via a GSM network. Contrasting with SMS, it offers real time connection during a session. A USSD message can be upto 182 alphanumeric characters in length. This is a WAP bearer service.

UT (upper tester) The representation in ISO/IEC 9646 of the means of providing, during test execution, control and observation of the upper service boundary of the IUT, as defined by the chosen Abstract Test Method.

Utility A small, useful program. Unix comes with some utilities like diff and sort.

Utility program A small program, or set of small programs, that supports the OS by providing additional services that the OS does not provide. Some services they commonly provide are: disk backup, disk optimization, file recovery, safe formatting, and resource editing.

UTMS Universal Mobile Phone System is the European implemention of the ETSI's 3G system. The advertised data rates for UTMS are: 144 Kb per second for vehicular transmissions, 384 Kb per second for oedestian and 2Mb per second for in-building communication.

UTOPIA (universal test & operations interface for ATM) Refers to an electrical interface between the TC and PMD sublayers of the PHY layer.

UTP (unshielded twisted pair) Cables that consist of pairs of unshielded wire twisted together. These cables are used for data and telephone networks. They are cheap to produce because they are unshielded, and they get their shielding by being twisted together in pairs.

UUCP (unix to unix copy protocol) A UNIX protocol and set of programs most often used to copy files across serial connections and telephone lines. UUCP was often used to transfer e-mail and Usenet news over phone lines when direct Internet connectivity was scarce in small and medium-sized companies.

UUCP (unix-to-unix copy program) This was initially a program run under the UNIX operating system that allowed one UNIX system to send files to another UNIX system via dial-up phone lines. Today, the term is more commonly used to describe the large international network which uses the UUCP protocol to pass news and electronic mail.

UV (ultraviolet) A spectrum of light with wavelengths from about four nanometers to 380 nanometers. Light below 4 nm is in the x-ray spectrum, and just above 380 nm is visible violet light, moving through the color spectrum of visible light as wavelengths get larger.

UXGA (ultra xga) A display with 1600x1200 pixel resolution.

V

V.32 A standard naming convention used in determining modem communications, all starting with "V." This one is for specifying the Hayes standard of bidirectional 9600 baud transmission.

V.32bis The standard that came after V.32 which increased the speed from 9600 baud to 14.4 Kbits per second.

V.34 This was a dramatic improvement for modem communications. It doubled the top speed of the V.32bis standard to 28.8Kbps.

V.34+ - This standard was made by US Robotics to indicate that its modems are superior to a standard V.34 modem in that they run at 33.6 KB baud instead of the slower 28.8 KB baud.

V.42 The name given to the standard for transmitting at 2400 baud.

V.42bis This is not a speed standard like V.32 and V.34, but an error correction and compression method that is hardware-based. Its major improvement comes from knowing when compression will be beneficial and when it will not be.

V.90 A standard for 56-Kpbs modems approved by the International Telecommunication Union.The V.90 standard resolves the battle between the two competing 56 Kbps technologies –X2 from 3COM and K56Flex from Rockwell Semiconductor. Both manufacturers have announced that their future modems will conform to V.90. In addition, most users who already purchased 56 Kbps modems will be able to apply a software upgrade to make their modems support V.90.

V.92 An extension to the V.90 modem transmission standard that adds three new features: quick connect, which speeds up the connection handshake; Modem-on-Hold, for receiving incoming calls without breaking your connection; and PCM Upstream, for speeding up upstream data rates to up to 48Kbps. Previously with V.90, upstream rates were limited to 33.6Kbps.

V.everything US Robotics' designation for its Courier Dual standard modems, which support all types of analog modem communications.

V.fast This standard was made between the time of V.32bis and V.34. It is also a 28.8 KB baud speed, but was not as reliable as the approved V.34 standard.

Vaccine An application program that removes and destroys a computer virus.

Vacuum tube An electronic device constructed of a sealed glass tube containing metal elements in a vacuum; used to control electrical signals

Valence A measure of the reactive nature of a chemical element or compound in relation to hydrogen.

Validation The process of evaluating software at the end of the development process to ensure compliance with software requirements.

Value added reseller (VAR) An individual or company that resells computer hardware and/ or software. They "add value" to the items they sell by integrating or customizing them as needed. VARs are part of the channel.

Value Anything that may be a legitimate (actual) parameter in a request. In particular, a value is an instance of an IDL data type.

Vandal Malicious auto-executable applications written into the code of Java applets, ActiveX objects, or other scripting language designed to enhance Web pages. Vandals can and have been used to steal money and secretly redirect modems. The "I Love You" vandal caused $7-9 billion of damage in just 5 days.

Vanity page A vanity page is a website placed on-line by an individual, not for commercial purposes, or as an informational resource, but simple because it tells something about the person that put the page up.

VAP (value-added process) To the NetWare operation system provided by a third party vendor.

Vaporware A sarcastic term applied to a product that has been announced but has missed its release date, often by a large margin, and so is not acutally available.

VAR (value added reseller) An individual or company that resells computer hardware and/ or software. They "add value" to the items they sell by integrating or customizing them as needed. VARs are part of the channel.

Variable A symbol, such as a string of letters, which may assume any one of a set of values known as the domain.

Variable bit rate (VBR) A type of encoding of compressed audio that allows for different bitrates in the same file. VBR can reduce file size and increase quality. The file size can be reduced by keeping bit rates low in non-complex parts of audio. Increased quality comes from allowing high bitrates in more complex segments of audio.

VAX (Virtual Address extension.) A line of 32-bit servers sold by the former Digital Equipment Corp. Initially, VAX computers ran only the VMS operating system, but later versions supported UNIX as well as VMS.

VB (visual basic) A software product developed by Microsoft. Its purpose is to bring programming down to a drag-and-drop level to speed up development cycles. In many ways that goal has been achieved. VB's main competitor at one time was Borland's Delphi. Both programs offer similar functionality, with VB based on the BASIC programming language and Delphi based on Pascal. The actual code generated by VB is BASIC, and you can go in and edit the nitty-gritty if you want to. VB was at one time very slow compared to C++, but it has been sped up significantly since those days.

VBR (variable bit rate) A type of encoding of compressed audio that allows for different bitrates in the same file. VBR can reduce file size and increase quality. The file size can be reduced by keeping bit rates low in non-complex parts of audio. Increased quality comes from allowing high bitrates in more complex segments of audio.

VBScript (visual basic script) A Microsoft scripting language that is embedded in many Microsoft applications. Although it allows for powerful interoperability and functionality, it also creates a great deal of security risks unless it is tightly controlled.

VCD (Video CD) This technology was developed by Sony and Philips in 1993, and allows around 70 minutes of compressed MPEG-1 video/audio to be stored on a CD. Typically VCD movies are shipped on two CDs. VCDs were very popular in Asia, and were available before DVD. Even though the VCD format was extended with SVCD, VCDs will probably eventually succumb to the higher quality of DVD. VCD resolution is 352x240 (NTSC) or 352x288 (PAL), which is fairly comparable to VHS resolution of 300x360.

Vbscript A scripting language developed by Microsoft, with syntax based on Visual Basic. Only Microsoft Internet Explorer supports VBScript.

Vcal Electronic or virtual Calendar, developed by the versit consortium and now controlled by the Internet Mail Consortium. This open specification defines the format of electronic personal calendar entry and scheduling information.

Vcard Elecronic or virtual card Developed by the versit consortium and now controlled by the Internet Mail Consortium. This open specification defines the format of an Electronic Business Card.

VCC (virtual channel connection) A concatenation of VCLs that extends between the points where the ATM service users access the ATM layer. The points at which the ATM cell payload is passed to, or received from, the users of the ATM Layer (i.e., a higher layer or ATM-entity) for processing signify the endpoints of a VCC. VCCs are unidirectional.

VCI (virtual channel identifier) A unique numerical tag as defined by a 16 bit field in the ATM cell header that identifies a virtual channel, over which the cell is to travel.

VCL (virtual channel link) A means of unidirectional transport of ATM cells between the point where a VCI value is assigned and the point where that value is translated or removed.

VCM (virtual channel memory) A type of memory developed by NEC. VCM memory adds some low latency SRAM registers onto standard SDRAM, much like EDO compared to Fast Page Mode memory. VC memory never took off, as DDR memory and RDRAM superseded SDRAM.

VCO (voltage controlled oscillator) An oscillator whose clock frequency is determined by the magnitude of the voltage presented at its input. The frequency changes when the voltage changes.

VCR (video cassette recorder) A device that can record and play back video to and from videotapes (video cassettes). Typical tapes can hold two to 6 hours of video, depending on quality.

VDD Stands for Virtual Device Driver.

VDL Vienna Definition Language: an algebraic definition language.

VDM Virtual Device Metafile.

VDT Acronym for video display terminal. In short, a monitor.

Vector A set of scalar numbers that refers to a point in space. Say, for example, you are in a two-dimensional space. A vector may be (5,6), which is 5 units across the X axis and 6 units up the Y axis.

Vector graphics As opposed to raster graphics, vector graphics are composed of groups of colored lines. If you've ever seen those old Atari arcade games like Tempest, Battlezone, or Asteroids, that's vector graphics. At one point a company even made a home game machine based on vector graphics—it was called the "Vectrex." Nowadays the only time you see things that look like vector graphics is when you are creating 3D models and you haven't rendered them yet.

Vector processing An approach to computing machine architecture that involves the manipulation of vectors (sequences of numbers) in single steps, rather than one number at a time

Vector supercomputer A highly optimized computing machine that provides high performance using a vector processing architecture.

Vectorial font Vectorial fonts handle the characters by representing their shape, thus being independent of the actual size. Contrarily, character set generated using a method which handles each character as a pixel set are called bitmap fonts.

Velocities Vector quantities that have a magnitude or speed and a direction.

Venn diagrams Diagrams used to demonstrate the relationships between sets of objects, named after John Venn, a British logician.

Venture capitalists Persons or agencies that speculate by providing financial resources to enable product development, in the expectation of larger returns with product maturity.

Verification The process of determining whether or not the products of a given phase in the life-cycle fulfill a set of established requirements.

Verilog A Hardware Description Language for electronic design and gate level simulation.

VERONICA (very easy rodent oriented net-wide index to computerized archives) Developed at the University of Nevada, Veronica is a constantly updated database of the names of almost every menu item on thousands of gopher servers.

Version A variant of the original value of an object.

Vertical frequency This indicates how many times per second the monitor can draw all the lines on an entire screen. A higher Vertical frequency or Refresh rate will produce less flicker.

Vertical market An industry or group of companies that can be marketed to in a similar manner because they have similar needs. Common examples of vertical markets include the government, healthcare, and insurance.

Vertical market application An application written specifically for a particular vertical market, as opposed to more generic multi-purpose applications such as office suites. One example is a program written for the insurance industry that computes insurance rates. Such an application is useless in any market besides the insurance industry.

Very Large database (VLDB) This refers, unsurprisingly, to a database that is very large in size. How large exactly is not specifically defined, but sizes of around a terabyte or more would fit this moniker. Database technology is driven by the need for fast VLDB solutions, and there are annual VLDB conferences and VLDB journals.

Very large scale integration (VLSI) The amount of transistors that are incorporated in a chip. A VLSI processor has on the order of 100,000 or more transistors, but not over a million.

Very long instruction word (VLIW) A microprocessor architecture different from CISC and RISC. VLIW uses encoded instructions that are even more complex than the instructions used in CISC. While RISC took instruction sets in a simpler direction by making instructions smaller, VLIW moves them in a more complex direction by encoding four or more instructions into a single operation. VLIW is used in the Hewlett Packard PA-RISC series of microprocessors, and formed the basis of some of the architecture used in Intel's IA-64 processors.

VESA (video electronics standards association) A group that sets standards for certain peripheral devices and their connectors, such as the VESA Local Bus and VESA standard monitor specification.

VESA local bus A 32-bit extension of a 16-bit ISA slot. This architecture predated PCI and allowed users to break the bottleneck that occurred when the ISA bus slowed down graphics speed. It allowed speeds of up to 40MHz, compared to ISA's measly 8.3MHz. The fact that it had twice as many pins to transmit data helped out as well. VL-Bus was big on 486-66 machines when it first came out, but was quickly displaced by PCI. PCI cards have some modest speed advantages and are much smaller. All VL-Bus cards were full-length cards.

VF (variance factor) VF is a relative measure of cell rate margin normalized by the variance of the aggregate cell rate on the link.

VGA (video graphics array) A video standard that allows for resolutions up to 640x480 with up to 16 colors at a time. It also allows for 320x200 resolution with 256 colors. Many older games were written to take advantage of the 320x200 resolution because of the comparatively high color depth. SVGA and XGA replaced VGA, but VGA compatibility remains an important part of most graphics cards. If your video driver is messed up, versions of Windows, starting with 95 and NT, let you go in under VGA mode to fix your graphics driver.

VHS Videotape having 240-325 lines of horizontal resolution. Super VHS (S-VHS) and videodiscs contain up to 425 lines of resolution. S-VHS tape decks can also play VHS formats.

Victim That which is the target of an attack. An entity may be a victim of either a successful or unsuccessful attack.

Video A term that was once used to refer almost exclusively to analog recordings of images on tape that can be replayed at 30 or more frames per second (fps) depicting "full motion video." Since the age of digitization, the term now refers to analog or digital recordings (e.g., digitized video in computer files and HDTV) that can be replayed at 30 fps or a reasonably close approximation of full motion video. The term differs somewhat from "animation" in that animations are successions of still frames not necessarily intended to be "full-motion" at speeds comparable to video full motion. The highest quality video connectors are termed S-video connectors, whereas the lowest quality connector is the RF connector. Because of the tremendous bandwidth required for network transmission of video between computers, it is not yet common to watch a movie on the Internet. The wave of the future isMPEG compression. However, until there are millions of computer users with enough computer hardware capacity to run MPEG digitized video, Microsoft Video for Windows and Apple QuickTime will probably remain more common in CD-ROM authoring of education materials. Video options for the PC with particular stress upon Intel's Indeo Video amd Smart Video Recorder are analyzed by.

Video accelerator A hardware component on a Video Card that is designed to consume all Local Bus bandwidth. Video Accelerators' software device drivers are often released according to the Stepwise Principle.

Video adapter The video hardware that determines the resolution and color depth of screen images. A k-bit adapter can display 2 to the kth power colors. For example, an 8-bit adapter displays up to 256 colors whereas a 24-bit adapter can display over 16 millions colors in a single screen. In hypermedia authoring, problems are created when the color depth of the authored image is higher than the color depth of the user (customer, student, reader) computer. Mac and PowerPC computers will usually dither to make the image reasonably good for users, whereas PC users may have terrible images if their video adapters are too low in color depth. The same thing can happen if the user's PC screen resolution adapter is lower than the authored PC screen. These are terribly frustrating problems for authors and users. For this reason, most of the commercial PC graphics and video CD-ROM files are authored for lower video adapters than the author's video adapter. For example, the author may be capable of presenting a graphics image in 30 million colors in a resolution of 1024 by 768. The author may elect, however, to only use no more than 256 colors in standard VGA resolution in order to have better images on user computers with lower powered video adapters.

Video board A somewhat misleading term that can apply to video capture and/or video playback hardware inside a computer. Video can be played back on computers without having video capture hardware. This enables CD-ROM users to view video and animations without having to install MPC or other standard video capture boards. However, if video capture boards are installed, users can also connect their computers to video sources (video recorders, video cameras, and television signals) in order to either view incoming video "on the fly" and/or capture segments of the video into digitized formats such as quicktime, avi, MPEG, or JPEG video formats.

Video capture A process of transforming a video (e.g., NTSC) image into a computer (digitized) image The process entails adding hardware and software designed to transform an analog (TV) image, say from a videotape, into a digital computer image. Usually a video capture board must be installed that is compatible with the bus of the computer. For example, a PC generally has an ISA, EISA, or MCA bus that in turn requires a compatible video capture board inside the computer. Video boards also enable computer users to view videotape or television images "on-the-fly" without necessarily capturing the images into computer files. Video capture boards vary greatly in price and quality. What is best for a given computer depends a great deal upon the amount of RAM, video RAM, graphics adapter, screen resolution, color depth, and speed of the computer.

Video capture cards Plug-in cards for a computer that accepts video input from devices like televisions and video cameras, allowing the user to record video data onto the computer.

Video cassette recorder (VCR) A device that can record and play back video to and from videotapes (video cassettes). Typical tapes can hold two to 6 hours of video, depending on quality.

Video compression algorithms Special algorithms applied to remove certain unnecessary parts of video images in an attempt to reduce their storage size.

Video electronics standards association (VESA) A group that sets standards for certain peripheral devices and their connectors, such as the VESA Local Bus and VESA standard monitor specification.

Video for Windows Animation and video files that originally were developed by Microsoft Corporation for PCs running under Windows. This has become a widely popular option for PCs operating under MCI standards. Like QuickTime, Video for Windows is a low cost and low fps option that will be common in CD-ROM authoring of education materials until MPEG compression options and video networking become more widespread. Although Microsoft's Video for Windows and Apple's QuickTime captured early market share leads in digital video, newer and better compression alternatives such as Indeo and MPEG probably will take over this market.

Video from digital (DV) Camcorders Camcorders that capture video directly into digital formats that offer many advantages for multimedia computer files. The captured video can be copied indefinitely with higher resolution, digitized audio, and no loss of frames. The mini-DV cassettes are smaller and have at least double the capacity of the Regular 8 and Hi8 analog cassettes.

Video graphics array (VGA) A video standard that allows for resolutions up to 640x480 with up to 16 colors at a time. It also allows for 320x200 resolution with 256 colors. Many older games were written to take advantage of the 320x200 resolution because of the comparatively high color depth. SVGA and XGA replaced VGA, but VGA compatibility remains an important part of most graphics cards. If your video driver is messed up, versions of Windows, starting with 95 and NT, let you go in under VGA mode to fix your graphics driver.

Video home system (VHS) A trademark and industry standard for the tape format used in VCRs. The VHS format features resolution of about 300x360 pixels.

Video RAM (VRAM) Dual-ported memory made specifically for video cards that was very similar to DRAM but was able to receive and send data at the same time. Due to the complexity of this, it was more expensive than DRAM. VRAM was common when Fast Page Mode memory was the best thing going for PCs.

Video server The combination of hardware and software that allows for storage and transmission of continuous animation and video in real time. The core of a video server is a continuous media operating system that allows animation, audio, and real-time video to be processed and transmitted across networks or over digital television satellites.

Video/audio networking (streaming) Refers to audio and video on network that commences to play before files are fully downloaded. The terms "real" and "streaming" are synomyms in terms of network video and audio.

Videoconferencing Remote communication in which two-way video images are transmitted with audio. Although this can be accomplished with video cameras on special telephone connections, it is now possible to become much more sophisticated with videoconferencing using computers.

Videodisc An antiquated "large" (more than 12 cm or 4.72 inches) injection-molded optical disc containing digitized information that has been recorded with a laser device and must be read on a laser device known as a videodisc player. The most common sizes are eight and 12-inch discs. A 12-inch disc will hold 54,000 video frames of super VHS quality. Full-length movies usually require more than one disc since only 30 minutes of video with audio can be stored on each side of a 12-inch CAV disc. A CLV disc can hold up to 60 minutes per side of a 12-inch disc. CLV holds more video but is more limited than CAV in terms of searching for individual frames. Two audio tracks can accompany a video track, thereby enabling educational audio to accompany entertainment audio. Although a videodisc resembles a CD-ROM in appearance, there are major differences. Relative to a CD-ROM disc, the laser disc is "large" in varying sizes of eight or more inches. Whereas a CD-ROM player can hold computer files and computer graphics images in common file extensions (e.g., GIF, BMP, PCX, TIF, JPG, etc.) and can be treated as a computer storage disc somewhat analogous to a high-capacity floppy disc, a videodisc cannot hold computer files. Videodiscs are more like videotape in that they are recorded in video formats such as NTSC or PAL or SECAM. Videodisc players are generally connected to television sets and will play on-the-fly in a computer only if that computer has a video board for any video source such as television inputs and VCR inputs. Videodisc and videotape images can be "captured" and transformed into computer files only if the computer has video capture hardware and software.

Virtual A seeming reality that lacks some elements of total reality. Since the early days of computing, simulation has become the most common form of achieving virtual worlds for learning and research. The term "virtual" is now loosely applied in many contexts. At one extreme it is applied to most anything connected with a computer or networks. For example, network chat lines may be viewed as "virtual communities." Interactive creation (by multiple persons) of artificial worlds (e.g., MUDs, MOOs, MUSHes, simulations, etc.) has become a major component in creating virtual communities. At the other extreme there is virtual reality in its most advanced stages with headgear, wired body suits, simulated odors, simulated tactle sensations, surrounding 3-D worlds, interactions of multiple people and machines in a shared cyberspace, etc. Entire courses are either using or devoting the course to "virtual communities." The term "virtual community" has evolved to where it usually refers to "conversations" that are not face-to-face and are often anonymous to at least the point where speakers cannot be identified (although groups to which they belong might be known). The key element is anonymity. Corporate boards of directors and other groups often pay to rent "silent meeting rooms" that are available. In a "silent meeting," participants can be face-to-face and still communicate anonymously. This is because the "conversations" are taking place within the computers in front of all participants. When a participant makes a point, none of the other participants can detect which person in the room made the comment.

Virtual Address extension (VAX) A line of 32-bit servers sold by the former Digital Equipment Corp. Initially, VAX computers ran only the VMS operating system, but later versions supported UNIX as well as VMS.

Virtual channel memory (VCM) A type of memory developed by NEC. VCM memory adds some low latency SRAM registers onto standard SDRAM, much like EDO compared to Fast Page Mode memory. VC memory never took off, as DDR memory and RDRAM superseded SDRAM.

Virtual channel switch A network element that connects VCLs. It terminates VPCs and translates VCI values. It is directed by Control Plane functions and relays the cells of a VC.

Virtual circuit Like a virtual channel connection, a virtual circuit appears to be a direct path between two elements, but is actually a managed collection of physical connections.

Virtual classroom Any means of live or pre-programmed Internet broadcast of information meant to function in a teaching capacity. For example, you could say "see you in the virtual classroom" and meet at a particular URL that is dispensing information.

Virtual device driver In Windows systems, a special type of device driver that has direct access to the operating system kernal. This allows them to interact with system and hardware resources at a very low level. In Windows 95, virtual device drivers are often called VxDs because the filenames end with the .vxd extension.

Virtual disk Main storage section configured as a disk unit, thus allowing faster read and write operations. Also called "VDISK" or "RAM disk".

Virtual host A shared hosting solution, the most basic of hosting types. Numerous Web sites are shared on one server.

Virtual lan (VLAN) This is created when a bunch of physically connected ports are grouped together by network hardware that supports VLANs. These VLANs are each treated as completely separate entities, and can only be joined together by a router. This scheme is useful for grouping departments together for security and minimizing network traffic.

Virtual machine Generally speaking, this is any non-physical construct that runs within the confines of another real (physical) or virtual machine. For example, an operating system is a type of virtual machine that runs on a computer's BIOS software, which runs on a physical computer. Any piece of software that runs on an operating system (or within the confines of another piece of software) can also be considered a virtual machine. The term and idea of a virtual machine has been used by Sun Microsystems in its description of a program launched by a browser that will run Java programs. Virtual machine also describes specific programs that mimic a computer within a computer, or a simulation of a physical device represented by computer software.

Virtual machine environment (VME) An operating system developed by ICL (International Computers Limited) for mainframe computers. ICL is a hardware and software manufacturer from the U.K.

Virtual memory A section of a hard drive used to augment a computer's RAM, or main memory. Different operating systems have different ways of dealing with virtual memory. UNIX and Linux often use a separate hard drive partition dedicated to virtual memory, while Windows uses a file or files on any number of hard drive partitions. However, Linux and UNIX can be configured to use a swap file as needed also. Virtual memory is used when the operating system runs low on physical memory. Virtual memory is also used to swap out lesser used portions of physical memory, freeing it up for other operations.

Virtual path A group of virtual circuits bundled together.

Virtual path switch A network element that connects VPLs. It translates VPI (not VCI) values and is directed by Control Plane functions. It relays the cell of the VP.

Virtual private network (VPN) A "virtual" network constructed by connecting computers together over the Internet and encrypting their communications so that other people cannot understand the communications. The benefit is that people can connect to a local LAN from anywhere on the Internet. This allows easier connectivity and lower phone bills for travelling salespeople. They just sign up with a national ISP and call local POPs from their hotels as they travel the country, easily connecting back to their company's local network.

Virtual reality (VR) A world that only exists in a computer, often experienced by looking through 3D goggles that detect which way you are looking and then display what should be there. Another form of virtual reality is a world created in your imagination by stories on the computer, such as a MUD.

Virtual reality Computer and video "VR" simulations that entail wearing headgear, electronic gloves, and possibly electronic body suits such that users are immersed in a cyberspace of simulated reality that gives the sensation of being in a three-dimensional world where objects can be moved about with hand movements and sensations of walking and touching are simulated using super computing power. The origins of virtual reality are in flight simulators of the military. There are now VR game arcades and laboratories where wide varieties of applications in entertainment, training, medical research, architectural design, data research, etc. are taking place. Virtual reality programs require massive computer power. Usually, the closer authors attempt to simulate the real world, the greater the computing power needed to achieve sensations of reality. In June 1994, Apple Corporation unveiled a new desktop computing software option (with a CD-ROM recorder) called QuickTime VR that takes a collection of photographs (e.g., photographs of numerous angles of the inside of a room) and assembles them into motion scenes that resemble more expensive virtual reality generated on super computers.

Virtual reality modeling language (VRML) Similar to SGML and HTML, the Virtual Reality Modeling Language (VRML) provides a way to textually represent objects in a three-dimensional virtual world, defining color, size, shape, lighting factors, and so forth.

Virtual server A Virtual Server is fully functioning Web Server that resides within the same physical location of a true Web Server. Multiple Virtual Servers can reside on a single Web Server. This technology sprang up in the mid 1990's and has allowed business and persons to have the benefits of a Web Server at a very feasible rate.

Virtual-image file A set of pointers to the files on your hard disk to be sent to the CD-R drive, rather than a duplicate physical-image of those files. Usually employed for on-the-fly recording.

Virtualization A process/software designed to reduce server management costs through automation, while providing more control over service levels.

Virus A program or piece of code that is loaded onto your computer without your knowledge and runs against your wishes. Most viruses can also replicate themselves. All computer viruses are manmade. A simple virus that can make a copy of itself over and over again is relatively easy to produce. Even such a simple virus is dangerous because it will quickly use all available memory and bring the system to a halt. An even more dangerous type of virus is one capable of transmitting itself across networks and bypassing security systems.

Virus-like activity An action which may be a legitimate action under certain circumstances, but can also be caused by a virus. You can change the default settings if you use software that causes a specific virus like activity under normal operation.

Visible speech A set of symbols, comprising an alphabet, that "spell" sounds instead of words.

Visitor When a user arrives on a website, he or she is considered one visitor regardless of how many pages at which he or she looks. If a visitor returns to that website later in the day, he or she may be counted as another visitor by logging programs unless you are looking for "unique" visitors and the visitor is identified by cookies or IP addresses.

Visual basic (VB) An extension of Microsoft Basic that allows for GUI controls, animations, and drag-and-drop features. Its main competitors are Borland's Delphi and Sun's Java. VB is used in many Microsoft products and in numerous applications by third parties.

Visual basic script (VBScript) A Microsoft scripting language that is embedded in many Microsoft applications. Although it allows for powerful interoperability and functionality, it also creates a great deal of security risks unless it is tightly controlled.

Visual C++ A Microsoft product that is basically. It features a similar visual interface with drag-and-drop functionality, but the code is C++, which is much more robust than BASIC. It's also faster when compiled.

Visualization A technique whereby complex systems are portrayed in a meaningful way using sophisticated computer graphics systems; e.g., chemical molecules.

VLAN (virtual LAN) This is created when a bunch of physically connected ports are grouped together by network hardware that supports VLANs. These VLANs are each treated as completely separate entities, and can only be joined together by a router. This scheme is useful for grouping departments together for security and minimizing network traffic.

VLDB (very large database) This refers, unsurprisingly, to a database that is very large in size. How large exactly is not specifically defined, but sizes of around a terabyte or more would fit this moniker. Database technology is driven by the need for fast VLDB solutions, and there are annual VLDB conferences and VLDB journals.

VLIW (very long instruction word) A microprocessor architecture different from CISC and RISC. VLIW uses encoded instructions that are even more complex than the instructions used in CISC. While RISC took instruction sets in a simpler direction by making instructions smaller, VLIW moves them in a more complex direction by encoding four or more instructions into a single operation. VLIW is used in the Hewlett Packard PA-RISC series of microprocessors, and formed the basis of some of the architecture used in Intel's IA-64 processors.

VLSI (very large scale integration) The amount of transistors that are incorporated in a chip. A VLSI processor has on the order of 100,000 or more transistors, but not over a million.

VM/CMS virtual machine/conversational monitor system An IBM operating system running on 43xx and 30xx series machines, providing efficient support for large numbers of interactive users.

VME (virtual machine environment) An operating system developed by ICL (International Computers Limited) for mainframe computers. ICL is a hardware and software manufacturer from the U.K.

VMS (virtual memory system) Designed in 1976, this is the operating system that ran on Digital Equipment Corp.'s VAX operating system. Eventually DEC ported VMS to run on the Alpha processor and added POSIX functions into the operating system, renaming it OpenVMS.

Voice activity detection (VAD) A technology that recognizes when a person is speaking and when a person is silent to suppress sending unnecessary noise across a telecommunications line.

Voice over IP (VoIP) The practice of using an Internet connection to pass voice data using IP instead of using the standard public switched telephone network. This allows a remote worker to function as if he or she were directly connected to a PBX even while at home or in a remote office. As well, it skips standard long distance charges, as the only connection is through an ISP. VoIP is being used more and more to keep corporate telephone costs down, as you can simply run two network cables to a desk instead of separate network and data cables. VoIP runs right over your standard network infrastructure, but it also demands a very well-configured network to run smoothly.

VoiceXML VoiceXML, a makeup language for speech, is standard being pushed by the VoiceXML the internet via a phone, whether wired or not.

Volatile Subject to rapid change; describes the character of data when current no longer flows to a device (that is, electrical power is switched off).

Volt The standard unit of electric potential. It is defined as the amount of electrical potential between two points on a conductor carrying a current of one ampere while one watt of power is dissipated between the two points.

Voltage A measure of an amount of volts.

Voltage regulator A device which maintains constant voltage in an electrical line in case of brownout.

Volume A drive or set of drives seen as a single entity by a Novell NetWare file server. It is the highest level of the NetWare directory structure. Volumes must be mounted to be recognized by the NetWare operating system, and can be unmounted to be taken offline.

VP (virtual path) A unidirectional logical association or bundle of VCs.

VPC (virtual path connection) A concatenation of VPLs between Virtual Path Terminators (VPTs). VPCs are unidirectional.

VPI (virtual path identifier) An eight bit field in the ATM cell header which indicates the virtual path over which the cell should be routed.

VPL (virtual path link) A means of unidirectional transport of ATM cells between the point where a VPI value is assigned and the point where that value is translated or removed.

VPN (virtual private network) A "virtual" network constructed by connecting computers together over the Internet and encrypting their communications so that other people cannot understand the communications. The benefit is that people can connect to a local LAN from anywhere on the Internet. This allows easier connectivity and lower phone bills for travelling salespeople. They just sign up with a national ISP and call local POPs from their hotels as they travel the country, easily connecting back to their company's local network.

VS/VD (virtual source/virtual destination) An ABR connection may be divided into two or more separately controlled ABR segments. Each ABR control segment, except the first, is sourced by a virtual source. A virtual source implements the behavior of an ABR source endpoint. Backwards RM-cells received by a virtual source are removed from the connection. Each ABR control segment, except the last, is terminated by a virtual destination. A virtual destination assumes the behavior of an ABR destination endpoint. Forward RM-cells received by a virtual destination are turned around and not forwarded to the next segment of the connection.

VTAM (virtual telecommunications access method) The SNA software that runs on IBM mainframes and implements the functions of network control, network management interface, and SNA support for host based application programs.

Vulnerability A software, hardware, or system flaw that leaves a network or device unprotected, or that prevents the successful implementation of a particular security policy. For example, a program with a buffer that can be overflowed with data supplied by a hacker, or a telephone procedure that provides private information about the caller without prior authentication.

Vulnerability analysis Systematic examination of a network or product to determine the adequacy of security measures, identify security deficiencies, provide data from which to predict the effectiveness of proposed security measures, and confirm the adequacy of such measures after implementation.

Vulnerability assessment The process of reviewing networks to identify weaknesses in procedures and technology that create vulnerabilities in the defenses of the company's networks. Once identified, corrective actions should be taken where technically and procedurally feasible. Vulnerability assessments need to be performed on an ongoing basis to keep pace with advances in technology and hacker techniques.

VxD (Virtual device Driver) A device driver that runs under the Windows operating system. It runs as part of the OS kernel and has access to kernel memory, running processes and hardware. Starting with Windows 95, these files have the file extension .vxd, and before that with Windows 3.x, they had the extension .386.

W

W3 W3 is a group of networking professionals, academia, scientists and corporations who have been charged with maintaining and developing the emerging internet technologies which apply to the web. W3 is also in charge of any new standards for HTML.

W3C (world wide web consortium) An industry group created to design and promote standards to increase the functionality of the Web. The W3C was initially established in collaboration with CERN, the creator of the World Wide Web.

WAE (wireless application environment) Part of the WAP stack of protocols. It consists framework containing all the elements allowing for the development of wireless applications. This includes WML, WMLScript, the WAE User Agent and supported media types.

Wafer A flat, round piece of silicon that is used in the manufacture of microprocessors. Fabrication plants, or fabs, typically will take a wafer and carve many microprocessors into it. Over the years wafer size has been increasing so that more chips can be fit on a single wafer, from 6" to 8" to 12" in diameter in some plants today. Wafers are created by taking a cylinder of silicon and slicing it, much like taking a loaf of bread and cutting slices, but to much more precise measurements.

WAIS (wide area information servers) A commercial software package that allows the indexing of huge quantities of information, then makes those indices searchable across networks and the Internet. A prominent feature of WAIS is the ranking (scoring) of the search results, according to how relevant the hits are.

WAIS gateway This term refers to a computer that is used to translate WAIS data so it can be made available to an otherwise incompatible network or application. Mosaic must use a WAIS gateway.

Wait state A brief delay added before a microprocessor executes an instruction, to allow time for slower memory chips or external devices to respond. A wait states may be one or more of the computer's clock cycles or may be timed differently. One wait state on each access of memory can make the processor up to 20% slower. With no wait state (called zero wait state) the processor will run faster.

Wake-on-lan (WOL) A technology developed by the IBM and Intel Advanced Manageability Alliance where a computer motherboard can turn itself on (and off) based on signals arriving at the computer's network card. Thus, if all your client machines support Wake-on-LAN you could remotely turn all your client machines on during a Saturday afternoon and perform a network-based upgrade without actually going to each machine and powering it on. WOL is certainly a useful technology for network administrators.

Wallpaper An optional background graphic used in a graphical user interface.

WAN (wide area network) A network in which computers are connected to each other over a long distance, using telephone lines and satellite communications. This is a network which spans a large geographic area relative to office and campus environment of LAN (Local Area Network).

WAP (wireless application protocol) A proposed standard that allows for transfer of data securely between wireless devices, such as PDAs, cellphones, pagers, or other combinations of those devices. WAP supports many different wireless networks.

WAP (wireless application protocol) Open global standard for wireless solutions. This technology permits the design of interactive, real time wireless devices.

Wares A slang term derived from the word "software." This term generally refers to pirated or cracked software. Chop off the "soft" part and you are left with "ware." There is no singular form of warez, or "wares" as they are also called.

Water cooling This type of cooling differs from air cooling in that water is used to remove heat from a heatsink that makes contact with a hot microprocessor or other device. Ultimately the water may actually exchange its heat with metal and air, or it could be cooled by a refrigeration unit. Water cooling is more efficient than air cooling, especially if the water is refrigerated.

Waterfall A software life-cycle life-cyclemodel showing the phases of the cycle and their interrelations on a characteristic diagram.

Watermark A background image in HTML documents that does not scroll like larger images that are not watermarks. For example, in the Microsoft FrontPage Editor, if you click on Page Properties and Background, one of the options is to import a watermark image for your web page.

Watt The electrical unit of power, which is energy transferred over a unit of time. Often it is used to describe the amount of heat generated by a microprocessor.

Wattage A measure of an amount of watts.

Wav (wave form audio) A sound file format introduced in Windows 3.1 with the .wav file extension. Files with the .wav extension are digital representations of sound and typically take up a good deal of space to store (typically 50 MB for a 5-minute song). If you use software to rip files from an audio CD the result is usually stored in .wav format. Standard Windows sounds are still in .wav format.

Wave division multiplexing (WDM) A means of multiplexing different wavelengths of light onto the same physical fiber-optic communications line pair, allowing up to a 40x increase in bandwidth. A single wavelength of light limits a T1 line to 1.4 Mb/s (+/- allowing for clocking); using different wavelengths of light allow the same fiber pair to carry 60Mb/s of data.

Wave file A wav file format used by Microsoft Windows for storing digitized audio. All information necessary to generate voice and music is stored in the file.

Waveform An abstraction used in the physical sciences to model energy transmission in the form of longitudinal or transverse waves.

Wavetable A bit of ROM on sound cards that stores standard sounds (as .wav files) for instruments instead of generating them from FM sounds. This gives a much more realistic sound to music in games and MIDI files. Ideally, sound cards also allow programs to load their own instruments in as well for added effects.

Wavetable synthesis A method of creating music based on a table of complex sounds. A wavetable could contain a realistic piano sound or guitar sound, which can then be manipulated to create very complex sounds.

WBMP (wireless bitmap) A graphic format optimized for the transmission of bitmaps over wireless networks.

WCDMA (wideband CDMA) A 3G standard that increases the throughput of data transmission of CDMA by using a wider 5MHz carrier than standard CDMA, which uses a 200KHz carrier. WCDMA allows for data transfer rates as high as 2Mbps.

WCMP (wireless control message protocol) Is a part of the WAP stack and provides an error reporting mechanism for the WDP(Wireless Datagram Protocol). These errors can be captured and managed.

Web browser A web browser is a software package that allows your computer, once connected to the Web, to fetch documents from Web Servers around the World, translate the HTML code in the documents and display the information to your screen. examples: Netscape Navigator, Mosaic, MS Internet Explorer.

Web clipping Palm proprietary format for the delivery of web based information to Palm devices via synchronization or wireless communication (Palm VII).

Web content Web surfing is the second most popular Internet activity, and it is the least secure. The newest Internet technologies, especially Java and ActiveX, are used to create dynamic, content-driven Web sites. Unfortunately, these compelling new technologies also pose the highest risk. Java applets and ActiveX controls are downloaded and executed automatically by simply viewing a Web page. By viewing the page, the user allows the Web page to copy an unknown program to the network and run it. Instructing browsers not to download any Java or ActiveX content is possible, but increasingly less practical as many Web sites require these technologies to provide full functionality.

Web developer Grown up Webmasters are Web Developers. Generally, if you are a Web Developer you have a range of Web skills, from managing a webserver to coding HTML, CGI scripts, and even creating spiffy graphics as needed.

Web document An HTML document, Gopher document, a PDF document, or some other document that is browsable on the Internet.

Web page A document created with HTML that is part of a group of hypertext documents or resources available on the World Wide Web.

Web portal A term coined to describe the large search engine sites, such as Yahoo! and Lycos, that have branched off to offer a wide variety of services. The idea is that a Web user would peer at the Web by using only one website: the portal. For example, you go to a portal to do searches, get stock quotes, buy things, etc. It would be your everything site. Each portal site wants to offer one of each type of service so that a user never has to leave the site.

Web server A Web Server is a computer on the World Wide Web (connected to the Internet Backbone) that stores HTML documents that can be retrieved via a Web Browser.

Web site The Web Site is a location on the Internet, specifically it refers to the POP location in which it resides. All Web Sites are referenced using a special addressing scheme called a URL. A Web Site can mean a single HTML file put up by an individual (called a personal page or vanity page) or hundreds of files placed on the net by a commercial venture.

Web surfers People who "surf" (search) the Internet frequently.

Web synonym for the term "World Wide Web," often referred to as "The Web."

Web walking Using a Web client program to move through the documents available on the World Wide Web. This casual browsing nature of navigating the WWW has also been referred to as strolling, crawling and jumping.

Webcasting Use of World Wide Web to broadcast information. Unlike typical surfing, which relies on a pull method of transferring web pages, webcasting uses a "push" combination of technologies to send information to users' computers. This is also referred to as "broadcasting, channel surfing, or "netcasting." Users get steady updates of streams of information in requested categories. Users can subscribe to a "channel," download software to a local computer, and then streams of automatic updates follow. The most popular webcasting service to date is PointCast, but several major companies, including Microsoft and Netscape, have announced their own webcasting products and services.

Webledger An online accounting system in which a vendor of accounting services (e.g., bookkeeping, receivables management, bill paying, inventory management, financial statement preparation, and tax services) are provided to multiple firms by a WebLedger vendor.

Weblog (Same as blog) This is a publicly accessible personal journal for an individual. Similar to a personal diary, but shared over the web. The activity of updating a blog is "blogging" and someone who keeps a blog is a "blogger." Blogs are typically updated daily using software that allows people with little or no technical background to update and maintain the blog. Postings on a blog are almost always arranged in chronological order with the most recent additions featured most prominently.

Webmaster A blanket term that refers to the person responsible for running a website. It is associated more with server administration and HTML coding than other Web development, such as CGI scripting.

Wellfleet compression protocol (WCP) The proprietary protocol that allows Wellfleet routers to make more efficient use of network bandwidth for inter-router communications.

WFM (wired for management baseline) An Intel hardware specification for easier management of desktop PCs in a networked environment. The specification calls for computers to be compatible with a pre-boot protocol that can be used to update the system or perform other management options. Also, the computer must be compatible with network/desktop management applications.

Wheel mouse A mouse controller that, besides the usual buttons, also has a wheel device built in that is most often used to scroll up and down windows that are longer than the screen, such as long Web pages or documents.

White hat A hacker with benign intentions. For example, if a hacker encounters a security hole and the first thing he or she does is explain the problem to the people who run the system that allows the security hole—without letting the knowledge out publicly—that hacker would be described as a white hat hacker. This term comes from old cowboy movies where the good guy wore a white hat.

White list List of known objects (Websites, script commands, etc.) that should be allowed, while all other objects of the same type are blocked.

White noise This is technically sound with a uniform frequency spectrum over a wide range of frequencies. Non-technically, white noise is any unobtrusive background noise, such as the hum of a fan, the sound of rain, or the sound of a channel that isn't coming in properly on an old television. Often white noise is imitated and generated to drown out other obtrusive sounds.

White paper A complete description of a particular technology, from overview to the nitty-gritty details. It is produced by the company that created that technology, as opposed to a FAQ, which can be created by anyone.

White point A movable reference point that defines the lightest area in an image, causing all other areas to be adjusted accordingly.

Whois A searchable database maintained by VeriSign, which contains information about networks, networking organizations, domain names, and the contacts associated with them for the com, org, net, edu, and ISO 3166 country code top level domains. Also, the protocol, or set of rules, that describes the application used to access the database. Other organizations have implemented the Whois protocol and maintain separate and distinct Whois databases for their respective domains.

Wide area information service (WAIS) A client/ server method of accessing databases stored on multiple servers. You use a WAIS client to connect to a WAIS server and search the databases that the WAIS server has cataloged. WAIS is not much use to the average Internet user today, but is still used by some to access information that is not readily available in HTML form yet.

Wide area network (WAN) Any network that spans more than one location. Typically at least one of the locations is fairly remote. Compare this to a MAN that may encompass several closely located buildings, such as a college campus.

Wide SCSI An improvement to the old narrow SCSI that allows for faster throughput by increasing the number of pins used to connect the drive to the controller from 50 to 68. Wide SCSI doubled the throughput of narrow versions of SCSI, but was generally more expensive due to the additional pins and marketing strategies.

Wideband CDMA (WCDMA) A 3G standard that increases the throughput of data transmission of CDMA by using a wider 5MHz carrier than standard CDMA, which uses a 200KHz carrier. WCDMA allows for data transfer rates as high as 2Mbps.

Widget In the X Window System X-Window-System, a window with its associated input and output functions. Widgets, provided by a library package, are used as building blocks to construct a wide variety of application environments.

Wildcard special character that acts like a joker when it is used in filenames or pathnames. Unix shells have two: and ?.

WIM (wireless identity module) Is part of WTLS that stores information necessary for te protocol to execute its security and authentication functions. SIM cards and Smartcards are implementation of WIM.

WIMPS windows, icons, menus, pointers, scroll bars A style of graphical user interface originally developed by Xerox and popularised by Apple Macintosh

Win95 1. A version of MS Windows that integrates 16 bit DOS device drivers, 24 bit memory management and 32 bit applications on 64 bit processors with 128 bit video cards.

2. An operating environment that promised an end to memory management problems, for which an entire range of third-party memory management programs is now available.

Window manager In a window system window-system, a program which manages windows on a screen. It is responsible for moving and resizing windows, and other practical functions.

Window system Software which supports windowing windowing. Examples are the X Window System X-Window-System, and proprietary systems on the Macintosh, NeXT and Sun.

Windowing A display technique that uses multiple screen segments to display different items of information. The display can take two forms: tiling (breaking up the screen into discrete segments) and overlapping (producing a three-dimensional effect by having a screen segment partially or fully obscure another segment)

Windows 2000 At first this operating system was called Windows NT 5, until Microsoft renamed it to Windows 2000. Windows 2000 was mainly a 32-bit operating system using the NT code base, but 64-bit versions also came out for Intel's Itanium processors. Windows 2000 ads new functionality into Windows NT, such as support for USB and other new devices, built-in DirectX 7.0, and many other features.

Windows 3.x The first accepted commercial version of Windows. There was a version 2.x that was available at one point, but Windows didn't achieve success until 3.x arrived, putting a Windows GUI directly on top of DOS 5.

Windows 95 A 16- and 32-bit operating system that builds on DOS and Windows 3.x to support 32-bit operations, additional hardware, and a more usable interface. This was a true breakthrough product for Microsoft, allowing game developers to run games inside of the Windows OS instead of separately in DOS. It was designed for the consumer market.

Windows 98 This operating system was designed by Microsoft and adds additional hardware support and integrated browsing onto the Windows 95 platform. This OS is still partially 16-bit, a full 15 years after Intel released its first 32-bit processor, the 386.

Windows A rectangular shaped area on the screen of any GUI that contains a program. It also refers to a family of operating systems developed by Microsoft. The family includes Windows 3.x, 9x, Me, NT, 2000, XP, and 2003.

Windows CE This was initially the name for Microsoft's mobile operating system designed for PDAs. Initial Windows CE devices offered color screens, and a fairly direct port of the Windows user interface. The Windows CE platform has been renamed by Microsoft to Pocket PC.

Windows for workgroups (WFW) Officially this was called Windows 3.11 for Workgroups, and it added some basic networking functionality to the standard Windows 3.1 operating system.

Windows internet naming service (WINS) A system that determines the IP address associated with a particular network computer. This is called name resolution. WINS supports network client and server computers running Windows and can provide name resolution for other computers with special arrangements. Determining the IP address for a computer is a complex process when DHCP servers assign IP addresses dynamically. For example, it is possible for DHCP to assign a different IP address to a client each time the machine logs on to the network.

Windows management instrumentation (WMI) Microsoft's answer to DMI. Microsoft felt that DMI didn't fully exploit Windows capabilities and was incomplete. Microsoft developed WMI to be an easier way of collecting management data from Windows OSes.

Windows ME (windows millennium edition) This Microsoft Windows operating system added many UI enhancements and clutter that actually made it less stable and more hated than Windows 95 and 98. No improvements to the core were made for stability or to enhance the combination 16- and 32-bit mess under the hood.

Windows media audio (WMA) A Microsoft-developed audio codec that offers sampling rates of 8 to 48KHz. Files of this type typically have the file extension ".wma," and Microsoft is aggressively pushing WMA as an alternative to the popular MP3 audio format, making WMA the default format for its Media Player, which now ships with Windows by default. WMA can create files that sound similar to MP3 files at a given quality and take up less disk space.

Windows Microsoft graphical environment, allowing to use simultaneously several applications, to exchange information between applications, and file management.

Windows NT (windows new technology) A full 32-bit operating system developed by Microsoft to be a very stable operating system to be used on servers and business machines. It was developed from the ground up to be fully 32-bit without much worry about DOS compatibility. The core of Windows NT code has been updated for Windows 2000 and XP.

Windows NT file system (NTFS) One of the file system for the Windows NT operating system (Windows NT also supports the FAT file system). NTFS has features to improve reliability, such as transaction logs to help recover from disk failures. To control access to files, you can set permissions for directories, individual files, or both. NTFS files are not accessible from other operating systems such as DOS.

Windows RAM A type of memory chip, or RAM, that was commonly used at one time in graphics cards on PCs. It is dual-ported so that graphics information can be displayed at the same time that it is being refreshed, much like with VRAM. This can give an increase in display speed over conventional memory.

Windows sockets An API designed to help inconsistent TCP/IP stacks talk together and be accessed properly by Windows 3.x programs.

Windows XP The friendly-faced, updated version of Windows 2000, with an almost cartoonish interface that will surely be looked back upon with a wince. XP started to take real "advantage" of the Internet by including numerous hooks and links to Microsoft's website to improve various functionality, and that is part of what made this operating system so controversial. Also, at long last, it moved the Windows NT code-base onto consumer machines, allowing home users to get the benefits of stability that Windows ME didn't offer.

Wine An implementation of Windows 3.x and Win32 APIs on top of X-Windows. Wine runs on Linux and UNIX, and allows Windows programs to run. Wine was created in 1993 and continues to be updated.

WinFS (windows file system) WinFS is the code name for the next generation storage platform in Windows "Longhorn." Taking advantage of database technologies, Microsoft is advancing the file system into an integrated store for file data, relational data, and XML data. Windows users will have intuitive new ways to find, relate, and act on their information, regardless of what application creates the data. Also, "WinFS" will have built-in support for multi-master data synchronization across other Longhorn machines ˑ .d other data sources. The platform supportˢ .ich managed Longhorn APIs as well as Win32 APIs.

WINS (windows internet naming service) A Windows-specific method of name resolution where a WINS server translates a NetBIOS name into an IP address.

Winsock A Microsoft Windows DLL file that provides the interface to TCP/IP services and allows Windows to use web browsers, FTP programs, and other Internet-related programs.

Wintel The common term for computers using Intel microprocessors and running Windows. Thus Windows/Intel becomes Wintel. Often this is used as a slur towards these type of machines; however, it can be a friendly reference as well. Many people have referred to the Wintel monopoly, since 90% of computers sold in the late 1990s had this configuration.

Wired for management baseline (WFM) An Intel hardware specification for easier management of desktop PCs in a networked environment. The specification calls for computers to be compatible with a pre-boot protocol that can be used to update the system or perform other management options. Also, the computer must be compatible with network/desktop management applications.

Wire-feet The actual length of the copper wire connecting the end user to the telephone company central office. This measure is used to determine the eligibility of the end user for receiving various DSL services.

Wireless application protocol (WAP) A proposed standard that allows for transfer of data securely between wireless devices, such as PDAs, cellphones, pagers, or other combinations of those devices. WAP supports many different wireless networks.

Wireless local area network (WLAN) An interconnected network of computers that uses radio and/or infrared communication channels, rather than cables

Wireless local loop (WLL) This is simply a wireless connection of a telephone in a home or office to a fixed telephone network. Using industry technology, it is an implementation of subscriber loops to connect devices over a multiple access radio system to the Public Switched Telephone Network (PSTN). It differs from a standard local loop in that the connection to the telephone system is made wirelessly instead of with cables.

Fig. Wireless local loop (WLL)

Wireless markup language (WML, formerly HDML) Part of the Wireless Application Protocol (WAP) , allowing text portions of Web content to be separated from graphical content for display on wireless devices.

WISE Web-Integrated Software Metrics Environment. A WWW based software management and metrics system from NASA.

WIT WWW Interactive Talk.

WMA (windows media audio) A Microsoft-developed audio codec that offers sampling rates of 8 to 48KHz. Files of this type typically have the file extension ".wma," and Microsoft is aggressively pushing WMA as an alternative to the popular MP3 audio format, making WMA the default format for its Media Player, which now ships with Windows by default. WMA can create files that sound similar to MP3 files at a given quality and take up less disk space.

WMI (windows management instrumentation) Microsoft's answer to DMI. Microsoft felt that DMI didn't fully exploit Windows capabilities and was incomplete. Microsoft developed WMI to be an easier way of collecting management data from Windows OSes.

WML (wireless markup language) Is a subset of XML and has been developed especially for WAP. It provides 4 major functionalities: allows for text display on a device, card and deck organization, navigation and linking, and stage management.

WOL (wake-on-lan) A technology developed by the IBM and Intel Advanced Manageability Alliance where a computer motherboard can turn itself on (and off) based on signals arriving at the computer's network card. Thus, if all your client machines support Wake-on-LAN you could remotely turn all your client machines on during a Saturday afternoon and perform a network-based upgrade without actually going to each machine and powering it on. WOL is certainly a useful technology for network administrators.

Word A group of bits of data regarded as a whole while programming or transferring data. Often a word is 8 bits in length, also referred to as a byte. This is also the name of Microsoft's word processor.

Word processor A program that lets you create documents—files that contain text, pictures, and formatting codes. Unix word processors include Wordperfect and Microsoft Word.

Word size The number of bits of data stored in a CPU register. Typically the number is a power of 2, with 8, 16, 32, and 64 being common. You have to deal with word size when doing certain data manipulations while programming.

Workflow The way in which work units (information or actions) are routed through an organisation. It can be formalised in terms of rules incorporating dependencies, staff roles etc. and hence automated.

Workgroup Persons sharing files and data between themselves.

Working directory The directory you are working in. The pwd command tells you your working directory.

Workstation A computer with a big screen, a keyboard, and a mouse. If it runs Unix, it's called a workstation; if it runs DOS, it's called a PC. And, if it runs Macintosh Finder it's called a Mac.

World wide web (WWW or web) This is basically a means of communicating text, graphics, and other multimedia objects over the Internet. Web servers on the Internet are set to respond to particular requests sent on TCP/IP port 80 by sending HTML documents to the requester. The requester usually uses a browser to receive this data. Think of the Internet as a 100-lane highway, and the Web as one of those lanes. Of course traffic in the Web lane is probably very high compared to traffic in most other lanes.

WORM (write once, read many) A digital, optical storage medium on which information can be recorded one and read many times. Provides for extremely compact storage of data at relatively low prices compared to traditional magnetic storage.

Worms A worm is an independent program. It reproduces by copying itself in full-blown fashion from one computer to another, usually over a network. Unlike a virus, it usually doesn't modify other programs. Also if worms don't destroy data (like the Internet Worm, they can cause the loss of communication with only eating up resources and spreading through the networks. A worm can also easily be modified so that data deletion or worse occurs.

WOSC World Organisation of Systemics and Cybernetics.

WRAM (Windows RAM) A type of memory chip, or RAM, that was commonly used at one time in graphics cards on PCs. It is dual-ported so that graphics information can be displayed at the same time that it is being refreshed, much like with VRAM. This can give an increase in display speed over conventional memory.

Write protect tab This phrase was initially coined for older floppy diskettes that needed to be write-protected by placing a tab or sticker over a notch that told a floppy drive that the disk was write-enabled. With the standard 3.5" floppy disks, the write protect tabs are replaced by small plastic parts that can be enabled by setting them to up or down positions.

Write time Time expended from the moment data is entered for storage to the time it is actually stored in the memory cell.

WYSIWYG (what you see is what you get) This term describes software that allows you to perform edits on a document that show you on-screen exactly what will print out. The Macintosh was one of the first computers to easily support WYSIWYG programs—that's why it was so popular in desktop publishing. Nowadays WYSIWYG programs are handy when editing HTML pages for display on the Web.

X

X An abbreviation for the X-Window-System.

X client An application process in the X Window System: it gains access to windowing services via the Xlib library. These are translated by the system into messages to an X-server.

X Window system (x windows) A consortium-developed, open-standard, device-independent GUI system that is most commonly found on UNIX and Linux operating systems and invoked with the "startx" command. The X Window System was initially developed in 1984 at MIT and called Project Athena. In 1986 the X Consortium was formed to further the development of the GUI. The torch was passed to the Open Group in 1997, and now resides at x.org on the Web. The GUI system works by running an X Server on the client machine that manages the windows, or X Clients. The X Window System uses the client/server architecture in and of itself.

X.25 An International Telegraph and Telephone Consultative Committee interface standard for connection of data terminal equipment to a public packet-switching network.

X.400 The International Telegraph and Telephone Consultative Committee series of recommendations that defines the basis for providing Message Handing Services, such as store-and-forward electronic mail.

X.desktop A desktop manager for UNIX from IXI.

X/open An international consortium of computer vendors that aims to create and promote a vendor-independent interface standard called the Common Applications Environment (CAE). CAE addresses the operating system interface, data management and languages, and will include networking and will include networking and a graphic user interface. X/Open was founded in Europe by European vendors, but has expanded to include a number of US companies (AT&T, Digital Equipment Corp., Hewlett-Packard, NCR, Unisys and Sun Microsystems) and office in the United States.

X2 A technology developed by U.S. Robotics (now 3COM) for delivering data rates up to 56 Kbps over plain old telephone service (POTS). It was long believed that the maximum data transmission rate over copper telephone wires was 33.6 Kbps, but X2 achieves higher rates by taking advantage of the fact that most phone switching stations are connected by high-speed digital lines. X2 bypasses the normal digital-to-analog conversion and sends the digital data over the telephone wires directly to your modem where it is decoded.

X86 The 32-bit instruction set used by most PCs. It originated with the Intel spec of the 8088, which then went to the 8086. Since then increments have come by changing the first number to 80286, 80386, "486", and then Pentium and beyond. The reason that the newer chips are actually named is because the numbers can't be copyrighted, and Intel needed to distinguish its chips from competitors' products.

XBRL (Extensible Business Reporting Language) This is an extension of XML metatag technology key terminologies in business, accounting, and financial reporting. The major purpose is to allow users to locate and analyze financial reports or portions of financial reports in a manner that is far more efficient and effective than using traditional search engines and EDGAR utilities.

X-designer A user interface builder for Motif from Imperial Software Technology.

Xerography A printing process that uses electrostatic elements derived from a photographic image to deposit the ink.

Xerox network systems (XNS) The network architecture developed by the Xerox Corporation in the 1970s. The XNS Internet protocol suite is similar to the TCP/IP suite. However, different packet formats and terminology are used. XNS protocols establish a means of transport for data across an interconnection of network or Internet. A sample library provides user applications for XNS, such as the courier, associate printing, filing, and clearinghouse protocols.

XGA This started out as IBM's term for a computer monitor resolution standard of 1024x768 pixels and 16-bit color. IBM released XGA monitors and graphics cards for its PS/2 computers, but unfortunately the standard was interlaced, and ran on 14" monitors. Nowadays XGA just means 1024x768. Laptop makers often mention that their screens are XGA, meaning that they support that resolution.

XLR cable (cannon cable, microphone cable) An analog audio cable normally used to connect microphones to professional audio devices. It has three pins and provides a balanced input, as opposed to an unbalanced or single-ended RCA connector.

XML (extensible markup language) A standard created by the W3C. It is a language with many similarities to HTML. What XML adds is the ability to define custom tags, such as , and define the meaning of those tags within the XML document itself—thus the term "extensible." You can extend the XML language easily. XML is becoming more and more common as more browsers and webservers support it. It is also a very flexible way to exchange data over the Web and interpret and use data from other websites.

Xmodem A protocol for transferring files during direct dial-up communications. Developed by Ward Christensen in 1977, Xmodem has basic error checking to ensure that information isn't lost or corrupted during transfer. It sends data in 128-byte blocks. Xmodem has undergone a couple of enhancements: Xmodem CRC uses a more reliable error-correction scheme, and Xmodem-1K transfers data faster by sending it in 1,024-byte blocks.

XMS (extended memory specification) A procedure developed jointly by AST Research, Intel Corporation, Lotus Development, and Microsoft Corporation, for using extended memory and DOS's high memory area, a 64K block just above 1MB.

Y

YB (yottabyte) This is 280 bytes, or 1024 zettabytes.

Yellow pages A system of network configuration files developed by Sun Microsystems and AT&T, extending the text-file setup concept of individual UNIX computers to UNIX LANs. The name was changed to NIS (network information system) because AT&T faced trademark problems with foreign TelCo's when marketing System V. NIS+, the latest version of YP, has largely been superceded by DNS, except for the local network password maintenance features.

Ymodem A protocol for transferring files during direct dial-up communications. It is so named because it builds on the earlier Xmodem protocol. Ymodem sends data in 1,024-byte blocks and is consequently faster than Xmodem; however, it doesn't work well on noisy phone lines. Ymodem has undergone a few enhancements: Ymodem-Batch can send several files in one session, and Ymodem-G drops software error-correction, which speeds up the process by removing the overhead used by error-correction. This works because all modems since the V.32 era have error-correction built into the hardware.

Yottabyte (YB) This is 280 bytes, or 1024 zettabytes.

YP (yellow pages) A name server in NFS to link clients desiring a service with servers who can provide it.

Z

Z A formal specification language developed at Oxford University for describing computing systems, based on set theory and predicate calculus.

Z39.50 Information Retrieval Service Definition and Protocol Specification for Library Applications. Developed by NISO, this standard specifies an OSI application layer service to allow an application on one computer to query a database on another; it is used by WAIS.

ZAK (zero administration kit) A software kit from Microsoft originally for Windows NT that can prevent various user actions, such as installing software or changing desktop configurations.

ZAW (zero administration windows) This version of the Windows operating system from Microsoft allows for various easy administration and management options, such as storing user software and settings on the network so that people can log into any machine on a network and retain the same personal settings. Basically it turns your PC into an NC.

Z-buffering (or hidden surface removal) This tracks the depth of each triangle in a 3D graphics representation, from the perspective of the viewer, to ensure that objects behind other objects in a scene don't appear until the viewer has them in his or her line of sight. This is why you can't see through walls to what lies behind, but why you can play multiplayer Quake and have people at many different areas in a level.

Zero insertion force socket (ZIF socket) A socket designed to accept a PGA chip, such as most common CPUs produced today. The ZIF socket allows you to plug in a PGA chip with no pressure required. This is a big advantage because older sockets required you to push the chip in with equal force on all sides or risk bending the pins.

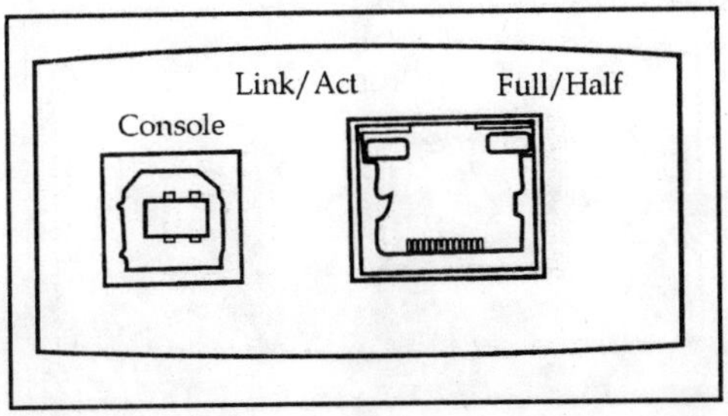

Fig. Zero insertion force socket (ZIF socket)

Zip A file extension added onto files created by the PKZip file compression program written by PKWare. Zip files are the most common compressed file format in existence and are supported by most compression and decompression programs, such as WinZip and WinRar.

Zipped Compressed version of a program or document.

Zmodem This protocol has many error-correcting properties. It can detect if a bad block (of 1,024 bytes) has come through and ask to have it resent. If the transfer gets interrupted for any reason, it can resume from where it left off. It is slightly slower than Ymodem-G, but is much more reliable.

Zone A portion of the total domain name space that is represented by the data stored on a particular name server. The name server has authority over the zone - or the particular portion of the domain name space - described by that data.

Zone file A file that contains data describing a portion of the domain name space. Zone files contain the information needed to resolve domain names to Internet Protocol (IP) numbers.

Zone transfer The act of replicating a zone file from one DNS server to another.

Zoo Collection of viruses. These can be found on Web sites, even though they are generally illegal.

Zoomed video A PC Card (PCMCIA) slot that is linked directly to the VGA controller. It allows easier implementation of MPEG video decoding and other video/TV features in laptops.